EXTENDING CITIZENSHIP, RECONFIGURING STATES

EXTENDING CITIZENSHIP, RECONFIGURING STATES

Edited by Michael Hanagan and Charles Tilly

ROWMAN & LITTLEFIELD PUBLISHERS, INC.
Lanham • Boulder • New York • Oxford

ROWMAN & LITTLEFIELD PUBLISHERS, INC.

Published in the United States of America
by Rowman & Littlefield Publishers, Inc.
4720 Boston Way, Lanham, Maryland 20706

12 Hid's Copse Road
Cumnor Hill, Oxford OX2 9JJ, England

The EuroSlavic font used to print this work is available from Linguist's
Software, Inc., PO Box 580, Edmonds, WA 98020-0580 USA tel (206)
775-1130.

British Library Cataloguing in Publication Information Available

Library of Congress Cataloging-in-Publication Data

Extending citizenship, reconfiguring states / edited by Michael
   Hanagan and Charles Tilly.
      p.   cm.
   Includes bibliographical references and index.
      ISBN 0–8476–9127–6 (cloth : alk. paper). — ISBN 0-8476-9128-4
   (paper : alk. paper)
      1. Citizenship.   I. Hanagan, Michael P., 1947–   .   II. Tilly,
   Charles.
   JF801.E97   1999
   323.6—dc21   98–21753
                                                                        CIP

Printed in the United States of America

To Eric Hobsbawm, World Citizen

Contents

1   Introduction: Changing Citizenship, Changing States   1
    Michael Hanagan

2   Burghers into Citizens: Urban and National Citizenship
    in the Netherlands during the Revolutionary Era (c. 1800)   17
    Maarten Prak

3   Citizens in Search of a State: The Limits of Political
    Participation in the Late Ottoman Empire   37
    Ariel Salzmann

4   Scripted Debates: Twentieth-Century Immigration and Citizenship
    Policy in Great Britain, Ireland, and the United States   67
    Suzanne Shanahan

5   Citizenship in Chinese History   97
    R. Bin Wong

6   The Right to Work and the Struggle against Unemployment:
    Britain, 1884–1914   123
    Michael Hanagan

7   Women's Collective Agency, Power Resources, and
    the Framing of Citizenship Rights   149
    Barbara Hobson

8   The Prospects for Transnational Social Policy: A Reappraisal   179
    Abram de Swaan

9   From *Special* to *Specialized* Rights: The Politics of Citizenship
    and Identity in the European Union   195
    Antje Wiener

10   From Center to Periphery and Back Again: Reflections on the
    Geography of Democratic Innovation   229
    John Markoff

11   Conclusion: Why Worry about Citizenship?   247
    Charles Tilly

12   A Bibliography of Citizenship   261
    Teal Rothschild

Index   273

About the Contributors   285

1

Introduction: Changing Citizenship, Changing States

Michael Hanagan

The official anthem of the European Union (EU) is Beethoven's Ninth Symphony, whose finale provides the setting for Schiller's "Ode to Joy." Adopting Schiller's celebration of friendship, domestic happiness, and the deity's beneficence as lyrics for its anthem does credit to the EU's nobler sentiments. Yet, what strange words for a European anthem! To fully understand the incongruity, let us compare its lyrics to those of European national anthems found in a widely used collection, compiled in 1960 (before the formidable challenge for Eastern European and Central Asian composers that came with the collapse of the USSR).[1]

Warmaking (61 percent) and territoriality (41 percent) are the two themes most frequently represented in European anthems. The principal theme is the celebration of war. The title of Eire's national hymn is simply "The Soldiers' Song." Bulgaria's pre-Communist anthem has the refrain "March, march with our General, Let's fly into battle and crush the enemy." Denmark and Holland celebrate the triumphs of military heroes and the personalities of King Christian IV and William of Nassau. Poland's pre-Communist national anthem lauds the actions of the Polish legions in Napoleon's army and was indeed composed and sung by these legionnaires. Even the smallest countries celebrate military prowess. Andorra boasts that "great Charlemagne, my Father, from the Saracens liberated me," while Monaco rejoices in the "Proud Fellows of the Civic Guard" who "listen to the Commander's voice" and urges that "Drums are beating, let us all march forward." Do Germans sleep more comfortably at night knowing that "stands dauntless Liechtenstein on Germany's guard"? The bloody lines of the French anthem, with its hope that the impure blood of foreign invaders will irrigate French fields, are well known; yet are they more brutal than the lines in the Danish national anthem exulting that King Christian's "sword was hammering so fast, through Gothic helm and brain it passed"?

1

Also prominent in national anthems is the theme of territorialism, by which we mean "the attempt by an individual or group to affect influence or control people, phenomena, and relationships, by delimiting and asserting control over a geographic area."[2] In part, European anthems derive national identity from topography. The Austrian anthem praises "Land of mountains, land of streams, land of fields, land of spires, land of hammers, with a rich future, you are the home of great sons, a nation blessed by its sense of beauty," and the refrain of the Czech anthem asserts that "this land of wond'rous beauty is the Czech land, home of mine." Estonia's anthem begins, "My native land, my joy, delight, How fair thou art and bright"; Lithuania's, "may the sun of our loved shore shine upon us evermore"; and Wales's, "Old land of the mountains, the Eden of bards, each gorge and each valley a loveliness guards."

The centrality of warmaking and territoriality in European anthems reflects their dominant role in the transformation that produced modern European states, and their absence in the EU anthem reflects their limited role in the processes currently driving EU development; in the contemporary EU, market expansion outside the control of individual states and conditions of divided sovereignty are the order of the day. Such significant differences necessitate thinking about current events in a broader historical and comparative context. The hurtling EU may or may not be off track, but it is clearly not on the same track as the nineteenth- and twentieth-century European states with which it has been so frequently compared. As the title of this book suggests, our concern is with expanding rights in reconfiguring states, and our interest is in looking at changes in both rights and states. The essays in this collection not only consider the "consolidated states" that contributed so powerfully to the growth of citizenship rights but also examine conflicts over rights in situations of mixed and fragmented sovereignty in the past. They investigate four linked questions: (1) What sorts of rights and obligations did Europeans attach to citizenship, how, and why? (2) How and why did those rights and obligations vary from regime to regime, including non-European systems? (3) What sorts of established citizenship rights and obligations are now threatened, and why? (4) What sorts of citizenship rights and obligations might soon come into being, under what circumstances, how, and why?

Before looking at how our authors address these questions, let us first define the "consolidated state," look briefly at the conditions that produced it and why they no longer obtain, and consider why a broader set of historical comparisons may be pertinent.

In the aftermath of the Versailles settlement of World War I, the territorially continuous, centralized, differentiated, coercion-monopolizing "consolidated state" dominated the European continent. Here, the term is employed in preference to the more commonly used "nation-state," for it refers to well-documented processes such as the introduction of direct taxation, more centralized administration, and general conscription, while "nation-state" refers to a conflation of identity and territory that was an integral, but seldom achieved, element of many nationalist programs. To refer to existing European states as nation states ignores the claims of Wales, Scotland, Catalonia, the Basque country, Occitania, Corsica, Alsace, Frisia, Macedonia, Flanders, and Wallonia as well as the minorities of Albanians, Austrians, Germans, Hungarians, Russians, and Rumanians residing in foreign states. It validates the goals of those engaged in "ethnic cleansing" while seriously exaggerating the effects of nineteenth- and twentieth-century state transformation in producing an homogenous national identity.

Though not a "nation-state," the consolidated state still represents a very substantial accomplishment for which its builders paid a high price. In return for new powers, they conceded "rights," defined as "a set of mutually enforceable claims relating categories of persons to agents or governments."[3] Rights depend on power. Our definition nods to Hobbes's claim that "Covenants without Swords are but Words, and of no strength to secure a man at all."[4] Governments must have power to enforce citizens' claims, yet citizens must possess sufficient power to defend rights even when they impede government policy. Throughout the last period of state transformation, rulers' needs for capital and conscripts have given populations bargaining power.[5]

As we approach the year 2000, the EU of today differs from the consolidated state of the French Revolution as the vague universalism of the "Ode to Joy" differs from the particularism and ferocity of earlier national anthems; the protectionism, militarism, and patriotism of the consolidated state contrast with the free market philosophy, disinclination to use military force, and lukewarm loyalties of the current EU. Though military competition has not been a driving force in EU development, the union's origins are rooted in warfare. Given the toll such sentiments had just exacted, after World War II assertions of nationalism were widely distrusted throughout Europe. Western European states survived by adhering to a common market that brought *les trente glorieuses,* the thirty years of economic growth after World War II. That portion of Europe rebuilt under American auspices first formed itself into the European Coal and Steel Community (ECSC) serving key interests in individual countries: for Belgian political leaders, it provided subsidies for inefficient coal producers; for frightened French businessmen, access to German coal resources and the deconcentration of the German steel industry; and for Germans, control over their natural resources. The ECSC was the precursor of the Common Market, the European Community and the present European Union.[6]

Economic growth within the Common Market went far toward restoring the damaged authority of Western European states, but it also tied them to a transnational union that limits national sovereignty in important respects. This tendency for states to relinquish sovereign power over trade and commerce to international bodies such as the GATT, the World Bank, and the IMF is one important characteristic feature of the contemporary period of state transformation. Coinciding with the growth of international trade has been the rise of multinational corporations and a new international division of labor in which capital has increased its investments outside its home state or territories controlled by the home state. To prosper economically, states have been forced to seriously compromise their own sovereignty and relinquish important controls over capital.

If the subordination of European states to Russian and American superpowers after World War II marked the end of the Westphalian system of balance of power among competitive states, the collapse of the Soviet Union in 1989 meant that, for the first time in a score of centuries, no credible military threat menaces the states of Western or Central Europe, either individually or collectively. Outside Europe, U.S. military power, with tacit or overt European support, has intervened to preserve a status quo that favors the West and particularly the United States, as in response to Iraq's invasion and annexation of Kuwait in 1990.

In the 1950s and 1960s, on the assumption that state formation was an inevitable process and the consolidated state its predestined end, neofunctionalists argued that the economic union would produce a consolidated state of a federal type.[7] But the conditions of military competition and patterns of capital concentration that underwrote the development of the consolidated state no longer obtain. Charles Tilly's survey of European state transformation over the last millennium reminds us that the preferred venue of uncontrolled capital was never the consolidated state but the city-state or confederations of city-states. Capitalists preferred rule by urban oligarchies, unconstrained by strong administrative bureaucracies; instead, they wanted their governments to focus attention on protecting commerce and on extracting revenue from the hinterlands they dominated.[8] The striking extent to which the contemporary EU fits this description suggests the shaping role of capital and, to the extent that capital continues to influence its growth, represents one plausible trajectory for its future development. The "capital-intensive" path of development represented by urban oligarchies is one of the historically recurrent lines of European state transformation. As late as the sixteenth and seventeenth centuries, autonomous cities in Italy, the Spanish Netherlands, and the Baltic established themselves as major powers that negotiated as equals with French kings and Holy Roman Emperors. The Holy Roman Empire was itself a vast confederation of kingdoms, principalities, and independent and semiautonomous cities. After 1648 the empire ceased to resemble a state at all but remained important as an institution organizing and guaranteeing the existing state order in central Europe. (Here, too, is a trajectory for the EU worth considering.)[9]

In the new Europe of the EU, multiple political allegiances marked by fragmented sovereignty and crosscutting jurisdictions are beginning to emerge. As the EU moves towards really achieving a single European market and also towards economic and monetary union (EMU), the most important mechanisms for regulating capital and redistributing wealth remain confined to the level of individual states. In contemporary Europe, the Schengen and Maastricht treaties were unable to agree on a unified border control policy, and German bankers have been unable to negotiate a common currency for all EU members. Recent extensions of power within the EU have come at the expense of shattering its territorial coherence.

But the unstable equilibrium between Brussels and EU member states is nothing new in European history. Fragmented sovereignty and crosscutting jurisdictions are far older European conditions than the reliance on undiluted sovereignty that figures so prominently in the last two or three centuries. Just so, sixteenth-century Europe was dominated by composite monarchies with representative assemblies, "coexisting with a myriad of smaller territorial and jurisdictional units."[10] In the Spanish Empire, the ruler was pledged to maintain the distinctive rights and identity of Aragon, Valencia, the principalities of Catalonia, the Kingdoms of Sicily and Naples, and the different provinces of the Netherlands. Even though the eighteenth-century French kingdom was largely territorially contiguous, still it contained sixteen separate representative estates, each with its own rights and privileges.

Although not unprecedented, the reconfiguration of the European state system has important ramifications for the European rights tradition, and in this area, too, there are historical parallels. The dilemmas of divided allegiance occurring within contemporary Europe would have been familiar to sixteenth- and seventeenth-century Europeans. As angry German artisans in seventeenth-century Reval (Tallinn) debated whether to direct their claims to their own oligarchical municipal council or to the court of their distant lord, the Swedish king, so English Muslims discuss whether to take their demands for religious equality to Parliament or to the European Court of Justice.[11] In today's Europe, social movements of feminists and of those demanding migrants' rights actively argue over whether Brussels or London/Paris/Rome/Berlin is most likely to respond favorably and effectively to their demands. Although casting an eye on events in Brussels, contemporary labor movements by and large continue to focus their attention on politics within individual member states; it is at this level, at an enormous cost of blood and collective perseverance, that labor movements have managed to carve out for themselves positions of power.

Having put the consolidated state and the rights tradition in a broad historical context, let us get down to cases. Let us look at how the essays in this collection deal with questions of the development of rights and their variation
across systems as well as the character of the contemporary attack on rights
and the future of rights-based political obligations.

What sorts of rights and obligations did Westerners attach to citizenship,
how, and why? The character of rights and their variation within and
between polities are best seen through comparison; Maarten Prak contrasts
the rights conferred by the new consolidated state with those then on offer by
existing semi-independent municipalities and city states, while Ariel Salzmann focuses on the Ottoman Empire's failed attempts to disseminate rights
in a large, unintegrated polity. Prak's discussion of the Dutch municipality of
Bois-le-Duc illustrates the triumph of one rights tradition over another, in
this case the triumph of the "thin" rights extending throughout an entire state
territory over the "thick" rights provided by semi-independent municipalities. Prak focuses on the case of one small eighteenth-century Dutch city,
Bois-le-Duc, and analyzes a "municipal citizenship" that, he maintains, was
the "norm throughout early modern Europe." Municipal citizenship retained
the hearts of Dutch urban dwellers because it offered incomparably more
benefits; urban citizenship conferred rights to work through membership in
corporate organizations, to participation in municipal affairs, to trial in local
courts, and, when combined with prolonged residence, to local welfare benefits. And in Bois-le-Duc, unlike in many municipalities, citizenship was
readily attainable.

Territorial reconfiguration is central to Prak's analysis. By bringing into
being a new creation, a Dutch consolidated state, elites were able to avoid
confrontation with the body of traditional rights vested in the municipality.
Prak laments that the new tradition of broad and equal rights derived from the
Enlightenment and inherent in "the people of the Netherlands" never confronted the richer communal social rights tradition of the municipality. But
the dialogue missed in 1796 only underlines the significance of spatial reorganization in political life. State reconfiguration can erode rights as easily as
broaden them. In Bois-le-Duc, the French Revolution contracted the community's rights but created an enlarged political venue in which populations
could fight for rights.

Ariel Salzmann's contribution to this collection reminds us of the intimate
relationship between military power and citizen rights. Faced with European
military threats and widespread internal discontent, the Ottoman Empire tried
to introduce rights and citizenship to win the loyalty of its population, but its
inability to resist foreign pressures and its own internal weakness doomed its
initiatives. Although ultimately they failed, their defeat was not predestined.

Reform was embraced by some imperial elites and won a measure of popular support as well.

In the end, different groups within the Ottoman Empire weighed the advantages conferred by participation in imperial politics against the benefits to be won by its dismantlement and the likelihood of the rise of independent states based on ethnicity.[12] While the move towards a secular Ottoman identity challenged many powerful interests within the empire and encouraged their support for resurgent despotism, the military pressure of Western consolidated states was crucial in tipping the balance in favor of imperial breakup. Demanding special rights for their citizens and recruiting local minority groups to European citizenship, they provided an alternative to Ottoman citizenship for minority elites; meanwhile, rivalries between Britain, France, Austria-Hungary, and the Russian Empire led to piecemeal annexations of Ottoman territory or support for national liberation movements and the population transfers that inevitably followed. Annexations, independence, and population transfers withdrew more and more of the Christian and Jewish populations from the empire and made the creation of a new Middle Eastern identity less politically rewarding for the Ottoman government.

How and why did those rights and obligations vary from regime to regime, including non-European systems? Essays by Suzanne Shanahan and R. Bin Wong deal especially with these questions. Shanahan shows the varying roots and quite different purposes of state social policies concerning migration in the United Kingdom, Ireland, and the United States, but she argues that involvement with the international community has served to standardize debate over migration in each of these countries.[13] Particularly in Britain and Ireland, ethnicity is used to justify grants of citizenship rights. What most strikes Shanahan is convergence, the participation of all three countries in a broader international discourse. While the language of racial exclusion has disappeared, the idea of ethnicity has been given increased legal sanction, particularly in the United Kingdom and Eire, where the idea that identity is transmitted by blood has gained ground.

Shanahan's chapter also deals with issues of divided sovereignty; in this case, she contrasts the evolution of imperial citizenship within the British Empire with that in Ireland and the United States, two imperial successor states. In some ways there is a remarkable similarity between Shanahan's British Empire and Salzmann's Ottoman Empire. Both developed very extensive definitions of citizenship to enhance the value of participation within the empire by those who had formerly been conquered peoples, and, in both, the character of citizenship was subject to dramatic narrowing in favor of the ethnicity in the imperial homeland as subject peoples exited the imperial framework.

Where Shanahan emphasizes convergence among regimes, R. Bin Wong stresses the differences between political cultures in China and Europe. The chapter by Bin Wong on China is particularly interesting because it focuses on the character of political obligation in two very different regimes. While the chapters by Prak and Salzmann identify important characteristics of European consolidated states by analyzing how different polities sought to adopt rights-based political obligations, the chapter by Bin Wong employs comparison but proceeds in a different direction; he identifies a Chinese approach to the question of political obligation, contrasting it to that of Europe. Bin Wong feels that the practice of formal and concrete commitment to the public good is as much a part of China's political culture as the rights tradition is part of Europe's. Looking at China, imperial, republican, and Communist, he examines how political culture might be reframed in contemporary China to attain the same kinds of egalitarian outcomes and social welfare measures as the rights tradition has won in Europe.

In comparative perspective, what is of most importance is the very different character of political obligation in China and Europe. Historically, "rights" were unknown within the Chinese Empire: instead, as Lowell Dittmer argues, "the public interest occupies a position of sacrosanct priority. . . . The tendency in Chinese political culture is for the public interest to subsume all private interests to the extent that the two may hardly be seen as separate or in conflict."[14]

An important aspect of the difference between European and Chinese citizenship is perhaps best captured by John Austin's distinction between "real law" and "moral law."[15] As Austin sees it, "real laws" are generated by states issuing commands and establishing institutions to enforce them. In contrast, "moral laws" are based on consensus about what is right but lack determinate institutions for enforcing that moral consensus. For Austin, Chinese imperial commitments would be better styled moral laws. In China the state committed itself publicly to tax lightly, to intervene in subsistence crises, to maintain dams and canals; but in some periods of Chinese history the concrete responsibility for carrying out these commitments was not "determinate and assignable"; indeed, the Chinese state increasingly tended to turn these responsibilities over to local elites.

Different approaches to rule shaped the character of European and Chinese protests. When the state did not enforce laws regulating the price of bread, European protestors often fixed the price of bread and auctioned it off themselves; but such initiatives were intended to prod established state authorities to assume their legal responsibilities. In the end, such popular pressure resulted in making public officials more accountable to citizens. In China, protestors were much more likely to establish organizations, levy taxes, and carry out responsibilities independent of the state. Private collectivities acted because formal organizations designed to carry out state commitments were lacking.[16]

Though China's commitments differ from Europe's enforceable rights, Chinese government commitments set important agendas for social action. If the state did not fulfill its pledges, then independent actors considered themselves empowered to take on these responsibilities. The character of those independent actors who assumed moral obligations necessarily varied from region to region to region, and tricorner conflicts often emerged between local groups formed to protect villagers from banditry, bandits, and state authorities who viewed with misgivings the development of private military organizations. When the state massively failed to carry out its obligations, rebels did not hesitate to use these failures to legitimate their insurrections. In so doing, they carried out the legacy of government commitment even as they overthrew governments.

What sorts of established citizenship rights and obligations are now under threat and why? Essays by Barbara Hobson and me address these issues. I focus on the emergence of new rights claims within the turn-of-the-century United Kingdom. I argue that new rights claims emerged from the appearance within the political arena of new social groups, in this case the growth of a dissatisfied industrial proletariat suffering from the effects of the second industrial revolution combined with the shifting loyalties of trade union organizations. But I also add that the character of new groups and their claims are shaped by the political arena in which they emerge. The competition of a rights-based Liberal Party with a state-oriented Conservative Party for the votes of newly enfranchised workers provided a favorable climate for the emergence of Labourism. While many early Labour Party leaders had a broad conception of the labor movement that included women and less skilled workers, the coalitions and allies available and the willingness of Labour leaders to form such coalitions established a male, skilled identity as the dominant element in the party.

Drawing on the distinction between enforceable rights and moral commitments discussed earlier, I show how the demand for a "right to work" was shunted from the former category to the latter. The initial efforts of British Labour were to cast the demand for a right to work in terms of an enforceable right, but Labour was unable to find support among either Liberals or Conservatives for this claim. Gradually, the right to work was displaced by promise of "full employment," which was really a moral claim. Such moral claims are not without force, for they give a special legitimacy to such claims within a particular political system. Nonetheless, as in Bin Wong's China, there is no available agent to prod into action when rights are not enforced. In the end, the ability of groups to give life to such claims depends on their own ability to act and to join with other groups in society to achieve goals recognized as legitimate.

Unlike rights, which are routinely enforced by states, claims depend more directly on the ability of groups to mobilize, and they decay as group strength and solidarity declines.

Barbara Hobson's essay emphasizes the struggles that expanded citizenship rights within consolidated states as well as reasons why many Europeans feel that their rights may be threatened by inclusion in the EU. In Sweden, a well-organized, modern labor movement was able to form broad coalitions and extract genuine concessions from capitalist elites. Decades of political struggle were needed to thicken the "thin" rights initially bestowed by the consolidated state. Hobson examines why Sweden was able to pass relatively generous entitlements for women in the 1930s at a time when feminists lacked strong independent organizations. Hobson puts particular weight on the strategizing of Social Democratic women who harnessed pro-natalist conservative rhetoric to Social Democratic purposes. While Hobson lauds Swedish Social Democratic women's cunning, she acknowledges that family entitlements were also the result of "cross-class coalitions" in which Swedish feminists and Conservatives had shared interests.

Hobson's Swedish case also reminds us that movements for rights within states possess some advantages for mobilization lacking in Prak's semi-independent municipalities. While guildsmen could muster their resources intensively towards city hall, Swedish workers organized extensively, formed strong central organizations, and found agrarian allies.[17] Swedish feminists were well placed in the centralized structure of national Swedish Social Democracy to launch their initial campaigns within a Swedish labor movement that possessed considerable political power.[18]

Indeed, feminist power within the consolidated state has made many Swedish women less enthusiastic about the EU. While many feminist movements within member states have turned to the EU with enthusiasm, Swedish women have worried about how the EU might try to reconcile German social policies that encourage married women to stay home with Swedish policies that encourage married women to participate in the labor force. Their location within the political structure of the consolidated state allows them to wield power that could be seriously weakened by entry into the EU.

What sorts of citizenship rights and obligations might soon come into being, under what circumstances, how, and why? The chapters by Abram de Swaan and Antje Wiener present contrasting images of the EU and project alternative visions of its prospects; considered together, they give a good idea of current debates among European social scientists about the EU's future. Both de Swaan and Wiener center their analysis on the kinds of rights and obligations that characterize the EU's development. De Swaan laments the EU's inability to formulate and implement a policy of European foreign aid.

He is intrigued by the inability of rich countries to aid poorer countries even though their best interest would be served by such aid. The effects of civil wars, environmental degradation, and the requirements of the labor market all illustrate the interdependence of rich and poor countries. But as they reach levels of prosperity undreamed of by previous generations, rich European states and the United States are failing in their commitment to poorer states.

While politicians in individual countries realize the need to deal with international problems while they can still be controlled, the lack of an effective coordinating agency for allocating costs among richer countries makes the problem of how to mobilize European aid insoluble. Why, asks de Swaan, cannot the EU serve as such an effective coordinating agency? De Swaan's response emphasizes the EU's market character and the declining European faith in state intervention. Although the EU has proved effective in regulating European markets, it has hardly increased Europeans' sense of community participation. De Swaan believes that, while Europeans understand that EU market regulations are decreasing the power of their own states, there is a sense that the EU has not gained in power.

De Swaan also reminds us of the EU's inability to act in a unified manner in world politics. By and large, the last decade has vindicated Stanley Hoffman's arguments that "low politics" covering economics and welfare would be more amenable to EU influence than the "high politics" of foreign policy and defense.[19] Formed in war, European states jealously preserve this legacy of their origins. The individual states' control of military force and foreign policy making constitute an almost invincible obstacle to any possible effort to construct a federative state in the foreseeable future. But we should also recall the very real limitations of the EU's capacities. The entire EU employs a staff of only thirteen thousand (three thousand of them translators), but even the Netherlands has more than twenty times that number of central government officials.[20] The budget of the EU is projected to reach 1.2 percent of total EU gross national product in 1999—a very large sum, to be sure, and one that makes the EU an important player in the politics of Europe's smaller states and in regional politics, but still a paltry proportion compared with that of its member states, which between 1995 and 1996 typically received around 30 to 40 percent of domestic product.[21]

In contrast to Abram de Swaan, Antje Wiener sees the EU as a more dynamic institution and is more optimistic about its possibilities. Taking up a theme of Bin Wong's chapter but adapting it to a European context, Wiener studies how EU commitments become rights" within a type of political organization that Wiener labels a "state-union" with fragmented citizenship.[22] Citizenship was not among the *acquis communautaire* that the EU inherited from its predecessors; rather it developed beginning with the Paris summit of the EU in

1973–1974, and Wiener traces its evolution through the Maastricht summit of 1991 and legal grounding in the Treaty of the Union in 1993.

The most common current interpretations of the transformation of moral commitments to "enforceable" legal rights stress the growing influence of international human rights law, the expanding power of the European Court of Justice, or the coalition of interests within individual powerful states including the appearance of "new social movements" throughout Europe. Such interpretations exaggerate the power of institutions whose enforcement powers are feeble and whose jurisdictions are increasingly limited, and they do not explain the highly discontinuous transformation of European states.[23] Wiener emphasizes the unlikelihood of a smooth expansion of across-the-board universal rights and points out that the evolution has been from special rights for Europeans in the direction of "specialized" rights defined according to what people did or who they were. Whether citizenship rights extended to European workers or students can be expanded to immigrant workers or students residing in Europe depends not on the inherent logic either of institutions or of political traditions but on the evolution of political opportunity and internal political mobilization.

In contrast, Wiener shows how political opportunity structures play a key role in political development, but the political opportunity structure that she considers is considerably more complicated than that within a single consolidated state. In terms of a single state, Sidney Tarrow defined political opportunity as "the opening up of access to power, shifting alignments, the availability of influential allies, and cleavages within and amongst elites."[24] But the character of political opportunities within the EU involves more intricate constellations of power, including the complicated division of powers among the Council of Ministers, the European Commission, and the European Parliament; the legacy of European understandings of the EU generated by decades of collective resolutions and agreements; the outbreak of a Europe-wide crisis beginning with the oil embargo of 1974; and the effects of political debates within individual countries in inclining British, French, and German politicians towards face-saving compromises.

Perhaps Wiener will prove correct in her hopes that a constellation of factors favoring the expansion of citizenship will crystallize within the EU. In any case, the consolidated state will not be suppressed automatically as were the Dutch municipalities described by Maarten Prak; divided sovereignty and the opportunities for maneuver and complicated alliance are likely to be with Europeans for a long time to come. But here it might be helpful to recall the Chinese case studied by Bin Wong. Both consolidated states and the European Union have made commitments to their citizens concerning opportunities and employment that they may not be able or willing to keep. In such an eventuality, migrants, feminists, and workers may have to organize outside the electoral arena to win for themselves rights that have been affirmed but not enforced by existing polities.

Whatever the outcome, it seems clear that in contemporary Europe democracy will need to be reconstructed if it is to be maintained. Markoff invites us to search around the world and in world history for examples that might serve as models for democratic development. Markoff points out the relative creativity of "semiperipheral" states in the development of democratic practices. Constitutionalism, women's suffrage, and the secret (or Australian) ballot were first enacted in relatively obscure states or regions. Markoff roughly links this pattern to the threefold division of Immanuel Wallerstein's world systems. He argues that entrenched power in core states was strong enough to fend off innovation, while the peripheries were too poor and too oppressed for such experiments. Precisely intermediate areas, often British or Spanish colonies, where most established institutions lacked deep roots were able to try new approaches.

Markoff's findings are significant, for they remind us of the potential importance of democratic inventions in countries far from the center of world political attention. In the modern period, states like South Africa and Brazil might well be locations where the democratic institutions of the future are forged. And Markoff's recognition of the continuing relevance of democratic experiment is perhaps his most important point of all. In the old homelands of democracy, the established democratic institutions of the consolidated state are proving increasingly inadequate. Democratic institutions must be reinvented for the future as they were invented in the past, and, as Markoff shows, there is no reason to think that the patterns of the future can be found in the strongest and most central consolidated states of the contemporary period.[25]

A case in point is the remarkable series of institutions for government worked out in contemporary Belgium, where the federal union, at least in the Brussels region, breaks definitively with territorialism and constitutes a truly transnational state. The Belgian constitution of 1995 recognizes the existence of communities conceived as linguistic/cultural units: French, Dutch, and the small German minority.[26] Portugal's recent decision to expand voting rights to Portuguese immigrant communities abroad represents an almost unprecedented action by a major emigrant country, and Haiti's periodic flirtation with elective representation for the migrant community as a group is also promising.

To discuss the democratic future, we must distinguish between democracy as a system of government and democracy as an ideal rooted in experience. Increasingly, the established system of democracy established in contemporary consolidated states is coming under challenge. Serious democrats must resist the temptation to identify these particular democratic systems with democracy per se. Nor should democrats commit themselves to untried utopian experiments.

Rather, as Markoff suggests, we must look to the democratic experiments of the present and learn from them what we can. Where they are successful, we should emulate them. As John Dewey argued:

> Regarded as an ideal, democracy is not an alternative to other principles of associated life. It is the idea of community life itself. It is an ideal in the only intelligible sense of an ideal; namely, the tendency and movement of things which exist carried to its final limit, viewed as completed, perfected.[27]

Notes

I would like to thank Miriam Cohen, Behrooz Moazami, and Charles Tilly for their helpful comments.

1.   Martin Shaw, Henry Coleman, and T. M. Cartledge, *National Anthems of the World* (Poole, England: Blandford Press, 1975). The comparison is not entirely consistent because the collection usually only contains the three or four best-known stanzas, and in most cases the attempt to convey rhyme yields translations more broad than precise. In the case of the then Communist nations, the collection sometimes gives both Communist and pre-Communist versions. In three cases—the Isle of Man, the Ukraine, and Wales—anthems are given for countries that are not (or were not at that time) independent. The Manx anthem seems an exotic, but our business is not to teach compilers but to learn from them.

2.   Robert David Sack, *Human Territoriality: Its Theory and History* (Cambridge: Cambridge University Press, 1986), 19.

3.   Charles Tilly, "A Primer on Citizenship," *Theory and Society* 26, no. 34 (1997): 599–602.

4.   Thomas Hobbes, *Leviathan,* ed. C. B. Macpherson (New York: Penguin Books, 1980), 223.

5.   Charles Tilly, *Coercion, Capital, and European States, A.D. 990–1990* (Cambridge, Mass.: Blackwell, 1990).

6.   Alan Milward, *The European Rescue of the Nation-State* (Berkeley and Los Angeles: University of California Press, 1992).

7.   Ernst Haas, *The Uniting of Europe; Political, Social, and Economic Forces, 1950–1957* (Stanford: Stanford University Press, 1958); and Leon N. Lindberg, *Political Dynamics of European Economic Integration* (Stanford: Stanford University Press, 1963).

8.   Tilly, *Coercion, Capital, and European States,* 143–51.

9.   John G. Gagliardo, *Reich and Nation: The Holy Roman Empire as Idea and Reality, 1763–1806* (Bloomington: Indiana University Press, 1980), 45.

10.   J. H. Elliott, "A Europe of Composite Monarchies," *Past and Present,* no. 137 (1992): 48–71.

11.   Christopher R. Friedrichs, "Artisans and Urban Politics in Seventeenth-Century

Germany," in *The Artisan and the European Town, 1500–1900*, ed. Geoffrey Crossick. (Aldershot, England: Scolar Press, 1997), 41–55.

12. On efforts at reform, see Caglar Keydar, "The Ottoman Empire" in *After Empire: Multiethnic Societies and Nation-Building: The Soviet Union and the Russian, Ottoman, and Hapsburg Empires,* ed. Karen Barkey and Mark Von Hagen (Boulder, Colo.: Westview Press, 1997), 19–29.

13. On transnational identities in the history of Irish nationalism, see Michael Hanagan, "Transnational Movements, Deterritorialized Immigrants, and the State System: A Nineteenth-Century Case Study," *Mobilization* 2, no. 1 (1998): 107–26.

14. Lowell Dittmer, "Public and Private Interests and the Participatory Ethic in China," in *Citizens and Group in Contemporary China,* ed. Victor C. Falkenheim (Ann Arbor, Mich.: Center for Chinese Studies, 1987), 17–44.

15. John Austin, *The Province of Jurisprudence Determined and the Uses of the Study of Jurisprudence* (London: Weidenfeld & Nicolson, 1954).

16. For a splendid study of Chinese protest and state making with consistent comparisons with Europe, see R. Bin Wong, *China Transformed: Economic Development, State Making, and Social Protests* (Ithaca: Cornell University Press, 1997).

17. Peter Gourevitch, "Breaking with Orthodoxy," in *Politics in Hard Times: Comparative Responses to International Economic Crises* (Ithaca: Cornell University Press, 1986), 124–80.

18. On this point, see Michael Hanagan, "Social Movements: Incorporation, Disengagement, and Opportunities: A Long View," in *How Movements Matter: Theoretical and Comparative Studies on the Consequences of Social Movements,* ed. Marco Guigni, Doug McAdam, and Charles Tilly (Minneapolis: University of Minnesota Press, 1998), 3–30.

19. Stanley Hoffman, "Obstinate or Obsolete? The Fate of the Nation State and the Case of Western Europe," *Daedalus* 95 (1966): 862–915.

20. Michael Newman, *Democracy, Sovereignty, and the European Union* (New York: St Martin's Press, 1996), 70. Peter Flora et al. vol. 1, 263.

21. For example, 39.7 percent in France, 31.4 percent in Germany, 29.3 percent in Italy, 44.2 percent in the Netherlands, 37.2 percent in Sweden, and 34.5 in the United Kingdom. Estimates from International Monetary Fund, *International Financial Statistics Yearbook, 1997* (Washington, D.C.: International Monetary Fund, 1997).

22. For a fuller statement, see Antje Wiener, *"European" Citizenship Practice: Building Institutions of a Non-State* (Boulder, Colo.: Westview Press, 1998).

23. See David Jackson, *Rights across Borders: Immigration and the Decline of Citizenship* (Baltimore: Johns Hopkins University Press, 1996); and Elizabeth Meehan, *Citizenship and the European Community* (London: Sage, 1993).

24. Sidney Tarrow, "States and Opportunities: The Political Structuring of Social Movements" in *Comparative Perspectives on Social Movements; Political Opportunities, Mobilizing Structures, and Cultural Framings*, ed. Doug McAdam, John D. McCarthy, and Mayer N. Zald (Cambridge: Cambridge University Press, 1996), 41–62, 54.

25. On the role of semiperiphery in political innovation, see Christopher Chase-

Dunn and Thomas D. Hall, *Rise and Demise: Comparing World Systems* (Boulder, Colo.: Westview Press, 1997).

26. William M. Downs, "Federalism Achieved: The Belgian Elections of May 1995," *West European Politics* 19, no. 1 (1996): 168–75; and "Belgium's Melting Fudge (Separatist Movements May Cause Flemish-Walloon Ethnic Split)," *Economist,* 16 March 1996. For background, see John Fitzmaurice, *The Politics of Belgium: A Unique Federalism* (London: Westview Press, 1996).

27. John Dewey, *The Public and Its Problems* (Athens, Ohio: Swallow Press, 1954), 148.

2

Burghers into Citizens: Urban and National Citizenship in the Netherlands during the Revolutionary Era (c. 1800)

Maarten Prak

> "I promise and swear . . . to support and remain loyal to the town of Bois-le-Duc and my fellow citizens until death us do part, so help me God." (18th c.)[1]

> "No one shall be admitted into any guilds who is not a citizen." (1675)[2]

> "Let it be known that all these offices will be open to citizens of Bois-le-Duc and none other." (1704)[3]

These quotes highlight various aspects of citizenship rights in the Dutch town of Bois-le-Duc during the eighteenth century. Obviously, they do not provide an exhaustive picture of early modern Dutch citizenship, but the quotes do bring out that citizenship was institutionalized and suggest that perhaps it was even of some relevance to the lives of the inhabitants of this particular town. This essay seeks to investigate the transformation of this early modern form of citizenship in the wake of the French Revolution. Before we look at the historical record, however, we need some sort of definition that will help us to chart the trajectory of Dutch citizenship during these turbulent years. As Charles Tilly has remarked, citizenship is "a continuing series of transactions between persons and agents of a given state in which each has enforceable rights and obligations uniquely by virtue of (1) the person's membership in an exclusive category and (2) the agent's relation to the state rather than any authority the agent may enjoy."[4] Three elements are crucial to this definition: the nature of the "persons," that is, citizens; the nature of the authority that Tilly foreshortens as "the state"; and, finally, the reciprocal relationship between these two actors. The importance of this definition is that it allows for variation through time and space and presents the bond between citizen and state as one that provides both parties with obligations on the other. The problem with such a wide definition, however, is that it makes it difficult to distinguish between various

17

types of ties between state officials and inhabitants of the state. In other words, when we let go of the formal aspect in the definition of citizenship, it tends to blur into a very wide range of issues.[5] This chapter will define the "exclusive category" from the outset as "citizenship" in the legal sense. Thus, the "people" discussed in this paper are citizens. The state presents problems too. Under the Old Regime, no such thing as Dutch citizenship existed. The state, that is, the Dutch Republic, was a federation composed of seven sovereign provinces. These provinces did not have citizens either, at least in the formal sense. Citizenship in the Dutch Republic was a local, more specifically an urban, phenomenon.[6] There was nothing unusual in this: urban citizenship was the norm throughout early modern Europe.[7] This changed radically during the Napoleonic era, in the Netherlands as much as in other European countries.[8] The French revolutionary regime and its collaborators in the occupied territories centralized government and administration and created new ties between themselves and their subjects in the form of modern citizenship.[9]

Much of the literature seems to suggest that this new form of citizenship was created in what was more or less a legal void, superficially occupied by the political theorists of the Italian Renaissance and, later on, absolutism, who took most of their inspiration from antiquity.[10] A recent survey of books on rights and citizens in Old Regime France bluntly sets out from the position that "until 1789, citizenship in France, and more broadly Europe, had little practical or ideological significance."[11] Looking at citizenship from that angle can easily circumvent any questions about the ways in which previous forms of citizenship were transformed or superseded by the citizenship of the French Revolution. That this was not at all an obvious development, however, can be deduced from the fact that in northwestern Europe the practical applications of early modern citizenship had very little to do with antiquity or Renaissance theories of classical republicanism. Instead, they were a function of the separate status that feudal society had bestowed on urban communities. And let us not forget that the very word "citizen" is derived from "city." To end these cities' privileged status was the mission of the emerging modern state. Therefore, it seems reasonable to assume with Brubaker that "[t]he modern state and state citizenship were constructed against urban autonomy and urban citizenship."[12]

This chapter tries to contribute some elements towards such an analysis.[13] It seeks to describe, not a simple creation of modern citizenship in the Netherlands around 1800, but a transition from one type of citizenship to another during the decades around 1800. This chapter demonstrates how citizenship in the Netherlands changed from a local, fragmented, and exclusive phenomenon that covered a wide range of social activities into one that was national, uniform, and inclusive, but restricted to the political and legal domains. To do this,

I discuss both a local form of citizenship of the type customary in the Dutch Republic under the Old Regime and the new, national type of citizenship introduced by subsequent revolutionary governments in the Netherlands.

Urban Citizenship under the Old Regime:
The Dutch Town of Bois-le-Duc

"The citizens of Bois-le-Duc," according to a multivolume, eighteenth-century description of the Dutch provinces, "are of two types: native and acceded."[14] Native citizens were all people born, or at least baptized, within the town. They had received their citizenship automatically and could never lose it. Other cities were less generous with their right of citizenship. In Amsterdam, for example, or the small city of Deventer, only children born within a citizen family were assured of immediate citizenship.[15] Of the almost five thousand heads of households in Bois-le-Duc in 1775, 48 percent gave their residence as place of birth.[16] The other half of the population was either deprived of the benefits of citizenship or required to obtain it through alternative means. Those who had acceded to citizenship status had bought that status and were therefore usually designated as the "purchased citizens." The purchase required a mere 17 guilders in Bois-le-Duc, a modest amount even by the standards of the time.[17] In Amsterdam the right of citizenship was for sale for 50 guilders, in eastern Nijmegen for 48.[18] The citizenship of Bois-le-Duc was also an easy buy because no extra qualifications were required. In Nijmegen or Deventer, Catholics were excluded from the privilege of citizenship.[19] Similar rules in Bois-le-Duc from the mid-seventeenth century were no longer observed in the eighteenth century.[20] Citizenship was confirmed by swearing an oath in the presence of the magistrate. The new citizen promised to remain loyal to the States-General (the government), to the Stadholder (an informal head of state), and finally to the city, "to remain loyal to my fellow citizens [male and female form], until death us do part."[21] The latter clause should not be taken lightly. In 1787, at the height of the Patriot rebellion, a group of people who introduced themselves as citizens stated that they were "prepared to defend the city and its privileges in every possible way, . . . if necessary with their blood and life."[22]

To swear the citizens' oath was to become a full member of the urban community of Bois-le-Duc. What did that mean for those involved? Why would anyone bother to become a citizen of a town like Bois-le-Duc? Contemporaries would probably list at least three obvious advantages of citizenship. First, they would point out that only citizens could be admitted to the guilds, which held a monopoly in the production of, and trade in, a wide range of goods. "Whoever is not a citizen cannot occupy himself in the burgher trades," was the brief and very clear expression of one commentator, whose opinion was echoed by many more.[23] The expression "burgher trade" was significant by itself, because in Dutch the word for citizen is actually "burger." In the fourteenth century, the guilds of Bois-le-Duc, like those of many other European towns at that time, had also gained seats on the local government, a right they were to hold until 1629, and every head of household was required to become a member of a guild, so as to ensure that all elements of the community were represented politically.[24] Since the fourteenth century, the political rights attached to citizenship had gradually diminished in Bois-le-Duc, but they had not completely disappeared. The old rule that only "native or purchased citizens" could be elected to the city's more important offices still applied.[25] Access to political office was thus a second clear advantage of citizenship in Bois-le-Duc. The third advantage of the citizen over noncitizens was that he (or she) could be tried only by a local court.[26] After one Martinus Dijkmans had been arrested in January 1788, suspected of murdering a Jew in Amsterdam, he went to great lengths to prove he was a citizen of Bois-le-Duc, to avoid extradition to Amsterdam. Dijkmans's wife was indeed able to produce an extract from the local register of baptisms, thereby proving that her husband was entitled to citizenship status. The complicating factor, however, was that he was also a citizen of Amsterdam. In the latter city Dijkmans had worked as a brazier, an occupation that required guild membership and, by implication, citizen status. On these grounds the Amsterdam magistrates insisted on bringing Dijkmans to trial before their own law court.[27]

Citizenship was not only a privilege, it also implied some obligations, as Tilly's definition of citizenship might lead us to suspect. This at least is what various authorities suggested, even though they were not always very clear about what these duties were. Some writers seemed to think that the citizens were responsible for the maintenance of the community in every conceivable way—paying taxes, performing duties in the citizen militias, helping out in case of fire, and so on.[28] If such activities had ever been the exclusive duty of the citizens, that had become a thing of the past by the eighteenth century. Such "onerous duties" were by then shouldered by citizens and ordinary inhabitants alike. References to any special burden on the citizens were ideological, a way to emphasize the special bond between citizen and community and perhaps also to justify the privileges of the citizen.

Some symbolic gestures did in fact underscore the special relationship between the purchased citizen and his town. The rite of accession, including the citizen's oath, is a case in point. Even more obvious, perhaps, was a 1783 proposal by the commission overseeing the fire equipment. Fire was still a serious threat to cities like Bois-le-Duc; one only has to think of the Great Fire of 1666 in London. In the eighteenth century, the magistrate presented medals of honor to any house-owner who replaced his wooden façade with one of stone. Bois-le-Duc did not have a professional fire brigade. In case of fire, large sections of the community were called up.[29] The commission's idea was to demand that every new citizen present a fire basket to the town.[30]

Besides citizens, the population of Bois-le-Duc, like that of other Dutch cities of the Old Regime, consisted of a second legal category, the inhabitants. Inhabitants were not legally protected by the local courts in the way citizens were. Inhabitants were not eligible for any major office. Inhabitants had no access to the guilds and could not establish themselves as independent craftsmen or shopkeepers in the trades covered by the guilds. To oversimplify somewhat, the inhabitant was without legal, political, and economic rights. In real life, however, the inhabitants' position was not that bad. They had access to normal juridical procedures; their property rights were respected like those of the citizens. Whereas in many German towns only citizens could own real estate,[31] no such restrictions were imposed in Dutch towns. Even if citizens had formal access to all local offices, the great majority of the citizens were not officeholders. By the eighteenth century the guilds in Bois-le-Duc (and most other Dutch towns), unlike their German and Belgian counterparts, did not have seats in local government.[32] In terms of direct advantages, the major difference between citizens and inhabitants thus boiled down to guild membership. It is, in fact, quite probable that most outsiders became citizens specifically to enter a guild.[33]

But differences between citizens and inhabitants did exist, not only juridically but also socially. The fact that everyone born (or baptized) in Bois-le-Duc was by definition a citizen to some extent obscures social differences. But if we look at the immigrants, who had to make a conscious effort to raise themselves from inhabitant to citizen, one cannot fail to notice the divide. A ledger from 1775 listing all heads of household with their place of birth, combined with a tax register from the same year, enables us to classify immigrants according to their wealth, as well as their status as citizens or inhabitants.[34] Whereas the native and immigrant halves of the population are remarkably alike in the way their wealth is distributed, the figures also clearly show a social differentiation within the immigrant community of Bois-le-Duc. The citizens among the immigrants are on average much better off than the mere inhabitants. Whereas the citizens are overrepresented among the upper middle class and the elite, the inhabitants are clearly overrepresented among the lower middle class and the poor.

Citizenship, in the eighteenth century no less than today, was not only a right but also an instrument of social regulation. By raising or lowering the fee to be paid for citizenship or by creating other obstacles, the authorities might try to vary the attractiveness of citizenship.[35] Established citizens of Bois-le-

Duc in fact recommended such a policy in 1786, when they proposed to admit new citizens only after a two-year residence in the town. This proposal was rejected by the magistrate, who argued, on the authority of "all political writers," "that it was absolutely necessary for the welfare of the town, to provoke and stimulate outsiders and aliens to establish themselves within the city." Merchants and artisans would be ruined if they were excluded from the guilds, and by implication from their trade, for two years.[36] This, of course, was precisely what the citizens' proposal hoped to achieve. It was even harder to regulate the influx of lower-class immigrants. Because any resident became an inhabitant without administrative ceremony, the authorities could not control the settlement of the poor, much to the despair of the directors of the welfare institutions. In the early 1770s they complained that the city was flooded with "poor aliens and beggars" who exhausted the financial resources of their institutions.[37] In 1772 it was stipulated that one could only be treated in the Great Hospital (an institution for the poor) after ten years of residence in town. To be eligible for poor relief from the municipal welfare institution, one had to prove fifteen years of residence.

Such negative reactions to outsiders point to a reflex that was central to the whole concept of early modern communities: the sharp distinction between "us" and "them."[38] When the city was looking for a new municipal architect in 1773, the advisory committee of the local government was of the opinion that an indigenous candidate "is far preferable to an alien of equal, and even of superior qualities, because he who has always lived here knows the pros and cons of every contractor, the best suppliers of building materials and finally the town's works."[39] Some years later the bakers' guild complained about competition from the surrounding villages, arguing that it was very hard on the "established burghers, who help carry the burdens of the town and whose help the city enjoys in every incident, such as fire, etc."[40] A regulation concerning the gold- and silversmiths was repealed in 1757 "as too favorable to the aliens."[41]

Aliens were not only an economic threat but also pests to society, inferior social types. Although diatribes against outsiders could be expressed generally, they were often specifically targeted at Jews and couched in terms that are shocking to twentieth-century sensibilities. The deans of the shopkeepers' guild of Bois-le-Duc claimed in 1775 that the established merchants and shopkeepers in the city were "undercut and disadvantaged ceaselessly by the illegal practices of aliens, particularly of the Jewish nation, who come and go, do not pay any taxes and carry stolen goods, from bankrupt estates into the city." To these people it made no difference where they lived, and "they do not care about moving from one place to another, leaving behind their debts." The guild's directors demanded that Jews be banned from citizenship in Bois-le-

Duc.[42] Two years later they repeated their request,[43] and this time they got their way: the admission of Jews, reestablished in 1768, was terminated again.[44] In the ten years that Jews had been admitted into Bois-le-Duc, seven had gained citizenship.[45] In fact, three had become members of the shopkeepers' guild.[46] Although the guild had clamored for their deportation, no documents suggest that this actually happened. Samuel Joseph claimed in 1790 that he had lived in the city for over twenty years and had had his marriage ceremony ratified by the aldermen in 1786.[47] Simon Hartog (or Hartogensis), who left town in 1777, returned in 1787. According to his own testimony, he "was known publicly by everyone as an established resident of the city, who has exercised his affairs, paid his taxes and truly owns three houses within the town."[48] In 1780, the magistrate himself had already noticed that the number of Jewish inhabitants kept growing, in spite of the prohibition against their establishment.[49]

Citizenship in the Age of the Democratic Revolution

During the 1770s and 1780s, new ideas about citizenship began to emerge among radical opponents of the regime then in power. This regime was headed by the Orange stadholder, who was nominally a servant of the sovereign provinces but in fact controlled the provincial estates through his patronage-based influence on major political appointments.[50] Against the hierarchical model of clientelism, opponents of the stadholder developed a model of participatory citizenship. Sources of inspiration were found among political essayists abroad, particularly in the writings of such British Enlightenment philosophers as Price, Priestley, and Hutcheson, whose ideas were disseminated through the traditional broadsheets and also discussed in the popular political press, which developed more or less overnight in the early 1780s, building on an earlier tradition of political pamphleteering.[51] The new conception of citizenship was no longer corporate and local but general and national. Citizens now became "the people of the Netherlands," to whom an instantly famous pamphlet in 1781 addressed itself.[52] Instead of merely conferring membership in corporate institution, the new citizenship required active participation in the affairs of the community, particularly in public administration. Citizenship, in other words, became strongly politicized, where before it had been just as much an economic and social institution. The political debate about citizenship linked up with the tradition of classical republicanism as it had been developed in the Italian city-states of the Renaissance and later picked up by seventeenth-century English political theorists.[53] The influence of classical republicanism was clearly visible in the appearance of authors and actors from Greek and Roman antiquity, who played no role whatsoever in the tradition of the "ancient constitution" but were now presented as exemplary models.[54]

These new ideas sat somewhat uncomfortably alongside the urban citizenship that was in many respects alive and well in the cities of the Dutch Republic. Urban citizenship, based on privileges and other texts of the ancient constitution, had in the past provided a rallying point for radical opposition movements.[55] The Patriots, even had they wanted to, could not afford to disregard this tradition. Political expediency dictated that attacks on the stadholder and his clients would be legitimized by arguments that appealed to the tradition at least as much as to new ideas.

As a consequence, elements common to both traditions came to be highlighted, both in the discourse and in everyday practices of the Patriot revolutionaries, during the 1780s. The citizen militias in particular provided a common ground.[56] In the tradition of classic republicanism—one has only to think of Machiavelli—the citizen's virtue was exemplified by his arms, which at one and the same time established him as an independent individual and as a member of the community willing to participate in the defense of the commonwealth. In the tradition of ancient constitutionalism, citizen militias signified the capacity of the urban community to maintain its independence. Hence, the militias could be, and in times of political troubles were, put forward as representing the body of the community, that is, the burghers of the town.

In most cities, Patriot demands contained, almost without exception, a large dose of good old urban constitutionalism. In the city of Deventer, a radical draft constitution (1787) managed to offend the guilds but nevertheless reserved the franchise for those who held (urban) citizenship status.[57] In radical Utrecht, similar requirements were included in the Patriot program. In Bois-le-Duc, the local militias rearticulated their traditional rights and contribution to the community. Citizens, and more particularly the "native citizens," pleaded their right to preferential treatment over those of alien stock.[58] For all these local movements, urban citizenship, even if it did not give the franchise to the citizenry, provided a basis for collective action. This was the situation when the Patriot movement was forcefully suppressed in the late summer of 1787.

The National Citizenship of the Revolutionary Era

In the winter of 1794–1795 the Dutch Republic was occupied by French revolutionary forces, an event that was to change the nature of the entire political system in the Netherlands.[59] Perforce, "transactions between persons and agents of state" went through a fundamental transformation as well. "Transformation" is perhaps the wrong word, because the men who came to power acted, as far as citizenship was concerned, as if they were confronted with a vacant lot. The new constitutions for the Batavian Republic, as they were put together in successive forms in 1796, 1797, and 1798, never even referred to urban citizenship. They simply created a hitherto nonexistent category of people: the citizens of the Netherlands. Although one could assume that citizenship in the Batavian Republic was of French making, nothing in fact points in that direction. The goal of the French occupation was to extract a maximum of financial support from the Dutch.[60] To this end, French policy was to leave the Dutch politicians to look after the details themselves. Of course, the Dutch were aware of the example the French had set. Quite a few Dutch revolutionaries had actually been in France in 1789 and subsequent years. There is, however, no evidence that the French pushed their own political creations as models for the Dutch.

The national citizen, as he began to take shape in the first constitutional draft of 1796, was not a well-defined character. The second article of the draft simply stated that "[t]he sovereignty rests with the People of the Netherlands," immediately followed by a third article that bound citizenship to the exercise of political rights: "3. This [sovereignty] is exercised by the enfranchised citizens."[61] The qualities that were required of a citizen were therefore spelled out in a chapter devoted to the franchise, which defined a citizen as someone registered as a voter. Article 9 of the draft explicitly stated: "Every Citizen of the Netherlands who registers as a voter . . . thereby agrees to renounce all relations with other nations, and to belong to no other than the Dutch Nation." Two further articles listed who could be registered as voters and who could not. Acceptable as voters, and implicitly as citizens (article 10), were those who had been born within the Dutch Republic and had permanent residence there and were twenty-two years of age; and (2) aliens who had lived in the republic for ten years, or for five years if married to a woman born in the Netherlands. A fourth clause stated that in ten years' time, it would be required of voters that they be able to read and write. The list of reasons for exclusion (article 11) was much longer, consisting of no fewer than nine categories: (1) those who went to live in another country; (2) those under legal restraint; (3) bankrupts; (4) those indicted or dishonored by a legal judgment; (5) everyone in the service of a foreign power, either ecclesiastical or secular, or receiving pensions from such powers; (6) members of foreign corporations that require their members to take an oath; (7-8) everyone supported by ecclesiastical or public welfare or living in a welfare institution; and, finally, (9) those who had bought or sold votes. Although this was not stated explicitly, the largest category excluded from citizenship, of course, consisted of women.

The 1796 draft never even got beyond the national parliament, which itself was a product of the revolution. The National Assembly was roughly divided between federalists and those in favor of a unified state. In 1796 the federalists still held the high ground, making it even more remarkable that no reference was made to urban citizenship and the way it might relate to national citizenship. Nonetheless, some important elements of citizenship as previously understood did survive, particularly in the categories of exclusion. The attempt to restrict voting, and by definition citizenship, to inhabitants who were economically and otherwise "independent" has strong overtones of the urban traditions of citizenship. At the same time, new elements were introduced that were very different from these traditions. From a social point of view, there was definitely much continuity. But politically, the picture suggests rupture much more than a development from one type of citizenship to another.

A new draft, presented in 1797, changed some details as far as citizenship was concerned but not the overall picture.[62] Aliens were now eligible for citizenship after six years of residence, instead of ten; for those married to a Dutch woman, three years' residence was sufficient. Newly added were four articles designed to make citizenship not merely a right but an obligation. All those qualified to vote were required to register. Those who did not register would lose whatever public office or pension they had. Another addition was the requirement, upon registration, to swear an oath condemning the previous regime. This draft was put before the electorate in August 1797—and rejected out of hand by a clear majority. The reasons for this rejection are not yet well understood. Most historians seem to think that the draft was not radical enough, that it contained too many traces of federalism.[63] Some contemporaries, however, were of the opinion that it was the other way around: the destruction of the guilds announced in the constitution had discredited it with the electorate.[64] After a few months, in January 1798, the deadlock created by the rejection of the constitution was broken by the radicals. With the help of the French army, they executed a coup d'état on 22 January and immediately proclaimed the unified state in which all other authorities—that is, provinces and cities—were reduced to "mere administrative bodies," according to the official proclamation. The new state of affairs was to be shortly legitimized by a constitution, which proved to be acceptable to a thoroughly purged electorate—potential dissidents were removed from the voting register.

The constitution of 1798 seemed to say that citizenship was of a very general nature but could only be exercised after one had registered as a voter.[65] The qualifications were the same as in the previous drafts, albeit with minor variations. Aliens now had to be able to read and write the Dutch language, and the oath required a declaration of adherence to the new regime and of abhorrence of federalism. To the list of those excluded was added a new category: private servants living with their masters.[66] Another new element was the formal certification of citizenship in the shape of certificate of citizenship that everyone who registered as a voter would receive.[67]

One remarkable aspect of the new conception of citizenship was the absence of any reference to the Jews. As we saw earlier, the urban constitutions considered them as the outsiders par excellence. Even if Jews were admitted to urban citizenship, they often remained subject to special clauses, such as a prohibition from joining a guild (as in Amsterdam) or a special tariff for registration. This special status was lifted in 1796, when the National Assembly decided that Jews could become citizens of the Batavian Republic. The debates on this issue were significant in at least two respects.[68] First, they established that citizenship was an individual quality. As one member remarked, a well-ordered civil society should consist of "collected individual citizens and not of collected corporations." Therefore, Jews were not admissible as a people but only individually. The second significant aspect was the firm decision not to allow the provincial or local bylaws concerning the Jews to interfere with this national policy.

The new citizenship defined the citizens' claim on the state very widely and at the same time provided very little in terms of practical arrangements, at least outside the realm of politics. The constitution of 1798 promised to "all members of society, . . . without distinction of birth, wealth, estate or rank, an equal claim on society's advantages" (art. iii). Freedom of speech (art. xvi), the right to petition the government (xvii), the right of assembly (xviii), of public worship in any church (xix), and so on, were all granted—rights that were not self-evident or in fact were explicitly missing (e.g., public worship outside the Dutch Reformed Church) from citizenship under the Old Regime.[70] Urban citizenship, on the other hand, had provided many more specific claims on the authorities, such as access to the guild trades, trial before a local court, and sometimes also privileged access to welfare institutions, which were absent from the new citizenship.

Significantly, the struggle between the old and the new citizenship was not over the issue itself but over the institutional corollaries of urban citizenship: urban political autonomy, the organization of the judiciary, and the guilds.[71] The political autonomy of Bois-le-Duc was reduced step by step from 1798 onwards. One significant phase, in 1803, demonstrates the process well. In 1802, all communities in the province of Brabant had received orders to draft a new local code. The draft from Bois-le-Duc contained references to the old regime, such as "city" instead of the neutral "community" now in vogue; it still demanded that members of the town council be citizens of Bois-le-Duc; it insisted on the continuation of the local court of law; and so on. All these elements were carefully removed when the provincial authorities edited the draft in January 1803. The council of Bois-le-Duc then refused to comply with these changes. It was prepared to do so only after several weeks of negotiations, which came to an end when the province threatened to publish the new code book on its own authority, as well as to "take such measures, the woeful consequences of which will harm the persons and families of the council and they will live to regret it."[72] By gradually limiting the scope of urban autonomy, the central government of the Dutch state and its provincial agencies indirectly subverted urban citizenship, which was withering away while national citizenship gained in significance.

Conclusion

The Dutch Republic had a rich civic tradition, not least because it was one of the most urbanized countries of early modern Europe. With as much as 35 percent of the population living in cities,[73] assuming that between a quarter and half of the inhabitants of towns were citizens, urban citizenship may have covered as much as 9 to 18 percent of the people of the Netherlands in the late eighteenth century. The example of Bois-le-Duc demonstrates that urban citizenship was a living institution.[74] Although the Enlightenment added new elements to the idea of citizenship, the radical Patriot movement of the 1780s still worked to a large extent within the boundaries set by this urban tradition of citizenship.[75] Only after the French Revolution and the invasion of the Dutch Republic by French revolutionary armies in the winter of 1794–1795 did new conceptions of citizenship emerge to dominate the debate henceforth.

The new national citizenship was neither a transformed version of the older urban citizenship nor a full break with the past. Socially, the two types displayed some distinctive common traits, particularly the emphasis on independence as a qualification for citizenship. Bankrupts, servants, and the poor could not be assumed to be able to decide for themselves. On this point, notions from the urban tradition were continued by the new regime. At the same time, citizenship was thrown open to rural folk as well as urbanites. But the national citizenship that was bestowed on them was more restricted than its urban predecessor. Instead of covering political, economic, social, and legal spheres, the new citizenship was restricted to the citizen's political capacities. Given this combination of old and new elements, it is remarkable that the emergence of the new citizenship in the Netherlands did not lead to a genuine confrontation with the urban tradition of citizenship. Contrary to Brubaker's statement that national citizenship was "constructed against urban autonomy and urban citizenship," the Dutch experience suggests that the two floated past each other, almost without taking notice of each other, it seems. In this sense, the political rupture outweighed the social continuities. The reason for that, I would suggest, is that national citizenship in the Netherlands—and probably everywhere else in continental Europe during the revolutionary era—was part of an effort to create something that had not existed before: domestic, in the sense of national, politics.[76] Insofar as the Dutch experience of citizenship had been distinctly local, the new national citizenship was a radical departure from the past. Taking the argument to its logical conclusion, one could say that given the distinctly local character of Dutch citizenship before the Revolution, the rupture in the Netherlands was perhaps even more radical than in France.[77]

Before the French Revolution, the state had provided legal and military protection to its subjects in exchange for a financial contribution in the form of taxes or loans. Relationships between subjects and the state's agents were usually indirect, as Tilly has pointed out. The revolutionary state instead sought to provide general "well-being" to its population, without the intermediate services of corporations and individual brokers. The national citizen became both the object of the state's new domestic services and the ultimate source of legitimacy of the state's policies. In the end, national citizenship would prove to be incompatible with urban citizenship and the local political autonomy it implied. But the Stadtbürger (urban citizen) was superseded by the Staatbürger (national citizen), not through direct confrontation, but through the creation of an alternative political domain. Within the national arena, new types of policies were appropriate, as well as new types of political strategy. Democracy, if that is what we want to call the rights given to the Dutch citizens, was the product, not of demands put forward by an oppressed population, but of a new institutional environment imposed upon the people by revolutionary elites.

Notes

This is a somewhat modified version of an article that was first published under the same title in *Theory and Society* 26 (1997): 403–20. An early version of the paper was presented at the Twentieth Social Science History Conference in Chicago in 1995, in a session convened by Michael Hanagan. I would like to thank him and Wayne te Brake for inviting me, and Katherine A. Lynch for her enthusiasm. The text was redrafted at the University of Exeter (England) and I want to acknowledge the hospitality of its Department of Archeology and History. I am particularly grateful to Jonathan Barry, whose comments on the manuscript improved the English and helped to clarify my thinking.

1. Citizens' oath for the town of Bois-le-Duc, as printed in the *'s Hertogenbossche Comptoir en Schryfalmanach* 1784, 112. On citizenship oaths, see also Rainer Koch, *Grundlagen bürgerlicher Herrschaft. Verfassungs- und sozialgeschichtliche Studien zur bürgerlichen Gesellschaft in Frankfurt am Main, 1612–1866,* Frankfurter historische Abhandlungen 27 (Wiesbaden: Franz Steiner, 1983), 76–77; and, more broadly, Paolo Prodi, *Der Eid in der europäischen Verfassungsgeschichte,* Schriften des Historischen Kollegs, Vorträge 33 (Munich: Stiftung Historisches Kolleg, 1992).

2. National archives (Rijksarchief) in North Brabant, Collection Martini, 123m: Codex Instructionem, vol. 1, fol. 28.

3. National archives in North Brabant, Collection Martini, Codex Instructionem, vol. 1, fol. 62; Collectanea Van Heurn, fol. 122ii.

4. Charles Tilly, "Citizenship, Identity, and Social History," *International Review of Social History* 40, (1995, supp. 3): 8; also published in 1998 by Cambridge University Press as Charles Tilly, ed., *Citizenship, Identity, and Social History.*

5. Rogers Brubaker, *Citizenship and Nationhood in France and Germany* (Cambridge: Harvard University Press, 1992), 21–23.

6. Some villages in the province of Holland had inhabitants who were known as "citizens." It is not entirely clear if there were special rights attached to this status. A. Th. van Deursen, *Een dorp in de polder: Graft in de zeventiende eeuw* (Amsterdam: Bert Bakker, 1994), 192.

7. See the papers collected in Simona Cerutti, Robert Descimon, and Maarten Prak, eds., "Cittadinanze," *Quaderni Storici* 30, no. 89 (1995): 281–513; and in Marc Boone and Maarten Prak, eds., *Statuts individuels, statuts corporatifs, et statuts judiciaires dans les villes européennes (moyen âge et temps modernes) Individual, Corporate, and Judicial Status in European Cities (Late Middle Ages and Early Modern Period)* (Leuven/Apeldoorn: Garant, 1996).

8. Derek Heater, *Citizenship: The Civic Ideal in World History, Politics, and Education* (London: Longman, 1990), 37–52.

9. The debates about citizenship during the Revolution are reviewed by William Sewell, "Le citoyen/la citoyenne: Activity, Passivity, and the Revolutionary Concept of Citizenship," in *The French Revolution and the Creation of Modern Political Culture,* vol. 2, *The Political Culture of the French Revolution,* ed. Colin Lucas (Oxford: Pergamon Press, 1988), 105–23. See also Pierre Rosanvallon, *Le sacre du citoyen: Histoire du suffrage universel en France* (Paris: Gallimard, 1992).

10. See the selection of primary texts in the reader by Paul Barry Clarke, ed., *Citizenship* (London: Pluto Press, 1994). T. H. Marshall, in his classic essay, acknowledged urban citizenship as "genuine" but considered it irrelevant to the development of national citizenship. See T. H. Marshall, *Citizenship and Social Class and Other Essays* (Cambridge: Cambridge University Press, 1950), 12. On Marshall's chronology, see also Anthony M. Rees, "T. H. Marshall and the Progress of Citizenship," in *Citizenship Today: The Contemporary Relevance of T .H. Marshall,* ed. Martin Bulmer and Anthony M. Rees (London: UCL Press, 1996), 8, 14–17.

11. Gail Bossenga, "Rights and Citizens in the Old Regime," *French Historical Studies* 20 (1997): 218.

12. Brubaker, *Citizenship and Nationhood,* 42.

13. The need for this type of research is underscored by recent work that claims that "civic" or "communal" traditions contribute to the success of democracy. See Robert D. Putnam, *Making Democracy Work: Civic Traditions in Modern Italy* (Princeton: Princeton University Press, 1993), esp. chap. 5; Antony Black, "Communal Democracy and Its History," *Political Studies* 45 (1997): 5–20.

14. *Teegenwoordige Staat der Nederlanden,* vol. 12, *Generaliteitslanden* (Amsterdam: Isaac Tirion, 1740), 47.

15. Hubert Nusteling, *Welvaart en werkgelegenheid in Amsterdam, 1540–1860. Een relaas over demografie, economie, en sociale politiek van een wereldstad* (Amsterdam: Bataafsche Leeuw, 1985), 146; Maarten Prak, "Cittadini, abitanti, e forestieri: Una classificazione della popolazione di Amsterdam nella prima età moderna," *Quaderni Storici* 30, no. 89 (1995): 335; G. Dumbar, *Het kerkelyk en wereltlyk Deventer . . .*, vol. 1 (Deventer: Lucas Leemhorst, 1788), 22.

16. These data have been reconstructed on the basis of Municipal archive Bois-le-Duc (BLD) (Stadsarchief 's Hertogenbosch), Old archive (Oud archief), C 106, "Blokboeken" 1775. The exact number was 2,315 heads of households born in Bois-le-Duc, of a total of 4,817 households.

17. Municipal archive BLD, Old archive, A 560, Register Van Heurn.

18. Prak, "Cittadini," 336; J. A. Schimmel, *Burgerrecht te Nijmegen, 1592–1810: Geschiedenis van de verlening en burgerlijst,* Bijdragen tot de Geschiedenis van het Zuiden van Nederland, vol. 7 (Tilburg: Stichting Zuidelijk Historisch Contact, 1966), 38–39.

19. F. M. H. C. Adriaens, *De magistraat van Nijmegen en de armenzorg, 1825–1846,* Bijdragen tot de sociale en economische geschiedenis van het Zuiden van Nederland, vol. 2 (Tilburg: Stichting tot bevordering van de studie der sociale en economische geschiedenis, 1956), 32–35; Wayne Ph. te Brake, *Regents and Rebels: The Revolutionary World of an Eighteenth-Century Dutch City* (Oxford: Blackwell, 1989), 93.

20. National archives in North Brabant, Collection Martini 63, Collectanea Van Heurn, fol. 426r.

21. *'s Hertogenbossche Comptoir en Schryfalmanach* 1784, 112

22. Municipal archive BLD, Old archive, A 314, Letters and reports, 16 May 1787.

23. National archives in North Brabant, Collection Martini, 62, Collectanea Van Heurn, fol. 122ii.

24. N. H. L. van den Heuvel, *De ambachtsgilden van 's Hertogenbosch voor 1629* ('s Hertogenbosch: Kemink, 1946), 277; B. C. M. Jacobs, *Justitie en politie in 's Hertogenbosch voor 1629,* Brabantse Rechtshistorische Reeks, vol. 1 (Assen: Van Gorcum, 1986), 59–60, 206 n 60. Cf. also Knut Schulz, "Die politische Zunft: Eine die spätmittelalterliche Stadt prägende Institution," in *Verwaltung und Politik in Städten Mitteleuropas: Beiträge zu Verfassungswirklichkeit in Altständischer Zeit,* Städteforschung, vol. A 34, ed. Wilfried Ehbrecht (Cologne: Böhlau Verlag, 1994), 1–20.

25. National archives in North Brabant, Collection Martini 123m, Codex Instructionem, fol. 28.

26. Municipal archive BLD, Old archive, A 560, Register Van Heurn, fol. 64v–65r.

27. Municipal archive BLD, Old archive, A 161, Resolutions, 5 February 1788, fol. 37r–42r.

28. Municipal archive BLD, Bossche schuttersgilden (Archives of the citizen militias) 66a, Memorie by forme van Replicq gedaen maeken . . . wegens de capiteijn en verdere officieren van de Jonge Schuts Bogaert, 1768.

29. *Brandt-keure der stadt 's Hertogenbosch* (Bois-le-Duc, 1739).

30. Municipal archive BLD, Old archive, A 310, Letters and reports, 5 March 1783.

31. Gerald L. Soliday, *A Community in Conflict: Frankfurt Society in the Seventeenth and Eighteenth Centuries* (Hanover: University Press of New Hampshire, 1974), 54–55; Dietrich Ebeling, *Bürgertum und Pöbel: Wirtschaft und Gesellschaft Kölns im 18. Jahrhundert*, Städteforschung, vol. A 26 (Cologne: Böhlau Verlag, 1987), 33, 111.

32. E.g., Karin Van Honacker, "De politieke cultuur van de Brusselse ambachten in de achttiende eeuw: conservatisme, corporatisme, od opportunisme?" in *Werken volgens de regels: Ambachten in Brabant en Vlaanderen, 1500–1800*, ed. Catharina Lis and Hugo Soly (Brussels: VUB University Press, 1994), 179–228.

33. Cf. Prak, "Cittadini," 344.

34. Municipal archive BLD, Old archive, C 106, "Blokboeken" and "Tauxen," 1775; Collection of additions, 8087, Citizens' register 1742–1775.

35. Nusteling, *Welvaart en werkgelegenheid*, 146–47; Prak, "Cittadini," 336–37.

36. Municipal archive BLD, Old archive, A 313, Letters and reports, 6 December 1786.

37. Municipal archive BLD, Old archive, Inventory Van Rooy, Resolutions of the "Blok" masters: Blok A, 26 January 1770, fol. 34r–v.

38. Maarten Prak, "Individual, Corporation, and Society: The Rhetoric of Dutch Guilds," in *Statuts individuels*, 255–79.

39. Municipal archive BLD, Old archive, A 146, Resolutions, 10 November 1773.

40. Municipal archive BLD, Old archive, A 316, Letters and reports, 21 October 1789.

41. Municipal archive BLD, Old archive, A 148, Resolutions, 20 December 1775, fol. 467r.

42. Municipal archive BLD, Old archive, A 148, Resolutions, 25 October 1775.

43. Municipal archive BLD, Old archive, A 304, Letters and reports, 12 March 1777.

44. Municipal archive BLD, Old archive, A 150, Resolutions, 26 March 1777.

45. Municipal archive BLD, Collections of additions 8087, Citizens' register: Isak Moses (4 May 1768), Jacob Joseph Cohen (30 May 1769), Salomon Levi Oppenheim (14 June 1769), Gerson Abraham Demorhansch, or de Morhansch (15 June 1769), Simon Israel Ulman (11 February 1771), Isak Benedictus (17 September 1771), Marcus Levi (17 May 1774).

46. Municipal archive of BLD, Guilds' archives BLD, 185, Masters' register of the shopkeepers' guild: Isak Moses 1768, Gerson Abaraham de Morhansch 1769, Isaak Benediktus 1772.

47. Municipal archive BLD, Old archive, A 317, Letters and reports, 15 December 1790.

48. Municipal archive BLD, Old archive, A 317, Letters and reports, 15 December 1790.

49. Municipal archive BLD, Old archive, A 153, Resolutions, 5 April 1780, fol. 100v–103r.

50. A. J. C. M. Gabriëls, *De heren als dienaren en de dienaar als heer: Het*

stadhouderlijk stelsel in de tweede helft van de achttiende eeuw, Hollandse Historische Reeks, vol. 14 (The Hague: Stichting HHR, 1990).

51. Nicolaas C. F. van Sas, "The Patriot Revolution: New Perspectives," in *The Dutch Republic in the Eighteenth Century: Decline, Enlightenment, and Revolution,* ed. Margaret C. Jacob and Wijnand W. Mijnhardt. (Ithaca: Cornell University Press, 1992), 99–106.

52. Joan Derk van der Capellen, *Aan het volk van Nederland: Het patriottisch program uit 1781,* ed. H. L. Zwitser (1781; reprint Amsterdam: De Bataafsche Leeuw, 1987).

53. Cf. J. G. A. Pocock, *The Machiavellian Moment: Florentine Political Thought and the Atlantic Republican Tradition* (Princeton: Princeton University Press, 1975). See also Daniel T. Rodgers, "Republicanism: The Career of a Concept," *Journal of American History* 79 (1992): 11–38.

54. S. R. E. Klein, *Patriots Republikanisme: Politieke cultuur in Nederland, 1766–1787* (Amsterdam: Amsterdam University Press, 1995), 212–14.

55. Maarten Prak, "Citizen Radicalism and Democracy in the Dutch Republic: The Patriot Movement of the 1780s," *Theory and Society* 20 (1991): 73–102; Wayne Ph. te Brake, "Provincial Histories and National Revolution in the Dutch Republic," in *The Dutch Republic,* 60–90; Marc Boone and Maarten Prak, "Rulers, Patricians and Burghers: The Great and the Little Traditions of Urban Revolt in the Low Countries," in *A Miracle Mirrored: The Dutch Republic in European Perspective,* ed. Karel Davids and Jan Lucassen (Cambridge: Cambridge University Press, 1995), 99–134.

56. Klein, *Patriots Republikanisme,* chap. 5; see also Paul Knevel, *Burgers in het geweer: De schutterijen in Holland, 1550–1700,* Hollandse Studiën, vol. 32 (Hilversum: Verloren, 1994), chap. 10.

57. te Brake, *Regents and Rebels,* 136 n 9.

58. Municipal archive BLD, Old archives, A 159, Resolutions, 4 January 1786.

59. For the general history of these years, see Simon Schama, *Patriots and Liberators: Revolution in the Netherlands, 1780–1813* (New York: Alfred A. Knopf, 1977).

60. Schama, *Patriots and Liberators,* 195–207.

61. Facsimile edition of the draft constitution, in *Het plan van constitutie van 1796,* ed. L. de Gou, Rijks Geschiedkundige Publicatiën, kleine serie, vol. 40 ('s Gravenhage, 1975).

62. Facsimile of the draft of the constitution of 1797, in *Het ontwerp van constitutie van 1797,* vol. 3, ed. L. de Gou, Rijks Geschiedkundige Publicatiën, kleine serie, vol. 57 ('s Gravenhage, 1985), articles 8–14.

63. See, e.g., Schama, *Patriots and Liberators,* 270.

64. According to a preprinted petition, to be signed by "Citizens of the Netherlands": "No doubt, among the reasons why the draft constitution that was recently put before the People of the Netherlands has been turned down by such a large majority not the least important has been the general destruction of all Guilds, Corporations, and Brotherhoods of Trades, as it was included in that draft." Municipal archive Amsterdam, Amsterdam Library, B 1798, no. 6.

65. Article X of title II reads: "Nobody, however, can, as a Batavian Citizen exercise

an immediate influence on the administration of Society, unless he has registered in the public Pollbook of the Community he belongs to." *De staatsregeling van 1798: Bronnen voor de totstandkoming,* vol. 2, ed. L. de Gou, Rijks Geschiedkundige Publicatiën, kleine serie, vol. 67 ('s Gravenhage, 1990), 114.

66. *De staatsregeling van 1798,* 115, title II, art. XIII.d.

67. *De staatsregeling van 1798,* 114, title II, art. XII.

68. This section is based on A. Huussen Jr., "De Gelijkstelling der Joden met andere Nederlandse Burgers in 1796," in *Religies en (on)gelijkheid in een plurale samenleving,* ed. Reender Kranenborg and Wessel Stoker. (Louvain: Garant, 1995), 149–60; quote on 155. See also Jozeph Michman, *Dutch Jewry during the Emancipation Period 1787–1815: Gothic Turrets on a Corinthian Building* (Amsterdam: Amsterdam University Press, 1995); and Hetty Berg, ed., *De Gelykstaat der Joden: Inburgering van een minderheid* (Amsterdam: Waanders, 1996)

69. Later constitutions did not diverge significantly from the pattern established in the 1790s, as is demonstrated by Eric J. M. Heijs, *Van vreemdeling tot Nederlander: De verlening van het Nederlanderschap aan vreemdelingen, 1813–1992: Een wetenschappelijke proeve op het gebied van de rechtsgeleerdheid* (Amsterdam: Het Spinhuis, 1995), chap. 2.

70. *Staatsregeling van 1798,* 106–9; quote on 106.

71. On the suppression of the guilds, see C. Wiskerke, *De afschaffing der gilden in Nederland* (Amsterdam: Paris, 1938).

72. Municipal archive BLD, New archives, 4, Minutes, 24 February 1803. Cf. Maarten Prak, "Van stadsregering naar gemeentebestuur: De veranderende plaats van de stad in het staatkundig bestel, 1770–1848," in *Bestuurders in het archief. Symposium ter gelegenheid van het 150-jarig bestaan van het Stadsarchief 's Hertogenbosch,* ed. Aart Vos, Publicaties van het Stadsarchief van 's Hertogenbosch, vol. 3 (Den Bosch: Stadsarchief, 1991), 16.

73. Estimate based on data from the first national census in 1795, provided in A. M. van der Woude, "Demografische ontwikkeling van de Noordelijke Nederlanden 1500–1800," in *Algemene geschiedenis der Nederlanden,* vol. 5, ed. D. P. Blok et al. (Bussum: Fibula–Van Dishoeck, 1980), 139.

74. Examples from other European countries can be found in Joseph di Corcia, "Bourg, Bourgeois, Bourgeois de Paris from the Eleventh to the Eighteenth Century," *Journal of Modern History* 50 (1978): 207–33; Robert Descimon, "'Bourgeois de Paris': Les migrations sociales d'un privilège (14e–17e siècles)," in *Histoire sociale, histoire globale?* ed. Christophe Charles (Paris: Editions de la Maison des Sciences de l'Homme, 1993), 173–82; Lothar Gall, ed., *Vom alten zum neuen Bürgertum: Die mitteleuropäische Stadt im Umbruch,* Stadt und Bürgertum, vol. 3 (Munich: Oldenbourg, 1991); Hans-Werner Hahn, *Altständische Bürgertum zwischen Beharrung und Wandel: Wetzlar 1689–1870,* Stadt und Bürgertum, vol. 2 (Munich: Oldenbourg, 1991); Steve Rappaport, *Worlds within Worlds: Structures of Life in Sixteenth-Century London* (Cambridge: Cambridge University Press, 1989), 29–31, 35, 53, 60, as well as in the collections of essays quoted in note 7.

75. Cf. Prak, "Citizen Radicalism."

76. The transition was not necessarily permanent. In many German towns, traditional urban citizenship was restored after Napoleon's defeat. See Koch, *Grundlagen bürgerlicher Herrschaft,* 78; Gall, *Vom alten zum neuen Bürgertum,* 56 (Bremen), 505 (Karlsruhe, Mannheim), 653 (Munich). For the broader dimensions of the debate about Bürgertum in Germany, see the review article by Jonathan Sperber, "Bürger, Bürgertum, Bürgerlichkeit, Bürgerliche Gesellschaft: Studies of the German (Upper) Middle Class and Its Sociocultural World," *Journal of Modern History* 69 (1997): 271–97, esp. 278–80.

77. I owe this idea to an unpublished conference paper by Wayne Ph. te Brake, "The Old Régime and the Dutch Revolution" (1997).

3

Citizens in Search of a State: The Limits of Political Participation in the Late Ottoman Empire

Ariel Salzmann

Restaging Late Empire

Social scientists return periodically to the spectacle known as the "end of empire."[1] Notwithstanding fresh perspectives on, and even a belated appreciation for, the multiethnic states of the past, depictions of the late Ottoman Empire continue to follow time-honored theatrical conventions. The curtain rises on the sultan's besieged seraglio. European battleships rescue the empire from unruly Janissaries and rebellious provincial lords. However, the same Western-inspired reforms and modern technology that sustain the sultan's rule also trouble the empire's "traditional" societies. As cultural awakening and revolutionary ideas drive Balkan Christians toward nation-states of their own, the cast dwindles. By the early twentieth century, only the sultan's loyal Middle Eastern subjects remain to interpret empire's delayed but inevitable demise.

Despite its epic sweep and aesthetic familiarity, this dramatization belies Ottoman realities.[2] The shifting geopolitical relations of the nineteenth century and the conflicting motivations of the empire's protagonists have more in common with modern theater than Greek tragedy. The great powers and, later, post-Ottoman nations resemble the intrusive stage manager in Pirandello's *Six Characters in Search of an Author*. Bursting onto the stage, they summarily cut short speech, draw the curtains, and determine the sequence of action—the "rules of the game." The flight of former subjects, exiles, and revolutionaries as well as the influx of refugees continues to reconstitute empire's dramatis personae and blur the boundaries between actors and audience, citizens and noncitizens. Before the curtain falls, Ottoman actors struggle to redefine their characters and identify new political communities as they salvage the remnants of a territorial state.[3]

Taking a cue from Pirandello, this essay proposes a restaging of the last Ottoman century. Using the complex and interactive processes that constitute

37

modern citizenship, it investigates the dynamic interaction between Ottoman actors and the changing parameters of state power in the context of a changing global order.[4] Citizenship-like rights in the Ottoman Empire—that is, claims premised on a direct relation between state and individual—date only to the middle decades of the nineteenth century, when sultanic regimes attempted to transform both the coercive and consensual means of rule. As elsewhere the processes of citizenship were protracted; new rights were unevenly conferred and irregularly enforced. However, Ottoman reformers also grappled with more than a century of decentralized rule that had encouraged a wide variety of "vernacular" political systems (socially, economically, and organizationally specific or spatially contained relations of power). Because of this, the liberal franchise took shape in tandem with efforts to create fundamentally new governmental powers.

Without minimizing the particularities of the Ottoman path to the modern state, the empire's political impasse at the end of the century should not be attributed to either an illiberal franchise or an unresponsive government. In fact, certain aspects of Ottoman legal reform actually anticipated similar legislation in much of the West. Rather, the instability of Ottoman citizenship was due to the overall lateness of the empire's organizational centralization and its limited infrastructure and economic development. These differences affected the institutionalization of new rights as well as leaving the empire vulnerable to escalating encroachment on its territories and resources.[5]

Yet the pattern of foreign intervention was not consistent over the nineteenth century. During the middle decades of the century, Istanbul's promise of rights and governmental reforms, particularly those facilitating capitalist expansion within the empire, served as points of diplomatic negotiation with the great powers and even allowed this Muslim state's inclusion in the Concert of Europe. Given the primacy of economic concerns and need to check rival territorial pretensions, French and British involvement in Ottoman affairs between 1838 and 1870 continued to respect, by and large, the empire's sovereignty over its lands and peoples.[6] Although such intervention constrained the definition of rights and institutional reform, Ottoman statesmen and protocitizens were also able to exploit outside pressure to advance specific domestic programs including the establishment of a constitutional monarchy.

The shifting foci and intensity of imperialist rivalry in Africa and Asia after 1870, however, proved antithetical to the consolidation of political rights. Ostensibly responding to the plight of the empire's non-Muslim citizens, European states now insisted on the resolution of social conflicts at the expense of the empire's territorial integrity in the form of new nation-states, adjusted national boundaries (in the Balkans), and, in the Mediterranean and Middle East, direct imposition of European administrative control. Such massive assaults on the empire's sovereignty and alteration of the very demographic makeup of the state helped overturn representative rule. For three decades, the Ottoman monarchy redirected citizens' demands while building the state's coercive capacity. Although the Ottoman parliament was restored after 1908, the beleaguered civilian government was able neither to secure its citizens' aspirations nor defend the empire's territorial boundaries.

From "Vernacular" Politics to Imperial Citizenship, 1800–1869

The new institutions and law codes of the *Tanzîmât-ı Hayriye,* the "Auspicious Reform," began with the promulgation of the *Gülhane* Rescript of 1839 and culminated in the convening of the Ottoman parliament in the spring of 1877.[7] These dates bracket decades of social conflict and profound economic and political change undergirding and defining Ottoman citizenship. From the outset, however, it is difficult to disentangle the rights and responsibilities of citizenship from the very bases of imperial sovereignty. The Gülhane Rescript, rightly considered an Ottoman "bill of rights," was announced only a year after the granting to Great Britain of the *Balta Limanı* Treaty, an open-door commercial agreement, and at a time when Russian, French, and British navies restrained Muhammad Ali's Egyptian armies in Syria from marching on Istanbul. The text, like others produced over the century by Tanzimat planners, New Ottoman philosophers, and Young Turk activists, reflected an ongoing engagement with European affairs and thought—from Enlightenment philosophy to positivism, social Darwinism, and nationalism—in addition to Ottoman history and Islamic ethics and jurisprudence.[8]

The timing and content of Tanzimat legislation also indicated the specificity of the Ottoman encounter with modern rights and governmental form.[9] More than political theory, history and geography provided compelling reference points for Ottoman practices and the Ottoman elite's perceptions of the world order. A glance at the Ottoman political endeavor on the world map circa 1800—an endeavor consisting of nearly three million square kilometers in west Asia and the Balkans alone—and consideration of the contrasting topographical and demographic contours reveal the sheer logistical problems in imposing a centralized and unitary form of administration.[10] Aside from modestly settled, agrarian central provinces in western Anatolia and the Balkans, the empire's largest territorial expanses, particularly those in North Africa and southwest Asia, were characterized by extremely low and uneven population densities. The limitations imposed by the scarcity of navigable rivers within Asia Minor and, before the middle of the nineteenth century, the lack of any rail transport whatsoever meant that integration of these lands depended on coastal shipping, caravan traffic using pack animals, barge and sail traffic on the Euphrates and Nile, and pilgrimage and religious networks, in addition to the official courier and military relay systems. Given that the empire was situated between two large multiethnic states in Central Europe and Eurasia, with its southern provinces abutting Britain's expanding Indian Ocean empire, it was the distribution of confessionally defined groups and distinct forms of social adaptation, such as pastoral nomadism, rather than ethnicity or "nation," that shaped the Ottoman understanding of its provincial structure and frontiers.

Although the geographic magnitude and the diversity of cultural forms within the Ottoman empire startle modern social scientists, they have also obscured the internal cohesion of the empire and its institutional parallels with contemporary regimes. Fiscal decentralization in the eighteenth century was one response to such logistical and organizational dilemmas, as well as to opportunities to tax urban production and global flows of commodities. Although Istanbul left powers of enforcement, tax collection, and even surveillance to local authorities, the regulation of transimperial exchange, taxation, and the legal mediation of contracts, debt, and transfer of property wove forms of state power into the fabric of everyday life and the reproduction of private wealth.[11] Astute appointments, sporadic military intervention, and fiscal blandishments placed conditions on the autonomy of a wide array of provincial actors that included not only the gentry but also tribes, military units, churches, and agricultural producers.[12]

As in other old regimes, Ottoman statesmen in the late eighteenth century became acutely aware of the limits to decentralized governance. Disruptions of commodity flows and finance following the Russian advance into the Black Sea in the last quarter of the century, and more intensely during the French Revolution and Napoleonic blockade (1789–1815), rendered provincial actors, especially tax farmers, less willing to cooperate with central authorities. Histories of the early nineteenth century provinces abound in tales of unruly provincial lords and urban gentry, an entrenched "vernacular" elite who served as the informal agents of central state rule. Yet it would be a mistake to think that only the provincial elite benefited from past accommodations with the central state. Vernacular politics subsumed diverse social, economic, and cultural relationships that spanned the gap between provincial practice and the official order. Merchants, peasants, guildsmen, and tribes, individually and in groups, defended themselves in vernacular terms against exploitation and abuse at the hands of both Istanbul and local officials; they employed vernacular means to carve and maintain a protective niche within local sociopolitical hierarchies and organizational arrangements.[13]

Early-nineteenth-century regimes confronted the resilience of such vernacular claims and claimants in the course of central state campaigns to impose direct rule and abolish tax farming. Ironically, the encounter between early centralizers under sultans Selim III (1789–1807) and Mahmud II (1808–1838) and vernacular actors, whose range of options and actions had been, by definition, spatially contained, led to a strengthening of provincial power brokers and a stiffening of provincial resistance to central state authority. The need for local troop recruitment expanded the power of local magnates and gentry. At the same time, attempts to rein in state finances and increase taxation helped forge unprecedented unity across economic and sociopolitical lines, as evidenced in the rebel urban "communes" of Aleppo (Syria) and Diyarbekir (Kurdistan) (1819–1821), as well as the protonational rural uprisings in Serbia (1804) and Greece (1821–1829).[14] Recognition of the Greek nation-state (1830) and autonomy for both Serbia (1835) and Egypt (1833–1841), in addition to the loss of Algeria to France, brought a reconsideration of the program of state centralization and the means of dissolving vernacular systems of power.

From its first edict, the Gülhane Rescript of 1839, the Tanzimat did not so much inaugurate modern state institutions as announce the end of vernacular patterns of political participation. It was not merely another order sent from Istanbul and entered silently into the judge's register. In the capital and provinces, the new franchise was proclaimed aloud before local authorities and "the people."[15] Symbolizing the new relationship between state and subject, the public event identified common interests and bonds and pledged the state to establish legal equality and universal obligations. Although succinct and simple, the Gülhane Rescript's main provisions—the abolition of tax farming and the implementation of a fair and universal system of military recruitment among Muslims—isolated a universal subject (an individual, adult male) as the basis for modern political practice. At the same time, it stripped away the collective obligations and privileges previously enjoyed by diverse sociopolitical bodies, including special military units, tribes, guilds, and other civil orders.

The proclamation of the Tanzimat also permitted the Ottoman elite to enter formally into an international diplomacy revolving around individual rights and governmental reform. Versions of the Gülhane Rescript in Western European languages did, as would later translations of the 1856 Reform Rescript, spotlight those clauses pertaining to the dignity and religious freedom of non-Muslim subjects ("the people of Islam and other groups").[16] Improving the status and social conditions of the empire's Christian populations in particular sought to stem the spread of nationalism in the Balkans as well as to counter long-standing French and Russian intervention on behalf of the Catholic and Orthodox churches and the holy sites in Palestine. Ottoman statesmen enlisted liberal rights to protect their own positions and properties as well as to pursue programs of state consolidation; European outrage at tribal persecution of Christians lent moral authority to Istanbul's own military repression in 1847 of Bedr Khan's protostate in Botan (Kurdistan), one of the more stubborn outposts of "vernacular" power in Asia Minor.[17]

The state's zeal to individuate, enumerate, and categorize subjects as well as to mobilize their resources and bodies responded to nearly continuous military and fiscal exigencies during the first three quarters of the century.[18] Before the Tanzimat, the 1831 census had brought central authorities a new awareness of the resources and distribution of wealth among the empire's populations. Accounts and surveys, the rationalization of the fiscal year according to a solar calendar, unification of the treasuries, and the ingathering of documents in a new state archive were expressions of a modern "governmentality." From the first attempts to rationalize revenues on urban wealth by means of a tax gauged on urban income and property (*temettü'ât vergisi*) to land reform and censuses of taxable rural subjects and potential male conscripts, the state also acquired new means for monitoring its populations. Yet realistic assessment of the sensitivity of such border areas as Erzurum, Baghdad, Basra, Libya, Yemen, and Hijaz postponed the application of censuses in many areas of the empire until the first decade of the twentieth century.[19]

In addition to standardizing processes and individuating taxpayers and soldiers, Tanzimat policies were aimed at the creation of a new juridical foundation for the government. In this regard, new legislation not only overturned older codes and practices but also resolved long-standing ambiguities and overlapping jurisdictions between palace and mosque[20] and established an independent legal field between statute, custom, and *Shari'ah*. The criminal code of 1840, overhauled in successive decades on the bases of Napoleonic codes, allowed the state to take charge of areas of social control and punishment, even cases involving conversion to and from Islam.[21] Criminal and commercial legislation would also extend governmental reach into emerging spheres of urban life, such as the press, international commercial transactions, and industrial relations. Compiled and printed in official gazettes and handbooks, the fruits of Tanzimat jurisprudence culminating in the master civil and procedural code, the *Mecelle-i Ahkâm-ı Adliye* (compiled between 1870 and 1876), were to be adjudicated in new venues, including interconfessional commercial tribunals and the reformed civil courts (*nizamiye*). As in many European states, even reform legislation avoided questions of women's rights and the household. Issues of personal status—marriage, divorce, inheritance (with the notable exception of the award of state land titles to women after 1847), as well as the purchase and treatment of domestic slaves—would remain under the control of relevant religious courts until the early twentieth century.[22]

Typically, the legal output of scholars and statesmen outstripped the actual institutional means. Although Ottoman military reforms had begun in earnest during the last decade of the eighteenth century, in formal bureaucratization the empire trailed behind both Prussia and Russia by at least half a century.[23] An immediate need to interpret, adjudicate, and enforce laws and staff provincial and foreign posts forced early Tanzimat governments to resort to familiar remedies: leading ulema and graduates of the religious colleges were drafted as jurists and central state and provincial officials;[24] soldiers and military officers performed police duties, carried out infrastructural projects, and collected taxes. Within a few years, tax farming itself was reinstated.[25] Important religious functionaries, such as the Muslim *kadı* (judge) or mufti (chief religious authority), and, for non-Muslims, the highest-ranking Greek Orthodox cleric, participated alongside the gentry and central state administrators in the first experimental provincial councils established in Gallipoli, Izmir, Salonika, Varna, Trabzon, and Samsun.[26]

Over the century the need to build a professional bureaucracy would inevitably open the gates of government service to broader social groups.[27] Education was key to the creation of a new civil service. Building on the intermediate schools (*rüşdiye*), state efforts first focused on primary education for Muslims and timid revisions of a curriculum based on literary and language studies in Persian, Arabic, and Ottoman. Military colleges took the lead in scientific and medical training, and only after midcentury did the state develop academies devoted to the training of diplomats, judges, bureaucrats, and teachers (both male and female).[28] Yet late bureaucratization, the limited number of places in state-sponsored institutions, and outmoded curricula were only partially to blame for the widening cultural divide among educated middle classes. Well-supplied Catholic and Protestant missionary schools together with the existing Ottoman parochial system educated proportionately greater numbers of Christians than government schools could accomplish for Muslims.[29] The educational divide, accentuated by the literary renaissance in the Slavic, Greek, Albanian, and Armenian languages, perpetuated the linguistic disadvantages of non-Muslims in a state where Ottoman Turkish remained the language of record.

The relatively limited advances in state education and the inability to build adequate government structures to implement reform were not simply a matter of miscalculation or misinvestment. The state's financial plight worsened as Russian and Austro-Hungarian pressure on the Balkans and Black Sea mounted. Its financial and technological dependency allowed European powers, France and Britain foremost among them, to set the terms of rights and dictate institutional priorities. The result of such intervention is seen most clearly in the 1856 Reform Decree, drafted with the strong input of its allies in advance of the Paris negotiations concluding the Crimean war.[30] The decree combined numerous provisions to satisfy European economic and financial concerns with programs that explicitly sought to redress non-Muslim inequality.

Considering the European record on minority rights, it is perhaps no coincidence that at least some of the remedies proposed by the 1856 reforms actually formalized past and emerging cultural cleavages. The new confession-specific (*millet*) councils and constitutions admitted—over the objections of established leaders and clerics—lay members to their deliberations. However, the millet system reconstituted communities in new and often conflictual ways. Protestant, Catholic, and Gregorian Armenians made up separate millets, each with its own constitution. By contrast, the Greek Orthodox Church was able to reconsolidate powers over the ritual and tithe of communities stretching from the Danubian provinces to Egypt—powers that had been lost or divided after the formation of the Greek state and an independent "national" church. Without reifying this institution, the millet served as a framework or baseline for subsequent formulations of both community and nation, especially in the form of autocephalous churches (e.g., the Bulgarian Exarchate after 1870), that entailed jurisdictional and, later, territorial boundaries.[31]

Thus, if the 1856 decree conformed to the spirit of the Tanzimat, it nonetheless departed in organizational terms from other, internally generated, projects for social and political reform dating from Mahmud II (1808–1838) that aimed at both centralizing institutions and disaggregating and dissolving vernacular forms of power. In comparison with the sweeping and often uncompromising application of the provincial reform laws of 1846 and 1864,[32] which rationalized the size of administrative units; removed the established privileges of local elites based on prior fiscal jurisdictions; and imposed direct, unmediated, central state control down to the village level, European intervention tended to fragment state authority regionally or encourage both European nationals and non-Muslim protocitizens to demand new forms of institutional autonomy. In acquiescing to foreign demands, Ottoman statesmen were forced to weigh their institutional and infrastructural priorities: whether to satisfy the needs of European capital or to develop civil institutions for social control and the provision of basic services. The strident lobbying of embassies and the foreign press on behalf of non-Muslim rights, packaged with demands for economic and political concessions ranging from banks and special tariffs to extraterritoriality for their citizens, made for a particularly unhappy equation in the minds of many Ottoman Muslims between the progress of religious equality and the decline of state authority.[33]

The elaboration of citizenship rights under the later Tanzimat must not be read only as a defense against nationalism or a means of resisting the dictatorial demands of the sultan on the individual subject. Parrying right with right,

Ottoman reformers attempted to reassert sovereign claims over land, persons, and resources within the nineteenth-century world order by building its military and civil institutions on one side and by fortifying the empire's protocitizens with basic rights and a universal political identity on the other. As the export of agricultural commodities and raw materials rose, the product of European industrialization and the extraordinarily low Ottoman tariff rate, the Tanzimat government granted its broadest social constituency, the peasantry, a new fiscal and economic franchise in the form of the 1858 Land Code. The Citizenship Law of 1869 was announced, to the consternation of European powers who feared retroactive demands for tax, two years after permitting foreign citizens to acquire land in much of the empire. In defining the empire's citizenry (albeit employing the word for "subject" [*tebaa-yı saltanat*] in combination with a dynastic qualifier, *Osmanlı*), the law merged the principles governing Islamic religious heredity with political affiliation by residence and birth (effectively, *jus soli* and *jus sanguinis* via paternal descent). Such a broad and inclusive citizenship did not simply recapitulate the individual's rights and duties. Rather, it bolstered the powers of government by delimiting the legal population from the increasing numbers of foreign residents and their protégés who appealed to international treaties for legal and fiscal immunity.[34]

Promises Unkept: Social and Economic Rights, 1839–1877

From the perspective of peasants, herders, and artisans, Istanbul's promises of social equality and impartial governance had always required more than a little credulity, perhaps never more so than in the nineteenth century, when famine, epidemic, war, and large-scale migrations provoked recurrent, massive social and economic dislocations. Notwithstanding notable efforts made by the Tanzimat government to build roads and bridges and promote public health, sanitation, and education, as well as to expand postal and telegraph service, the extremely limited state of communications hampered efforts to improve popular welfare.[35] Despite fiscal reform, local lords continued to impose illegal duties on peasants; Christians and Jews were still subject to discrimination, intimidation, and forced conversion. Tanzimat's provisions struck at the very bases of cultural identities and social hierarchies formed over centuries. Even those inequalities perpetuated by government reform, such as the conversion of the poll tax into a tax exempting non-Muslims from military service, may well have appeared to be a special favor, given the unenviable lot of the Ottoman soldier in battles from the Crimea to Yemen.

Although economic historians continue to debate the impact of commercial treaties on Ottoman trade patterns and urban production,[36] the new political and institutional manifestations of state power are no less relevant to an understanding of the success or failure of the Tanzimat franchise. For the majority of Ottoman protocitizens, next to conscription the most immediate face of the government remained taxation and encounters with state representatives in the field, pasture, marketplace, custom station, and workshop. Despite the relatively low level of capitalist investment and restricted entry of industrial goods to local markets,[37] the deregulation of internal trade (the end of state monopolies) and the establishment of border controls and quarantine facilities at ports and internal transit stations, as well as international efforts to curtail the trade in African and Caucasian slaves, exemplified the new regime. Ottoman traders—from Pontic Greeks to the *Chalabi* Muslims of Iraq—continued to ply domestic circuits. However, the advent of steam-powered foreign transportation companies on internal waterways politicized the customary lines of interregional social and cultural exchange. Foreign consulates and trade missions, which often provided fiscal immunities, educational services, and commercial connections and credit selectively to their Ottoman protégés, created distrust among Muslim, Jewish, and Christian traders and artisans. Such new political realities in the context of economic dislocations undermined long standing patterns of social interaction between religious communities based on craft specialties, interreligious partnerships, shared residence, and occupations.[38]

In agriculture, the backbone of the Ottoman economy, the terms of trade were not unfavorable to cultivators during the middle decades of the century.[39] Tanzimat agrarian policies began cautiously with commissions of inquiry, followed by the adoption of largely legal, financial, and organizational remedies. In addition to a redefinition of the legal status of peasant tenure as per the 1858 code, the government offered tax inducements to bring new lands under cultivation and established new sources of credit. Yet even in its most limited and legalistic form, the redefinition of state power, as Halil İnalcık's research on the Bulgarian provinces demonstrates,[40] exposed multiple contenders for land titles and peasant labor and produce. Muslim tax lords chose to interpret the Gülhane Rescript as confirmation of earlier writs according them property rights over land; peasants regarded the Tanzimat as the end of generations of onerous labor and monetary duties, while Christian tithe collectors (*çorbacıs*) realized that the abolition of tax farming threatened their income. In the decades of social unrest that engulfed the Bulgarian provinces, repeated confrontations between tax lord and peasant, bloody reprisals, and brutal government repression hardened confessional divisions and fueled separatist movements.

There can be little doubt that the use of excessive force to quell social conflict embittered the populace toward the Tanzimat government. Yet both the means and the goals of Ottoman policymakers merit consideration in their historical context. In its legal formulation, the 1858 land reform remains a milestone in the social and economic rights of the period, which should be compared with the czarist emancipation of the serf and the postindependence agrarian policies of Balkan states.[41] The actual impact of the land reform in improving conditions for the peasantry varied from one end of the empire to the other, and especially in regions such as Kurdistan and southern Iraq where the state's concern for sedentarization of the tribal population seems to have taken precedence over enforcement of peasant claims. In some areas and periods, the reforms that allowed for registration and alienation of land as private property permitted more powerful individuals and families to obtain peasant titles through debt or deception. However, in other provinces, peasants not only acquired hereditary rights to their fields but also were allowed to take possession of formerly uncultivated state lands.[42] In one of the few fiscal success stories of the modernizing state, the reformed agricultural tithe's contribution to the Ottoman budget increased steadily over the century.[43]

It is difficult to recover peasant perspectives on these political and legal changes. A rare eyewitness account documenting the uprising of Maronite peasants against Maronite land-controlling elites in the Kisrawan district of Mount Lebanon in 1858 sheds light on what may have been the philosophy motivating the peasants' actions.[44] The leader of the revolt, a certain Tanyus Shahin, is reputed to have brandished the Gülhane writ—in particular the clause demanding respect for all of the sultan's subjects—to protest the injustice of the lords. Such evidence suggests that this uprising was more than an economic conflict pitting a middle peasantry engaged in silk production for export against the ebbing power of an old tax-farming elite. It was also a demand for rights and enforcement by a new governmental authority. No longer able to contain cultivators by threat of local force, personal ties, or withdrawal of seed and credit, local elites must have regarded this challenge as a critical test of regional power. What might have once been a vernacular peasant-landlord contest assumed larger import and, with the entry of the Druze land-controlling elites, ignited an intersectarian conflict of wider scale and longer duration.[45]

Not only the Kisrawan uprising but also its resolution illustrates another key aspect of the Tanzimat dilemma. French and British diplomatic and military intervention in Mount Lebanon and Beirut resulted in international conventions that established a special governmental status for the region and a confessional formula for representation in councils and high provincial office. This agreement brought "enlightened" Western influence into the processes of Ottoman reform. However, once Europe's moral pretenses and material interests were

satisfied, the convention accorded this province neutrality and secure boundaries under great power guarantees. It was this framework, as Engin Akarlı's
research makes clear, that allowed Ottoman bureaucrats leeway to build (with
substantial central state subsidies) efficient, interconfessional government institutions that kept the peace in this region until the end of Ottoman rule.[46]

The singularity of Lebanon's peaceful transition is highly suggestive. Unresolved struggles over land, labor, and rights to rents after 1860, particularly in
Bulgaria, Herzegovina, Crete, and eastern Anatolia, spelled the end of vernacular politics and the steady, although uneven, encroachment of Tanzimat government. However, the assertion of new peasant rights on the one hand and the
refusal of tax lords to cede long-standing claims on the other, in the context of
broader European demands for Christian equality, accentuated the ethnic
dimensions of these conflicts and subjected Ottoman domestic policy to
unequal international scrutiny and sanction. Meanwhile, the explicitly expan-
sionist aims of neighboring states such as Austria-Hungary, Russia, and
Greece heightened the fears of Ottoman Muslims in these provinces, while
holding out more immediate possibilities for Ottoman Christians to realize
new rights or recover older privileges outside the imperial state.

Constitutionalism Derailed, 1878–1907

Without ignoring the violence that accompanied the application of the new
franchise, Roderic Davison argued that the Tanzimat instilled "a principle of
representative government" in Ottoman society.[47] As in Western Europe, myriad problems and stark social inequalities encumbered even the most limited
meanings of citizenship in the last quarter of the nineteenth century: government decisions excluded most of "the people," discrimination against religious
minorities continued in many areas of life, and slavery survived, especially
among the elite, although sales of human beings were no longer conducted in
public view.[48] Yet the Tanzimat process had opened new sites for institutional
participation. The rudiments of a representative system could be found in the
partial decentralization of legislative processes in provincial, district, and,
later, municipal assemblies composed of largely appointed or indirectly "elected" elites. It could be seen in the self-governing codes, "constitutions" granted
outlying provinces, such as Serbia, the Black Sea principalities, Tunisia, and
Egypt. Although a small clique of high-ranking ministers dominated discussions of reforms and international policy, central government operations had
grown too numerous and complex for any individual to dominate personally.
Specialization of operations; widening jurisdictions; codification of criminal,
commercial, and civil laws; and creation of new courts led to the division of

the Tanzimat's executive commission into a Council of State (*Şura-ı devlet*) and a Supreme Court (*Divan-ı ahkâm-ı adliye*), the latter being composed of nearly one-third Christians and Jews.[49]

The evolution of an Ottoman civil society may be observed from a variety of social and cultural angles.[50] It is seen in the doubling of enrollments in state schools and the religious and ethnic diversity of the graduates of its specialized academies, especially the well-regarded Mekteb-i Mülkiye (founded in 1859) and Galatasaray lycée (founded in 1868). It may be measured by the participation of lay elites—merchants, intellectuals, and artisans—in millet deliberations and by the range of topics covered within the official gazettes and multilingual private newspapers printed in Istanbul, Cairo, and less prominent provincial centers, as well as in an underground press published abroad. The "New Ottoman" intelligentsia of the second half of the century is distinguished by its social breadth. Ranging from the editor and son of a craftsman, Ali Suavi (1826–1871), who preached in mosques, to a Freemason prince who briefly assumed the Ottoman throne as Murad V in 1876, these individuals coined new terms of association, formulated novel demands of government, sought to transfer loyalty from the sultan to the state, and debated the interconfessional content of citizenship.

Without the existence of this new social milieu, it is unlikely that the viziers alone could have carried out the constitutional coup d'état that placed Abdulhamid II (r. 1876–1909) on the throne. The constitution brought into being a bicameral parliament. While provincial elections tended to follow the indirect patterns established by the assemblies, in Istanbul, elections were carried out directly and required a non-Muslim and a Muslim representative for each city quarter. Pledging allegiance to the empire and sultan by means of a nondenominational oath, Muslims, Christians, and Jews worked together. Debates and discussions in the lower house, *Meclis-i Umumi,* among the 115 deputies (47 of whom were non-Muslim) representing the Balkans, Anatolia, the Mediterranean islands, Africa, and Istanbul were conducted in vernacular Turkish, rather than the ornate language of the chancellery.[51]

The constitution itself was offered as a pledge of change to the Austrian, Russian, English, French, Prussian, and Italian diplomats who gathered in Istanbul to consider remedies for the interconfessional strife in Ottoman Bulgarian lands. Political reform did not, however, prevent the resumption of hostilities with Russia and Austria one month after the parliament's opening. Default on its debt, famine in Anatolia, France's defeat by Germany, and strong anti-Ottoman public opinion in Britain deprived the empire of allies and resources to conduct its defense. Despite diplomatic mediation, the 1878 Berlin Congress granted Serbia, Romania, and Montenegro full independence and brought into being a new Bulgarian state. Bosnia and Herzegovina were turned over to an Austrian mandate, Tunisia was assigned to French administration, while Britain occupied Cyprus. Four years later, the semiautonomous Ottoman province of Egypt, with its newly opened Suez Canal (1869), also fell under a "veiled" British protectorate after defying its creditors.

The forfeiture of approximately one-third of its lands at one blow (and with one out every five former Ottomans now a citizen of a new nation-state or subjects of a European empire) destroyed the coalition supporting the representative government. Taking advantage of divisions between junior and senior bureaucrats as well as provincial resentment against the Istanbul elite, Abdulhamid II shut the presses and exiled officials in the name of domestic security. Without rescinding the constitution itself, the prorogation of the parliament in 1878 made political rights a dead letter.

Settling accounts with European bankers and governments proved more time-consuming for the regime. Throughout the Hamidian period, this would require a skillful balancing of interests among the European powers, which attempted, often successfully, to dictate Ottoman policy though the sultan's cabinet and ministers.[52] French, British, and Belgian creditors assumed direct oversight of the Ottoman debt, swollen from war expenses and indemnities. Between 1882 and its dissolution in 1924, the Public Debt Administration skimmed off over a quarter of the state's income and dictated administrative reform and funding priorities. Given a stronger domestic economy (Ottoman trade doubled and foreign investment tripled between the 1890s and the outbreak of World War I), the regime was still able to devote considerable resources to expanding and modernizing its military.[53]

The Hamidian regime did not abandon Ottomanism. Instead it was guided by a new demographic reality. Stripped of large Christian populations in Europe with the exception of Albania, Thrace, and Macedonia, the problem of religious pluralism had ceased and the question of ethnic minorities had begun. Without explicit rejection of international conventions bearing on the protection and rights of Christian populations in Macedonia and the eastern provinces of Anatolia, the regime's practices, particularly at the level of local administrations, suggest halfhearted and even cynical enforcement.[54] In eastern Anatolia, for example, the numbers of Armenians and Greeks in provincial governments continued to rise. However, as the employment of officials in Bitlis, Van, Erzurum, Diyarbekir, and Sivas demonstrates, non-Muslim officials were concentrated almost exclusively in translation, technical, and educational departments and in the judiciary; almost no Christian officers were found in the provincial military or police. The regime's decision to create a special rural security force of Kurdish tribesmen (named after the sultan and modeled on the czar's Cossack brigades) only widened the breach between the civil administration of the cities and the countryside. After a peasant protest against illegal taxation in 1894, the Hamidiye cavalry took law and order into its own hands, unleashing a campaign of pillage and murder that took the lives and property of thousands of Armenian civilians in eastern Anatolia.[55]

The Hamidian regime also reinterpreted the meaning of citizenship to suit the empire's Turkish-, Arabic-, and Kurdish-speaking Muslims, who comprised nearly three-quarters of the empire's population. Although Ottoman intellectuals had long felt the need for greater unity among world Muslims, Pan-Islamic ideas had gained greater currency and attention through the activism of the Iranian-born Jamal al-Din al-Afghani (1838–1897).[56] Championing Muslim rights in the face of British and Russian imperialism in India and Central Asia, al-Afghani's critique did not spare Muslim governments that, like the Qajar Shah of Iran, granted concessions to European companies. Rather than a return to the Prophet's ideal community or a literal interpretation of Scripture, Pan-Islam offered Muslims a type of spiritual "citizenship" within an imaginary *"umma"* superimposed over the modern political map. Domestically, Abdulhamid II's defense of Muslim resources and lands deflected the discussion of rights beyond the state.[57] Abroad, Pan-Islam furnished the Ottoman sultan-caliph with a moral mantle no less grandiose than the Pan-Germanism, Pan-Slavism, and the Megali Idea (the pan-Hellenist aspiration to resurrect the Byzantine Empire) assumed by his contemporaries.[58]

Citizens of a Precarious State, 1908–1914

Selim Deringil's vivid characterization of the regime's quintessentially modern use of government institutions and cultural postures explains how the sultan was able to captivate the imagination of his citizens.[59] Those unconvinced encountered the sultan's security forces, which, with increasing efficiency after 1890, purged, exiled, and assassinated the regime's opponents in greater numbers. Networks of informers, copious files maintained on its officials, strict censorship, more efficient postal and telegraph services, and new forms of identification and certification permitted the state to monitor its citizens and restrict their movement within the empire.[60] Large infrastructure projects that appealed to the Muslim desire for technological parity with the West, notably the Syria-Hijaz railroad, completed in 1908, kept the more distant reaches of the empire (in this case, the Islamic Holy Cities and their dignitaries, the Sherifs of Mecca) on a tighter leash.[61] Still, the contradiction between the regime's modernizing self-image and its meticulous censorship of the press allowed unpredictable cultural spaces where new demands and constituencies could grow, as research on the women's journals and education during this period emphasizes.[62]

Fig. 3.1. The Ottoman Empire. From *The Columbia History of the World,*
ed. John Garraty © 1990 Columbia University Press. Reprinted with the
permission of the publisher.

Thirty years of police-state tactics achieved their larger aims: the Hamidian
regime decisively broke the connection between state modernization and the
liberal franchise. Discussion of political and social rights took place in underground cells or abroad among political exiles of socialist, nationalist, and
Ottomanist persuasions. Founded by students of the Royal Medical Academy
in 1889, the forerunner of the era's most important political movement and
Turkish nationalism itself, the Ittihad ve Terakki Cemiyeti (the Committee of
Union and Progress, hereafter, the CUP) developed cells throughout the
empire, from army barrack to artisan's workshop. Strongly patriotic, with an
as yet ill-defined political program, the CUP cultivated contacts with Islamic
religious orders as well as non-Muslim nationalist parties.[63]
    The regime's indiscriminate repression forged a certain unity across the

ideological spectrum. However, by the first congress of Ottoman opposition (the so-called *Jeunes Turcs*) which met in Paris in 1902, opinions diverged not only on the basis of ideological and nationalist agendas but also on the meaning of citizenship itself. Polarized in particular over the means of restoring the constitution, the "minority" represented by individuals who would play an important ideological role in the reorganized CUP, vehemently opposed the "majority" platform. This platform was backed by a coalition of Turkish, Greek, Albanian, and Armenian groups and called for immediate foreign intervention to depose the regime. With memories of the Anatolian massacres fresh, the two Armenian committees, the Armenian Revolutionary Federation, or Dashnaktsutiun (founded in Tiblis in 1890), and the Hunchakian Revolutionary Party (founded in Geneva in 1887), were understandably intransigent on the issue of foreign guarantees. On the other side, the minority position held by individuals who both feared the destruction of the empire and believed in the power of legal reform, considered the call for foreign intervention a violation of the social contract itself: social, religious, and political rights derived from the Ottoman state and its constitution alone.[64]

It would not be left to the exile community to resolve these questions. The looming "Eastern Question" in Macedonia, the changing balance of power in Asia after Japan's victory over Russia in 1905, and the Iranian Constitutional Revolution in 1906, as well as increasing civil unrest within the empire due to the regime's economic policies, offered the moment to strike against the autocratic regime.[65] Demanding restoration of the constitution and reopening of the parliament, junior officers in the Third Imperial Army in Salonika mutinied in 1908. Word of the insurrection spread quickly by telegraph and awakened the long-repressed desires for political change throughout the empire. Too strategically located for the regime to suppress militarily without inviting foreign intervention, the Macedonian insurrection soon became too well publicized to contain within the Balkan province.[66]

The restoration of parliament and the constitution, still considered by many to be the panacea for the country's domestic and international woes, allowed Ottoman citizens to exercise political rights checked for decades by Hamidian police. Workers' pent-up demands exploded in an unprecedented series of strikes over the summer and fall of 1908.[67] Despite improved communications, especially within the central provinces, years of censorship and political repression deprived most parties of the means to channel grievances and thus to take advantage of the democratic opening. As a result, the first elections sent a largely Muslim and Turkish delegation to the parliament. The absence of transimperial political alternatives in part explains pro-CUP regional voting patterns, particularly among minorities.[68] In Istanbul, fearing the imminent loss of subsidies and positions, the sultan's special military detachments and members of the ulema fomented counterrevolution. Before the civilian authorities could restore order, partisan politics and unabated ethnic tensions triggered anti-Armenian pogroms that swept southeastern Anatolia, from the coastal city of Adana inland to Marash.

The Third Army restored the parliament in 1909. Deposing Abdulhamid II and redrafting the constitution to curtail sharply the dynasty's political and military prerogatives, the parliament absorbed full legislative and diplomatic authority.[69] The CUP-dominated parliament dissolved special police and military units and equalized the duties of citizens on the basis of universal male conscription. Its pursuit of provincial reform, new public works projects, and institutional centralization at a rapid clip, especially its attempts to standardize court and office procedures in Turkish, soon provoked anger among Arabic speakers. Although the increasing sensitivity to the language question appears to bespeak emergent ethnic nationalism, it is important to remember that the Ottoman constitution recognized only one language of government. Perhaps more indicative of shifting perspectives were the CUP's economic policies, which aimed at freeing the empire from dependency on the European financial order and the semicolonial terms of commercial treaties. A progressive shrinking of the operating conception of citizenship can be surmised from government attempts to promote a "national" economy, with German aid, in precisely those sectors, such as trade and industry, where Ottoman Christian and Jewish investments predominated.[70]

The CUP government did not abrogate the constitution or disregard all Tanzimat rights and liberties. However, its record in promoting social and cultural rights remains at best mixed. In the midst of passing important legislation bearing on the family and women, the government also suppressed strikes and increasingly resorted to the monarchy's secret police and information networks to harass and even assassinate its opposition.[71] Such tactics paralyzed the growth of political parties, particularly those with the greatest potential for intercommunal and transimperial constituencies, such as the Liberal Union (Osmanlı Ahrar Firkası), which advocated a platform of economic liberalism and federalism.[72] Sensitivity to criticism and fear of separatist movements induced the government to repress both the explicitly nationalist organizations formed by Albanians and the purely literary and cultural societies initiated by Kurds and Arabs. Some Arab leaders accused the government of concerted attempts to deny the provinces proper representation in parliamentary elections.[73] Yet neither regional nor religious bias appears to have motivated the widespread irregularities that characterized the prewar election of 1912. Undemocratic measures notwithstanding, the CUP government continued to command the loyalty of its citizens, including the non-Muslims who defended the Macedonian front in 1912 and 1913.[74]

With the loss of Macedonia to Greece in 1913 and the influx of thousands of Muslim and Jewish refugees, few parties or individuals could ignore the precariousness of the empire itself. Neighboring states had wasted no time in taking advantage of the revolutionary upheaval. Austria-Hungary welcomed the restoration of the Ottoman constitution with its formal annexation of Bosnia and Herzegovina; Greece captured Crete. Italy, a latecomer to imperialism, followed suit three years later by occupying the last Ottoman province in North Africa, Libya and the Dodecanese Islands. Only the military putsch of 23 January 1913 and immediate resumption of war prevented the civilian government from surrendering the last remnant of Ottoman Europe, Eastern Thrace, to Bulgaria.[75]

From the first Balkan war to the outbreak of World War I, it is impossible to imagine government policy or citizen reaction without appreciating the pervasive sense of political uncertainty. Fighting for greater autonomy for decades, Albania declared its independence during the Balkan wars. Armenians, who had endured the upheavals of the Tanzimat and Hamidian oppression and now confronted resettlement of Muslim immigrants from the Balkans on disputed agricultural lands, no longer expected justice from the parliament.[76] Yet it should not be assumed that nationalism, although already well articulated among certain Ottoman communities, inspired all on the eve of the war. Sherif Husayn of Mecca, who negotiated with British agents during the summer of 1915, must have based his actions not only on the opportunity to establish an Arab monarchy but also on the prospects of imperial dismemberment.[77] Leaving to one side the question of the Ottoman (as well as the Austro-Hungarian) miscalculation of German military strategy, the decision to sign a secret pact with Berlin, according to Erik Zürcher, was to a large degree a reaction to Britain's demeaning and dismissive treatment of Istanbul's earlier overtures.[78] Evoking prewar sentiments and referring to the secret agreements to divide the empire that appeared on drawing tables in Paris and London in 1915 and 1916, Mustafa Kemal would exclaim: "The Ottoman Empire whose heirs we were, had no value, no merit, no authority in the eyes of the world. It was regarded as being beyond the pale of international right."[79]

Citizenship: The Unacknowledged Narrative of Late Empire

"Turkos, djudios, i kristianos/Todos ottomanos/Mos tomimos de las manos/ Djurimos de ser ermanos (Muslims, Jews, and Christians, all Ottomans hand-in-hand, We swear to be brothers)" went the refrain to a Ladino song of the 1908 revolution.[80] As a vernacular chorus for what might have been an Ottoman republic, this song is a fitting testament to nearly a century of social and institutional change in this European, Asian, and African state. Although historians have recognized Salonika's role as the cradle of new social movements, far too little attention has been paid to the relationship between the loss of such cosmopolitan constituencies and the collapse of Ottomanism itself as an overarching category of citizenship.[81] The birthplace of the Second Constitutional movement and the home of the father of the Turkish nation-state, Mustafa Kemal, Salonika was amputated from the empire in 1913; this, with the Entente occupation of Istanbul after World War I and the Greek invasion of Izmir (which culminated with the population exchange a decade later), meant that all major industrial and commercial cities of the Ottoman Mediterranean and their multireligious populations would cease being ideological and social reference points for the late empire's statesmen and citizens.

Although an inclusive notion of citizenship no longer informed the empire's last regime, the Ottoman reform movement deserves recognition as one of the more significant examples of the nineteenth-century liberal franchise. Neither Ottomanism nor citizenship had been the central project of the Tanzimat architects. As elsewhere, they were by-products of government practice and the transformation of the subject's expectations and demands of the state. The meaning of citizenship was continually reshaped by discussion and contention between majority and minority; between individuals, semiautonomous bodies, and an emerging legal and public sphere. These discussions were never contained within the state's territorial boundaries. The great powers, international institutions and lobbies, as well as post-Ottoman nation-states—empire's phantom limbs—continued to influence the debate about rights as well as the content of an Ottomanist identity. Prompted by their large and increasingly organized non-Muslim cocitizenry, Tanzimat politicians and ordinary Ottoman citizens formulated a new form of civic identity that resisted a purely majoritarian, religiously or ethnically exclusive definition of community.[82]

Having said this, it must be recognized that citizenship rights in the empire came at an unusually high price for all Ottomans.[83] Because universalization of rights across the religious spectrum long preceded revolutionary mobilization or a meaningful consensus on the nature of popular sovereignty, many imperial subjects, especially Muslims, experienced a relative loss in social status before they could appreciate new social and political rights. The timing of economic rights brought political disaffection and social disconsonance, particularly in regions where the granting of land titles to peasants weakened the primary bonds linking lords, tax farmers, and tribes to the Istanbul government. Precisely because it asked citizens to shoulder new burdens before formalizing its civil government (uniform administrative institutions, legal codes, social welfare programs, and a modern bureaucracy) and building its infrastructure, the state was unable to enforce reforms or shield its citizens from the uncertainties of global capitalism or the vicissitudes of war. Though seemingly better served by the new social contract, Christians and Jews were also asked to wager the vestiges of a system based on equity in the past on an imperfectly delivered equality in the present.[84]

Not characters in Greek tragedy, empire's last protagonists were not predestined to expiate the Ottomanist legacy. Rights deferred and abridged over the first half of the century fueled domestic conflicts and seemingly irreconcilable social and cultural claims. However, these conditions were due not only to administrative mishandling, social and religious prejudice, and defects in the franchise but also, and in far larger measure, to the modalities and timing of great-power intervention. Selective enforcement of religious rights and wide-ranging economic concessions to European states and companies undermined channels of interreligious communication. Repeated violation of treaties and occupation of Ottoman territory heightened mistrust between communities and, ultimately, undermined attempts to institutionalize some modicum of popular sovereignty. The creation of new nation-states from some Ottoman provinces and the absorption of others into the colonial empires of Britain, France, Russia, Austria-Hungary, and Italy preempted or redirected the struggle for social and economic rights in new political units.[85] Within what remained of empire, the hemorrhage of resources and citizens skewed relations between minorities and majorities. The loss of some of its most important investments, industries and revenues, particularly those in the European provinces, ultimately emphasized the social, infrastructural, and economic imbalances among provinces and provincial elites within the Ottoman Middle East.

Against this Pirandello-esque backdrop, one might, indeed, be tempted to reassess all the ideologies that accompanied or succeeded late Ottomanism.With demands for social and cultural equality subverted by the Hamidian regime, the refinement of the terms of inclusion and institutions for political participation, which was carried out in less than two years of the first constitutional period (1876–1878),and the crucible of the 1908–1912 revolution were too brief to reconcile the programs and interests of repeatedly fragmented and increasingly apprehensive constituencies. From particularist nationalisms to panethnic and religious movements such as Pan-Turanism and Pan-Islam, intellectuals and ordinary citizens attempted to grapple culturally with the conundrum posed by citizenship itself: how to maintain the loyalty of rights-demanding individuals and the cohesion of political communities within a state whose jurisdictional boundaries and human contents remained vulnerable to repeated redefinition from outside.[86]

All the same, there could be no return to being merely subjects of the sultan. By the end of the century Ottoman citizens had come into possession of rights that were fragmentary but cumulative. Many of these rights depended on local adjudication or enforcement by government agents. However, as the out-pouring of orientalist and colonialist writings on Islamic and Ottoman jurisprudence during this period attests, these claims would remain embedded in the very status of property, labor relations, and land.[87] Concessions, codes, and provisions, especially those pertaining to international political and finan-cial agreements, as Yasemin Soysal notes in more contemporary settings,[88] could prove compelling as well. Many of these legal relationships bore the considerable moral and economic weight of the foreign states, banks, compa-nies, and international bodies that had helped bring them into being.

So too it must be understood that the citizen's rights dissipated neither with the collapse of representative rule nor with the end of state sovereignty. Despite the suppression of political rights during the Hamidian era and after 1913, no Ottoman government contemplated revoking the Tanzimat franchise in its totality. Notwithstanding the presence of Armenian troops among the czar's armies and Arab military support for the British invasion, no ethnic or religious group ever comprehensively renounced its citizenship.[89] In fact, in the midst of world war, it was the persistence of rights, as much as their denial, that informed policymakers, revolutionaries, and military strategists.[90] For as armies erased boundaries, each citizen's claim could potentially be weighed against another's in any settlement after empire. Thus, the often unhappy reassignment of persons and festering borders created after 1918 are not only the issue of imperialism, nationalism, and the cruel scramble for land that marks the end of empire;[91] they are also reflections of the outstanding and unresolved claims of citizens on what was once a multiethnic and multireli-gious state.

Notes

Thanks go to Michael Hanagan and Charles Tilly for their critique and encouragement, as well as to Stuart Schaar and Marvin Gettleman for prodding me, several years past, to consider the contradictory experience of modernity in the Middle East. In tracing a path through a voluminous secondary literature, the advice of Selim Deringil, Donald Quataert, Aram Arkun, Jenny White, Faruk Tabak, Waheguru Pal Singh Sidhu, Eliza-beth Frierson, and Serpil Bagcı has proved invaluable. A 1998 graduate colloquium on late Ottoman history (New York University) offered me the opportunity to "test drive" these ideas and to benefit from student perspectives on them.

1. For versions of the classical drama, see, among others, S. N. Eisenstadt, *The Political System of Empires* (New York: Free Press, 1963); and Bernard Lewis, *The Emergence of Modern Turkey* (Oxford: Oxford University Press, 1961). For a recent

attempt to place the Ottomans in a comparative context, see Karen Barkey and Mark Von Hagen, eds., *After Empire: Multiethnic Societies and Nation-Building: The Soviet Union and the Russian, Ottoman, and Habsburg Empires* (Boulder, Colo.: Westview Press, 1997).

2. The Ottoman archives and libraries of the Turkish Republic contain voluminous materials on the empire's last century, including legislation, memoirs, parliamentary deliberations, newspapers, journals, literature, government documents, and handbooks. In an effort to reconceptualize the late imperial dilemma, this essay draws upon the research of the following scholars in particular: Roderic Davison, *Reforms in the Ottoman Empire, 1856–1876* (Princeton: Princeton University Press, 1963); Halil İnalcık, "The Application of the Tanzimat and Its Social Effects," *Archivum Ottomanicum* 5 (1973): 97–128; Şerif Mardin, *The Genesis of Young Ottoman Thought: A Study in the Modernization of Turkish Political Ideas* (Princeton: Princeton University Press, 1962); İlber Ortaylı, *Imparatorlugun En Uzun Yüzyılı* (Istanbul: Hil Yayınları, 1987); Engin Akarlı, *The Long Peace: Ottoman Lebanon, 1861–1920* (Berkeley and Los Angeles: University of California, 1993); Donald Quataert, "The Age of Reforms," in *An Economic and Social History of the Ottoman Empire,* ed. Halil İnalcık with Donald Quataert (Cambridge: Cambridge University Press, 1994), 759–933; Selim Deringil, *The Well-Protected Domains: Ideology and the Legitimation of Power in the Ottoman Empire, 1876–1909* (London: I. B. Tauris, 1998); Erik J. Zürcher, *Turkey: A Modern History* (London: I. B. Tauris, 1997); M. Şükrü Hanioğlu, *The Young Turks in Opposition* (Oxford: Oxford University Press, 1995); Feroz Ahmad, *The Young Turks: The Committee of Union and Progress in Turkish Politics, 1908–1914* (Oxford: Oxford University Press, 1969). For a more detailed and topical analysis, see Murat Belge, ed., *Tanzimat'tan Cumhuriyet'e Türkiye Ansiklopedisi* (Istanbul: Iletişim, 1986).

3. Cf. Mark R. Beissinger, "The Persisting Ambiguity of Empire," *Post-Soviet Affairs* 2 (1995): 149–84.

4. I rely on Charles Tilly's definition of citizenship ("Citizenship, Identity, and Social History," in *Citizenship, Identity, and Social History* [Cambridge: Cambridge University Press, 1995], 1–18), amplified by Margaret R. Somers's ("Citizenship and the Place of the Public Sphere: Law, Community, and Political Culture in the Transition to Democracy," *American Sociological Review* 58 [1993]: 587–620) special attention to the legal sphere.

5. For an overview of eighteenth-century decentralization and its impact, see Ariel Salzmann, "An Ancien Régime Revisited: Privatization and Political Economy in the Eighteenth–Century Ottoman Empire," *Politics & Society* 21, no. 4 (1993): 393–423; on the geopolitical dimensions in the nineteenth century, see Roderic Davison, "Foreign and Environmental Contributions to the Political Modernization of Turkey," in *Political Modernization in Japan and Turkey,* ed. Dankwart A. Rustow and Robert E. Ward (Princeton: Princeton University Press, 1964), 91–116. Major treaties and international conventions are found in J. C. Hurewitz, ed., *The Middle East and North Africa in World Politics: A Documentary Record* (New Haven: Yale University Press, 1975).

6. For an overview of events, see Matthew S. Anderson, *The Eastern Question, 1774–1923: A Study in International Relations* (London: Macmillan, 1972).

7. For important legislation, see *Düstür Meclisi Tanzimat'ın Teşkilinden berü Tertib ve Tanzim Olunan Kavânin ve Nizâmet* (Istanbul, 1299–1862) (Wiesbaden: Otto Harrassowitz, 1984); for an annotated bibliography of published compilations of Tanzimat legislation in different languages, see Davison, *Reforms in the Ottoman Empire,* 426–29.

8. As one example of the Ottoman understanding of the impact of the French Revolution, note the report on Toussaint L'Ouverture's revolt in Haiti (Document No. 14,127), found in the *Hatt-ı Humâyün* Series (Başbakanlık Archives, Istanbul). See also Virginia Aksan, "Ottoman Political Writing, 1768–1808," *International Journal of Middle Eastern Studies* 23 (1993): 53–69; Hanioğlu, *Young Turks in Opposition,* 10–14; Butrus Abu Manneh, "The Islamic Roots of the Gülhane Rescript," *Die Welt des Islam* 34 (1994): 173–203.

9. Cf. Pierre Birnbaum and Ira Katznelson, eds., *Paths of Emancipation: Jews, States, and Citizenship* (Princeton: Princeton University Press, 1995).

10. Quataert, "Age of Reforms," 777–78; see also Mehmet Hurşid [Paşa]'s account of the 1847 border settlement with Iran, *Seyâhatnâme-i Hudûd,* ed. Alâattin Eser (Istanbul: Simurg, 1997).

11. See Mehmet Genç, "Osmanlı Ekonomisi ve Savaş" (The Ottoman economy and war), *Yapıt* 49, no. 4 (April-May 1984): 52–61, tables in 49, no. 5 (June-July 1984): 86–93; Rhoads Murphey, ed. and trans., *Regional Structure in the Ottoman Economy* (Wiesbaden: Otto Harrassowitz, 1987); and Haim Gerber, *State, Society, and Law in Islam: Ottoman Law in Comparative Perspective* (Albany: State University of New York Press, 1994).

12. On the intertwining of fiscal, military, and political structure in the eighteenth century, see Ariel Salzmann, *Rewriting Sovereignty: Fiscal Decentralization and the Constitution of the Ottoman Ancien Régime* (Leiden: Brill, forthcoming); on religious autonomy, see Joseph R. Hacker, "Jewish Autonomy in the Ottoman Empire, Its Scope and Limits: The Jewish Courts from the Sixteenth to the Eighteenth Centuries," in *The Jews in the Ottoman Empire,* ed. Avigdor Levy (Princeton: Darwin Press, 1994), 153–202.

13. Invoking enduring principles of justice found in custom, religious precept, or statute, these protests were rooted in local contexts and translated rights and wrongs into more authoritative languages of the state in order to obtain justice. See Suraiya Faroqhi, "Political Initiatives 'from the Bottom Up' in the Sixteenth- and Seventeenth-Century Ottoman Empire," in *Osmanische Studien zur Wirtschafts-und Sozialgeschichte: In Memoriam Vančo Boškov,* ed. Hans Georg Mayer (Wiesbaden: O. Harrassowitz, 1986), 24–33; cf. James C. Scott, *Domination and the Arts of Resistance: Hidden Transcripts* (New Haven: Yale University Press, 1990), 45–69.

14. On the relationship between eighteenth-century vernacular politics and revolts in Diyarbekir and Aleppo, see Salzmann, *Rewriting Sovereignty,* as well as Herbert L. Bodman, *Political Factions in Aleppo, 1760–1826* (Chapel Hill: University of North Carolina Press, 1963); on Greece, see William W. McGrew, "The Land Issue in the

Greek War of Independence," in *Hellenism and the First Greek War of Liberation (1821–1830): Continuity and Change,* ed. Nikiforos P. Diamandouros et al. (Thessaloniki: Institute for Balkan Studies, 1976), 111–29.

15. İnalcık, "Application of the Tanzimat," 97–98.

16. Davison, *Reforms in the Ottoman Empire,* 101.

17. Martin Van Bruinessen, *Aga, Shaikh, and State: The Social and Political Structures of Kurdistan* (London: Zed, 1992), 180–81.

18. Cf. the Egyptian experience; see Khaled Fahmy, *All the Pasha's Men: Mehmet Ali, His Army, and the Making of Modern Egypt* (Cambridge: Cambridge University Press, 1997).

19. For a comprehensive study of these institutions, see Ali Akyıldız, *Tanzimat Dönemi Osmanlı Merkez Teşkilâtında Reform, 1836–1856* (Istanbul: Eren, 1993); for an overview of fiscal developments, see also Mahır Aydin, "Sultan II Mahmud Doneminde Yapılan Nufus Tahrirleri," in *Sultan II Mahmud ve Reformları Semineri,* ed. Mübahat Kütükoğlu (Istanbul: Edebiyat Fakultesi Basımevi, 1990), 81–106; and Stanford J. Shaw, "The Nineteenth-Century Ottoman Tax Reforms and Revenue System," *International Journal of Middle Eastern Studies* 76 (1975): 421–59. Cf. discussions in Graham Burchell, Colin Gordon, and Peter Miller, eds., *The Foucault Effect: Studies in Governmentality with Two Lectures by, and an Interview with, Michel Foucault* (Chicago: University of Chicago Press, 1991).

20. Criminal law, as Uriel Heyd noted (in *Studies in Old Ottoman Criminal Law,* ed. V. L. Menage [Oxford: Oxford University Press, 1973]), is an important case in point.

21. Deringil, *Well-Protected Domains,* 84–91.

22. Aron Rodrique, "From Millet to Minority: Turkish Jewry," in *Paths of Emancipation,* 238–61; Y. Hakan Erdem, *Slavery in the Ottoman Empire and Its Demise, 1800–1900* (New York: St. Martin's Press, 1996), 94–125.

23. On central state bureaucracy, see Carter V. Findley, *Bureaucratic Reform in the Ottoman Empire: The Sublime Porte, 1789–1922* (Princeton: Princeton University Press, 1980).

24. David Kushner, "The Place of the Ulema in the Ottoman Empire during the Age of Reform, 1839–1918," *Turcica* 19 (1997): 51–74.

25. Stanford J. Shaw, "Local Administrations in the Tanzimat," in *150. Yılında Tanzimat,* ed. Hakkı Dursun Yıldız (Ankara: Türk Tarih Kurumu Yayınları, 1992), 35.

26. The admission of local elites into provincial governance meant that they were well placed to take advantage of new powers for "class interests," particularly with the reintroduction of tax-farming contracts for many rural taxes. Yet they also, as demonstrated by Elizabeth Thompson ("Ottoman Political Reform in the Provinces: The Damascus Advisory Council in 1844–45," *International Journal of Middle East Studies* 25 [1993]: 457–75), exercised real and responsive legislative authority in local matters.

27. Ruth Roded, "Ottoman Service as a Vehicle for the Rise of New Upstarts among the Urban Elite Families of Syria in the Last Decades of Ottoman Rule," *Asian and African Studies* 17 (1983): 63–94; cf. Arno Mayer, *The Persistence of the Old Regime: Europe to the Great War* (New York: Pantheon, 1981), 177.

28. Metin Kunt et al., *Türkiye Tarihi III: Osmanlı Devleti: 1600–1908* (Ankara: Cem Yayınevi, 1988), 127; Bayram Kodaman and Abdullah Saydam, "Tanzimat Devri Eğitim Sistemi," in *150. Yılında Tanzimat*, 475–96.

29. On the relations between missionaries, the state, and local Christians, see Jeremy Salt, *Imperialism, Evangelism, and the Ottoman Empire* (London: Frank Cass, 1992).

30. Davison, *Reform in the Ottoman Empire*, 52–80.

31. Marin V. Pundeff, "Bulgarian Nationalism," in *Nationalism in Eastern Europe*, ed. Peter F. Sugar and Ivo John Lederer (Seattle: University of Washington Press, 1994), 115.

32. Maria Todorova, "Midhat Paşa's Governorship of the Danube Province," in *Decision Making and Change in the Ottoman Empire*, ed. Caesar E. Farah (Kirksville, Mo.: Thomas Jefferson University Press, 1993), 115–27.

33. For majority reaction, see Ufuk Gülsoy, "1856 Islahât Fermanı'na Tepkiler ve Maraş Olayları," in *Prof. Dr. Bekir Kütükoğlu'na Armağan*, ed. Mübahat S. Kütükoğlu (Istanbul: Edebiyat Fakültesi Basımevi, 1991), 443–58; on the quarantine regime, see Gülden Sarıyıldız, *Hicaz Karantina Teşkilatı: 1865–1914* (Ankara: Türk Tarih Kurumu, 1996).

34. Davison, *Reform in the Ottoman Empire*, 56 n 14, 262–63; Kemal Karpat, "Millets and Nationality: The Roots of the Incongruity of Nation and State in the Post-Ottoman Era," in *Christians and Jews in the Ottoman Empire: The Functioning of a Plural Society*, vol. 1, *The Central Lands*, ed. Benjamin Braude and Bernard Lewis (New York: Holmes & Meier, 1982), 163. For the wrangling between the British, Russian, and Ottoman authorities over the status of Russian Jews, see Albert M. Hyamson, *The British Consultate in Jerusalem in Relation to the Jews of Palestine, 1838–1914* (London: Edward Goldston, 1989).

35. Quataert, "Age of Reforms," 804–5.

36. Orhan Kurmuş, "The 1838 Treaty of Commerce Re-examined," in *Economie et sociétés dans l'Empire Ottoman*, ed. Jean-Louis Bacqué-Grammont and Paul Dumont (Paris: Éditions C.N.R.S., 1983), 411–17.

37. See Donald Quataert, *Ottoman Manufacturing in the Age of the Industrial Revolution* (Cambridge: Cambridge University Press, 1993).

38. For an exploration of economic reasons behind the anti-Christian riots in Damascus in 1860, see Linda Schilcher, *Families in Politics: Damascene Factions and Estates of the Eighteenth and Nineteenth Centuries* (Stuttgart: Steiner Verlag, 1985), chap. 4.

39. Şevket Pamuk, *The Ottoman Empire and European Capitalism, 1820–1913* (Cambridge: Cambridge University Press, 1987), 13–15; Tevfik Güran, "Tanzimat Döneminde Tarım Politikası," in *Türkiye'nin Sosyal ve Ekonomik Tarihi, 1071–1920*, ed. Osman Okyar and Halil İnalcık (Ankara: Meteksan, 1980), 271–77.

40. See Halil İnalcık, *Tanzimat ve Bulgar Meselesi* (Ankara: Türk Tarih Kurumu, 1943).

41. For taxation and other social conditions in comparative perspective, see Fikret Adanır, "The Macedonian Question: The Socioeconomic Reality and Problems of Its

Historiographhical Interpretation," *International Journal of Turkish Studies* 3 (1984): 43–64.

42. Albertine Jwaideh, "Midhat Pasha and the Land System of Lower Iraq," *St. Anthony's Papers: Middle Eastern Affairs* 16 (1963): 106–36; Haim Gerber's overview of the impact of the 1858 code (*The Social Origins of the Modern Middle East* [Boulder, Colo.: Lynne Rienner, 1987], 67–82) suggests that it reinstated a "classical age" approach to land, without emphasizing the radical implications of such a document in the context of substantial changes in taxation, peasant status, and circulation that took place between the seventeenth and early nineteenth centuries.

43. Güran, "Tanzimat Döneminde Tarım Politikası," 274–75.

44. Malcolm Kerr, ed. and trans., *Lebanon in the Last Years of Feudalism, 1848–1868* (Beirut: American University, 1959).

45. Kerr, *Lebanon in the Last Years,* 50–55, 65, 98; Marwan Buheiry, "The Peasant Revolt of 1858 in Mount Lebanon: Rising Expectations, Economic Malaise, and the Incentive to Arm," in *Land Tenure and Social Transformation in the Middle East,* ed. Tarif Khalidi (Beirut: American University, 1984), 291–302; on intersectarian conflict in Damascus, see Linda Schilcher, *Families in Politics.*

46. Akarlı, *Long Peace,* 36–43, 84–93.

47. Roderic Davison, "The Advent of the Principle of Representation in the Government of the Ottoman Empire," in *Essays in Ottoman and Turkish History, 1774–1923: The Impact of the West* (Austin: University of Texas Press, 1990), 96–111.

48. Akarlı, *Long Peace,* 156–62; Erdem, *Slavery in the Ottoman Empire,* 130–31; Hagop Barsoumian, "The Eastern Question and the Tanzimat Era," in *The Armenian People from Ancient to Modern Times,* ed. Richard G. Hovanissian (New York: St. Martin's Press, 1997), 2:175–202.

49. Akyıldız, *Tanzimat Dönemi,* 212–18; Steven Rosenthal, "Minorities and Municipal Reform in Istanbul, 1850–1870," in *Christians and Jews in the Ottoman Empire,* 1:369–400; Vartan Artinian, "A Study of the Historic Development of the Armenian Constitutional System in the Ottoman Empire, 1839–1863" (Ph.D. diss., Brandeis University, 1970).

50. İlber Ortaylı's *İmparatorluğun en Uzun Yüzyılı* (The Ottoman Empire's longest century) (Istanbul: Hil Yayınları, 1987) remains one of the best syntheses of these cultural developments with a comparative slant. For urban society, see Musa Çadırcı, *Tanzimat Döneminde Anadolu Kentleri'nin Sosyal ve Ekonomik Yapıları* (Ankara: Türk Tarih Kurumu Basımevi, 1991).

51. Enver Ziya Karal, "Non-Muslim Representatives in the First Constitutional Assembly, 1876–1877," *Christians and Jews in the Ottoman Empire,* 1:387–400. Generally, see Robert Devereux, *The First Constitutional Period* (Baltimore: Johns Hopkins University Press, 1963).

52. Engin Akarlı, "Friction and Discord within the Ottoman Government under Abdulhamid II (1876–1909)," *Boğaziçi University Journal* (Istanbul) 7 (1979): 3–26.

53. Engin Akarlı, "The Problem of External Pressures, Power Struggles, and Budgetary Deficits under Abdulhamid II, 1876–1909" (Ph.D. diss., Princeton University,

64   *Ariel Salzmann*

1976), 178–220. On mobilization and demobilization of the army, see Sabri Yetkin, *Ege'de Eskiyalar* (Istanbul: Tarih Vakfı Yurt Yayinlar, 1990), 62–82.

54. Mesrob K. Krikorian, *Armenians in the Service of the Ottoman Empire, 1860–1908* (London: Routledge & Kegan Paul, 1977), 11–12, 41–44, 108–10.

55. Van Bruinessen, *Aga, Shaikh, and Tribe,* 188–89.

56. Nikki Keddie, "The Pan-Islamic Appeal: Afghani and Abdulhamid II," *Middle Eastern Studies* 3 (1966): 46–68.

57. Hasan Kayalı, *Arabs and Young Turks: Ottomanism, Arabism, and Islamism in the Ottoman Empire, 1908–1918* (Berkeley and Los Angeles: University of California Press, 1997), 141.

58. Deringil, *Well-Protected Domains,* 44–67; cf. Hans Kohn, *Nationalism* (Princeton: Van Nostrand, 1955), 69–73.

59. Deringil, *Well-Protected Domains,* 16–43.

60. Ceasar Farah, "Censorship and Freedom of Expression in Ottoman Syria and Egypt," in *Nationalism in a Non-National State: The Dissolution of the Ottoman Empire,* ed. William W. Haddad and William Ochsenwald (Columbus: Ohio State University Press, 1977), 151–93; Kunt et al., *Türkiye Tarihi III,* 164.

61. For Pan-Islamic technology, see William Oschenwald, *The Hijaz Railroad* (Charlottesville: University Press of Virgina, 1980).

62. Elizabeth D. Frierson, "Unimagined Communities: Women and Education in the Late Ottoman Empire, 1876–1909," *Critical Matrix* 9 (1995): 55–90.

63. Hanioğlu, *Young Turks in Opposition,* 71–109.

64. Hanioğlu, *Young Turks in Opposition,* 181–98; cf. Dov Yaroshevski, "Empire and Citizenship," in *Russia's Orient: Imperial Borderlands and Peoples, 1700–1917,* ed. Daniel R. Brower and Edward J. Lazzerini (Bloomington: Indiana University Press, 1997), 58–79.

65. For political and social conditions, see Aykut Kansu, *The Revolution of 1908 in Turkey* (Leiden: Brill, 1997); Donald Quataert, *Social Disintegration and Popular Resistance in the Ottoman Empire, 1881–1908: Reactions to European Economic Penetration* (New York: New York University Press, 1983).

66. Kansu, *Revolution of 1908,* 32.

67. Yavuz Selim Karakışla, "The Emergence of the Ottoman Industrial Working Class, 1839–1923," in *Workers and the Working Class in the Ottoman Empire and the Turkish Republic, 1839–1950,* ed. Erik J. Zürcher and Donald Quataert (London: I. B. Tauris, 1995), 31.

68. Kansu, *Revolution of 1908,* 181–82; 206–10.

69. On party politics, see Feroz Ahmad, *Young Turks*; Zürcher, *Turkey,* 98–105.

70. As for the prehistory of the "national" economy, see Zafer Toprak, *Türkiye'de "Milli Iktisat," 1908–1918* (Ankara: Yurt Yayınları, 1982).

71. Zürcher, *Turkey,* 98

72. Cağlar Keyder, "The Ottoman Empire," in *After Empire,* 30–44.

73. Rashid Khalidi, "Arab Nationalism in Syria: The Formative Years, 1908–1914," in *Nationalism in a Non-National State,* 219–23.

74. Richard G. Hovanissian, "The Armenian Question in the Ottoman Empire, 1876

to 1914" in *Foreign Dominion to Statehood: The Fifteenth Century to the Twentieth Century,* ed. Richard G. Hovanissian (New York: St.Martin's Press, 1997), 1:203–38.

75. Ahmad, *Young Turks,* 144.

76. Richard G. Hovanissian, *Armenia on the Road to Independence* (Berkeley and Los Angeles: University of California, 1967), 27.

77. William Cleveland, *Islam against the West: Shakib Arslan and the Campaign for Islamic Nationalism* (Austin: University of Texas Press, 1985), 1–28; Kayalı, *Arabs and Young Turks,* 14.

78. Zürcher, *Turkey,* 117.

79. Ghazi Mustapha Kemal, *A Speech* [delivered by Ghazi Mustapha Kemal, President of the Turkish Republic October 1927] (Leipzig: K. F. Koehler, 1929), 526

80. Pamela J. Dorin Sezgin, "Hakhamim, Dervishes, and Court Singers: The Relationship of Ottoman Jewish Music to Classical Turkish Music," in *Jews in the Ottoman Empire,* 586.

81. Donald Quataert, "The Workers of Salonica, 1850–1912," in *Workers and the Working Class,* 59–74. Hanioğlu, *Young Turks in Opposition,* 10.

82. Mardin, *Genesis of Young Ottoman Thought,* 71–72, 206–26.

83. Pierre Birnbaum and Ira Katznelson, introduction to *Paths of Emancipation,* 24–25.

84. For the minority predicament, see Kamal S. Salibi, "The Two Worlds of Assaad Y. Kayat," in *Christians and Jews in the Ottoman Empire,* 2:134–58.

85. National settlements often, according to István Deák ("The Habsburg Empire," in *After Empire,* 130), offered a redistribution of institutional and political resources among elites. However, as Michael Palairet's study *The Balkan Economies, c. 1800–1914: Evolution without Development* ([Cambridge: Cambridge University Press, 1997], 357–70) concludes, in terms of overall development, the price of independence may have been more onerous than endurance of the Ottoman "yoke." For lingering identities and other questions, see Thanos Veremis, "From the National State to the Stateless Nation," in *Modern Greece: Nationalism and Nationality,* ed. Martin Blinkhorn and Thanos Veremis (Athens: Sage-Eliamep, 1990), 9–22.

86. Consider the fluctuating ideological transformation of Turkish nationalism's greatest exponent, Ziya Gökalp (see Taha Parla, *The Social and Political Thought of Ziya Gökalp, 1876–1924* [Leiden: Brill, 1985]) as well as the contradictory declarations, alliances, and policies of the founder of the Turkish nation-state, Mustafa Kemal (Atatürk), between 1918 and 1924 (see Stéphane Yerasimos, "The Monoparty Period," in *Turkey in Transition,* ed. Irvin C. Schick and Ertuğrul Ahmet Tonak [Oxford: Oxford University Press, 1987], 67–101).

87. The heyday of orientalist scholarship on Islamic and Ottoman law coincided, not surprisingly, with British, French, Dutch, and Italian colonialism. In addition to the numerous British handbooks on Ottoman land laws in Palestine, one notes the critical importance in contemporary social and political conflicts of qualifying the status of land in Palestine and later in Israel, from *miri* (pertaining to the Ottoman state) and private peasant *tapu* (deed) to the inalienable trust of the Jewish state and people.

88. Yasemin Nuhoğlu Soysal, *Limits of Citizenship: Migrants and Postnational Membership in Europe* (Chicago: University of Chicago Press, 1994), 119–35.

89. Nor could they under Ottoman law; Article 8 of the constitution of 1876 reads: "All subjects of the Empire are called Ottomans, without distinction, whatever faith they profess; the status of *an Ottoman* is acquired and lost, according to conditions specified by law" (emphasis added); see Edward Hertslet, *The Map of Europe by Treaty . . . since the General Peace of 1814* London: Harrison & Sons, 1891), 4: 2533).

90. The distinction between subjects and citizens is, I would venture, a critical one for discussions of human rights violations and genocide. Cf. essays in George J. Andreopoulos, ed., *Genocide: Conceptual and Historical Dimensions* (Philadelphia: University of Pennsylvania Press, 1994).

91. Cf. David Fromkin, *The Peace to End All Peace: The Fall of the Ottoman Empire* (New York: Henry Holt, 1990); Eric Hobsbawm, *The Age of Extremes: A History of the World, 1914–1991* (New York: Penguin, 1994).

4

Scripted Debates: Twentieth-Century Immigration and Citizenship Policy in Great Britain, Ireland, and the United States

Suzanne Shanahan

In the fall of 1997, the United States Commission on Immigration Reform published recommendations for changing naturalization law.[1] The report, "Becoming an American: Immigration and Immigrant Policy," draws upon familiar themes to characterize the American nation as a community of immigrants. Barbara Jordan, the late chair of the commission, explained:

> We are a nation of immigrants, dedicated to the rule of law. That is our history—and it is our challenge to ourselves. . . . It is literally a matter of who we are as a nation and who we become as a people. *E Pluribus Unum.* Out of many, one. One people. The American People.[2]

The commission self-consciously reclaimed the controversial 1920s language of "Americanization" to reaffirm the conceptual and legal link between citizenship and nationality. "That word earned a bad reputation when it was stolen by racists and xenophobes in the 1920s. But it is our word, and we want to back."[3] Americanization is depicted as a contract between immigrants and existing citizens. It is an individual, voluntary effort to cultivate a shared commitment to American values of liberty, democracy, and equal opportunity. Immigrants, the report insists, must be ready to undergo Americanization to make them worthy of the benefits (rights) of American citizenship. Citizenship is participation in the national community.

In one sense this report provides a policy analogue to the flurry of social scientific interest in the institutions of citizenship and nationality in the 1990s. National citizenship is once again fashionable fodder for both official and social scientific debates.[4] In another sense, however, this report appears somewhat at odds with this social scientific literature, or at least with a common interpretation of the literature. The emergence of "world citizenship" or postnational membership illustrates how changing notions of citizenship,[5] particularly in the face of a global human rights regime, have separated the historical link between citizenship and nationality institutionalized as an inherent feature of the post-World War II nation-state. A worldwide philosophy of human rights has decoupled rights (citizenship) and identity (nationality).[6] Globalization has fostered the development of particularistic identities[7] that often contravene national ones. Increasingly, one's humanity is a more secure guarantor of rights than one's nationality.[8] According to some, both nationhood and citizenship have declined in importance as the language of nation is deployed on behalf of a myriad of collective formations and as citizenship becomes a largely instrumental venue for the distribution of varied economic, cultural, and political rights.[9] That is, if any group can package itself as a nation and if rights of individuals and groups are no longer contingent on the status of national citizenship but are increasingly attributes of universal humanity, perhaps nation and citizen are outmoded—or at least fundamentally altered—concepts.

And yet, the report of the U.S. commission quite deliberately attempted to concretize the union of citizenship and nationality through the concept of Americanization. Perhaps this effort was a desperate attempt to salvage what is no longer tenable. Or perhaps, as I suggest, the effort speaks to the tenacity of the relationship between nationalism and citizenship even in the face of the dramatic social and economic changes attendant to the rapid process of globalization. Indeed, globalization has undermined neither nations nor citizenship; it has fortified them both. As always, "[c]ontemporary debates about citizenship are simultaneously debates about nationhood. They are debates about what it means, and ought to mean, to be a member of a nation-state in today's increasingly international world.[10]

In this chapter I illustrate how three different nation-states have attempted to reconcile notions of nation, state, and citizenship in the context of changing international norms. Accordingly, I examine the major post–World War I immigration and citizenship debates in Great Britain, Ireland, and the United States. The continued importance of nationality and citizenship are patent in these debates.

Drawing on perspectives that situate nation-state policies within a worldwide cultural environment that influences both their constitution and activity through exposure to world norms and standards, I demonstrate how policy debates within these three countries increasingly have become part of a single international discourse. Participation in this broader discourse means that policy debate and policy decisions have become more similar during the twentieth century than the extant literature might predict. In many ways, debate becomes ritualized and standardized both in language and objective. "These policies are depicted as if they were autonomous decisions because nation-states are defined as sovereign, responsible, and essentially autonomous actors. Taking into account the larger culture in which states are embedded, however, the policies look more like enactments of conventionalized scripts."[12] Even attempts to deviate from international consensual standards and discourse become formalistic. Nations (and their policies binding and consolidating nationality) are expected to vary, but only in highly circumscribed ways. Thus, while these three nation-states try to articulate their unique situations, their special characters, they do so in surprisingly similar ways, yielding fairly similar national identities. National differences are highly stylized and draw upon models codified by international standards and norms.

I am not merely arguing that there has been a convergence in language, although this is considerable. Immigration terminology is certainly standardized: "The principal metaphor is aquatic and references aquatic: floods, torrents, rivers, streams, pools, flows, trickles, dams, barriers and floodgates."[13] To be sure, some of the broader consistency of language can be attributed to the circumscribed parameters of legitimate discussion of immigration policy.[14] Nonetheless, concerns that debate and policy will be labeled "racist" rarely prevent rather frank and explicit discussion of diverse social groups and the relative merits of their members as potential citizens. More important, the patterning of immigration and citizenship debates is far more than an issue of language. Following Brubaker (1995), "I argue that in immigration policy debates, as in other policy domains, the boundaries of legitimate discussion are one of the crucial stakes of the debates, and that these boundaries change over time in response to broader developments in the environing culture and polity."[15] Linguistic convergence is symptomatic of a more fundamental isomorphism in ideals and values.

I argue that world cultural norms provide a standardized script for immigration and citizenship debates. An incorporative logic of national citizenship proposed first, perhaps, by the French, begins to be institutionalized through international norms and organizations in the post–World War I era. [16] It is this normative frame that determines the contours of legitimate discourse, contours that are fixed irrespective of national demographic trends, political changes, or crises. While conventional accounts often portray immigration policies as a response to localized, exogenous, and usually material shocks[17]—economic crisis, war, etc.—immigration and citizenship debate tends to highlight universal cultural concerns. I argue that just as the style of imagining nation-states is standardized, so, too, are the ways in which nation-states rhetorically bind their nations via immigration and citizenship policy. Nations are not the product, however, of idiosyncratic thought but of a certain standard of thought. Nationalism constitutes a global phenomenon and a molding power that, rather than giving rise to new and original cultural phenomena, instead reorients, revitalizes, and rearranges existing cultural frames, tailoring a comprehensive ideology that was assumed to be a unique and natural historical production. "That is, modern nationalism emerged as a sculptural will that recast its appropriated raw materials: traditions, customs, social and scientific ideas, and history. As a result, we live in a world of nationalist nations, in which each appears to be an exceptional and inimitable product of the same sculptor."[18] The imagining of nations is not unbounded, and neither are the parameters of the debate over immigration and citizenship.

This is not to imply that all states eagerly and without trepidation embrace these norms. Nor do the three cases here consistently parrot twentieth-century international conventions. Rather, the potency of this logic has increased continuously over the past sixty years. These exogenous world standards are a destination toward which Great Britain, Ireland, and the United States are slowly drifting. Sometimes they fight the tide and sometimes they ride it. And it is the particular needs and requisites of their respective national identities, not economies or governments, that determine this flow.

Points of Departure: Cases and Their Context

Cases

The three countries from which case materials are drawn share—if only because of a common experience with colonialism—a roughly similar liberal political and legal heritage. Today, these countries are loosely configured liberal democracies[19] supported by some form of bourgeois legal structure. Their historical experiences with immigration are, however, quite different. In each of the three nation-states, policies reflect particular experiences and immigration assumes a distinct place in national mythology. In each case policy debates are reflexive exercises in the management of a unique national identity.[20] The interpretation of international standards and the nationalization of world models are important dimensions of this exercise. These models are differentially negotiated.

The political imperatives of a global empire were critical in shaping Great Britain's approach to immigration and citizenship. The ambiguous sociocultural relationship between England the long-standing early modern territorial nation and Great Britain the modern juridical state, itself a by-product of the imperial form, was critical in the development of a national system of citizenship and immigration legislation in the twentieth century. While the purity of Anglo blood and homogeneity dominate British folk mythology and historical ideology, immigration has been an important fact throughout British history.[21]

Indeed, the long-standing principle of *jus soli* (the right to citizenship by birth in the territory) has provided a tacit assumption of assimilation in English culture. Few would seriously argue for an ancient purity of English blood. However, prior to the dramatic increases in postcolonial immigration into Britain following both World War I and World War II, Britain had experienced very little immigration since the Reformation. Emigration had been much more dominant throughout the seventeenth, eighteenth, and nineteenth centuries. Indeed, the first modern immigration exclusion did not occur until the 1905 Aliens Act.[22] But more recently, in the wake of decolonization, the end of the British Empire, and the eventual demise of the Commonwealth, immigration flows have increased. This unprecedented immigration sparked considerable reconsideration of English culture and resulted in the comparatively late articulation of British nationality in 1948. That is, while one might argue that English nationality and nationalism have a long history,[23] Great Britain lacked an identifiable nationality. Until the 1948 legislation, citizenship and nationality were two distinct principles, unlike the celebrated French model, where citizenship and nationality were linked by the revolutionary changes of the eighteenth century. Until 1948, allegiance to the crown was the fundamental principle of citizenship. Since the 1948 Nationality Act there have been six major alterations in immigration policy through which Great Britain has reconstructed a national identity and a national citizenry for itself. And while immigrants now constitute between 4 and 5 percent of the total population and new immigrants totaled more than fifty thousand in recent years, Britain aggressively resists even the slightest hint that it is a country of immigrants.[24] Indeed, technically Britain still exports more people than it imports.[25]

The United States is the clearest example of a settler society[26] where a principle of jus soli has been both a legal statute and a national philosophy. A long and continuous history of immigration has meant that, for more than a century, the United States has been engaged in a continuous debate about immigration policy. This debate has yielded the most highly elaborated system of regulations of the three cases. Since the 1790 Naturalization Act, the United States has passed more than 130 immigration and citizenship acts. Forty-seven of these acts were directed at promoting the immigration of people with certain skills, 30 imposed racial or ethnic exclusions, 30 promoted family reunification, 26 outlined character qualifications for potential immigrants and citizens, and 19 protected the rights of refugees, Since World War II alone, the United States has passed 45 immigration acts.[27] Moreover, many more bills have been introduced than the 133 that have been entered into law. In the 86th United States Congress (1959–1960), for example, more than 125 bills and resolutions relating to refugees, aliens, and immigrants were introduced. Only three bills became law, and none was considered major legislation. Furthermore, in every presidential election since 1848, debate over the purpose and role of immigration policy in defining America has been a central platform issue. "Whether it was 300 years ago or 100 years ago, it was immigration and immigration policy that really defined how America became America."[28] Today, immigration flows continue. Indeed, despite mounting tensions concerning the economic costs of immigration, particularly in California and Florida, and a general ethos of exclusionism, entrance has never been easier. About 3,000 new immigrants arrive daily. In the 1990s annual immigration has hovered around 1 million persons, with 850,000 of this total made up of legal entrants.[29]

The case of Ireland is perhaps the most distinctive. Ireland is a country of "senders, not receivers." Emigration, not immigration, has had an important effect upon Irish national culture and the definition of "Irishmen." Accordingly, Ireland has had only four major immigration and citizenship acts. And while most immigration and citizenship policies in Great Britain and the United States have operated under a logic of selective exclusion, inclusion has dominated discussions of nationality in Ireland, at least in one important respect: a principle of *jus sanguinis* (citizenship on the basis of descent) governs citizenship law and shapes the contours of immigration debate. Indeed, Irish citizenship policy has deliberately fostered the notion of Irish diaspora, consisting of many generations of Irish men and woman scattered across the globe. And yet, while promoting a diasporic identity, the Irish are considerably more apprehensive about facilitating immigration and extending citizenship to those outside this community of descent than either the British or the Americans.

Context

While particularistic histories and experiences in Great Britain, Ireland, and the United States shape immigration and citizenship debate, the broader shared context of these debates ultimately produces policies that are far more alike than even a common, liberal legal structure might predict. Around the turn of the century a new international system began to emerge. This new system manifested itself in a set of conferences, conventions, and organizations, reaching a critical point in 1919 with the founding of the League of Nations. This system had a logic and purpose that went beyond the interests and needs of its participating nation-states. Indeed, it developed a set of semiautonomous norms and conventions that guided the behavior of states. In ways both explicit and implicit, this system endorsed and valorized one form of polity—the citizen-based nation-state—from among the range of existing political arrangements. The Versailles treaty and the League of Nations ideologically and organizationally enshrined the nation-state form, which became the natural model of political development.[30] This international system supported the notion that the globe was divided among nation-states or potential nation-states that were themselves made up of national citizens or potential national citizens. The system, then, both lent legitimacy to, and derived its own legitimacy from, this form. It was, after all, a club whose members were citizen-based nation-states.

This system sought to ensure the transition from potential to actual nation-state, to coordinate peaceful relations among nation states, and, above all, to define the very contours and being of the nation-state. Not only did this system shape relations between nation-states, it also shaped relationships within nation-states. It increasingly defined legitimate relations between peoples and polities. Indeed, national boundaries were inherently international. Likewise, the category of national citizen is an international category.

The Logic of Debate: Immigration and Citizenship Policy

The close of World War I found each of these three countries in a different moment of nation-building—in a certain spot on this road from potential to actual nation-state. It also found that each case had different cultural and material needs and resources that would undoubtedly promote or constrain this transition. The differences were a critical factor in determining the extent to which international ideas would be embraced or accommodated.

From a certain perspective the Irish and the British nation-states suffered from opposite problems. The Irish state was but a quarter of a century old. The fit between the new state and long-standing nation was still awkward and incomplete. In Britain, a long-standing state was confronted with the task of recasting a nation that would map onto the new territorial scope of this state. The United States was probably the most self-confident in its sense of nation and state. The United States was working toward policies that could be reconciled with the more prominent place of the United States within the world economy and world politics. And yet the international political framework within which the three nation-states would struggle to solve specific immigration problems was the same. The tension between international standards governing ways of doing citizenship and ways of being a nation and the more local pressures to define and bound a unique nation-state became patent in this era. The discussion that follows highlights the peculiarly national reconciliation of these tensions. Both the extent and the limits of variation are noted.

Great Britain

In contrast to the tentativeness of the Irish and the confidence of the Americans, the British were almost cavalier about changes in immigration policy prior to World War II. For the Irish, policy changes were palpable indicators of the nature of the Irish nation-state, while for the British, policy changes were a solution to a specific problem. British policies were more functional and less symbolic. Policy changes in 1914 and 1919 also lacked the drama surrounding changes occurring at the same time in the United States. If there was a theme to debates during this period in Great Britain, it was security. Immigration policy was broadly defined under the rubric of wartime legislation. As in the United States, there was considerable uncertainty over the political loyalties of certain immigrant populations. Fears that some groups, including German Jews, did not behave in the best interest of Great Britain were considerable. Targeting "enemy aliens," the Alien Registration Act of 1914 gave the home secretary broad discretionary powers in the quest to protect the "safety of the realm."[31] Some years later, this freewheeling power, which included the right to detain or intern "suspicious" aliens, was depicted as "one of the least liberal and one of the most arbitrary systems of immigration law in the world."[32] Nonetheless, the 1919 act extended these provisions into peacetime. The act also served to regulate further the activities of aliens. Sedition and labor agitation were deemed unlawful. Civil service employment of aliens was banned. Moreover, an elaborate registration system was established to record the place of residence and employment status of aliens. The right of the state to govern its borders was paramount. Thus in 1924 the home secretary asserted, "If, when considering the desirability or otherwise of an alien's presence in the UK, doubt arises, benefit would be given to the country, not the alien."[33] And it was this hard line that also dominated British refugee policy during the international refugee crises of the 1930s and 1940s. The boundaries of the United Kingdom were the sole jurisdiction of Great Britain.

During this era, in contrast to the situation in the United States, immigration was subject to only limited debate in Great Britain. This absence of debate, and thus attention, provides insight into the logic of the British nation-state. In some sense, the British did not understand Great Britain to be a nation-state.[34] It was the capital of the empire. Thus, the question of who could or could not immigrate or emigrate was far less significant. The boundary of the nation did not need the same sort of tending as that of other territorially framed nation-states.

While Ireland was a state born of the twentieth century, Great Britain has been a state in one form or another for centuries. It is ironic, then, that it was Britain for which the definition of nation and state was most problematic in the post-war era. For Britain it was the inevitable decline of the British Empire that sparked a reevaluation of "Britain." In 1948, the British drafted their first Nationality Act.[35] The 1948 act was symbolic in that it redefined membership in the British nation and reconfigured the relationship between the state and the population by vesting in policy a notion of citizenship. In short, subjects became citizens. On one level, the act appeared to give quiet consent to the changing nature of social membership in the colonies and shifting forms of state sovereignty. But on another level, the 1948 act was a desperate attempt to hold the empire together.[36] "We must give these people [colonial subjects] a feeling that on the homespun dignity of man we recognize them as fellow citizens and that our object, as far as they are concerned, is to hope to raise them to such a position of education, of training and of experience that they too shall be able to share in the grant of full self-government."[37] The common, even expected, connection between nationality and citizenship was never directly made. The right of citizenship would not make a person British. Thus, while citizenship was introduced, the notion of the British subject remained. Ambiguity dominated interpretations of both statuses. Canadians might be citizens of Canada, but they were also British subjects. The Commonwealth would remain intact. Citizenship and nation remained distinct. Britishness was to remain an exclusive attribute of the indigenous population of the mother country. The boundaries of the British people would not correspond with the boundaries of British citizenry. Indeed, it was through a manipulation of the terms and meaning of citizenship that Britishness was delimited. The difficulty with these manipulations is the reason that, even today, the contours of this identity are deliberately imprecise.

The 1948 act evoked a certain self-satisfaction within Parliament. "We are proud that we impose no colour bar restrictions making it difficult for them when they come here. . . . we must maintain our great metropolitan tradition of hospitality to everyone from every part of our Empire."[38] Racial and ethnic neutrality in national policy was a norm quickly established in international debate following World War II and institutionalized in the 1948 United Nations Human Rights Charter. British MPs gloated over the fact that they — in contrast to the United States—were in line with this thinking. Britain publicly demonstrated its solidarity with the colonies. The British quickly mastered the language of human rights and deployed human rights principles as a means of rationalizing legislation. But it was always filtered to suit their particular objectives.

Because postwar changes in citizenship were an attempt to hold together the quickly dissolving empire, little attention was paid to the fact that, technically, British citizenship would entitle colonists to certain rights. Thus when the colonists—understanding citizenship quite correctly as their right—began to migrate to Britain, many in Britain were thoroughly unprepared and even aghast. A multiracial empire was one thing; a multiracial Britain was unthinkable. Almost as soon as the Nationality Act of 1948 was passed and celebrated as color blind, policy debate began to center on the issue of race and color. During the 1950s Irish immigration into Great Britain continued apace. More than fifty thousand Irish would migrate annually to Britain in search for work. The fewer-than-three-thousand colonial immigrants per year were, however, perceived as far more problematic because they were not of the same race. "In fact, the outstanding difference is that the Irish are not-whether they like it or not-a different race from the ordinary inhabitants of Great Britain."[39]

Ironically, the Irish had for centuries been labeled a separate race, often even a barbarian race. But during the 1950s black commonwealth immigrants became the new barbarians. While the skin color of the new immigrants was an easy marker of their difference, immutable biological notions of race were not the operative logic. That is, commonwealth immigrants could conceivably be well integrated into British society as long as their numbers were manageable. This notion of race is evocative of Victorian usages. Difference was a matter of character (and its perceived consequences) not biological or genetic capacity. The Commonwealth populations brought with them different standards of health and sanitation; a broader tolerance for poverty, vice, and immorality; and a tendency toward criminality. They were deemed uncivilized, just as the Irish had been.

To many, British society was under siege. members of Parliament (MPs) commonly depicted it as breaking under the insurmountable task of integrating two racially distinct populations. The immigration of nonwhite colonists disrupted the social harmony of British society. The only solution was stricter immigration controls. Introduction of the 1962 Commonwealth Immigrants Acts was an attempt to deal with the "problem" of immigration from the Commonwealth countries. According to the government, the torrent of postwar immigration was overwhelming British society. "If they come in small numbers they can be assimilated into the life of the country. If they come in tens of thousands they clot together in communities and preserve the characteristics they brought with them." In 1962 there was no sense that Britain was a multicultural society. The empire incorporated a diversity of peoples, but Britain would not. "The real question is at what rate can this country accept immigrants from whatever source so they can be absorbed in the community with minimum dislocation and tension."[40] Limits on the number of immigrants from different countries were set and residency requirements for citizenship were extended.

Great pains were taken to cast this legislation so that it would be immune from charges of racism. The government proposed that, in the name of fairness, white immigration from the Republic of Ireland also be restricted, although this proposal was eventually abandoned as unfeasible. The issue was also linked to the apparently racially neutral issue of the economy. Controlling immigration from former colonies was said to be one of the duties of the postwar welfare state. The British state had primary responsibility for control of labor markets. Accordingly, much of the discussion centered upon the occupational needs of the country. Chinese immigration, for example, would have to be limited because the restaurant market had been saturated. And while more than one MP claimed that West Indian women, for example, made wonderful nurses, this field, too, was limited. Certain racial and ethnic groups were assumed to have particular aptitudes. Here race marked character, mores, and social practice. The "clotting of immigrants" and the "slum problem" were seen to undermine the perception of otherwise harmonious social relations across Britain.[41] Overcrowding and the presence of large numbers of immigrants, it was argued, were responsible for vice, including drug use, petty theft, prostitution, and street fighting.

While the 1962 act did pass, many denounced the measure. The act, one MP charged, was one in which "race discrimination is now written, not only into its spirit and its practice, but its very letter. . . . This Act will be interpreted throughout the world as a failure to face up to the problem of colour presented to England for the first time in history."[42] But perhaps quite the contrary is true: the act made color an inextricable element of British policy. What Parliament had failed to do here was create a sense of the British nation. Instead, by manipulating the rights associated with British citizenship, they clung to an anachronistic vision of the empire. Both the 1968 Commonwealth Immigration Bill and the 1971 Immigration Bill continued in the tradition of the 1962 bill by making some connection to the United Kingdom a requirement of citizenship. Commonwealth membership would not confer full rights. Using the concept of patriality, the 1971 bill tried to reconcile notions of belonging and notions of citizenship. Being "British" would mean being a descendant of someone born in the United Kingdom. As in Ireland, national identity meant membership in a broader community of descent. The principle of jus soli that had been the ancient mechanism that made Normans, Saxons, Bretons, and other migrants the heart of the English nation was now at risk.

Here the case of Britain also sheds light on how idiosyncratic national systems of understanding social differentiation mediate broader international shifts. While international norms were validating the removal of racial barriers to immigration,[43] Britain's tenuous national identity made this transition more difficult. The rhetorical defiance evidenced in immigration and citizenship legislation was further demonstrated in race relations legislation, which emerged in tandem with immigration law as a means of confronting the problems of a changing British society. Indeed, this rhetorical defiance of international norms was one means of bolstering British nationalism. Flaunting these norms became a source, and continues to be a source, of British identity. And yet, as discussion of Great Britain's race relations legislation below will illustrate, British defiance was more often bravado; there were clear limits to British opposition to dominant models. In some sense the energies devoted to the negotiation of world norms with British needs provide key evidence of the broader importance of world norms. That is, while Britain may never have been in the vanguard of internationalism, its immigration and citizenship debates were firmly entrenched in a global discourse that would shape and mold almost every policy made during this period.

During the 1960s and 1970s Great Britain passed three separate race relations acts (1965, 1968, 1976). With each subsequent act, greater protections against largely racial and ethnic discrimination were set into law. The 1965 act defined a limited sphere of protection for racial and ethnic groups. Only discrimination in public facilities based on color, race, ethnic or national origins was deemed unlawful. In the 1968 act, the scope of antidiscrimination legislation was expanded to include employment, housing, and the provision of goods and services. And in 1976, all forms of discrimination, direct or indirect, on the basis of race, ethnicity, or national origin were deemed unlawful. Discrimination did not have to be intentional to be illicit.

Each act was initially introduced as a mechanism to improve "community relations" and abate mounting "civil unrest." The government minister charged with introducing the 1965 Act explained that the act "is concerned with public order."[44] In no case was the objective to expressly enhance the rights of immigrant minorities. Rather, such legislation was designed to protect the security of indigenous communities, though ultimately such minority rights were enhanced. Concessions made to minority rights were agreed upon in exchange for limiting future immigrant flows. "We must accept the fact that we have many thousands of these people here who cannot be integrated or assimilated. They will never learn English, they will never change their customs or their religious practices, their cooking habits or their sanitary standards. We want to see them fairly treated, but the condition precedent to their being fairly treated is that their numbers should not be added to."[45] Even in the 1976 debates a trade-off between increased minority protections and more limited immigration was demanded. "I believe that no Government has the right to carry out such a fundamental act without the most specific consent of the people. Successive governments are gradually depriving the English people of their birthright, and in time, if this procedure is not stopped, the local populations will be swamped."[46]

While demands for domestic peace sparked the debate, international discourse about the rights of individuals and the rights of racial and ethnic groups provided its shape. During the 1965 debates, attempts were made to reconcile the treatment of minorities in Great Britain with protocols established by the United Nations Committee for the Elimination of Racial Discrimination. Nondiscriminatory legislation was touted as a fundamental protector of human rights. Furthermore there was much discussion of the fact that many Commonwealth countries, including a number in Africa, already had nondiscrimination clauses built into their constitutions. Britain's reluctance to initiate such legislation was depicted as anachronistic and misplaced. "It would be a tragedy of the first order if our country, with its unrivaled tradition of tolerance and fair play . . . should see the beginnings of the development of a distinction between first and second class citizens."[47] The fair treatment of races across the globe was touted as, in large part, an accomplishment of the British people. To establish such standards at home would then be natural and right.

Nonetheless, the considerable uneasiness many legislators experienced during each of these three debates was further evidenced by numerous discussions of terms and the efforts to define race and ethnicity. In Britain as elsewhere, race and ethnicity were undergoing profound and continued semantic revolutions during this period. Concern arose almost immediately in the context of the 1965 debate about the ambiguity of the terms race, ethnicity, color, and nationality.[48] Ten years later only minimal progress had been made. Thus when the Commission for Racial Equality was established as part of the 1976 Race Relations Act. much confusion ensued.

> To purport to establish a commission to secure equality between things which cannot be defined with any certainty is inherently absurd and improper for the purposes of a statute. . . . Is there a Caucasian race? Are the Germans a race? Is there a Welsh race or an English race? . . . So, without even being able to state what is meant by "race", without any means of identifying a race, we are setting up a commission in the name of which denotes that its purpose is to secure equality between the races. That is a pretty ridiculous proposition.[49]

These struggles reflect the tenuous process of integrating these concepts, categories, and way of thinking into British traditions of identity and social differentiation. Indeed, at numerous points in the debates, the United States was held responsible for the Parliament's quandary and its inability to define, let alone understand, race and ethnicity. The obsession with race and ethnicity as well as the excessive attention to discrimination was an "American disease" fraught with all the combustibility of the "French disease" two hundred years earlier. The notion that postwar immigration had somehow made Great Britain a multiracial society and that this was a welcome form was deemed utterly "bizarre."[50] While multiculturalism might be a fashionable international trend, many British were skeptical. Thus, even as late as 1990, some advocated the abolition of all official racial and ethnic census categories. Again, perhaps if one didn't have racial and ethnic categories, there might be no race or ethnicity and thus none of the attendant problems and obligations. An assault on the categories might yield a return to a more individually based notion of social rights and obligations and of national citizenship.

Since World War II, the United States has more or less (and often begrudgingly) accepted immigration control as a bounded and constrained right of sovereign states. In contrast, in the past twenty years Great Britain has been quicker to exercise (or sometimes just vocalize) the option of state discretion. "Few people in the United Kingdom seem yet to have grasped that the British government no longer has absolute control over entry and settlement in the United Kingdom, and that what power it has now will diminish within the bounds of Community law."[51] British policymakers will frequently invoke their rights as statesmen to defend their sovereign borders even at the expense of individual minorities. Thus, in immigration and citizenship debates, they often draw on the existing contradictions in international norms that simultaneously protect the state and the individual to defend a culturally exclusive form of membership. The tension between international convention and these exclusionary impulses creates an often-muddled set of policy initiatives.

Much of Britain's muddled policy logic stems from the still-incomplete transition from dynasty to empire and from empire to nation-state. Remnants of both shifts linger in the confused distinctions between British subjects, British nationals, and British citizens and the seemingly ad hominem rights associated with these categories. States have tended more readily to adopt policies, rationales, and frameworks of the period in which they are constituted. Thus, we see Ireland adopting conventional citizenship policies and practices available in the international sphere at the time of its independence in the 1930s. Drawing consciously or unconsciously from existing international models, Ireland located its sovereignty in the individual citizen. In contrast Britain first layered a notion of parliamentary sovereignty onto an existing monarchical system and later introduced a notion of individual citizenship without eradicating either aristocratic authority or parliamentary control. This layering of political forms has been further exacerbated by a form of economic liberalism that, while privileging the individual unit of action, was never able to fully integrate itself into the political sphere. Simply put, British society is still dominated by an aristocratic or class system. Society is still largely defined in political and economic terms, not the cultural terms we associate with a prototypical "national" society. Moreover, this layering of models has left the place of the individual largely indistinct. Britain, for example, has no modern bill of rights. These lingering ambiguities surrounding the contours of the British nation-state—the boundaries of its territory and the definition of its population—have produced a set of immigration policies that may often appear to be at the margins of acceptable international norms. Ironically, as the discussion that follows will illustrate, these imprecise, contradictory, multiple, and muddled conceptions of citizenship and nationality have ultimately produced a way of understanding human differentiation that is often very similar to that in the United States.

"British immigration policy is simple. For twenty years or more it has been, in the words of the Conservative Party manifesto of 1974, 'to reduce and keep new immigration to a small and inescapable minimum.'"[52] Despite this outward claim, there were in Britain, as in most countries that engaged in a discourse of restriction, few dramatic revisions of immigration policy. Immigration was not a centerpiece in the 1983, 1987, or 1992 general elections. Nor was it an important issue in the 1997 general elections. The three most representative pieces of British immigration and citizenship policy during this period are the 1981 and 1988 Nationality Acts and the 1993 Asylum Act.

The 1981 British Nationality Act revised the 1948 act, which directly linked nationality and citizenship. Rights and privileges would be linked to a territorial and cultural belonging. In actuality the act largely served to degrade further the notion of British citizenship by creating a series of membership categories: British citizens, British overseas citizens, British protected persons, and British subjects. It marked a refusal to give up the historic myth that England was still at the center of world politics. Each category was due different rights and privileges within Britain, but only one category conferred the right to settle in the United Kingdom. Furthermore, the ancient rule of jus soli would stay firmly in place. The result of this policy was "that virtually all the existing British nationals who were non-European and who were outside the United Kingdom were to receive a practically valueless form of nationality."[53]

This policy was defended with language that echoed anticolonial discourses of oppression. The British appropriated the relevant international language and categories and deployed it in an ingenious manner. They framed their situation as that of an oppressed and besieged society whose indigenous culture was at risk. In the crudest sense they simply did not want to be "over run" by immigrants from the Third World states they had once ruled. Once again, nationality was conceptualized as a tool of immigration control policy.[54] "We who are the native, indigenous population of the country have the right to say to the legislators, 'We shall have no more of this. We are the people of England; we are the people who have lived in this land all our lives. We shall have no more of the nonsense that people are equal with us, because we are the people who live here.'" Other MPs went on to bemoan the inadequacy of current legislation, indicating a misplaced loyalty to international norms of behavior above a concern for the "people." "I believe that all Governments have failed to protect the indigenous people of this country. Not only does our Government lack the moral courage to put into force the natural controls on immigration that exist in almost all other parts of the world; for many years there has been a sort of brainwashing of anybody who has tried to control immigration as if he were an un-Christian and horrible beast instead of somebody expressing a perfectly normal and natural point of view which is supported by 90% of the population."[55] The lack of immigration control continues to be viewed as a fundamental violation of rights. The indigenous population, it was argued, has a unique, inviolable birthright. The 1981 Nationality Act was but further evidence of the difficulty of reconciling citizenship and nationality in modern England.

Even during the debate surrounding the 1988 Nationality Act, the essential function of which was to terminate the natural right of family reunification, a strong denial of the empirical reality of British demography was in evidence. There was some faint hope that by not attaching racial and ethnic labels to groups, by simply refusing to have a system of social differentiation, objective differences between members of the population would disappear. "We say that people who are in this country are British, whether they are black, Asian or Caucasian. If one seeks to create a divide between those people, by noting in immigration and nationality policy, by creating such categories for use in censuses and other government statistics, by noting it in welfare and housing policies and via the 1965, 1968 and 1975 Race Relations Acts as the Labour party seeks to do, that is racist."[56]

Like many other states, Britain has grown increasingly wary of international refugee policy and the respective obligations of states. A growing refugee population, along with refugee applications nearing fifty thousand annually, made policymakers nervous.[57] The 1993 Asylum Act, first published in 1991, targeted fraudulent refugees. The chief characteristics of this bill included the fingerprinting of all refugees, new appeal procedures that curtailed the right to an oral hearing, rapid deportation of "bogus" applicants, and elimination of a family's right to state housing pending determination of status. Taken as a whole, the bill sought to do far more than these administrative changes imply. In essence the bill sought to reorient the base approach to asylum by beginning with a presumption of fraud and then requiring the applicant to disprove it. This approach was met with considerable ethical objection. "To work on the basis that such claims are likely to be fraudulent unless proved otherwise, is to brand many of the world's most vulnerable with the accusation of deceit and to run the risk of sending people to torture and death."[58] The government was made to appear petty: "It will cost the Government nothing to be generous."[59] The Asylum Bill came to be known as the "exclusion bill" in certain circles and was heavily denounced as political pandering that was both "opportunistic and mean-spirit-ed."[60] Above all, the bill clearly pushed the boundaries of international norms regarding the treatment of refugees. The United Nations expressed concerns.[61]

But British participation in a overarching discourse reinforces two general points. First, a notion of human rights has affected the articulation of national identity. While Britain may seek to deny a refugee certain appeal rights, this refugee is depicted equally as human as any British citizen. In his or her humanity, in his or her personhood, no distinction is made. As human beings, both citizens and aliens are entitled to their cultural identity. In addition, identities are increasingly organized by extra-nation-state politics (institutions, organizations, and norms). States still control the rights associated with citizenship but not necessarily the personal meaning of nationality. Identities are no longer the exclusive purview of the nation-state.

The United States

Immigration and citizenship debate in the United States was, as in Great Britain, initially somewhat impervious to international norms following World War I. But over the course of the following eighty years, international logics would be subsumed into a national one. Indeed, by the 1960s the distinction between the two seems negligible. And while Britain continues to struggle to negotiate a balance between national identity and international convention, the United States has made international convention part of national identity. One could even argue that the United States often, perhaps erroneously, takes credit for the inspiration behind these broader norms in an global form of Americanization. In doing so, the possible tensions between world and national norms are minimized and made more palatable within the nation-state.

Citizenship and immigration policy in the United States were premised from the very outset on a set of racial or ethnic exclusions. American citizenship was initially the right of free white men, leaving Native Americans, African Americans, and women clearly outside the vision of nation. A principle of selectivity would be the guardian of the American way of life. The distinction between selectivity and hyper-restriction and exclusion often blurred. "All laws heretofore enacted on this subject have been of a selective rather than restrictive character. None of the existing selective features have been omitted in preparing this act; on the contrary, they have been strengthened."[62] Debates that began in 1914 against the background of the massive 1911 Immigration Commission Report culminated in the 1917 Immigration Act. This act was about preserving and protecting a particular kind of society. Growing municipal poverty, rising crime, labor unrest, and fears of massive postwar immigration prompted reassessment of immigration policy logic. Criminality, poverty, and immorality were viewed as a plague that threatened the American nation. The need to slow the pace of social change is evident in the debates of this period. "The statement that present immigration is affecting injuriously our democratic institutions is not the expression of mere opinion; it is the recording of a well-considered conclusion, . . . self-defense is the first law of nature and of nations. . . . No nation in human history ever undertook to deal with such masses of alien population."[63]

The targets of restriction were the "defective" classes: the unskilled, alcoholic, infirm, poor, criminally inclined, and lawless. The major contribution of the 1917 act was a literacy requirement for new immigrants, a notion that had been circulated in policy circles since the late nineteenth century. A literacy test was seen as a general filter to "separate the ignorant, vicious, and the lazy from the intelligent and industrious."[64] The passage of this act is an important indicator of the declining role of purely racial barriers to immigration. While it was understood that particular groups and races would have a clear advantage with this literacy requirement, the category of distinction was literacy, not race. The significance of this change is critical. It illustrates that already, race was, in and of itself, an insufficient means of categorizing immigrant populations, and that many U.S. legislators were very uncomfortable with policies based purely on race. Discrimination may well have been rampant, but race would not be the key boundary in the American nation-state. Certainly an easy argument can be made that race was unquestionably the central division in American society. Opportunities were clearly unequal across different social groups (races) at this time, and continue to be so today. Nonetheless, a narrowly construed notion of race would not be the logical foundation of immigration policy—a policy designed to preserve the integrity and sovereignty of the nation-state. The cultural legacy of the American nation was not perceived to be one of race; thus, the features that separated aliens from citizens could not be exclusively racial. Immigration policy sought to reject any attempt to construct the American nation-state as race-based.

The 1921 and 1924 immigration acts established national origin quotas as an alternative to more narrowly racial restrictions. Fears that postwar immigration was threatening standards of social life—materially, spiritually, and politically—prompted further demands to limit the inflow of immigrants. The ultimate decision to make national origins the basis for determining entrance quotas was not an undisputed move. Many legislators still preferred a notion of race that was more clearly grounded in biology and less prone to more changeable principles of geography. Race was scientific and nationality was political. As the 1921 act was unveiled, Senator Reed cautioned his colleagues against national origins categories: "I can not agree to the proposition that, because a human being happens to be born in some other country, he is therefore a menace to this Republic. I can not subscribe to the doctrine that, because there are some people in other countries who will not make good citizens of this country or of their own, therefore we should exclude all people indiscriminately. . . . We are a very hysterical people. We get excited very quickly about things that are purely temporary."[65]

The choice of national origins as a criterion was perhaps a compromise between those seeking rigid categorical racial barriers and those opting for a more subjective, case-by-case criterion. For many, the notion of heredity categories, whether based on race or nationality, seemed inappropriate. That is, these categories masked more important and substantive bases of inclusion or exclusion.[66] National origin was nonetheless deemed a far more accurate indicator of people's potential either to succeed or to corrupt the American vision. Thus, for example, people from democratic nations would be a logical fit for the United States, while those who lived historically under the yoke of despotism were deemed unlikely to have the requisite tools or appreciation of a democratic way of life. Traits of nations were slowly replacing traits of races as the relevant boundary markers, thereby becoming salient and significant categories of differentiation.

Thus in this period the principle of selection turned to one of restriction. First was the 1921 Quota Law and its more stringent amendment in the 1924 Immigration Act. By 1929, the U.S. Congress had developed an elaborate structure for both limiting the potential flow of immigrants and selecting among the remaining group. While not significantly altered during the Depression era, these limitations were reinforced by an increasing call for an end to immigration. Seen as a means to steady a unstable economy, a ban on immigration was a favored tactic of many legislators. No such absolute ban passed, however.

But economic concerns were not the sole worry of most policymakers. Warnings were voiced throughout the interwar years against the promotion of a "mongrel" society. Diverse immigration represented a direct threat to the "American nation" and the "American spirit." Homogeneity was understood to present a cure to social ills. "If that does not exist, there can not be homogeneousness of race; there can not be homogeneousness of purpose; there can not be homogeneousness of ideals; and there can not be a common patriotism."[67] In 1920, Congressman Box and others feared for the "de-Americanization" of the United States and the division of allegiances through the development of a "hyphenated population."[68] In the postwar context, hyphenation signaled a lack of allegiance. To consider oneself Irish-American or German-American was to commit "moral treason."[69] As naive as it might seem, it was not until after World War I that legislators fully realized the extent to which immigrant populations were actually quite distinct and not necessarily fully "Americanized."[70] Mere habitation in the United States would not automatically assimilate diverse peoples. Nation building and the maintenance of national boundaries would have to be a "deliberate formative process, not an . . . accidental arrangement."[71]

This concern about loyalties was related to the increasing fear of political subversion. Political agitators posed a dual threat to American society. They undermined both the authority of the state and the democratic ideology of the national community. Concern about criminal and subversive elements in society mounted as World War II ended. Indeed, more bills were introduced with these concerns than those inspired by economic depression.[72] During the 72nd Congress (1931–1932), eight bills called for the exclusion and/or expulsion of Communists.[73] It was during this period that deportation became a key tool of immigration control. The mounting fear of subversive activities—dissemination of foreign propaganda, espionage, or merely belonging to the Communist Party—made certain previously unnoticed behaviors grounds for deportation. When there was a mass deportation of a group of Wobblies, The *New York Times* lauded the government's efforts to rid the United States of "bewhiskered, ranting, howling, mentally warped, law defying aliens."[74] Radicalism was not only the product of intellectual deficiencies but also was more likely than not a genetic trait. Again, threats to a vision of American democracy were the motive behind this new target of exclusion. It was this concern for the integrity of American nationality that sparked debate around the 1940 Nationality Act. Here the concern was more about the naturalization of immigrants and the perceived ease with which aliens become citizens. "The existing law is so lax that it confers citizenship upon persons who are not at all likely to be American in character or become imbued with American principles."[75] There was little concern about international reprisals. Indeed, U.S. legislators showed little concern for policy norms elsewhere. Immigration law lay clearly and undisputedly in the domestic domain. These policy initiatives and the debate that surrounded them do speak, however, to the growing importance of these exogenous norms. That is, by strongly asserting the rights of nation-states to territorial sovereignty, the United States was, consciously or not, participating in a broader debate about the relative importance of international and national prerogatives. International norms may not have been embraced, but they nonetheless shaped both policy and debate.

Post–World War II policy sought to initiate a break from lingering racial and ethnic exclusions and base policy more on a vision of a "good American." The 1952 Walter-McCarran Nationality Act opened up naturalization rights to formerly excluded groups and tried for the first time to actually define American character and establish the basis for immigrant undesirability. A set of excludable traits drawn from previous legislation was advanced as the antithesis of a good, 100 percent American. In all there were thirty-one excludable attributes falling into six categories: (1) those with intellectual, emotional or physical problems; (2) those prone to criminality and vice, including drug and alcohol addiction; (3) those whose sexual practices were somehow deviant; (4) those who either lacked employable skills or who might create market competition; (5) those who did not seek admission via legislated routes; and (6) those who might potentially be considered subversive.

International human rights rhetoric was often adopted without reflection. A concession to basic individual human rights was implicit in this policy shift. "Of course, we must properly screen those whom we admit in order to keep out undesirable such as chronic malcontents, habitual criminals, hatemongers, and subversives of all types. But with proper safeguards, I believe in a liberal policy: one based upon individual evaluation instead of race or nationality characteristics. Our concept of human rights and individual dignity should bar us from judging alien or anyone else en masse."[76] All peoples are to be treated "as equal human beings."[77]

Legislators were quick to draw parallels between the global process of decolonization and the American revolutionary spirit while distancing themselves from any hint of racial superiority:

> The United States was founded and developed in the realization of a revolutionary dream. . . . Today, . . . the fires of revolution are burning in many parts of the world. . . . Both nationalism and imperialism have served as powerful revolutionary factors. . . . [T]he upsurge of new nationalism . . . is the passionate desire for independence dignity and self-realization. . . . We Americans put no faith in a master race. . . . Ours had been a land in which men and women of all races, all creeds, and national origins could live and work together. Ours is a land where all could seek a place of dignity, where each could try to make a contribution of importance, where all may strive for fundamental civil rights, and where each can seek to develop through his own voluntary effort the best that is in him.[78]

While the British debate inadvertently resembled that of a colonized people, American discourse portrayed the United States as champion of the cause of colonized people.

The 1965 U.S. Immigration Act sought to rid the country not only of racial prejudice but also of discrimination based on national origins. The debate reflected a highly individualized notion of identity. "You judge a man by his worth and not by his birth. We honor the uniqueness of a man, the boundaries of his mind and his soul, not the geographical boundaries of his place of birth."[79] To be sure, there was not complete agreement on the abolition of racial and ethnic immigration and naturalization exclusions. Nor did attempts to construct identity as an individual, expressive attribute go uncontested. In arguments reminiscent of both the British debate over Commonwealth immigration and earlier debates within the Untied States, some saw for the need to consider the cultural tendencies of particular groups. "There is no question of 'superior' or 'inferior' races . . . [but] [c]ertain groups not only do not fuse easily, but consistently endeavor to keep alive their racial distinctions when they settle among us. They perpetuate the hyphen which is but another way of saying that they seek to create foreign blocs in our midst."[80] Concerns also emerged that the United States was acting out of some misperceived sense of international norms. Perhaps, it was thought, the U.S. policy was too quick to eliminate notions of exclusivity. A survey sponsored by Congress found that immigration controls were universal. Noting that neither Japan or Switzerland allowed any immigration, that Britain even limits access by its own colonists, that Israel has a Jews-only policy, Liberia has a no-whites statute, and Australia has a no-blacks act, the survey concluded that the United States has misjudged the global liberalization of immigration controls and misperceived a loosening of borders.[81] Senator McClellan noted that discrimination "is a natural compulsion of the human kind," reminding the Senate that discriminating tastes in food and clothing are considered admirable traits.[82] He implied that attempts to rid policy of any hint of discrimination were utopian.

Discussions about a balance between international standards and national expectations continued in debates of the 1986 and 1990 immigration acts. The 1986 Immigration Reform Act grappled with the social and economic realities of increasing illegal immigration. Pressure to stem illegal immigration had increased in border regions throughout the 1970s and early 1980s. The 1986 act sought to manage this problem, but within the parameters of perceived international standards.

Like the 1986 act, the 1990 Immigration Act tried to address both international and domestic concerns. "While we cannot absorb an unending stream of immigrants who wish to enter the United States, our immigration policy must be flexible and balance this country's economic needs with its humanitarian principles." But in certain key ways the 1990 act was couched in different terms. International principles were framed as "American" principles. Thus the act's basic tenets, including the promotion of diversity, were most suitable for the post-cold-war era, heralding a new age of global social relations. As Senator Edward Kennedy of Massachusetts said in introducing the bill, "More than any other nation, we are a nation of diversity and this bill reflects our historic diversity."[83] What was depicted as a global or universal respect for diversity would be the backbone of U.S. policies.

This diversity—whether characterized by ethnicity, occupation or family heritage—was quite clearly to be understood as an attribute of individuals. The anecdotal and personal tone of much of the debate highlights this fact. Policymakers in the United States knew well that their own ethnic history was relevant to public debate. Thus, in the context of debate over the 1990 immigration act, numerous members of Congress felt compelled to reveal their cultural legacy and their ethnicity, and those less familiar with their heritage felt obligated to apologize for their ignorance.[84] Both the preferential immigration status for families and skilled labor established by the 1990 legislation and the Immigration Commission's 1997 report further illustrate this individualism.

Ireland

In sharp contrast to the extensive postwar debates in the United States and the certitude of the British, the Irish were comparatively ambivalent and perhaps even uncertain in their approach to immigration. Indeed, their immigration and citizenship policy reflected their tentative sense of statehood. The debates reveal lingering ambiguities about the nature of the Irish nation and Irish nationalism. Furthermore, the uncomfortable fit between nation and state manifested in the division between the Irish Republic and Northern Ireland was a consistent theme in the debates about the 1935 Citizenship and Nationality Act. This tension lingered well into the decades following World War II. In 1935, the boundary between a newly independent Ireland and Great Britain needed bolstering in order to enhance confidence in domestic sovereignty. These earlier debates reflect the struggle to adhere to international standards and models while carving space for a distinctive Irish nation. It is a dilemma that would be echoed in many national immigration and citizenship debates throughout the 1940s, 1950s, and 1960s. The issue of whether to admit Jewish refugees in the 1930s provides one example of this tension. Refugees had rights, and many of these refugees would be welcome additions to the comparatively undereducated Irish labor supply. But how would Jews fit into a Catholic nation? Were there costs? In many ways, the Irish debates reveal a far greater consciousness of and attention to international norms that were demonstrated in the United States. The Irish Republic was conceived as a nation-state with clear cultural, moral, and organizational commitments to the international system—its primary source of legitimacy.

But sorting out the logic and language of citizenship policy without repudiating the centuries of Irish struggle against Britain did pose a significant problem. Ironically, the 1935 Citizenship Bill was modeled after the 1914 British Nationality Act. "Anyone who has examined the two Bills," one TD explained, "must recognize that not only is this Bill modeled on the British Act, but that whole chunks of the phraseology of the British Act have been embodied in the Bill. I make no adverse comment on that, but surely, when we are repudiating the criminal mother of Parliaments, we ought to try to secure a native basis for our statutes.."[85]

In the 1950s, Irish policy once again sought to reconceptualize the nation through the instrument of citizenship. Here too, the issue was the mismatch between the Irish nation and the Irish state. "The Irish nationalist myth is that there was always a strong sense of national identity and separate sense of self in the Irish community. Modern Irish national identity drew on a long series of events and some sense of Irishness."[86] The belief that this Irish nation ought to have expression in the form of a sovereign state was, however, a far more recent invention. Thus an even broader notion of the Irish nation and the Irish people was advanced. Numerous pleas were made to liberalize citizenship. "I feel that we should liberalize as far as it is possible our legislation in order to permit the acceptance of those people who can prove Irish descent."[87] If people with "queer names" can be granted citizenship, then so, too, should those with a "natural" claim to it. The 1935 act made citizenship a right of birth; the 1956 act made citizenship also a right of blood. Irishness—as a national or ethnic identity—was a matter of descent; it was both figuratively and technically in the veins. Speaking of the millions of Irish ex-patriots who had fled into exile during centuries of colonial blight, Mr. Walsh noted, "Ireland is indeed a mother country and her sons and daughters have peopled many lands. They brought the Faith to many races and have assisted in the building up and have contributed to the development and administration of many countries throughout the world. . . . I believe that one day most of them hope to return to end their days in their own country, to be buried beneath the green sod, to be mourned by those near and dear to them in their native land."[88] These generations are of Irish stock and this Bill provides for their Irish citizenship without the fulfillment of any artificial requirements on their part such as registration. Citizenship is, in our opinion, their birthright."[89] Indeed, some officials went so far as to claim that bloodlines were a more fitting way to determine citizenship. "It is of course, desirable in one sense that anyone who was born in Ireland should be entitled to be an Irish citizen, but it seems to me to carry a certain amount of danger with it as well. . . . It is undesirable that we should have people in this country with rights of citizenship who might be not exactly satisfactory, from the standpoint of Irish culture and Irish thought or to the overwhelming majority of the Irish people."[90]

By redefining citizenship as a right of descent, a broader notion of a greater Ireland and an Irish diaspora was born, along with a new notion of social differentiation. In the 1930s, the Irish timidly approached the definition of Irish citizenship. They relied heavily upon a legal and juridical concept of citizenship that was closely tied to international political norms and formal organizations. The 1950s legislation reflects a greater national self-confidence. The earlier, narrow definition was replaced by a notion of citizenship and nationality that lay loosely in a shared culture and a shared history. Commonality was possible through lived experience but more likely derived from genetic heritage. People of Irish descent were of a special character. But even an Irishness passed on by heredity was a communal trait, not an expression of individualism. A communal logic embedded in the traditional values of both the Catholic Church and Gaelic society meant that individuals were still second to the community. Ireland was not alone in its reliance on biological metaphors to ground national citizenship; this was also the norm in the United States throughout much of its history.

Largely because of its increasing integration into the European Community—it held the EC presidency in 1996–1997—Ireland has been forced to consider the issue of immigration. There are now about 40,000 legal aliens living among the 4 million Irish in the Republic.[91] In 1996 there were 5,700 more immigrants than emigrants, marking a dramatic reversal of the historical negative population flow. Immigration and the problems that many nation-states have come to associate with it are unfamiliar to the Irish.

The most recent changes in Irish immigration and citizenship law occurred in 1986 and 1994. The changes did not fundamentally alter the terms or meaning of citizenship or revise the system of social differentiation. Moreover, neither act addressed the issues of immigration, citizenship, or race relations to the degree these issues have been addressed by many of Ireland's fellow European Community members in the past two decades. Ireland, by deploying a myth of homogeneity that comes closer to reality than most such fantasies, has sidestepped many of these concerns. In 1986, gender distinctions in immigration law were removed and a three-year waiting period for citizenship via marriage was instituted. Both wives and husbands of Irish nationals would have the same access to citizenship. Under the 1956 act, wives of nationals had an automatic right of citizenship, while husbands did not. The removal of such discrimination was touted as a vital "symbolic" step toward the eradication of gender discrimination in Ireland.[92] Moreover, with this change, Ireland would move into line with international standards regarding gender equality that both the United Nations and the European Union were then advocating. Antiquated and unnecessary distinctions between men and women that had unthinkingly been instituted in the 1950s were summarily removed. In 1994, the right of citizenship was made slightly less accessible; the capacity of persons of distant Irish descent to make direct claims on the Irish state was limited. The Irish nation was brought more closely into line with the Irish state, but not at the expense of international standards.

Standardized Difference, Discursive Uniformity, and the Importance of Ethnicity

In each of these three nation-states, a full account of post–World War I immigration and citizenship debate must attend to the broader international discourse from which they emerged. This discursive field determines not the precise content of either debate or policy but rather the range of imaginable discussion and policy. Defining the scope of the possible does not mean that international influences are not nationally or locally mediated. National or local politics often reframe international norms and co-opt definitions. For example, some British officials defended discriminatory immigration policies as a way to challenge the perceived hegemony of the United States in international politics. In this sense, exogenous influences might be said to have more effect on determining what nation-states don't do than with what they actually do. But ultimately, both are important. As Great Britain sought to replace empire with state, as the United States tried to position itself as a nation-state central to world politics, and as Ireland tried to find a state to accompany its nation, each via the creation of sociocultural and political membership of national citizenship, they differentially drew from and relied upon international ideas, principles, and frameworks to guide them. The evidence of this international context is manifest in the language, tone, and timing of policies and laws. Racial exclusions were phased out and refugee liberalization was instituted, for example, at similar times in all three nations in the name of the same universal principles and international norms.

Perhaps one unintended consequence of these efforts to bound the nation and create social and political closure through immigration and citizenship policy is the increasing standardization of social identity and social differentiation. These debates created a conceptual convergence around particular conceptions of personhood, human rights, and collective solidarities. Thus, certain categories of personhood—both national and subnational—have become more salient and more legitimate. In particular, the prevalence of ethnic notions of identity in the 1980s and 1990s is largely a result of the international advocacy of national citizenship. Ethnicity and the significance ascribed to it are products of this scripted immigration and citizenship debate. Ethnicity has emerged from these debates as a "sanctioned identity."[94] And like the debates around nationhood and citizenship, discussion of ethnicity is now part of a broader world discourse that tames and homogenizes its meaning.

Notes

1. This bipartisan commission was established in accordance with the Immigration Act of 1990 (PL 101–649). In 1994 the commission issued a separate report on the control of illegal immigration.

2. Barbara Jordan, 1997, as cited in U.S. Commission on Immigration Reform, *Becoming an American: Immigration and Immigration Policy* (Washington, D.C.: Government Printing Office), i.

3. Commission on Immigration Reform, *Becoming an American,* 6.

4. Will Kymlicka and Wayne J. Norman, "Return of the Citizen," *Ethics* 104 (1994): 352–81.

5. See Joseph Rotblat, *World Citizenship: Allegiance to Humanity* (New York: St. Martin's Press, 1997); Yasemin Soysal, *The Limits of Citizenship: Migrants and Postnational Membership in Europe.* (Chicago: University of Chicago Press, 1994).

6. Will Kymlicka, *Multicultural Citizenship* (Oxford: Clarendon Press, 1995); Kymlicka, *Limits of Citizenship.*

7. Roland Robertson, *Globalization: Social Theory and Global Culture* (London: Sage, 1992).

8. John W. Meyer et al., "World Society and the Nation-State," *American Journal of Sociology* 103 (1997): 144–81.

9. Recently, others have argued that this separation between rights and identity is quickly reaching its logical and logistical limits, claiming that the dynamics of 1990s identity politics will be short-lived. See, e.g., David Hollinger, *Postethnic America: Beyond Multiculturalism* (New York: Basic Books, 1995).

10. William Rogers Brubaker, ed., *Immigration and the Politics of Citizenship in Europe and North America* (New York: University Press of America, 1989).

11. George M. Thomas et al., eds., *Institutional Structure: Constituting State, Society, and the Individual* (New York: Sage, 1987); Meyer et al., "World Society."

12. Meyer et al., "World Society," 159.

13. Vaughan Bevan, *The Development of British Immigration Law* (London: Croon Helm, 1993), 28.

14. Teun A. VanDijk, "Discourse and the Denial of Racism," *Discourse and Society* 3 (1992): 87–118.

15. Rogers Brubaker, "Comments on Immigration Politics in Liberal Democratic States," *International Migration Review* 29 (1995): 903–8.

16. Francisco O. Ramirez, Yasemin Soysal, and Suzanne Shanahan, "The Changing Logic of Political Citizenship," *American Sociological Review* 62 (1997): 735–45.

17. See, e.g., Michael C. LeMay, *From Open Door to Dutch Door: An Analysis of U.S. Immigration Policy since 1820* (New York: Praeger, 1987).

18. Mauricio Trillo Tenorio, *Mexico at the World's Fairs: Crafting a Modern Nation* (Berkeley and Los Angeles: University of California Press, 1996), 241.

19. Gary Freeman has argued that liberal democracies exhibit key similarities in their immigration debates and policies. See Gary Freeman, "Modes of Immigration Politics in Liberal Democratic States," *International Migration Review 29 (1995): 881–902;* Audrey Smedley, *Race in North America: Origins and Evolution of a Worldview* (San Francisco: Westview Press, 1993); Paul Starr, "Social Categories and Claims in the Liberal State," *Social Research* 50 (1992): 263–95.

20. Rogers Brubaker, *Citizenship and Nationhood in France and Germany* (Cambridge: Harvard University Press, 1992).

21. Tom Nairn, *The Enchanted Glass: Britain and Its Monarchy* (London: Radius, 1988); Ann Dummet and Andrew Nicol, *Subjects, Citizens, Aliens, and Others* (London: Weidenfeld & Nicolson, 1990), 258.

22. Vaughan Bevan, *The Development of British Immigration Law* (London: Croon Helm, 1993); Zig Layton-Henry, *The Politics of Immigration* (Oxford: Blackwell, 1992).

23. Liah Greenfeld, *Nationalism: Five Roads to Modernity* (Cambridge: Harvard University Press, 1992).

24. David Coleman, "The United Kingdom and International Migration: A Changing Balance," in *European Migration in the Late Twentieth Century,* ed. Heinz Fassman and Rainer Munz (Laxenburg, Austria: IIASA, 1995), 38–66.

25. Office of Population, Censuses, and Surveys, *Annual Abstract of Statistics* (London: HMSO, 1990).

26. Freeman, "Modes of Immigration."

27. Department of Justice, *Immigration and Naturalization Statistical Yearbook* (Washington, D.C.: Government Printing Office, 1994).

28. From speech of Senator Kennedy of Massachusetts during debate of Immigration Act of 1990 (*Congressional Record* Computer File, 101st Congress, Senate Proceedings, 2 November 1990).

29. Philip L. Martin, "The United States: Benign Neglect toward Immigration," in *Controlling Immigration: A Global Perspective,* ed. Wayne A. Cornelius, Phillip L. Martin, and James F. Hollifield (Stanford: Stanford University Press, 1994), 83–99.

30. Nairn, *Enchanted Glass,* 129.

31. House of Commons, 5 August 1914, *Hansard Parliamentary Debates,* 1986.

32. House of Commons, 22 January 1969, *Parliamentary Debates,* 750: 504.

33. Bevan, *Development of British Immigration Law,* 74.

34. Nairn, *Enchanted Glass.*

35. According to agreements made at the Commonwealth Conference of 1947, while each dominion could determine its own criterion of citizenship, all such citizens would also be British subjects. See Bevan, *Development of British Immigration Law.*

36. David Reynolds, *Britannia Overruled: British Policy and World Power in the Twentieth Century* (London: Longman, 1991); David Sanders, *Losing an Empire, Finding a Role: British Foreign Policy since 1945* (London: MacMillan, 1990).

37. Home Secretary Chuter-Ede as cited in Bob Carter, Marci Green, and Rick Halpern, "Immigration Policy and the Racialization of Migrant Labour: The Construction of National Identities in the USA and Britain," *Ethnic and Racial Studies* 19 (1996): 135–57, quote at 143.

38. House of Commons, 7 July 1948, *Parliamentary Debates,* 453: 405.

39. Committee on the Social and Economic Problems, *Report,* 3 August 1955, 3.

40. House of Commons, 1962, *Parliamentary Debates,* 650: 1212, 1226, 1251.

41. House of Commons, 1962, *Parliamentary Debates,* 649: 716–18.

42. House of Commons, 1962, *Parliamentary Debates,* 649: 706, 731.

43. Note, e.g., that during this same time both Canada and the United States moved to eliminate explicit racial restrictions in their immigration and naturalization legislation.

44. House of Commons,1965, *Parliamentary Debates,* 711: 983, 928

45. House of Commons, 1976, *Parliamentary Debates,* 914: 1643.

46. House of Commons, 1965, *Parliamentary Debates,* 711: 983.

47. House of Commons, 1965, *Parliamentary Debates,* 711: 926, 1045, 1048.
48. House of Commons, 1965, *Parliamentary Debates,* 716: 969–75.
49. House of Commons, 1976, *Parliamentary Debates,* 914: 1913.
50. House of Commons, 1976, *Parliamentary Debates,* 914: 1787, 1888.
51. Nicol, *Subjects, Citizens, Aliens,* 258.
52. Coleman, "United Kingdom and International Migration," 58.
53. Nicol, *Subjects, Citizens, Aliens,* 245.
54. Nicol, *Subjects, Citizens, Aliens.*
55. House of Commons 1976, *Parliamentary Debates,* 914: 1726, 1644.
56. House of Commons, 1987, *Parliamentary Debates,* 122: 832
57. Satvinder S. Juss, *Immigration, Nationality, and Citizenship* (London: Mansell, 1993).
58. Right Reverend Peter Selby, Bishop of Kingston upon Thames, *Guardian,* 12 November 1991.
59. Lord Ackner as cited in Juss, *Immigration, Nationality, and Citizenship,* 25.
60. *Guardian,* 31 October 1991.
61. Juss, *Immigration, Nationality, and Citizenship.*
62. Burnett Bill, 19 March 1914, Senate Report 355 (63-II), 1.
63. Congressman Moss, citing Dr. Frank Julian Warne, *Congressional Record,* 3 February 1914, 51: 2827.
64. Senator Underwood,*Congressional Record,* 25 June 1906, 40: 9155.
65. Senator Reed, *Congressional Record,* 2 May 1921, 61: 948.
66. *Congressional Record,* 3 May 3 1921, 61: 951.
67. Senator Williams, *Congressional Record,* 13 December 1914, 52: 806.
68. Congressman Box, *Congressional Record,* 9 December 1920, 60: 1: 173–74.
69. John Higham, *Strangers in the Land: Patterns of American Nativism* (New Brunswick, N.J.: Rutgers University Press), 199.
70. Higham, *Strangers in the Land.*
71. Frances Kellor as cited in Higham, *Strangers in the Land,* 234.
72. Edward Price Hutchinson, *Legislative History of American Immigration Policy: 1789–1965* (Philadelphia: University of Pennsylvania Press, 1981).
73. Hutchinson, *Legislative History.*
74. *New York Times,* 10 February 1919, 1.
75. Congressman Rees, *Congressional Record,* 11 September 1940, 86: 1: 11948.
76. Congressman Yorty, *Congressional Record,* 1952, 98: 4: 441.
77. Congressman Judd, *Congressional Record,* 1952, 98: 4: 440.
78. Senator Benton, *Congressional Record,* 1952, 98: 4: 5149.
79. Congressman Celler, *Congressional Record,* 1965, 111: 16: 21579.
80. *New York Times* article from 1 March 1924 reprinted in *Congressional Record,* 1965, 111: 18: 24552.
81. Harris Poll cited in *Congressional Record,* 1965, 111: 18: 24447.
82. Senator McClellan, *Congressional Record,* 1965, 111: 18: 24554.
83. *Congressional Record* Computer File, 101st Congress, Senate Proceedings, 2 November 1990.

84. *Congressional Record* Computer File, 101st Congress, Senate Proceedings, 2 November 1990.

85. Mr. Milroy, Seanad Eireann, *Parliamentary Debates,* 17 January 1935, 19: 1042.

86. Gretchen M. MacMillan, *State, Society, and Authority in Ireland: Foundations of the Modern State* (Dublin: Gill & MacMillan, 1993), 124.

87. Dail Eireann, *Parliamentary Debates,* 29 February 1956, 154: 1014.

88. Seanad Eireann, *Parliamentary Debates,* 16 May 1956–19 December 1956, 46: 88.

89. Dail Eireann, *Parliamentary Debates,* 29 February 1956, 154: 1000.

90. Dail Eireann, *Parliamentary Debates,* 29 February 1956, 154: 1014.

91. *Irish Times,* 1 March 1997, 11.

92. Dail Eireann, *Parliamentary Debates,* 21 March 1986, 364: 2611–662.

93. Robert Carter, Marci Green, and Rick Halpern, "Immigration Policy and the Racialization of Migrant Labour" *Ethical and Racial Studies* 19 (1996): 135–57.

94. Jane F. Collier, Bill Maurer, and Liliana Suarez-Navaz, "Sanctioned Identities: Legal Construction of Modern Personhood," *Identities* 2 (1995): 1–27.

5

Citizenship in Chinese History

R. Bin Wong

The concept of citizenship as a way to characterize a particular range of relations between states and the people they rule first emerges historically in European experiences of state formation. To understand citizenship in a non-European setting, it helps to consider two ways in which the term is used: first, as a
general analytical category used by analysts seeking to examine a variety of
cases; and second, as a concept used by non-European actors to understand
their own political situations. There is little reason to assume that the meanings
of citizenship for late-nineteenth- and twentieth-century Chinese actors and the
relationships between their state and themselves will mirror the trajectory of
changes in European citizenship, yet there are good reasons to consider how the
concept of citizenship might help illuminate relations between the Chinese government and the people it rules. In this chapter I will compare the broad outlines
of state-society relations in China and Europe since 1600. A sense of what is
similar and different in these historical experiences helps us appreciate the contemporary situations of each. The possible futures for citizenship in China continue to be shaped by the arc of changes connecting the Chinese state and its
subjects over the past several centuries. The concept of citizenship has had historically specific formulations in China, where a tradition of political statecraft
has stressed, at least since the tenth century, state initiative and superiority but-
tressed by nongovernmental elite support. Late-twentieth-century democratic
reformers' calls for a radically different formulation of Chinese citizenship
upon principles more akin to those developed historically in the West echo the
hopes of Chinese reformers a century ago as they continue to face the challenge
of dislodging far older Chinese political practices and sensibilities.

   In a recent essay, Charles Tilly offers some guidelines for thinking about
citizenship.[1] He suggests that citizenship is a relationship between government agents and people composed of transactions clustered around mutual
rights and obligations that are formed through bargaining and protest leading

to settlements of various kinds. At the heart of rights and obligations is the presence of some third party that can enforce the claims that one party can make on another. But such a party is often absent or ineffectual since, Tilly tells us, most claim-making by citizens fails. But it bears stressing, I think, that the *potential* for adjudication and enforcement of claims, represented by the development of an institutional apparatus to implement an ideological belief in rights, is a feature of situations in which we can anticipate a transformation of state-subject relations into state-citizen relations. A second feature of citizenship in Tilly's formulation worth highlighting is its focus on transactions between state and citizens that proceed from an assumption of exchange: state and citizens do not have the same interests, but they share a mutual dependence that is best satisfied by meeting the distinct demands of each. This manner of formulating the relation of the state relations to the people it rules is by no means universal; officials and groups of people need not imagine their engagements to be defined by an interest-based calculus of exchange. With these features of citizenship in mind, let us turn to state-subject relations in late imperial China.

Late Imperial Chinese State-Subject Relations

Late imperial Chinese political ideology and government institutions created settings between the fourteenth and twentieth centuries in which officials and people interacted about a range of topics including taxation, famine relief, religious practices, and violations of law. Both government and its subjects held expectations for what was appropriate and acceptable behavior by the other. But people could not exercise any *claims* on the government, in the sense of having some third-party enforcement. Rather, the government made *commitments* to people—to tax lightly, to intervene in subsistence crises, to help maintain water-control operations, and more generally to promote broadly-based agrarian economic prosperity and social order. When officials failed to meet these commitments, people could protest. Agricultural taxes, the source of much of the government's revenue, were levied according to the quality of the harvests and varied according to the productivity of the land. When peasants felt that adjustments for harvests were inadequate or assessment procedures unfair, they protested. Similarly, when grain prices rose owing to bad harvests or the shipment of grain from the local area and officials did not intervene to stabilize prices and grain availability, peasants made protests.[2] Thus, there were mechanisms for people to express their expectations of officials and by so doing to elicit official responses more considerate of popular concerns, but people in late imperial China possessed no claim-making machinery and thus were not, in Tilly's terms, "citizens." They did not make claims on the state.

Taxation issues highlight the contrast between European claim-making and Chinese commitments. Early modern European state makers gathered new taxes in a range of ways. When new impositions were made on a broad range of subjects, widespread popular resistance could follow, as the mid-seventeenth-century French Fronde reminds us. On a more modest scale, when French kings levied new charges on particular towns or provinces, the inhabitants attempted to negotiate some defense of former privileges in return for some new tax payment; sometimes these efforts also ended in resistance.[3] In England, parliamentary procedures were developed whereby the king could not in general raise new taxes without the agreement of Parliament. By the nineteenth century, taxation in Western Europe more generally was increasingly enmeshed with a broader cluster of rights and duties that comprised citizenship. T. H. Marshall has presented one of the classic analyses of citizenship, based on the British case, that captures this expansion of citizenship features in nineteenth-century Europe.[4] Marshall explains that citizenship rights began with civil rights and then came to include political rights and finally, in the twentieth century, a set of social rights. He argues that citizenship was an important vehicle for creating political equalities in societies increasingly dominated by capitalism, which divided people into separate economic classes. Returning to the contrast between claims and commitments, Europeans became able to make a set of claims on their states as states expanded their authority over society. This process was not a simple one of governments simply granting new rights to their citizens but rather was a claim-making process in which participants in social movements made demands of their governments, many of whose leaders saw citizenship rights as a means for securing social order.

China, in contrast, did not have social movements pressing for a set of claims. There were no institutional mechanisms through which taxes could be negotiated in a legally meaningful manner. Nor, it should be added, was there much need for such mechanisms, since there were no statutory increases in land taxes, the main source of government revenues, between 1712 and 1853. People unhappy with tax levies had the options of protesting collectively when they deemed taxes unfair or individually seeking to avoid making payments. Their grievances prompted officials to address their dissatisfactions to avoid a breakdown of social control. Individual avoidance could be tolerated, but only to a certain degree, without undermining government resources and credibility. Chinese protests were embedded in a set of expectations about what proper official behavior should be—a willingness to reduce land taxes in years of poor harvest, an ability to provide relief in years of especially short supplies.

These expectations were grounded in the commitments both the people and the officials recognized were made by morally proper governments. Some of the popular expectations of officials were also held by common people of their elites: wealthy landlords, rich merchants, and scholars, some of whom were considered gentry because they had received degrees upon passing government civil service examinations and becoming eligible for bureaucratic appointment. These elites were expected to reduce rents in years of poor harvest; sell, lend, or give away grain in years of serious dearth; and organize community demands of the government for relief. Thus, late imperial Chinese elites and common people exercised no "claims," despite their ideologically grounded expectations for proper actions from the state. Local elites in China did not stake out separate spheres of autonomy that they sought to demarcate sharply from the state's realm. For their part, officials of the Chinese imperial state had an incentive to define people's expectations in a manner that they believed the state could meet, thus establishing the government's credibility and legitimacy. Confucian commitments to social stability and popular welfare were believed by leaders to be the basis of their political authority. Eighteenth-century Confucian paternalism, for instance, created a scale of government granary reserves for food-supply management that dwarfed similar efforts by European governments.[5] Chinese political practice created popular expectations through official commitments, while European governments negotiated with their elites, who sought to make claims. European claim-making was part of a broader effort made by European elites to defend their autonomous spaces through negotiation and struggle.

In European history claims were first made on the state by corporately organized elites—nobles, clergy, burghers. In domestic social terms the process of European state formation centered on relations among elite groups and officials, as the chapters by Shanahan and Prak in this volume make clear.[6] Citizenship as a relationship of transactions centered on mutual rights and obligations between European states and the people they rule was first entered into by governments and social elites. The process of claim-making at the heart of this relationship was not present in China, where a very different set of social relations obtained.

Late imperial China (1368–1911) had no corporately organized elites; the only nobility were individuals related to the emperor and thus members of the imperial lineage. There was no institutionalized religion that enjoyed earthly privileges as well as heavenly virtue. There were no city administrations organized prior to, and independently of, the central government. Instead of the European contest between a centralizing state and elites staking out their own spheres of power and authority, Chinese officials and elites shared a common Confucian agenda for creating local social order that depended crucially on landlords and merchants infused with a Confucian set of beliefs and willing to help pay for and manage local granaries and schools, as well as repair roads, bridges, and temples. In the seventeenth and nineteenth centuries elites would also mobilize men and resources to form militia to defend their locales in the Ming-Qing transition and the great mid-nineteenth-century rebellions. To stress the overlap of official and elite commitments and a shared willingness to establish and maintain local institutions in which both played roles does not, of course, mean that officials and elites enjoyed identical interests or outlooks. Beyond the obvious desire to avoid paying taxes, elites in some areas on occasion constructed spaces of social practice separate from government supervision; elite styles of consumption were one arena beyond state control, religious practice another, an example being patronage of Buddhist monasteries in the sixteenth century.[7] But most important for the construction of political order, and in contrast to European state-elite relations, Chinese elites and officials shared a Confucian agenda for creating social stability in which they jointly shouldered commitments toward common people. Meeting this agenda for social stability assured social control for both officials and elites. There were no "claims" of the kind that European elites, and later in the nineteenth century more ordinary European people, put upon their states, no notions of "rights" or "privileges" to be negotiated over as basic to the relationship between state and subject. Thus, in at least one sense, late imperial Chinese state-elite relations, as well as state-commoner relations, did not fit the criteria of citizenship.

Little of the ideological and institutional nexus that created European citizenship amid processes of state formation existed in late imperial China. China lacked a tradition of municipal autonomy and of corporately organized elites. In addition, European conceptions of sovereignty and the shift in location of the right to rule from kings to people were absent in China's domestic scene.[8] The absence of similar processes of political change raises the question of whether citizenship can be created in ways different from those in Europe. Bryan Turner expresses serious reservations when he concludes an assessment of citizenship with the thought, "It appears doubtful, therefore, that 'citizenship' could apply easily to societies which have had very different urban histories, or which have very different notions of 'the public.'"[9] European elites forged a "public sphere," a realm of public opinion and political activity that accompanied the state-making process and attempted to influence its direction toward democratic ends.[10] They constructed new kinds of civil society in which autonomous spaces—before the nineteenth century, especially those for elites—became demarcated from the spaces in which state power was expanding. Sharp divisions between state and society depended upon the institutional resources of elites to create their own organizations and social practices and safeguard them from government interference. These ideological and institutional conditions that supported European constructions of citizenship did not exist in China in the eighteenth century—indeed, they couldn't even be imagined at that time. In the late nineteenth century when Western ideas about citizenship were introduced to China, they could not easily replace older political sensibilities and social practices. Instead, they were introduced as components of larger visions of political reform, whose agreed-upon purpose was to strengthen China to withstand the pressures of international competition that threatened to dismember the empire. Kang Youwei and Liang Qichao, two of the most famous late Qing reformers, both understood citizenship as the relationship between the people on the one hand and the state and nation on the other.[11] The strength of the state and nation depended upon mobilizing the people to support and defend the government.

Consider how ideas of Western citizenship fit within broader late-nineteenth-century Chinese agendas of political reform and how these were in turn still linked to older strategies of rule within which there was no obvious space for European notions of citizenship. Of Marshall's three components of citizenship, civil, political, and social, the political was most salient in turn-of-the-century China. The key institutional innovation supporting the late-nineteenth-century Chinese development of citizenship was representative assemblies, which sought to create a new political role for elites who advocated constitutional monarchy. Inspired by Western examples, these assemblies created China's first citizens, in the sense of individuals with a claim on a form of political participation, from those propertied and educated men who were eligible to vote for representatives, who were drawn from a still smaller pool of men. The formation of representative assemblies was part of a broader set of institutional innovations intended to make Chinese government more effective and, in particular, responsive to challenges created and imposed by Western powers. Representative assemblies were flanked by other institutions, like newspapers and study societies, that aimed to forge a set of political reforms whose basic purpose was to promote the state's capacity to resist foreign threats. The freedom that officials and elites were both seeking in this period was the freedom of the Chinese nation.

For Liang Qichao, citizenship concerned the "pursuit of 'public morality' through political activism."[12] He imagined democracy as communication between government and people through study societies.[13] This notion of democracy was in turn based upon a logic of official-elite cooperation typical of the previous several centuries. The members of the study societies were to be the same degree-holding elites who previously played roles in sustaining local social order. These societies, in Liang's view, were to be sites at which elites could discuss policies and enact rules for effecting local order, but administrative officials were still the leaders who would carry out any projects proposed.[14]

For example, officials and elites in the late Qing reform era were allies in the effort to suppress opium. The state's strategy depended fundamentally on mobilizing gentry elites to share in this project of recreating a social order morally reinvigorated by the eradication of the opium blight. The central government began in 1906 to promote the founding of local anti-opium societies to be headed by local elites. The government wanted to mobilize elite support for promoting social order without sanctioning a more formal political role with enhanced and specified powers.[15] From the government's point of view, these anti-opium associations were an extension of government capacity and commitments to eradicate opium use; no notion of individual rights accompanied their creation. Indeed, a 1906 imperial edict granted anti-opium societies "full authority to enter any place for examination and plac[ed] at their disposal officers to enforce their demands for admittance or to make arrests where ordered by such committees."[16] The elites mounting anti-opium campaigns increasingly regarded their efforts, as Michael Tsin argues for the Canton case, as a means to establish a strong society quite separate from the government.[17]

In the late Qing effort to eradicate opium, the officials and elites employed a range of instruments, including new techniques, such as magazines. But many of the strategies, as well as the underlying social logic of opium suppression, engaged officials and elites together in an effort to resecure a Confucian social order. Members of the elite did not always agree to play subordinate roles to officials in implementing social programs like opium suppression; in addition, some felt strongly that they should have a more active role in influencing government foreign affairs policies.

The Chinese state had begun dealing with the serious problems created by Europeans with the Opium War (1839–1842) against the British. For roughly half a century Chinese government officials appeared to be doing a pretty reasonable job; they developed new bureaucratic capacities to deal with European-style international relations and avoided the subordination of colonialism. But after the country's defeat in the Sino-Japanese War (1894–1895), an increasing urgency over China's military and political weaknesses began to form the central concern of both many officials and many elites. Chinese leaders developed a new sense of the "nation" from the country's dealings with foreign powers. Saving the nation from dismemberment by foreign powers became a widely shared goal.

Studies of nationalism sometimes distinguish between two basic kinds of nations, one composed of citizens, modeled on nineteenth-century France; and one based on an ethnic definition of group. The first kind of nation includes expectations for how the relationships between governments and the people they rule will be forged, while the second makes no such statements. The nationalism that emerged around the notion of a "Chinese nation" at the turn of the century was more like the second type than the first. The elites' desire to play a larger role in government diplomacy did not translate easily into an institutionalized system of government with state-citizen relations at its foundation. While officials and elites could agree that a serious threat faced their nation, they did not always agree on what role elites should play in addressing this crisis. High officials of the government had little desire to delegate any new authority or power to provincial representative assemblies or study groups. Officials continued to view elites as groups whose members could help them implement strategies of rule and control. As long as both officials and elites agreed that their primary task was to save the country from dismemberment and destruction, they shared a common, overriding goal despite their disagreements about how to achieve it.[18] Elites began in the late nineteenth century to create new organizational bases for defining new relations to government authority, but their efforts failed to yield institutionalized results. Many envisioned the formation of citizens as the foundation of a revived nation distinct from the dynasty headed by Manchus.[19] The collapse of the dynasty in 1911 created an ideological and institutional vacuum within which ideas about citizenship and representation floated, unanchored by either a coherent political vision or a concrete set of institutions upon which to build a new state. The context within which Chinese used the concept of citizen lacked much of the substance associated with the term in Western discourse. Concern for political rights lacked the urgency of concerns for the nation's survival. Concern for civil rights was even less immediately important. Social rights, the third component of Marshall's discussion of British citizenship, did not exist in quite the same terms in China. Chinese officials and elites had long made commitments through their Confucian paternalism to popular social welfare; the substantive content of European social rights was broadly mirrored in Chinese welfare concerns, even if the processes creating these traits differed. There was also an important temporal difference. As European social rights were becoming a more prominent feature of citizenship, the end of imperial rule meant that Chinese capacities and commitments to sustain welfare were declining. Europeans had achieved their rights through negotiations and struggles over what citizen rights and obligations should be. As China's last dynasty fell in 1911, state-subject relations lacked the kind of transactions basis that formed the foundation of European citizenship.

Creating Chinese Citizens: Postimperial Possibilities

The late imperial Chinese state had been a unitary state in the sense that its power was not divided among different types of government authorities. There were no aristocracies, estates, provincial parliaments, or independent cities, each with its own bases of governmental authority. The late imperial state's vertical integration rested upon the central government's control of finances and personnel decisions; there were no institutionally separate power holders who independently laid claim to resources or selected officials. The collapse of the dynasty brought a halt to central control over finances and personnel decisions. The prospects for creating a unitary state in postimperial times looked less promising than they had under the agrarian empire.

Postimperial state formation in China was a complex process taking place at the central, provincial, and local government levels. From 1916 to 1927 there was no central government that could even make a plausible case for controlling the entire country. From 1927 until 1937 when the Japanese invasion severed whatever putative political unity had existed, the Nationalist Party (GMD) made such an assertion despite having only very limited bureaucratic reach beyond the five provinces it controlled near the capital of Nanking. Within many of the more than 1,300 counties, the lowest level of Chinese government administration, government capacities were expanded. At provincial levels, the development of new institutions of civilian rule competed with the growth of new forms of military power. Finally, at the central government level, new bureaucracies were formed and older ones reformed. The postimperial possibilities of Chinese state making were defined by the dynamics at each of these three levels and the linkages that were being created among them. Chinese elites and common people developed different relationships to expanding government power at each of these levels. These relationships in turn established the context for what citizenship could mean in the Republican era (1912–1949).

The penetration of local government into local society in the Republican period continued complex processes that first began in the late nineteenth century. Elites became more formally involved in local affairs, making even fuzzier the distinction between official and elite. The dynamics of local government expansion varied across China, in part at least conforming to the roles of officials and elites in the various provinces or regions during late imperial times. Political conditions at the local level varied dramatically across China depending on the area's wealth, its social structure, and degree of urban development. For example, in Jiangnan, the rich area near Shanghai, elites took on ever more formal roles through their own initiatives. [20] Continuing the trend of taking on material, coercive, and normative means of social control that began no later than the sixteenth century, consultative gentry assemblies were established in the late nineteenth century. In early-twentieth-century Shanghai, a city council was formed with separate executive and legislative branches to carry out a range of tasks entrusted to the gentry by imperial government officials, including selling cheap rice, suppressing opium dens, dredging waterways, building and repairing roads and bridges, removing garbage, and lighting streets.[21] The scale and sophistication of local government developed by Shanghai gentry may have exceeded practices implemented elsewhere, but the proactive role of gentry in forming local governments was hardly unique to Shanghai elites.

Keith Schoppa has reconstructed Zhejiang province's spatial variations in elite organization and action according to a social and political ecology that found fewer elite organizations in more peripheral parts of the province.[22] In less wealthy areas officials played a larger role in expanding local government and in the process asserted the importance of administrative hierarchy, seeking to integrate local government into a system of state control reaching the provincial level. The north China governors of Shanxi and Zhili provinces were ordered by the central government to experiment with local self-government in the early 1900s, just as they and other north China governors had been ordered a little more than a century and a half earlier to experiment with charity granary reserves.[23] Governor Zhao Erxun in Shanxi followed an authoritarian model, while Yuan Shikai developed a set of less authoritarian institutions more similar to Japanese practices.[24] The elaboration of local government under strong official control continued in the postimperial period as well; Shanxi governor Yan Xishan, for instance, created a village system that replicated late imperial practices of tax collection (*lijia*) and mutual surveillance (*baojia*). A program for stronger local government in Guangxi province also resulted from provincial-level official initiatives, in this case to serve military mobilization.[25] But there was no movement mobilizing common people to press for larger roles in either local government or national politics; common people did not engage in citizenship struggles as nineteenth-century Europeans did.

In some areas, local government was largely in the hands of elites who organized basic municipal institutions. In Europe, traditions of municipal autonomy formed a context for developing participatory democracy that in turn became basic to ideas about citizenship. In China elite engagement was part of a Confucian agenda of rule in which officials often looked positively upon elite roles in local rule but always saw such actions as ultimately subordinated to centralized official authority. Elites could call themselves citizens (*shimin*), but their efforts at local self-government were framed within their ongoing dialogue with bureaucratic authority. As Murata Yujiro tells us, these Chinese citizens "cannot be compared to the tradition of urban self-government in Europe."[26]

Because twentieth-century Chinese state-building initiatives at the local level often meant extracting revenue and men for increased levels of conflict, people in many local settings mobilized to protect themselves against what was experienced as a kind of government predation lacking both the customary status of late imperial collections and the traditions of negotiation that characterized early modern European tax expansion. Since villages rather than households were increasingly taxed as a unit, local communities shared an interest in resisting taxation. Villages also attempted to resist bandits, whose numbers were augmented by demobilized and unemployed soldiers. Efforts to expand the capacities of local government took place at the same time that local government's ability to ensure stability and peace was ever less certain and communities developed greater incentives to keep government out.

At provincial levels, the second tier of government expansion between county and nation, two new dynamics beginning in the last decade of the Qing continued into postimperial times. First, the formation of assemblies mentioned previously held out the possibility of new institutions for civilian rule. Second, the mobilization of armies to engage in fighting among China's regions increased the importance of military interventions in political decision making. The relative importance of civilian and military expansion varied among provinces. At one extreme, Yunnan in southwest China was basically under military rule.[27] At the other extreme, government in the lower Yangzi region around Shanghai featured far more participation by civilian elites. In between fall the cases of Hubei and Hunan in central China.[28] Assemblies tended to be more prominent in economically more developed areas with strong civilian elites, while military strongmen emerged in less wealthy areas with weaker civilian elites. Assemblies raised the issues of political rights for the elites who were represented in such assemblies. But assemblies never had a clearly defined role in government decision making at the county, provincial, or national level, and hence the kinds of citizenship associated with political rights in European traditions were never established in republican-era China.

The Nationalist government excelled at the third level of state building in postimperial times, the central government level; here officials established new specialized bureaucracies and reformed older ones. The central government improved its capacities in key areas that enhanced its control over major urban centers, facilitated economic development, and improved performance in international diplomacy. Separate from these positive signs of state building growth were the signs that the central government no longer controlled the governments that ruled beneath it. Outside the specialized central bureaucracies, republican-era government was plagued by corruption and cynicism. China was no longer structurally a unitary state, and the behavior of Chinese officials often seemed a far cry from the Confucian ideals of late imperial times. While corruption had also been an issue in earlier centuries, public trust in the state was far lower in republican times. In these circumstances, some elites sought to create new political rights for themselves.

The desire of elites to assert themselves more pointedly with respect to an emerging range of national issues and to promote effective local self-government challenged the structures and sensibilities of a unitary state. The Nationalist government's antidote to elite efforts to promote self-government within the county and representative assemblies at the provincial and national levels was to argue that representative institutions should be subordinated to a tutelary government under Nationalist Party control. Under the "tutelary state"—a term coined by revolutionary leader Sun Yatsen and promoted by later Nationalist Party leaders—the people were to enjoy "popular sovereignty," but only as a political abstraction. Various proposals were made for parliamentary-like bodies to transform rhetoric into practice, but little was achieved.

The fate of the People's Political Council (*guomin canzheng hui*) gives a sense of how political possibilities played themselves out. Initially formed in 1933, the People's Political Council was a body composed of representative leaders of different elite interest groups. The political role of the council was debated several times during the following decade among political activists and with Nationalist government officials, but it never assumed more than a policy advisory role.[29] As long as the council largely agreed with what the Nationalist government chose to do, its presence was tolerated by the government; but when the non-GMD members became critical of government policies, in particular the way in which the Nationalists were undermining the united front with the Communists against the Japanese, the government turned against the council. Dissident council members then formed the Federation of Democratic Parties to express their opinions about government policy; this move intensified government opposition to the council.[30] The transformation of a quasi-representative institution into a partylike opposition group under a one-party state helps explain the absence of parliamentary institutions during the republican era. More generally, both the Nationalist and Communist states under one-party rule have conceived of representative bodies as opportunities for other political parties to advise and consent without the abilities to oppose, dissent, or, even less, participate in ruling.

For their part, a major goal of Chinese elites was to stake out a role in helping the country in its time of national crisis. The focus of elites and common people was not on carving out their own spheres of activity free of state interference. Thus, the concerns for civil rights that figured so prominently in nineteenth-century Europe were not salient in republican-era China. When some Chinese elite assessments of policy became more sharply distinguished from official ones, these differences were crystallized politically in party affiliations, those of the party-state, first Nationalist and then Communist, and those of other elites. Thus, there was little place in early- and mid-twentieth-century China for the social and political dynamics that created European citizens in the late eighteenth and nineteenth centuries.

Constructing Communist Citizens

Chinese Communists, whose power grew steadily after the founding of their party in 1921, developed their own ideas about democracy, ideas within which there was no clear room for European "citizens." The Communist concept of democracy developed in the 1940s during the war against the Japanese; it was rooted in the idea of a "mass line," or the flow of ideas between party cadres and peasants. Peasants' ideas were solicited by cadres who then "system-atized" these suggestions and presented them back to the peasants. This defined the norms for political participation at local levels. The Communists stressed political involvement at local levels and the informal selection of leaders within the village as more meaningful than any formal procedure of voting for distant politicians. In the 1990s, village self-government has been more widely promoted with elections of three to seven village members to oversee village affairs. These elections replace the practice of the party appointing village leaders and are seen by some Western analysts as helping form real democratic habits.[31] Other foreign analysts, however, note that Chinese discussions of village self-government in the 1990s stress the role of elections in affording villagers the opportunity to select those people who they believe will best promote the village's economic interests, largely through the development of small-scale industries from which the village as a whole will benefit. For central government officials, promoting village self-government, in this view, is a means to meet a crisis in authority that has threatened the state since the destructive Cultural Revolution. The crisis was exacerbated by economic reforms that undermined the vertically integrated bureaucracy through which communication, control, and extraction flowed between center and locality.[32] The nature of political rights associated with voting for local government is therefore unclear, and as a result its significance for Chinese citizenship is ambiguous. If villagers are voting for people according to the candidate's perceived abilities to lead local industries, they are making as much an economic decision as a political one. If the Communist Party promotes elections in order to gain credibility and voters have little voice beyond the selection of village leaders, then the extent of political democracy is limited.

Regarding civil rights, individuals have "rights" offered by the government and stipulated in successive constitutions. But these rights are all conditional and can be qualified or suspended as the government deems appropriate, a situation similar to that under the Nationalist government.[33] In practice, since 1949 cycles of strict and loose surveillance over various popular activities have occurred, cycles sometimes in harmony with other official policies but rarely, if ever, taking popular sentiments into account. For instance, religious freedoms guaranteed by the constitution have at times been severely abridged and at others allowed, if not encouraged. The rhetoric of rights in the Chinese constitutions of 1954, 1975, 1978, and 1982 has granted citizens a variety of freedoms—of assembly, religion, and expression, among others. But citizens have been unable to act confidently because they lack the institutional means with which to bargain or negotiate to guarantee these rights. Civil rights are further qualified by the categories of people to whom they are denied. European citizenship depends upon formal juridical equality of individuals, who are denied some of their civil rights only when they violate certain laws. The Chinese government, however, until 1979 retained a class-based taxonomy that denied all civil and political rights to people deemed "rightists" or "enemies of the people." Even today. the arbitrary label of "counter-revolutionary" denies individuals rights stipulated in the Chinese constitution.

The fluctuating degree of individual freedoms or civil rights reflects the absence in Chinese state-society relations of any formally protected autonomous spaces with boundaries that can be contested or arenas where disagreements can be adjudicated by a third party. If citizenship depends on individuals enjoying some basis of autonomy from which they can negotiate with their governments, defend certain rights, and acknowledge various obligations, then Chinese subjects lack the institutional foundation to be citizens. In place of separate spaces with demarcated borders marking off public spheres and civil societies, there continues to be, as in late imperial times, a continuum along which state leaders assume their prerogative to intervene when and where they see fit, even if they choose not to do so for some period of time. The party-state from the 1950s into the 1980s routinely expected to engage in forms of political education to bring people into line with what the party deemed appropriate attitudes and behaviors. There was no clear public/private split, no sharp divide between official and non-official arenas of activity.

The public sphere and civil society so lacking in late imperial China have developed in fits and starts during the twentieth century. Western ideas about a state and civil society have hardly developed naturally in modern China. The continued association between *wuguanfang* (nonofficial) with *buzhengtong* (unorthodox) affirms the absence of an autonomous sphere for the expression of group interests.[34] Similarly, a Chinese historian's quip to American scholar Perry Link about "government-organized non-government organizations" replicates a structural ambiguity present in late imperial times.[35] The bureaucracy's scale and penetration of society, both in late imperial and postimperial times, has determined the scale and complexity of nonstate organizations. The ability of the state's bureaucracy to penetrate has been a function of its capacity to create new organizations and at least influence, if not control, those that are nongovernmental. The Communist government's relationship to merchants and entrepreneurs is an important example of this phenomenon. Earlier in the twentieth century, between 1911 and 1927, business leaders enjoyed a high point of autonomy when government control was at a minimum. In Qing times and especially after 1949, state supervision has been far greater than in the immediate postimperial period.[36] The absence of autonomous realms of social and political activity limits the possible elements of Chinese citizenship.

In place of a relationship of citizenship, Communist leaders into the 1980s relied on mass movements, which in Mao's day offered an alternative to political engagement by voting citizens who enjoy a public sphere and civil society. Participating in a mass movement educated individuals in the norms of behavior and levels of effort the party-state hoped to inculcate in order to make dramatic changes, whether economic, as in the Great Leap Forward, or political, as in the Cultural Revolution. Tang Tsou has explained the contrast: "Citizenship begins with the view of members of society as isolated individuals with a set of abstract and equal rights who voluntarily form themselves into social groups exercising these rights. . . . In contrast, the notion of the masses, the mass movement and the mass line begin with the position of individuals as members of segments of society with demands not for abstract, legal, civil rights but for substantive socio-economic entitlements."[37] These entitlements that Tsou contrasts with rights are built upon peasants' expectations of the state in the late imperial period. The differences in the way entitlements and rights developed in Western Europe and China can be illustrated by comparing French peasant engagement in politics during the 1840s with that of Chinese peasants a century later.

When the Second Republic proclaimed universal male suffrage in the aftermath of the 1848 revolution, rural people became active in elections. Many voiced their opposition to new indirect taxes by voting for Louis-Napoléon. Peasants also joined political clubs and participated in debates waged in the popular press. Rural political mobilization frightened some of the powerful, who maneuvered to change electoral qualifications to disenfranchise roughly one-third of the electorate. When Louis-Napoléon executed his military coup d'état on 2 December 1851, republican resistance spread across much of the country, with peasants coming to understand and defend democratic principles.[38] How different the roles played by Chinese peasants mobilized by the Communist revolutionaries in the 1940s. Communists promised to improve the peasants' bundle of social and economic entitlements; peasants were promised land and women, entitlements that won their allegiance to the Communist cause. Chinese peasants became part of a social movement not citizens in a representative political system.

Becoming participants to a party-led social movement created a different basis for relating state and subject. Focused on social and economic entitlements, Chinese social movements did not articulate issues of political participation and procedure, issues that nineteenth-century European social movements put at the center of efforts to improve the conditions of common people. Where nineteenth-century European constructions of citizenship grew out of earlier rounds of negotiations between states and elites, Chinese Communist notions of relations between state and subject were developed out of a political tradition in which the Communists shifted from a Confucian focus on state-elite relations to party relations with peasant masses, but with a common concern for substantive social and economic entitlements rather than political rights. French peasants joined French workers in becoming citizens in the nineteenth century. This spread of citizenship rights to the working classes was part of the process whereby European countries became politically and socially integrated. By extending rights and duties to working people, propertied elites hoped to tame what they believed to be the unruly nature of ordinary people. Being given positions within the state's political community made common men members of a nation; rights and duties, voting and military service marched forward together in creating nineteenth-century European societies of citizens. Chinese political strategies of social integration continued in the twentieth century to be based on a paternalism in which Communist visions had displaced but also overlay Confucian ones. Mobilizing and channeling populist enthusiasm made this paternalism different from Confucian strategies of rule but did little to create an ideological and institutionalized alternative to centralized and unitary state rule. How then should we characterize changes in Chinese state-subject relations since 1949?

Let's return to T. H. Marshall's classic taxonomy of three elements of citizenship: civil, social, and political. Having noted the differences between Chinese state-subject relations and European state-citizen relations, let us also agree to apply the term "citizenship" to China to evaluate changing features of post-1949 conditions and compare them with both earlier Chinese and European situations. We can now use the term citizenship with reference to China aware that the term is likely to have different meanings and associations than it does in the European context. The Chinese since 1949 have lacked both civil rights (e.g., secure rights to association and combination) and political rights (e.g., meaningful elections, at least before the 1990s), but they have enjoyed a number of social rights. When we think of the bundle of rights associated with citizenship, a fundamental distinction emerges between urban and rural residents. Most urban Chinese from the early 1950s to the 1980s worked for some state organization, be it an industrial enterprise, a government bureaucracy, or some service-sector operation. They enjoyed secure employment, euphemistically known as the "iron rice bowl," as well as health care benefits, heavily subsidized housing, and subsidized prices on daily necessities including grain, flour, oil, and cotton cloth. For rural populations, as members of rural collectives and then communes between the mid-1950s and early 1980s, the collective provision of basic subsistence, medical care, and education was a more modest bundle of entitlements than that enjoyed by urban dwellers. Peasants were left in economically inferior conditions to those typical of cities. Subject to periodic political campaigns designed to mobilize their energy and enthusiasm, peasants were "masses" for whom European notions of citizenship and its associated forms of political participation remained quite foreign. Their responses to political campaigns engaged them in state-directed struggles unlike those typical of European citizens.[39] The institutional framework within which nineteenth-century Europeans made claims that clustered into mutual rights and obligations helped build an ideological momentum to direct state-citizen relations in an arc quite different from that relating state and subjects in twentieth-century China, at least before the onset of major economic changes beginning in the late 1970s.

The economic reforms since 1978 have gradually created far greater options for peasants than existed in earlier years of Communist rule. Decisions on land use and labor allocations on and off the farm have led to a dramatic rise in rural incomes in much of China. The development of small-scale industries in towns and villages has been especially important in raising incomes. These industries have also created a rural alternative to the situation in urban state-run enterprises with their many social entitlements for city dwellers. Both these new enterprises and the larger-scale, foreign-invested joint venture enterprises found in the special economic zones along the coast create employment conditions generally without the bundle of social rights typical of state enterprises. For their part, many state enterprises are beleaguered, money-losing operations. With their probable demise or transformation, the social entitlements that many Chinese workers enjoyed for more than four decades are shrinking. At the same time, the recent industrialization of China has created far more factory employment and made possible marketing and service opportunities that were unavailable in the past. From the vantage point of citizenship rights, the ability of rural people to migrate more freely, coupled with the decline of the state sector and its attendant benefits, means that the gap between the social entitlements of urban and rural people has begun to diminish, even as a new gap is being created in China's cities between those who retain diminished social and economic entitlements and new migrants who lack them altogether.[40] The promise of better incomes has reached far more people in the reform era, but these economic opportunities are made possible as much by the reduction of state constraints, such as those governing migration, as by any increase in state-supplied rights or privileges. Indeed, social welfare rights are a less salient feature of Chinese citizenship today than they were twenty years ago; both urban and rural dwellers enjoy fewer economic entitlements than before.

As people make more money, they have to purchase more of the goods and services that were previously subsidized or even free. Market allocation of resources, goods, and opportunities has increased as government-controlled distribution has decreased. For European countries, some analysts have seen this structural shift as signaling a decline in citizenship rights. From a Marshallian perspective in which citizenship rights form a buffer against the inequalities of wealth and quality of life generated by capitalism, a contraction of social rights means that global capitalism has indeed gained at the expense of national states and their citizenship-granting powers. Peter Saunders argues against this common view, suggesting that increased incomes in advanced capitalist societies allows people to make more choices about what goods to purchase without worries over basic welfare needs. For those who lack adequate incomes to make these choices, he argues that monetary transfers are superior to the provision of goods and services, as financial resources allow the poor to make their own decisions.[41] The Chinese don't have a system of transfer payments and income levels remain well below those of advanced capitalist societies, but a change from state-provided entitlements to market-purchased goods and services has taken place.

If social rights and economic entitlements are less prominent aspects of Chinese citizenship than before, what about civil and political rights? Have they increased? How is Chinese citizenship affected by political reform? Evaluating the varieties of political reform advocated in the 1980s, Kokubun Ryosei identifies three types: party-centered efforts to strengthen central authority; political changes to support economic reforms, in particular those that reduce party-state control over economic decision making; and a more fundamental challenge to the institutions of the party-state by democratization advocates.[42] More recently, Baogang He has noted three broad varieties of political reform:[43] a government effort to rid bureaucracy of its corrupt behavior, streamline organization and encourage popular participation to affirm legitimacy; a populist movement to rein in the state; and democratic reforms based on ideological and institutional models from the West. Listing the reform approaches according to their potential for radical political change, the two extreme views of reform are the same for Kokubun and He: the efforts of party-state leaders to reaffirm their power in a changing economic system; and a fundamental challenge to the basic ideological and institutional logic of the

Communist party-state. Together these authors point out two more moderate alternatives: a populist critique of government practices; and political reforms that reduce the government's role in ways believed to be beneficial for economic reforms. Each of these approaches to political reform offers a different possible future for Chinese citizenship.

Government-sponsored efforts at reform proceed from a belief that if government works better, then state-society relations can be improved without any fundamental change in the basic assumptions about state-subject relations. In particular, the state can continue to be grant civil rights subject to conditions that allow for their revocation at government will. This sort of state-subject relationship promises little, if any, room for elaborating new claims by citizens as the social rights previously guaranteed become eroded.

A second variety of political reform is that mounted by popular demonstrations against government policies. This form of political participation has bases in Chinese tradition at two levels: (1) small-scale popular protests against state actions, like tax resistance; (2) large-scale protests or movements. The party-state has a more complex relationship to this second kind of collective action. On the one hand, Mao Zedong and his associates promoted now discredited party-directed social movements as a means to create swift change, especially during the Great Leap Forward and the Cultural Revolution. On the other hand, any large-scale demonstration, protest, or series of such actions that emerges independently of the government is a challenge to government authority. It is difficult for the party-state to sanction such actions and if such actions cannot be defused, repression like that in June 1989 follows. In the aftermath of repression, social control remains a major source of concern to leaders. Populist movements to date have not sustained themselves for any significant duration; nor have they created institutionalized political reform. Citizens and their claims on the state have not become more similar to European cases through either small-scale or large-scale protests.

A third variety of political reform results from efforts to contain the influence of the state in economic and social affairs by deflecting its penetration and creating spheres of activity beyond its control. With economic reforms has come the creation of numerous organizations with varying degrees of day-to-day autonomy from government bureaucracies. The explicit political reforms involve reduction of party-state supervision of production and distribution decisions. Party cadres may still play important roles in gaining favors, permissions, or resources, but the operation of enterprises is not under any form of routine political control. Economic reforms more generally have created increased and more varied production, exchange, and service provision, which in turn means more forms of consumption and leisure-time activities. As a consequence of the enabling political and economic reforms, cultural activities have proliferated, from restaurants to magazines to visual arts, all of which have developed since 1978 through cycles of loosening and tightening state social control. While the party-state has allowed the development of social and cultural spaces beyond the government's daily supervision, it faces no institutionalized barriers to intervening whenever and wherever it chooses.[44] This capacity for extraordinary intervention resembles the kind of capacity that the late imperial state maintained for monitoring social activities, on the alert for socially subversive actions and ready to assert itself when it perceived a danger to its orthodoxy and control. The recent multiplication of spaces for people to work and play outside direct state control has promoted visions of a public sphere and a civil society; but as I noted earlier, since these arenas are not defensible against state encroachment, it is difficult to find much room in these spaces for "citizens," in the sense of people with enforceable claims on the state.

The fourth and final framing of reform calls for the development of institutions flowing from an ideology at odds with Chinese government assumptions about politically granted rights. Within an alternative frame of reference that argues that people have inalienable natural rights, some Chinese reformers, like Fang Lizhi and Liu Binyan, seek to apply some ideas of citizenship forged in the West. To succeed, they must dislodge an earlier model of state-subject relations spanning late and postimperial times within which the category of citizen has been at most fragile and conditional, reflecting a political tradition in which state-subject relations have always found the state in a superior position without effective challenge from below. Much of the push for radical reform has been mounted by intellectuals and students, those people who are in a certain sense the descendants of the well-educated, scholarly elite of gentry degree-holders who previously worked with officials to promote social order. Thus, the push to create a Chinese citizenship more fully on a Western ideological basis is also an implicit statement that the official–scholar elite link typical of the unitary state in the late imperial period, and which Communists previously also attempted to strengthen, is not attractive or persuasive.

Political reform in China is at a stage of open-ended competition among different visions of how to define the state's relations with the people it rules. China's unitary state, typical of both late imperial and Communist practices, is perhaps on its last legs. The delegation of authority in economic matters both to lower levels of government and to individual firms has narrowed the duties and designs of central government bureaucracies. Local and provincial governments have become far more assertive in making their bids to extract and control new sources of revenue; with increased revenues comes an increased ability to make policy decisions separate from the central government. At the same time, Communist Party willingness since 1990 to allow more open local elections is consistent both with long-standing Communist beliefs professed by Mao and many others that local-level political participation was the key to democratic engagement and with efforts to integrate politically China's vast village population.[45]

Some social scientists and even more journalists have seen the radical efforts at political reform in China as part of the larger Eurasian rejections of Communist governmental forms. Similarities are certainly present, but the differences also matter. East European protestors in the 1980s clearly believed that they could make claims on their governments in ways quite different from Chinese protestors' efforts to force the government to make good on its commitments. Perhaps this contrast is related to earlier historical differences. Although both Eastern Europe and China have been ruled by Leninist parties, Eastern Europe's earlier experiences include a history of municipal autonomy and estates that is absent in China. Perhaps East European political reformers, compared to Chinese reformers, have more easily constructed the ideals, if not always the realities, of civil society and public sphere because of these distinctions. I do not mean to suggest that Chinese reformers are historically condemned to an impotence that precludes the birth of Western-inspired political practices. But I do wish to underline the importance of considering carefully the repertoire of ideas and institutions to which reformers can appeal in the struggle against their governments.

For much of this chapter I use a definition of citizenship according to which the subjects of many authoritarian regimes are not citizens. I have done so to highlight the kinds of conditions historically associated with citizenship in Western Europe and stress the presence of different conditions in China. I also relax the criteria for citizenship in order to consider post-1949 Chinese citizenship conditions. Together the two approaches offer some perspective on ways in which the relationship between the state and the governed are both similar and different in Chinese and European experiences.[46] There are at least two other strategies that deserve consideration in future treatments of Chinese citizenship in a comparative perspective. One way to develop this assessment further would be to consider more fully the ways in which translations of "citizen" into Chinese have been used in the twentieth century. By further analyzing what Chinese have meant by the term, we can avoid easy assumptions inferred from European practices about what "citizenship" has meant in Chinese contexts at the same time that we recognize the appropriateness, or even necessity, of using a term that Chinese themselves began to use a century ago. A second way to compare Chinese and European experiences would be to think of "citizen" and "subject" less as binary alternatives and more as endpoints of a political continuum along which states' relations with the people they rule can change. If we think of citizenship as being composed of multiple elements, then a variety of citizenship compounds can be considered according to the different mixes of claim-making and entitlements that are present. In such a manner, we can more easily note the ebb and flow of changes in state-society relations as social groups and government officials struggle to define what both can consider as acceptable, if not proper or ideal, relations.

For now, consider one final comparison of Chinese and European changes. The possible breakdown of the unitary state in China offers a vantage point from which to note some parallels with changes in Europe. As European states delegate some of their authority to a supranational body, the Chinese state is delegating some of its power to lower levels of government. These changes are making new spatial distributions of power in China and Europe that create a similarity not present before. A new level of more centralized political power, however weak, has certain authorities over European national governments, while the increased power of provincial and county governments in China, however limited, means that the national government no longer has the capacities it once did. The challenges of distinguishing among types of power to be held by authorities responsible for different spatial scales of territory is similar in both situations. And in each case, the decisions taken will affect what citizenship means. But even if recent movement toward European unity and away from a unitary state in China raise similar issues, the future of citizenship continues to look quite different at the ends of Eurasia. The party-state has proved quite willing to make all manner of institutional innovations to accommodate growing foreign economic ties but has demonstrated a desire to protect its domestic principles and practices of party-state rule. The central government shows relatively little enthusiasm for changing its basic logic of relating to the people it rules, and when it has done so, as recent work on the role of law demonstrates, it has enjoyed at best mixed success in persuading people it is doing the right thing.[47]

Rarely have governments given much of value to their subjects without taking or at least expecting something in return. The possible transactions that Tilly has stressed as key to analyzing citizenship become limited when officials and people cannot agree on what is negotiable. Can radical political reformers really expect the Communist party-state to accept their understanding of citizenship? The chances do not seem terribly high in the late twentieth century. The state will likely continue to labor to shape and then meet popular expectations for a government that meets its commitments rather than become a state willing to entertain claims. If the party-state is forced to accept the kinds of changes that radical democracy advocates have in mind, a fundamentally new kind of Chinese citizenship will be created, cast in a mold that bears European outlines and filled with a Chinese content quite different from any we have seen in the past.

Notes

Thanks to Kenneth Pomeranz, Dorothy Solinger, Vivienne Shue, and Elizabeth Wishnick for their suggestions on earlier drafts of this essay. Dorothy Solinger in particular shared both critical insights and bibliographic suggestions to improve the final product.

1. Charles Tilly, "A Primer on Citizenship," *Theory and Society* 26 (1997).
2. I develop the contrast between claims and commitments as part of a discussion of Chinese and European state formation and transformation in R. Bin Wong, *China Transformed: Historical Change and the Limits of European Experience* (Ithaca: Cornell University Press, 1997), 71–104; tax resistance and grain seizures are examined on 209–51.
3. René Pillorget, "The *Cascaveoux:* The Insurrection at Aix in the Autumn of 1630," and J. Gallet, "Research on the Popular Movements at Amiens in 1635 and 1636," both in *State and Society in Seventeenth-Century France*, ed. Raymond F. Kierstead (New York: New Viewpoints, 1975).
4. T. H. Marshall, *Citizenship and Social Class and Other Essays* (Cambridge, Cambridge University Press, 1950).
5. Pierre-Etienne Will and R. Bin Wong, *Nourish the People: The State Civilian Granary System in China, 1650–1850* (Ann Arbor: University of Michigan Center for Chinese Studies, 1991).
6. I develop the contrast between state-elite relations in late imperial China and in early modern Europe more fully in Wong, *China Transformed,* 73–104.
7. Craig Clunas, *Superfluous Things: Material Culture and Social Status in Early Modern China* (Cambridge, England: Polity Press, 1991); and Timothy Brook, *Praying for Power: Buddhism and the Formation of Gentry Society in Late Ming China* (Cambridge: Harvard University Council on East Asian Studies, 1993).
8. The Chinese emperor's mandate to rule was conditioned by the possibility of peasants rising up in righteous opposition, but this did not become a basis for sovereignty being vested in the people.
9. Bryan Turner, "Outline of the Theory of Human Rights," in in *Citizenship and Social Theory*, ed. Bryan Turner (London: Sage Publications, 1993).
10. The term "public sphere" has been made famous, of course, by Jürgen Habermas. For an evaluation of its relevance for China, see R. Bin Wong, "Great Expectations: The 'Public Sphere' and the Search for Modern Times in Chinese History," *Chūgokushi gaku* (Studies in Chinese history) 3 (1993): 7–50.
11. Peter Zarrow, "Introduction: Citizenship in China and the West," in *Imagining the People: Chinese Intellectuals and the Concept of Citizenship, 1890–1920,* ed. Joshua A. Fogel and Peter G. Zarrow (Armonk, N.Y.: M. E. Sharpe, 1997), 20.
12. Zarrow, "Introduction," 49.
13. Andrew Nathan. *Chinese Democracy* (New York: Knopf, 1985), 13.
14. Nathan, *Chinese Democracy*, 50.
15. Thus a set of government regulations on opium suppression with regard to anti-opium societies states, "Such society shall be purely for the anti-opium smoking, and the society shall not discuss any other matters, such as political questions bearing on

topical affairs or local administration, or any similar matter." International Opium Commission, *Report of the International Opium Commission, Shanghai, China February 1–26, 1909* (London: P. S. King & Son, 1909), 2:81. Another set of regulations called on all local officials to "instruct reputable gentry and merchants in their jurisdictions to organize Anti-Opium Associations and to publish pamphlets and magazines in simple language to exhort people to break off opium smoking. These publications should not interfere with politics or subjects outside of their province." (International Opium Commission, *Report,* 2:85).

16. International Opium Commission, *Report,* 2:115.

17. Michael Tsin, *Nation, Governance, and Modernity in Early Twentieth-Century China: Canton, 1900–1927* (Stanford: Stanford University Press, forthcoming).

18. Elites did, however, come to doubt the sincerity of the Manchu court, which seemed unable to lead very effectively the government's resistance to Western pressures.

19. Joan Judge, *Print and Politics: "Shibao" and the Culture of Reform in Late Qing China* (Stanford: Stanford University Press, 1996).

20. On merchant roles, see Susan Mann, *Local Merchants and the Chinese Bureaucracy, 1750–1950* (Stanford: Stanford University Press, 1987); for examples from Zhejiang. see Mary Backus Rankin, *Elite Activism and Political Transformation in China, Zhejiang Province, 1865–1911* (Stanford: Stanford University Press, 1986).

21. Mark Elvin, "The Gentry Democracy in Chinese Shanghai, 1905–1914," *Modern China's Search for a Political Form,* ed. Jack Gray (Oxford: Oxford University Press, 1969).

22. Keith R. Schoppa, *Chinese Elites and Political Change: Zhejiang Province in the Early Twentieth Century* (Cambridge: Harvard University Press, 1982).

23. Will and Wong, *Nourish the People,* 69–72.

24. Roger Thompson, *China's Local Councils in the Age of Constitutional Reform, 1898–1911* (Cambridge: Harvard University Council on East Asian Studies, 1995).

25. Philip Kuhn, "The Development of Local Government," in *The Cambridge History of China,* vol. 13, *Republican China, 1912–1949,* ed. John K. Fairbank and Albert Feuerwerker (Cambridge: Cambridge University Press, 1986), 2:340–43.

26. Yujiro Murata, "Dynasty, State, and Society: The Case of Modern China," in *Imagining the People,* 137.

27. Donald Sutton, *Provincial Militarism and the Chinese Republic: The Yunnan Army, 1905–1925* (Ann Arbor: University of Michigan Press, 1980).

28. Edward McCord, *The Power of the Gun: The Emergence of Modern Chinese Warlordism* (Berkeley and Los Angeles: University of California Press, 1993).

29. Shigeo Nishimura, *Chugoku nashynarizumu to minshu shugi* (Chinese nationalism and democracy). (Tokyo: Kenbun shuppan, 1991), 117–50.

30. Lloyd Eastman, "Nationalist China during the Sino-Japanese War, 1937–1945" in *Cambridge History of China,* vol. 13, 2:602.

31. Amy Epstein, "Village Elections in China: Experimenting with Democracy," in *China's Economic Future: Challenges to U.S. Policy,* ed. Joint Economic Committee, Congress of the United States (Armonk, N.Y.: M. E. Sharpe, 1997).

32. Daniel Kelliher, "The Chinese Debate over Village Self-Government," *China Journal* 37(1997): 63–86.

33. Nathan, *Chinese Democracy,* 111.

34. The association between *wuguanfang* and *buzhengtong* is pointed out in Perry Link, Richard Madsen, and Paul Pickowicz, eds., *Unofficial China* (Boulder, Colo.: Westview Press, 1989), 2.

35. Perry Link, "The Old Man's New China," *New York Review of Books* 41, no. 11 (1994): 31–36, quote on 35.

36. Margaret Pearson, *China's New Business Elite: The Political Consequences of Economic Reform* (Berkeley and Los Angeles: University of California Press, 1997)

37. Tang Tsou, "Marxism, the Leninist Party, the Masses, and the Citizens in the Rebuilding of the Chinese State," in *Foundations and Limits of State Power in China,* ed. Stuart R. Schram (Hong Kong: Chinese University Press, 1987), 265.

38. Edward Berenson, Theodore Margadant, John Merriman, and Charles Tilly have all seen a politically informed activism diffused from urban centers into the countryside. (See Edward Berenson, *Populist Religion and Left-Wing Politics in France, 1830–1852* (Princeton: Princeton University Press, 1984); Theodore Margadant, *French Peasants in Revolt: The Insurrection of 1851* (Princeton: Princeton University Press, 1979); John Merriman, *The Agony of the Republic: The Repression of the Left in Revolutionary France, 1848–1851* (New Haven: Yale University Press, 1978); and Charles Tilly, "How Protest Modernized in France," in *The Dimensions of Quantitative Research in History,* ed. William Aydelotte, Allan Bogue, and Robert Fogel (Princeton: Princeton University Press, 1972).

39. Two excellent accounts of village life in post-1949 China give a sense of how peasants worked to adjust policy changes to local conditions; see Anita Chan, Richard Madsen, and Jonathan Unger, *Chen Village: Under Mao and Deng* (Berkeley and Los Angeles: University of California Press, 1992); and Edward Friedman, Paul G. Pickowicz, and Mark Selden, *Chinese Village, Socialist State* (New Haven: Yale University Press, 1991).

40. Kam Wing Chan, "Post-Mao China: A Two-Class Urban Society in the Making," *International Journal of Urban and Regional Research* 20, no. 1 (1996): 134–50; and Dorothy Solinger, *Contesting Citizenship in Urban China: Peasant Migrants, the State, and the Logic of the Market* (Berkeley and Los Angeles: University of California Press, forthcoming).

41. Peter Saunders, "Citizenship in a Liberal Society" in *Citizenship and Social Theory.*

42. Ryosei Kokubun, *Chukogu seiji to minshuka* (Chinese politics and democratization) (Tokyo: Simul Press, 1991), 152–53.

43. Baogang He, *The Democratization of China* (London: Routledge, 1996).

44. Shaoguang Wang, "The Politics of Private Time: Changing Leisure Patterns in Urban China," in *Urban Spaces in Contemporary China: The Potential for Autonomy and Community in Post-Mao China,* ed. Deborah S. Davis et al. (Cambridge: Cambridge University Press, 1995).

45. John B. Starr, *Continuing the Revolution: The Political Thought of Mao* (Princeton: Princeton University Press, 1979), 212.

46. Joan Judge's book on the culture of reform in which journalism played an important new role in the closing years of the Qing dynasty helps us understand how Chinese used the concept of "citizen" in that period. See Judge, *Print and Politics*.

47. Pittman B. Potter, "Riding the Tiger: Legitimacy and Legal Culture in Post-Mao China," *China Quarterly,* 138 (1994): 325–58.

6

The Right to Work and the Struggle against Unemployment: Britain, 1884–1914

Michael Hanagan

The decade after the collapse of the USSR in 1989 has witnessed a vast output of triumphalist literature extolling the virtues of capitalism as a system rewarding hard work. Such praises sound hollow in a European Union (EU) where, on average, 8 percent of the labor force has been unemployed since 1980.[1] Continuing high unemployment has made a mockery of post–world War II European government commitments to full employment. Despite the fact that the "right to work" is enshrined in the United Nations' Universal Declaration of Human Rights of 1948, no government operating within a capitalist economic order has effectively provided general access to employment in the last half century.

In view of this failure, recent authors have suggested that it is time to abandon claims to a right to work. Social commentators such as Ralf Dahrendorf have demanded that European societies concede their inability to provide employment for all and recognize a "right not to work"; invoking economic citizenship rights, Dahrendorf advocates a basic income guarantee for all citizens, which he hopes will prevent the growth of an underclass and enhance the economic freedom of citizens.[2] Klaus Offe concurs and argues that it is time for the formation of a "post-industrial left" that will draw up a "non-productivist design for social policies."[3] A recent book by Jeremy Rifkin, *The End of Work*, has taken up the call for a guaranteed annual income combined with tax write-offs to encourage volunteerism.[4]

This chapter argues that the work/entitlement nexus remains important for extending social and political rights within modern states because: (1) work remains important within modern society and can generate powerful solidarities and collective identities; (2) struggles to redistribute work can promote political coalitions among diverse groups; and (3) the contradiction between capitalism's claim to reward work and its frequent inability to provide it, though a liability for society, is an opportunity for reformers; by highlighting the existence of unemployment, social movements greatly increase pressure on defenders of the system to make concessions. But while the demand for a right to work has historically been widespread and popular in working-class politics, it is also susceptible to selective application based on gendered assumptions about who should work, elitist disregard for some types of labor, and nativist or racist prejudice. A final section of this chapter argues that these dangers are significantly less in today's labor and social movements than at the end of the nineteenth century.

A Right to Work or a Right Not to Work?

A proper debate must regard the context in which demands are raised; the slogan "land, peace, and bread" served admirably in 1917 Russia but is scarcely likely to rally contemporary Europeans. The best-suited demands will not work when protesting groups are poorly mobilized and confront a united political establishment. Demands stand little chance of being met unless they can be transformed into concrete proposals that can withstand the scrutiny of social policy experts and political opponents; in practice, such scrutiny inevitably involves political compromises that weaken or distort intended goals. Sometimes these compromises will be acceptable and sometimes not.

Critics of the right to work view it as the relic of an age when unemployment was less menacing, class, more salient, and social movements, nonexistent. Such misconceptions partly motivate our study of the battle for the right to work in the United Kingdom between 1884 and 1914. As we shall see, in this period, the United Kingdom struggled with problems of enduring unemployment intensified by new competitors in the world market and by the introduction of the new technologies of the second industrial revolution. During this period large sections of the working class were felt to be politically uncommitted and their allegiance potentially winnable by either major party. Finally, the United Kingdom was a democratizing society in which both orthodox political economy and liberal political values were long established and in which social movements flourished. Observers who see similarities between the political situation in the EU and in North America today should view this case with interest. Understanding why the United Kingdom should have been at the forefront of social policy innovation in the area of unemployment may alert us to possibilities within the contemporary political order.

Political Opportunities, Proletarians, and Social Policy

The character of demands merits debate only within a political environment in which demands have a chance of being met. Certainly between 1884 and 1911 the United Kingdom exhibited all four elements of political opportunity as defined by Sidney Tarrow: "the opening up of access to power, shifting alignments, the availability of influential allies, and cleavages within and amongst elites."[5] The 1884 enfranchisement of a large number of males and the efforts of both major British parties to recruit these new voters opened a remarkable period of volatility in the political context for social movements.[6] Over the course of the period 1884–1911, two distinct though related currents contributed to the instability of the opportunity structure. The first current, beginning in 1885 and continuing through 1906, was an ongoing competition between Conservatives and Liberals for the new electorate; as part of this competition Joseph Chamberlain and his Unionists bolted the Liberal Party to join the Conservatives. During this phase, both parties sought to win the loyalty of the newly enfranchised by promoting social reforms and by portraying themselves as advocates for the working classes.

The date with which we begin our analysis, 1884, marks the passage of a reform bill that brought many British men into the electoral arena. The Local Government Act, passed in the same year, also redistributed seats in favor of urban areas.[7] The precise extent to which the suffrage law of 1884 enlarged the political arena is difficult to determine. Not everyone eligible to vote did so, and in normal times the poor are less likely to vote than the rich. British franchise requirements were notoriously intricate and these difficulties were increased by the complex nature of registration laws and the existence of multiple votes. Between the elections of 1886 and 1900, however, the number of votes increased by 53.7 percent. Most male household heads received the right to vote. Beyond that, it is easier to say who could not vote. No woman could vote. Avoiding the suffrage's many colorful eccentricities and focusing only on large groups of the excluded, we list: domestic servants resident with their employers, sons living with their parents, those receiving Poor Law relief, migrant workers, soldiers in barracks, and most lodgers. Perhaps as much as 70 percent of the adult population of the British Isles were still without the suffrage in 1885.[8] In sum, while many workers received the right to vote in 1884, the poorest sections—those on welfare, many migratory workers, and working women—were still disenfranchised.

Many of the new electors were undoubtedly concerned about unemployment. The magnitude of the unemployment problem is difficult to measure, but Deane and Cole see a pronounced economic slowdown between 1860 and 1913, and during this period urban industrial workers first begin to emigrate in large numbers.[9] The years after 1880 witnessed growing rounds of joblessness as the traditional staple industries, textiles, mining, and iron and steelmaking, failed to grow, while the unskilled and semiskilled workers whom they released were unprepared for work in the newly developing industries. While local relief offered a temporary alternative, many Liberals emphasized emigration. Reinforcing their faith in the self-regulating market for wage laborers, nineteenth-century Liberal policymakers believed that the operation of the international labor market would ensure that unemployment would not be a permanent presence in English society, at least among able-bodied workers.[10]

Liberal emphases on emigration were unpalatable to many of the newly enfranchised voters who had had personal experience with unemployment and dreaded its recurrence. Because many were second- or third-generation proletarians, the British unemployed lacked the ties to agriculture possessed by many European workers who were seasonal or short-term migrants from peasant agriculture.[11] Because industrial employment was more subject to the fluctuations of economic cycles than services, Britain, with a large proportion of such workers, was particularly vulnerable.

By 1885 both Conservatives and Liberals realized that many of the newly enfranchised workers were not necessarily committed to any one party. The elections of 1885 belied Conservative fears that the new electorate would rally en masse behind the Liberal standard. Internal divisions explain Liberal ineffectiveness. The Liberals were split between a conservative, "Whig," wing that feared social reform and a radical wing, led by Joseph Chamberlain, that attacked agrarian conditions, the established church, and the character of British popular education. Over the Whig heads of his party, Chamberlain attempted to fashion a political language that would appeal to the recently enfranchised. But militant as it might sound to Conservatives and Whigs, the radicalism of 1885 offered relatively little to the recently enfranchised urban dwellers who joined the ranks of the electorate. While suffrage expansion increased the Liberals' hold in the industrial cities, centers of trade unionism, it weakened their hold in London, where nonunionized, sweated industry was strong, and it did nothing to win votes in Chamberlain's own Birmingham, where discontent with the gentrification of the center city led many of the town's displaced poorer population to vote Conservative.[12] Attacks on the established church and its privileged position in public education did not stir the urban masses, nor did the growing Liberal commitment to Irish Home Rule.[13]

Conservatives sensed opportunities. The attempt to define this new electorate as concerned with class issues actually arose first among Conservatives. In the immediate aftermath of suffrage expansion, the most noteworthy effort to attract new supporters was made by Randolph Churchill, who compounded a rather vague New Conservatism with a nebulous Tory Democracy. Rhetorically Churchill denounced the exploitation of workers by a rapacious elite as furiously as Chamberlain.[14] Although Churchill swiftly departed the political scene, he was soon replaced in Conservative ranks by Chamberlain himself, who, revolting against Gladstone's leadership and support of the Whigs, led his political supporters into the Conservative Party in 1886. Once there, Chamberlain struggled valiantly to make the Conservatives the party of social reform and to complete the task, already begun in 1885, of refashioning a program to attract urban voters. To meet Chamberlain's challenge, Liberals developed their own reform programs, while lamenting, in Herbert Gladstone's words, that "Conservatives had lost all their principles and had disappeared: it had become a race between two parties, one outbidding the other."[15]

Between 1885 and 1910, the existence of elements within both major parties determined to win support from the enlarged electorate by offers of social reform fundamentally changed the pattern of reform movements. In the previous decade, between 1877 and 1885, Chamberlain had established the National Liberal Federation (NLF) as a reformist pressure group within the Liberal Party. The power and organization of the federation made it a force to be reckoned with and, increasingly, it exerted a magnetic influence on social reformers. By 1886, the Liberal Party had begun to establish an almost hegemonic relationship with reform movements; existing movements drew closer to the Liberals, while participation in Liberal associations, most notably the NLF, became the most effective way for up-and-coming social reformers to exert political influence. As a result, however, the political fate of reform was tied to that of the Liberal Party and, to a degree, subject to the political priorities of Liberal politicians.

In the 1880s, however, a new kind of independent social movement emerged. Although the NLF continued to attract reformers, Liberal political hegemony over reform movements was shattered by the growing bipartisan competition to win the loyalties of the new electorate. The competition between Conservatives and Liberals opened the possibility of forging a new political culture in which the language of social reform was no longer confined to that of a Liberalism deeply suspicious of the role of government and committed to an atomistic individualism. Political competition between Liberals and Conservatives not only created an opportunity for the appearance of new political contenders but also helped shape the character of the contending groups.

With both Liberals and Conservatives demonstrating their solicitude for the working classes, it was no wonder that a variety of ad hoc reformist groups, independent of both parties, proclaimed their interests in labor and their ability to speak in the name of particular categories of oppressed workers, their wives, or their families. Feminist organizations also grew up alongside these movements, and many feminist organizations shared overlapping concerns. Even powerful established groups such as the Trades Union Council, which, though never affiliated with the Liberal Party, had maintained close ties to it, began to assert their political independence. The small but influential Fabian Society's close links to the Liberal Party also weakened in the climate of the late 1880s and 1890s; leading Fabians like the Webbs cultivated prominent reform-oriented Conservatives.

Coalitions between the labor movement and Liberal reform groups were formed when it was a question of imposing legal restrictions on child and female labor; the growth of unemployment made organized workers sensitive to issues of harsh supervision, low wages, and long hours. British trade unionists supported compulsory schooling, partly for its own sake and partly because it withdrew even more labor from the market.[16] Trade unionists also joined movements against sweated labor. Campaigns to restrict homework and prohibit many forms of child labor came all the easier to trade unionists, because the wives and children of craftsmen and many semiskilled workers had already dropped out of the workforce as a result of rising male incomes or declining demand. In 1909 reformers and trade unionists won the creation of wage boards, which set wages in specified underpaid occupations and were designed to set wage limits within legally specified sweated industries.

The social movements and pressure groups that sprang up in the 1890s and 1900s were a melange of single-issue and general-reform organizations. While some reform movements were predominantly middle class and others were predominantly working class, and while there were often intense political differences within and between movement organizations, they nonetheless possessed a coherence that marked them as belonging to the same family of reform movements. For one, most leaders in these social movements belonged either to the Liberal Party or to a socialist organization. Among the socialist parties, social reformers usually belonged to the Fabian Society or the Independent Labour Party (ILP), but many working-class reformers originally entered politics through the Social Democratic Federation (SDF). Although sections of the Conservatives or Unionists might support the demands of these reform movements, those parties' members were rarely represented in the movements' leadership. Conservative-dominated reform movements such as the Anti-Socialist Union and Conservative popular issues such as anti-alienism did not attract these reformers.[17] Furthermore, while many leading reformers supported the cause of Irish Home Rule, few Irish nationalists played leading roles in other reform movements.

Other common bonds that brought these emerging reform movements together were the overlapping networks of well-known political leaders who were involved in a wide variety of such movements. For example, at one time or another, James Ramsay MacDonald was active in the Fabian Society, the ILP, the Labour Party, the organization of the Anti-Sweating Exhibition, and the National Right to Work Council. His wife, Margaret Ethel MacDonald, was active in the National Union of Women Workers, the Women Industrial Council, the Women Labour League, the organization of the Anti-Sweating

Exhibition, and the National Union of Women Suffrage Societies. Before World War I, William Beveridge had publicly supported movements for old-age pensions, meals for schoolchildren, and unemployment relief. Networks of prominent individuals belonging to a multiplicity of organizations, such as the MacDonalds and William Beveridge, architect of the Unemployment Insurance Act, were particularly important in hammering out compromises and articulating common purposes across social movements.

Recruitment patterns within reform institutions, government bureaucracies, and political parties helped to extend the influence of small networks of political leaders to the larger political world. Undoubtedly the most famous of these patrons were Sidney and Beatrice Webb; Beveridge was one of their protégés. Charles Booth was another powerful patron. Still another important patronage network was composed of those social reformers, mostly Liberals, who had spent time at Canon Barnett's Toynbee Hall. Among the prominent social reformers Toynbee Hall helped to produce were Ernest Aves, collaborator with Charles Booth in the London survey; William Beveridge; T. Hancock Nunn, member of the 1909 Royal Commission on the Poor Laws; Hubert Llewellyn Smith, first head of the Labour Department at the Board of Trade; R. H. Tawney, author and social theorist; and E. J. Urwick, first director of the London School of Sociology.[18]

The competition for the newly enfranchised voters created a fertile territory for the appearance of independent reform-oriented organizations concerned with labor and the conditions of working-class life and operating in the territory between Conservative statism and Liberal preoccupation with individual rights. While social movements were the first beneficiaries of these circumstances, the competition soon began to take a partisan form. In February 1900 the participants in a conference convened by the Parliamentary Committee of the Trades Union Congress was called upon to decide whether workers should demand independent political representation. After declaring that workers needed representation, the Workers Representation Committee next had to confront the question of the nature of the working class they claimed to represent. Opinions differed. Some, such as W. C. Steadman, called for a resolution in favor of working-class opinion being represented in the House of Commons by men sympathetic to the aims and demands of the Labour movement.[19] Others, primarily the Marxists in the SDF, challenged the narrow identification of the working class with the trade union movement and argued that it must include all wage laborers. They called for recognition of the class struggle and the nationalization of industry. Deftly avoiding the question of the identity of the working classes, the committee passed a resolution asking candidates to orient themselves towards the "direct interests of labour."[20] To carry out its resolutions, the conference elected a twelve-member executive committee, appointing Ramsay MacDonald as secretary. The ambiguities of the committee's report gave the executive the leeway to formulate a political agenda aimed expressly at working-class voters.

The second current of shifting political opportunities that made it possible for the newly enfranchised to articulate their demands came after 1903 with the emerging split within the established order caused by Chamberlain's advocacy of protectionism. As a result, for a time, unemployment became a high-profile issue in British politics.[21] This stage was to prove the most decisive for those concerned with unemployment because the specific issues raised between battling elites in the protectionist dispute, the economic condition of England and the debate over industrial backwardness, were extremely relevant to their concerns. In their eagerness to disseminate their views, protectionists emphasized that free trade meant unemployment, while Liberals were forced to deny any such relationship.

Chamberlain had thrust unemployment into the spotlight on earlier occasions. As early as 1886, he had encouraged a limited use of public works as a way of dealing with unemployment.[22] But the realignment of Conservatives around protectionism enabled him to rally sections of the party to his cause. Chamberlain's support of protectionism, a cause dear to many of his fellow Birmingham industrialists, was designed to appeal not only to employers threatened by foreign competition but also to all those whose jobs and working conditions were threatened by lower foreign wages and working conditions. Chamberlain's public advocacy of protectionism split the British elite down the middle, with many, but not all, large industrialists coming down on the side of protectionism. Chamberlain tried to use protectionism to appeal to workers, noting that "alien legislation, sweating legislation, fair wages legislation—is absolutely contrary to Free Trade."[23] The Unemployed Workmen Act of 1905 was undoubtedly the most important of the Conservatives' efforts. This measure provided for the establishment of rate-subsidized local committees charged with providing local works to relieve unemployment. But despite the Conservatives' social policy rhetoric, their actions in power were quite restrained. The 1905 Unemployment Act's sponsor, Walter Long, admitted that one of his chief purposes was to head off the growing demand for the intervention of the national state in unemployment policy.[24]

The Liberal landslide of 1906 revealed that Chamberlain had failed to make protectionism popular among the electorate.[25] Although Labour's victories (29 seats) could not compare with the Liberal triumph (401 seats), they were still significant. By itself, even the overwhelming character of the Liberal victory would not have resulted in reforms outside of the specific promises on legislation made before the election. The Liberal prime minister, Henry Campbell-Bannerman, was in the Gladstone mold, a principled anti-imperialist, deeply suspicious of social reforms. Only the onset of fatal illness forced Campbell-Bannerman to resign and paved the way for the appointment of Herbert Asquith, making possible serious social reform.

But the great Liberal landslide of 1906 also forced the party to transform itself. The program of the party's moderate leadership was enacted almost immediately. With those issues on which there was a Liberal consensus easily accomplished, the government had to decide what to do next. And when unemployment rates rose steeply in 1908 and 1909, Liberals who defended free trade were forced to reconsider the entire issue of unemployment policy. Conservatives and Unionists used the increase to justify their accusations that free trade meant unemployment. Many Liberals felt called upon to show that free trade did not mean the poorhouse for British workers. In 1908, Asquith himself stated that he had realized from the first that if it could not be proved that social reform (not Socialism) can be financed on Free Trade lines "a return to Protection is a moral certainty."[26] The Liberal sense of urgency was greatly intensified by demonstrations and rallies supporting a Labour Party–sponsored bill demanding the right to work.

The Right to Work and the Emergence of a New Social Policy

In some ways, it is not too much to say that the demand for a right to work made the Labour Party. But the kind of Labour Party that the battle against unemployment made changed considerably as demands gave way to actual programs. In its origins the right to work had been a radical and relatively encompassing demand. The sweeping and vague universalism expressed in early proposals addressed the plight of all "workers"; only as unemployment legislation began to take concrete form under the shaping hands of Liberal social policy experts did it identify male skilled workers as the major group requiring protection.

In asserting a right to work, Labour challenged a long-standing consensus within British politics that maintained that unemployment was a question of individual character and best dealt with at the local level—at the national level, there was nothing to talk about at all. The prestigious economists, who dominated academic discourse, asserted that the state could do nothing to increase the level of aggregate employment and the major problem was the refusal of workers to accept lower wages.[27] In 1902, Conservative prime minister Arthur Balfour refused to meet deputations from the SDF and the London Trades Council to discuss unemployment. The president of the Local Government Board, Walter Long, also refused to meet a delegation from the London Trades Council that wanted to inform him about the extent of unemployment in London.[28]

In pre–World War I Britain, the dominant voluntary charity organizations and the Poor-Law unions generally embraced this view and organized social welfare around its assumptions.[29] A foremost spokesman of established arrangements was the highly influential Charity Organization Society (COS). The assumptions and principles of the COS have been well studied and will be summarized quickly here for the purposes of comparison with less familiar views. Like other perspectives discussed later in this chapter, the most important of the COS views of unemployment were cast in narrative form. These narratives were the true heart of the matter, for they connected political slogans to the actual implementation of social policy. The COS narrative, a retelling of the parable of the good and bad servants, justified the basic welfare categories and represented the most important set of stories behind the British welfare system between 1834 and 1909.[30] The first part of the story concerns the improvident worker. In good times, he chooses free time over steady employment or seeks out irregular, factitious, and superfluous work, such as servicing the working-class community. In bad times, this worker is the first fired or finds his services beyond the means of his hard-strapped working-class customers. In the COS view, such a worker bore responsibility for his own unemployment. The second part of the story concerns the prudent worker, the ideal economic man, overwhelmed by misfortunes not of his making. Even the COS admitted that being born crippled or blind was outside the individual's control and might affect his or her chances of unemployment. Many cases were less clear-cut. A long illness, an industrial accident, or the desertion of a husband might have been unprovoked tragedies, or they might be due to some culpable individual failing. Only personal contact with a COS volunteer could enable the authorities to determine the extent of individual accountability.

Basing itself on these narratives, between 1834 and 1909, mainstream social policy had centered on the character of the individual recipient. By the 1880s and 1890s in many municipalities, a carrot-and-stick approach was employed. The "stick" for the improvident worker was provided by the Poor Law Unions supported by local property taxes; for the most part, these reflected, at least in theory, the savage principles of 1834—the "workhouse test," "less eligibility," and administrative centrality and uniformity. Although in practice the punitive regulations of 1834 were never fully applied and many groups were exempted, they remained the dominant principles in social welfare in Britain.

The carrot for the unfortunately impoverished was supplied by private, voluntary organizations such as the COS working hand-in-hand with the state. The COS's job was to make a preliminary investigation of individual poverty cases. When poverty was due to circumstances beyond the control of the average worker, the COS would provide temporary assistance. When poverty was due to individual inadequacy, however, the COS would remand the pauper to the grim mercy of the secular law, that is, the poorhouse. Although conceding that there were deserving individuals who might become impoverished through overwhelming misfortune, the COS was concerned that even these individuals might become lazy and shiftless if carried on the lists for too long. Continual inspection and investigation by middle-class volunteers was necessary to ensure that those whose poverty began with unmerited misfortune did not slip into the residuum of those who had lost their gumption from overlong dependence on charity.

Needless to say, to those who shared the perspective of political economy and the COS, the idea of a right to work was anathema. And many Liberals, historically the descendants of the Whig party that had enacted the Poor Law of 1834, felt that the political economy that justified the Poor Law was their true heritage.

The sudden emergence in 1905 of a demand for a right to work surprised and disturbed politicians who thought they had seen the last of it in on the French barricades in 1848. The appearance of the demand was bound up with the emergence of the Labour Party. The party's decision to campaign for the right to work allowed it to demarcate itself from the Liberal Party and establish an independent voice on an issue that had great resonance throughout the entire working-class community. After all, fear of unemployment was one of the few things that all workers, from boatwright to barrow boy, feared. According to Kenneth D. Brown, at the national level, the right to work represented the Edwardian Labour Party's main claim to originality, the sole area where there was a principled difference between the nascent Labour Party and the dominant Liberals.[31]

Certainly, unemployment was a serious concern of workers during the key years of the debate. At the time, no really adequate system of measuring unemployment existed; after all, a system of measurement depended on definitions of the nature of work and the character of unemployment that were a by-product of the policy debate under way. Trade union returns sent to the Board of Trade show that unemployment in 1909 was exceeded only in two years, 1878 and 1886.[32] The issue resonated in a party where most Labour members of parliament (MPs) had intimate knowledge of unemployment, either personally or through the experiences of friends and relations.[33]

With the raising of the right to work questions, Labour had identified an issue that it wanted to make peculiarly its own, because it knew that the issue had wide appeal among its core supporters and because it was a demand that would not be co-opted.[34] Up to that point, the Labour Party and the trade unions and social movements with which it was associated had generally sought to pose demands acceptable to reform-oriented Liberalism and Conservatism.

Generally, demands for legislation to protect nonunionized women workers and child laborers were couched in the established language of dependence.[35] Labor legislation affecting trade unions, including women trade unionists, was justified as promoting free market bargaining within the acknowledged field of individual rights. With the call for a right to work Labour asserted its own distinctive identity. Embracing the "rights talk" so beloved by Gladstone, the demand for the right to work asserted long-held working-class feelings. It was only partially a claim on citizenship. The right to work was labeled a universal right by Thomas Paine and a moral right by medieval theologians, thus the call was a demand that the state recognize an entitlement already firmly established in economic and religious thought. The demand was clearly an extension of the traditional liberal political framework.[36] But when extended this far, the whole framework began to crack and splinter.

The actual right-to-work bill drawn up in 1906 by Labour Party politicians that served as the focus of the campaign proposed relatively moderate practical measures, such as the creation of a central unemployment committee to plan public works and the appointment of local authorities to implement these plans through local taxes. Labour leaders were willing to promote a rather anemic practical proposal for dealing with unemployment if they could win the Liberal commitment to the right to work. In truth, Labour did not have a well-worked-out scheme for implementing its proposals, and acceptance of the principle would have constituted only the beginning of a debate about the extent to which it might be carried out. The bill was introduced in Parliament in July 1907 by James Ramsay MacDonald, an enthusiastic supporter. Everyone recognized that the real thrust of the law was its statement of a general principle that "Where a workman has registered himself as unemployed, it shall be the duty of the local unemployment authority to provide work for him in connection with one or other of the schemes hereinafter provided, or otherwise, or failing the provision of work, to provide maintenance should necessity exist for the person and for those depending on that person for the necessities of life."[37] Thus, Labour's bill moved from an assertion of local government's duty to provide work to its duty to provide a respectable maintenance for the unemployed, who was distinguished from the shiftless pauper.

Like the COS interpretation of unemployment, the Labour proposal contained its own narrative of unemployment and suggested new ways of classifying the unemployed. Such narratives are crucial to the invocation of general principles because they define situations in ways that make their application meaningful and appropriate. The story implicit in the bill is artfully portrayed from the perspective of an unemployed worker. In the bill, quoted above, the worker is presented as willing to work and unable to find employment. While the bill does not not state who exactly was to blame for the lack of work, it is clear that the worker is absolved of any responsibility. The "willing worker" without employment is the bill's image of the unemployed. There were many ambiguities to this phrasing. Nothing is stated about the previous work experience of the worker, and, while the legislation is cast in the usual gendered language of the time (e.g., "where the workman has registered himself"), Ramsay MacDonald's published explication of the text of the bill insisted that working women should be included.[38] Nor is anything stated about the kind of work that might be given workers. Although no contemporary political leader really expected the right to work to be implemented in its widest possible sense, at least initially, still everyone realized that Liberal acceptance of this demand would open up an immense terrain for clarification, debate, and conflict.

The bill asserted that it was local government's responsibility to ascertain the state of the local labor market so as to certify whether work was available. In many ways this was the genius of the bill, for it dared local committees to deny the existence of genuinely unemployed men and women when confronted with real cases. Local committees were also to organize labor exchanges, regulate public works, promote industrial education, and assist emigration. Local government itself would be required to document the inadequacies of a political economy that denied the existence of unemployment[39] Further, Labour proposed a right to work that was enforceable in that a specific administrative agent was responsible for carrying out a program towards an identifiable group of individuals. Unemployed workers would presumably be able to demand that local representatives of labor exchanges either find them jobs or give them relief.

Confident of support for a demand that it alone advocated, the Labour Party took unusual steps to rally popular support for the measure. In these early years, the Labour Party leadership was more willing than later to combine extra-parliamentary pressure with electoral action.[40] A joint conference representing the Labour Party, the Trades Union Congress, and the General Federation of Trade Unions declared that "At tens of hundreds of Socialist meetings during the year the demand that the Bill be Passed must be made, and at every meeting in the constituencies addressed by members who voted against the Bill their action must be challenged."[41] Trade unions, trades councils, and socialist societies were all circularized to this end. Although nothing so dramatic as the Hyde Park riots of 1886 and 1887 occurred, at times the agitation against unemployment verged on violence.[42] The Right to Work Council and the ILP organized hunger marches to demonstrate the extent of unemployment.

Institutions and Outcomes:
Turning Demands into Social Policies

Although the Labour Party did not win legal acknowledgment of the right to work, its campaign was not futile. Rejecting a right to work, the Liberal government was nonetheless forced to recognize the existence of genuine unemployment and the need to elaborate social policies in this field. If the issue of unemployment arose from the enfranchisement of a large section of the male working class and reached political status through the Labour Party's adoption of the demand for a right to work, it remained for this demand to affect the field of social policy formulation. Here we acknowledge Theda Skocpol and Dietrich Rueschemeyer's insistence on the importance of government bureaucracy in the development of social policy.[43] The overlapping networks between Labour and Liberal social policy analysts gave Labour access to those in government who could draw up and defend reform proposals, and the willingness of Labour leaders to compromise made such reform possible. Unfortunately, the character of this compromise would go far toward alienating Labour leaders from many of their former social movement allies.

When the demand for a right to work was first introduced, most Liberals rejected such an open-ended commitment, yet they also recognized that unemployment was a key area for renegotiating their relationship with a growing Labour Party. They accepted the premises of the COS while also wanting to make concessions to Labour. Upon assuming power in 1908, the Liberal prime minister, Herbert Asquith, assured the king that a right to work was "obviously inadmissible," but he felt that something must be done "for the sake of appearances." Sidney Buxton, the Liberal MP from Poplar and president of the Board of Trade from 1910 to 1914, also agreed that the bill went too far but that "we ought to at least . . . have an alternative."[44]

Searching for an alternative to the right to work, Liberals looked to social reformers, government bureaucrats, and moderate Labour leaders; if a compromise could be attained, these were the agents who could achieve it. Within the party, a group of extraordinarily talented, ambitious young men, including Winston Churchill and David Lloyd George, saw a chance to make their reputations as social reformers. Meanwhile, the shift of taxation from local to national sources, the reorganization of the British tax structure, and the introduction of progressive income taxes provided the indispensable fiscal base for any large program of social reform.[45]

Just as important, in a British bureaucracy renowned for its conservatism and lethargy, one small section of the bureaucracy was a hive of reformist activity, the Labour Department of the Board of Trade. These reformers knew that official dogma was wrong and that unemployment really existed, for they had seen it and studied it; but they had their own diagnosis of its causes and their own remedies. Under the leadership of Hubert Llewellyn Smith, the first head of the Labour Department, which had been created in 1893, the department had been systematically colonized by a Liberal network formed in the reform movements of the 1890s and 1900s, particularly from Barnett's Toynbee Hall.[46] In 1909, Llewellyn Smith was appointed permanent secretary of the Board of Trade. These bureaucrats, men like William Beveridge, were to provide the expertise for discussing the problems of the unemployed and for drafting legislation both was both practical and accommodated the political needs of the Liberal Party and the Labour Party. His tenure as head of the Board of Trade between 1906 and 1908 provided David Lloyd George with drafts of social reforms that were finally carried out during his years as chancellor of the exchequer. Nor was it coincidental that his successor at the Board of Trade, Winston Churchill, undertook the responsibility of developing unemployment policy.

Thus, Labour's demands paved the way for ideas previously consigned to the margins of British politics. Seeking to hold its own substantial working-class constituency and to accommodate Labour, the Liberal Party turned to groups of Liberal social reformers with long records of reform activity, men and women who had worked together with networks of social reformers in the Labour Party. Government bureaucrats unsympathetic to the voluntarism of the COS and Liberal social reformers expert in the area of unemployment intervened in this new debate and, together with Labour leaders, broke decisively with the COS, institutionalizing a new image of work and of workers. Not that all these groups agreed on a particular solution. The Unemployment Act of 1911 was a compromise that left many unsatisfied on all sides. A new vision of work, worker, and unemployment was fashioned, as well as a language corresponding to the public policy domain required for Labour's growing incorporation into the political order.

These approaches to unemployment broke decisively with past conventions and shared important features. Acknowledging the existence of genuinely unemployed workers who were not slackers or work shy, Liberal policy experts devised policies that attempted to remedy the problem without fundamentally challenging their own liberal commitments. The new convention can be summarized in the title of William Beveridge's celebrated book, first published in 1909, *Unemployment: A Problem of Industry*.[47] Beveridge's book drew on arguments developed by a generation of British social reformers that included Charles Booth and the Webbs. His account of unemployment provided a striking contrast with that of both the COS and the principle of the right to work. Instead of concentrating on the personal aspects or responding to the concrete needs of the unemployed, Beveridge focused on unemployment as a "problem of industry." Using the language of an impartial and objective social science, he found neither capital nor labor was at fault.

Basically, Beveridge focused on what economists have labeled "frictional unemployment," that is, the amount of unemployment flowing from the necessary, and ultimately beneficial, processes of economic change. Beveridge wanted to oil the cogs of industry and decrease frictional unemployment by providing information about jobs and tiding workers over the temporary hardships of unemployment. Beveridge's analysis also was based on a set of stories. According to this analysis, fluctuations in employment were characteristic of all industries. In some industrial regions, technological change or industrial restructuring led to declining employment. In these circumstances, municipally administered labor exchanges should promote the smooth transition of unemployed workers to jobs in other industries or other areas that require similar or related skills. In regions where casual or seasonal labor markets dominated, labor exchanges would act to promote and encourage the growth of a more permanent labor force by rehiring previously employed adult males.[48] As adult male employment increased, that of women and children would decrease, because the male household head would earn enough to support his family. José Harris's evaluation of Beveridge's scheme is to the point:

> far more important than its administrative thoroughness was its political plausibility. . . . It was content with the realization of many different kinds of social and political principle—with socialism and individualism, trade unionism and charitable organization, the laws of the 'free market' and the inculcation of self-help.[49]

Beveridge's scheme had further advantages. Depending on the assumptions of orthodox political economists, it still assumed that only faulty communication prevented workers in one region from learning about the availability of work in another. The plan was also unenforceable in that it contained no linkage between a specific worker and an agency charged with providing a job. A labor exchange could tell a worker about the availability of labor in a distant region but could guarantee neither that the information was reliable nor that work would still be available when the worker arrived. Since the British state generally played little role in providing job training, there was little standardization with regard to job qualifications; except where union apprenticeship programs provided some degree of homogenization or in a local context, it was difficult to communicate accurately the skills required or to vouch that a job candidate had the required skills. Moreover, the incorporation of the labor exchanges into the Unemployment Insurance Act as the agents for enforcing the "work-seeking" provision made them unattractive to the most skilled workers, who were their intended clientele.[50]

The assumption of self-clearing markets and the emphasis on frictional unemployment focused reformers' attention away from the problems of the most poverty-stricken workers. The key to the new social insurance system was promoting continuous employment for adult males rather than providing work.[51] Concerned about the cost of the scheme and determined to keep it actuarially sound, Churchill's lieutenants at the Board of Trade gave up any effort to design a scheme that would cover the majority of the working class. Hubert Llewellyn Smith drafted an unemployment plan, based on Beveridge's principles, concentrating on those sectors of the economy that were subject to cyclical change, where the state of "employment" was distinct from that of "unemployment."[52] Thus, the program would not deal with the problems of casual labor. Even at this early stage, a distinction was made between "regular workers" on whom contributions could be levied, thus creating entitlements, and "irregular workers" outside the social insurance system to whom aid could only be given as a gift.

Instead, the plan focused on those industries where frictional unemployment was prevalent but workers were able to bear the costs of insurance. There were the areas, it was felt, where government aid might be most effective. Unemployment insurance was made compulsory in shipbuilding, engineering, and building and construction work. These were male-dominated trades that employed mainly skilled workers. Poorer and less skilled workers, even those not employed in "sweated" industries, were left entirely outside the plan, and only male workers were offered the option of voluntary contribution. Women workers were prohibited from becoming voluntary contributors because it was felt that they composed a higher percentage of malingers and would threaten the actuarial soundness of the plan. The new system gave short shrift to female domestic workers who moved between family concerns and commodity production, to skilled workers who alternated between selling their own products and laboring in workshops, and to migratory workers who moved between seasonal agriculture and industry. Socialist leaders such as Keir Hardie and George Lansbury opposed the plan because they felt that less skilled workers would be unable to afford the contribution and because of the exclusion of women.[53]

Not surprisingly, those Labour Party leaders who had sought most to consolidate the party's alliance with the Liberals were the most enthusiastic about unemployment insurance. To justify their participation in an alliance with the Liberals, they were anxious to portray unemployment insurance as a concession won by Labour. To work out a common agreement for unemployment insurance, they substantially adopted the viewpoint of Beveridge and the Webbs. Writing in

1911, in the course of the debate over unemployment insurance, Ramsay Mac-
Donald abandoned the principles of the 1905 bill, claiming that unemployment
insurance was his own preferred means for implementing the right to work. He
argued that "a scheme of insurance, the premiums of which are provided by the
state, the trade, and the body of workman. . . . is much nearer to the general principles of Socialism, and in that form this part of the Right to Work Claim is now
being advocated and enforced by the Socialist parties of the world."[54] Ramsay
MacDonald also insisted that the right to work required "the decasualization of
labour by the prohibition of the engagement of casual workers except through
exchanges. The effect of this will be to increase the number of chronically unemployed men, for which the state must assume responsibility."[55] MacDonald was
anxious to remove the least capable from the labor force and felt that, as the
number of these unemployables rose, the government and society would be
forced to take further measures to deal with the problem. In fact, his view on this
question was also congruent with his conviction, shared by the Webbs and Beveridge, that married women with children did not belong in the workforce and
should be encouraged to return home to their families.

Ramsay MacDonald's usage of the right to work slogan changed in fundamental ways. Basically, he attempted to retain Labour's old slogan while substituting Beveridge's narrative. Instead of the "willing worker," Ramsay MacDonald embraced the concept of "frictional unemployment," shifting his focus
inevitably from a potentially inclusive attention to the plight of all the unemployed to an emphasis on that of its more mobile and skilled, those who were best
able to contribute to an insurance fund. The contributory character of unemployment insurance further reinforced these distinctions by tying benefits to contributions, thus creating a special sense of entitlement among contributing workers.

In the end, Ramsay MacDonald and the majority of the Labour Party came
to articulate a position that disproportionately favored privileged sections of
the working class that were continuously employed, that is, more skilled
males. But this is not to suggest that they represented such interests continuously and consistently throughout the entire debate between 1901 and 1911.
Pat Thane is persuasive when she says that:

> it is difficult to interpret the language of Edwardian Labour politics as the clear
> expression either of sectionalism or of class unity. . . . the often passionate, reit-
> erated defence of the exploited and low paid from Barnes or MacDonald and
> many more cannot be described as a mere expression of the interests of a work-
> ing class elite. Labour spoke for a mass of people whose interests it knew to be
> varied and often conflicting.[56]

But still the point is that when interests conflicted and choices had to be made, they were made in favor of the skilled male workers who were the base of the electoral party. While male skilled workers represented an important section of the Labour Party electorate, the leaders of the party had grown up among social movements concerned with the casual laboring poor and with women workers, both unionized and nonunionized, as well as with women's groups and feminist organizations. Their championship of the right to work expressed their sense of the variety and differing conditions of the unemployed. Unlike the Liberals, Labour was never committed to the doctrine of self-clearing markets and, in fact, was inherently suspicious of the "fairness" of competition. But in securing reforms for any portion of the unemployed, Labour Party leaders had to depend on shifting political circumstances and on the willingness of Liberals to compromise. To win support, they had to extol compromises as victories. In this process, however, Labour underwent its own process of self-definition. By championing the cause of the continuously employed male worker, Labour clarified and shaped its own self-image. The drafting of the unemployment insurance provisions of the National Insurance Act of 1911 provided a sharper, more searching answer to the question posed in 1901: What labor does the Labour Party represent? The interests and identity of Labour were not a priori constructs, to which men like Ramsay MacDonald were consistently faithful, but contingent determinations shaped by the very character of the struggle in which they were engaged. In fact, this chapter argues that all social policy shares this characteristic.

The Right to Work Today

Many British citizens were surprised by the repudiation in the 1970s and 1980s of the post–World War II "social contract." Like Beveridge's 1911 National Insurance Act, the employment commitment implicit in the Beveridge-inspired social welfare legislation of 1946 had never been enforceable, but millions accepted the pledges of successive Labour and Conservative governments that they would never permit the return of mass unemployment. Although Labour had long pledged to defend full employment, it found itself torn between economists urging wage and price stabilization and resistant trade unions; the Conservative Thatcher government repudiated the commitment entirely. Similar pledges were violated in many EU member nations in the 1980s and 1990s.

Nonetheless, trade unions generally still defend a right to work, and as unemployment has continued, some trade unions and socialist parties have fought to generalize labor participation. In common with Dahrendorf and Offe, they agree on the need to prevent their societies from being divided between underclass and working class. Instead of offering some a minimum income while others work for wages, they seek to increase social equality on the basis of general participation in work.

To achieve the goal of general labor participation, they fight to redistribute the labor burden more equitably from those who labor a grueling forty- or fifty-hour week to those who feel excluded from society because they have no work at all. Within the European Union, the last two decades have seen a renewed interest in shortening the workweek. In France, the Mitterrand government's one-hour reduction of the workday was a symbolic step in this direction; and Lionel Jospin, the current socialist prime minister, is planning to introduce a thirty-five-hour week; the French trade union federation, the CFDT, has vowed to demonstrate its solidarity with the unemployed by fighting for the thirty-two-hour week. Along this same line, in 1985, German metalworkers fought to reduce their workday to thirty-five hours, and the Norwegian Socialist Party has sought to experiment with a six-hour day with no reduction in pay. In France, Germany, and Italy, trade unions have agreed to "unemployment sharing," which involves lowering hours of work to prevent layoffs.

The new concern with unemployment has led many trade unions to involve themselves in reform movements that they had in the past ignored. Demands to allow time off for workers to engage in retraining have been adopted in many nations. Numerous unions have begun to increase their interest in extending the school-leaving age and in encouraging early retirement. Spain has encouraged early retirement on the theory that less productive older workers will be replaced by more productive younger workers. France has lowered the retirement age for some categories of workers, and some French companies have offered "partial retirement" arrangements to workers over fifty-five in which they work part time but agree to tutor young workers.[58]

One of the most exciting developments of the period, however, has been trade union support for lengthy paid leaves for child care or tending sick family members, responsibilities that often have fallen disproportionately on women. Paid absences for education, child minding, and sabbaticals have become a popular feature in Denmark. The large-scale entry of women into the market over the last forty years and widespread feminist political mobilization have created a new constituency within many trade unions capable of preventing the patriarchal biases evident in past applications of the right to work.

Of course, today as in the past, demands to generalize participation in work must stand or fall on their ability to mobilize workers as well as on their ability to find political allies and support among social policy makers. Advocates of the right to work hope that the same sense of unity and identity engendered in male skilled workers in the late nineteenth-century United Kingdom can today be spread to the entire labor force. The power of the right to work is that it draws on the very principles inculcated by capitalism's defenders. It builds on the deep and abiding contradiction within a system that insists on the necessity of work but is unable to provide it. Time and again, as in pre–World War I Britain, social reformers using the right to work have forced politicians and social policy makers to confront this disturbing reality and to make concessions benefiting at least some sections of the working class. But we also believe that, in the current context, demands for generalizing work can overcome some of the conservative aspects of previous struggles. In the contemporary period, the struggle to generalize work can bring together feminists and trade unionists as well as educational reformers and associations of the retired.

Demands for a right to work appeal to principles of equity, working-class solidarity, and universal justice as well as to citizenship. The multistranded character of this claim is important, for a reliance on citizenship alone is dangerous. One of the menaces hovering over the demand for the right to work concerns the situation of migrant workers. Most laws governing working conditions and hours of work apply to migrants as well as to natives. But there is also popular support for the view of the French right-wing leader Jean-Marie Le Pen that unemployment can be solved by deporting migrant workers. In the 1970s, Switzerland dealt with its unemployment problem by failing to renew the annual work permits of temporary workers, and French governments have increased the number of government jobs that can be held only by French citizens.[59]

Today in many EU countries, conservative parties are making new appeals to sections of the working class formerly seen as staunch supporters of socialism. Just as the competition between Liberal and Conservative Parties helped to create a new and more left-wing political space in pre–World War I Britain, so we believe that this possibility may be available today. We argue that, given a competitive battle for working-class allegiances and divided elites, the right to work can help create new and broader identities, forge wide and encompassing coalitions, and prevent debates on social policy from dividing those who work and those on welfare.

Notes

1. Hugh Compson, introduction to *The New Politics of Unemployment: Radical Policy Initiatives in Western Europe* (London: Routledge, 1997), 1–5, quote on 1.

2. Ralf Dahrendorf, *The Modern Social Conflict: An Essay on the Politics of Liberty* (New York: Weidenfeld & Nicolson, 1988), 33.

3. Klaus Offe, "A Non-Productivist Design for Social Policies," in *Work and Citizenship in the New Europe,* ed. Harry Coenen and Peter Leisink (Cambridge: Edward Elger, 1993): 215–32, quote on 227–28.

4. Jeremy Rifkin, *The End of Work: The Decline of the Global Labor Force and the Dawn of the Post-Market Era* (New York: G. P. Putnam's Sons, 1995).

5. Sidney Tarrow, "States and Opportunities: The Political Structuring of Social Movements," in *Comparative Perspectives on Social Movements: Political Opportunities, Mobilizing Structures, and Cultural Framings,* ed. Doug McAdam, John D. McCarthy, and Mayer N. Zald (Cambridge: Cambridge University Press, 1996): 41–62, quote on 54.

6. Doug McAdam, *Political Process and the Development of Black Insurgency, 1930–1970* (Chicago: University of Chicago Press, 1982), 41.

7. The 1832 battle for suffrage expansion has recently been studied by Charles Tilly, *Popular Contention in Great Britain 1758–1834* (Cambridge: Harvard University Press, 1995).

8. Neal Blewett, "The Franchise in the United Kingdom 1885–1918," *Past and Present,* no. 32 (December 1965): 27–56.

9. François Crouzet, *The Victorian Economy* (New York: Columbia University Press, 1982); Dudley Baines, *Migration in a Mature Economy: Emigration and Internal Migration in England and Wales, 1861–1900* (Cambridge: Cambridge University Press, 1985), 88; and Charlotte Erickson, "Who Were the English and Scots Emigrants to the United States in the Late Nineteenth Century?" in *Leaving England: Essays on British Emigration in the Nineteenth Century* (Ithaca: Cornell University Press, 1994), 87–125.

10. In 1868, for instance, John Stuart Mill emphasized the importance of emigration as a solution for unemployment.*The Collected Works of John Stuart Mill: Late Letters, 1849–1873* (Toronto: University of Toronto Press, 1972), 1454.

11. For a comparison with French workers, see Michael Hanagan, "Population Change, Labor Markets, and Working-Class Militancy: The Regions around Birmingham and Saint-Etienne, 1840–1880," in *The European Experience of Declining Fertility: A Quiet Revolution, 1850–1970,* ed. John R. Gillis, Louise A. Tilly, and David Levine (Oxford: Blackwell, 1989), 127–45.

12. Christopher Green, "Birmingham's Politics, 1873–1891: The Local Basis of Change," *Midland History* 2, no. 2 (1973): 84–98.

13. D. A. Hamer, *John Morley: Liberal Intellectual in Politics* (Oxford: Oxford University Press 1968), 255–66.

14. W. S. Churchill, *Lord Randolph Churchill* (New York: Macmillan, 1906), 1:465.

15. In November 1885, Sir William Harcourt had written that "The rapid conversion of the Tories to Radical measures quickens the speed of Radical progress." Hamer, *John Morley,* 220.

16. Clive Griggs, *The Trades Union Congress and the Struggle for Education, 1868–1925* (Barcombe, England: Falmer Press, 1983), 25.

17. See Edward Jay Bristow, "The Defence of Liberty and Property in Britain, 1880–1914," (Ph.D. diss., Yale, 1970); and Kenneth D. Brown, "The Anti-Socialist Union, 1908–49," in *Essays in Anti-Labour History: Responses to the Rise of Labour in Britain* (London: Macmillan, 1974), 234–61.

18. Standish Meacham, *Toynbee Hall and Social Reform, 1880–1914* (New Haven: Yale University Press, 1987).

19. Philip P. Poirier, *The Advent of the British Labour Party* (New York: Columbia University Press, 1958), 82.

20. Frank Bealey and Henry Pelling, *Labour and Politics: 1900–1906* (London: Macmillan, 1958), 28.

21. This point is developed by Doug McAdam in "Initiator and Spin-off Movements: Diffusion Processes in Protest Cycles," in *Repertoires and Cycles of Collective Action,* ed. Mark Traugott (Durham, N.C.: Duke University Press, 1995), 217–40.

22. Harris points out the tentative and incomplete character of Chamberlain's early suggestions. See José Harris, *Unemployment and Politics: A Study in English Social Policy, 1886–1914* (Oxford: Clarendon Press, 1974), 77.

23. Joseph Chamberlain, "Trade Unionism and Tariff Reform," London, 17 May 1905, in *Mr. Chamberlain's Speeches,* ed. Charles W. Boyd (London: Constable, 1914), 2:320

24. Kenneth D. Brown, *Labour and Unemployment, 1900–1914* (London: Rowman & Littlefield, 1971), 47.

25. For the details of these negotiations, see Bealey and Pelling, *Labour and Politics,* 125–59.

26. Harris, *Unemployment and Politics,* 270.

27. Such views were widely held by prestigious economists as late as 1932. See Guy Routh, *The Origin of Economic Ideas* (White Plains, N.Y.: International Arts & Sciences Press, 1975), 267–70.

28. Brown, *Labour and Unemployment,* 20–21.

29. Although many versions of the COS narrative can be discovered, the particular source I used for my summary is H. Denby, "The Industrial Residuum," in *Aspects of the Social Problem,* ed. Bernard Bosanquet (London: Macmillan, 1895), 82–102. The description of work in service industries in working-class areas as factitious and superfluous work is found on p. 89. For a discussion of the differences between the COS and the Webbs, see A. M. McBriar, *An Edwardian Mixed Doubles: The Bosanquets versus the Webbs: A Study in British Social Policy, 1890–1929* (Oxford: Clarendon Press, 1987).

30. On narratives and institutions, see Harrison White, "Networks and Stories," in *Identity and Control: A Structural Theory of Social Action* (Princeton: Princeton University Press, 1992), 85–115.

31. Kenneth D. Brown, "The Edwardian Labour Party," in *The First Labour Party, 1906–1914,* ed. Kenneth D. Brown (London: Croom-Helm, 1985), 1–16, quote on 9.

32. Table 2, Trade Union Unemployed Recorded by the Board of Trade, 1870–1912, cited in Harris, *Unemployment and Politics,* 374.

33. David Martin, "Ideology and Composition," in *First Labour Party,* 17–37, quote on 25.

34. On language shifts, see Harrison White, "Where Do Languages Come From? Switching Talk" (Center for the Social Sciences, Columbia University, New York, 1995).

35. In this regard, events in Britain seem to have followed a similar track to the

United States. See Nancy Fraser and Linda Gordon, "A Genealogy of Dependency: Tracing a Keyword of the U.S. Welfare State," *Signs* 19, no. 2 (1994): 309–36.

36. On the history of the right to work, see Michael Rath, *Die Garantie des Rechts auf Arbeit* (Göttingen, Otto Schwartz & Co. 1974), 24–47; and Heinrich Hanm, *Arbeit—Ethik—Menschenreit—Sicherung der Arbeitsplätze als sozialethische Forderung* (Limburg: Lanh, 1976), 11–61.

37. Brown, *Labour and Unemployment* 83.

38. "There are thousands of men and women living to-day whose labor is so sweated that their wages are not high enough to replace the wear and tear of life. . . . The State has a duty to these people. The duty is to tax the wealth which they have created (but that has gone to enrich other people) so that they might be rescued from deterioration and helped during the most trying times of their poverty-stricken lives—e.g.,when they are underfed children, unemployed adult men and women, aged workers." In *The New Unemployed Bill of the Labour Party* (London: ILP Publication Department, 1907), 1–2.

39. Harris, *Unemployment and Politics,* 242.

40. On the varying relationship between electoral politics and social movements, see Ronald Aminzade, "Between Movement and Party: The Transformation of Mid-Nineteenth-Century French Republicanism," in *The Politics of Protest: Comparative Perspectives on States and Social Movements,* ed. J. Craig Jenkins and Bert Klandermans (Minneapolis: University of Minnesota Press, 1995), 39–62.

41. Brown, *Labour and Unemployment,* 93.

42. In 1907 there were violent clashes of the unemployed in Birmingham. In September 1908 in Glasgow, two hundred unemployed broke into the council chamber. Two days later, the visit of Prince Arthur of Connaught was interfered with by the singing of "Red Flag." In Manchester, police broke up demonstrations of the unemployed with baton charges, and a silent gathering of ten thousand unemployed outside the Sheffield town hall succeeded in getting the councilors to vote £10,000 for relief works. See Brown, *Labour and Unemployment,* 92–99.

43. Theda Skocpol and Dietrich Rueschemeyer, introduction to *States, Social Knowledge, and the Origins of Modern Social Policies,* ed. Dietrich Rueschemeyer and Theda Skocpol (Princeton: Princeton University Press, 1996), 3–14.

44. Brown, *Labour and Unemployment,* 90.

45. José Harris points this out in "The Transition to High Politics in English Social Policy, 1880–1914," in *High and Low Politics in Modern Britain: Ten Studies,* ed. Michael Bentley and John Stevenson (Oxford: Clarendon Press, 1983), 58–79.

46. Roger Davidson and Rodney Lowe, "Bureaucracy and Innovation in British Welfare Policy, 1870–1945," in T*he Emergence of the Welfare State in Britain and Germany, 1850–1950,* ed. W. J. Mommsen (London: Croom Helm 1981), 263–95.

47. W. H. Beveridge, *Unemployment; A Problem of Industry* (London: Longmans, Green, 1910). For Alfred Marshall, see "Memoranda and Evidence before the Gold and Silver Commission," (1887) in *Official Papers by Alfred Marshall,* ed. J. M. Keynes (London: Macmillan, 1926), 17–196, quote on 92–93.

Far and away the best discussion of changing conceptions of unemployment adopted by governments is Christian Topalov, *Naissance du chômeur, 1880–1910* (Paris: Albin Michel, 1994). I have not always followed Topalov's interpretation, but I have always learned a lot from his study.

48. An important discussion of the role of labor exchanges in actual practice in the United Kingdom and the United States is Desmond King, *Actively Seeking Work? The Politics of Unemployment and Welfare Policy in the United States and Great Britain* (Chicago: University of Chicago Press, 1995).

49. Harris, *Unemployment and Politics,* 207.

50. King, *Actively Seeking Work?*

51. See Krishan Kumar, "From Work to Employment and Unemployment: The English Experience," in *On Work: Historical, Comparative, and Theoretical Approaches,* ed. R. E. Pahl (Oxford: Basil Blackwell, 1988), 138–66.

52. Harris, *Unemployment and Industry.*

53. Pat Thane, "The Labour Party and State 'Welfare,'" in *First Labour Party,* 183–216.

54. James Ramsey MacDonald, *The Socialist Movement* (London: Williams & Norgate, 1911), 166. An important interpretation of MacDonald's place in the Edwardian Labour movements is Duncan Tanner, "Ideological Debate in Edwardian Labour Politics: Radicalism, Revisionism, and Socialism," in *Currents of Radicalism: Popular Radicalism, Organized Labour and Party Politics in Britain, 1850–1914,* ed. Eugenio F. Biagini and Alastair V. Reid (Cambridge: Cambridge University Press, 1991), 271–93.

55. MacDonald, *Socialist Movement,* 167.

56. Thane, "Labour Party and State 'Welfare,'" in *First Labour Party,* 191.

57. See Jean-Pierre Jallade, "Working-Time Policies in France," in *Working Time in Transition: The Political Economy of Working Hours in Industrial Nations,* ed. Karl Hinrichs, William Roche, and Carmen Sirianni (Philadelphia: Temple University Press, 1991), 61–86.

58. Compton, *New Politics of Unemployment,* passim.

59. Alec G. Hargreaves, *Immigration, "Race," and Ethnicity in Contemporary France* (London: Routledge, 1995), 50.

7

Women's Collective Agency, Power Resources, and the Framing of Citizenship Rights

Barbara Hobson

Not too long ago, one would have had a hard time imagining a set of debates about the concept of citizenship in gender terms. The contours of citizenship were bound by notions of universality; a citizen was a person who embodied a bundle of obligations and rights. However, within the universal framework was a gendered inner frame that contained a male citizen: he was the independent paterfamilias in the liberal state, or the male breadwinner and his family in T. H. Marshall's framework of social citizenship.[1] Applying a gendered lens to citizenship, feminist research began decoding keywords that form the basis of dominant theories, such as dependence/independence and private/public.

Recent feminist research has reintroduced the dimension of participatory citizenship rooted in traditions of the Greek democratic forum and Rousseau's idea of civic republicanism. These are traditions in which women were left out of the script. But some feminist researchers have made the case that this framework of active citizenship produces a theoretical terrain for recognizing the role of women as social actors in the construction of citizenship.[2]

But the focus on the practice of citizenship tends to obscure the complex relationship between participation and power.[3] One could say that participation is empowering in the sense that it builds competence, power over oneself.[4] Also, meeting others who share interests and experiences can empower individuals and groups to delegitimize negative constructions of themselves. But this does not imply either a collective agency to represent group interests or command over power resources to influence outcomes. What is not made explicit is the relationship between the practice of citizenship and the articulation of claims and the exercise of power, nor how these power resources might lead to the redistribution of social goods and political influence in societies, or extensions in citizenship rights.

This study develops a framework that allows for analyses of women's collective agency, power resources, and extensions in citizenship rights and

149

reveals interdependencies in women's collective identity formation, organizational and discursive resources, and accumulation of power resources.

Power resource theorizing has not provided space for the role of women's agency in the development of citizenship rights, since it is built around working-class mobilization. Walter Korpi has argued that the power of workers resides in the "politics of numbers and voting strength," and the contests between capital and labor are seen in terms of workers' ability to use political resources through political representation to modify market processes. His current research introduces gender as a category in the analysis of the development of social citizenship. Women appear within organizations for collective action with rights but without power resources. Though his approach differs from Korpi's, Gösta Esping-Andersen also discusses women in policy regimes through analyses of postindustrial economic transformation and its effects on women's employment in public sector work.[5]

Power resource theory and policy regime studies have made crucial theoretical contributions to the study of welfare states by bringing in social actors and institutions. However, social actors who lack access to, or have weak positions within, unions or political parties are not given agency in the making of welfare states. The loose organizational framework in most women's movements and their lack of formalized institutional bases of power require a more process-oriented model of women's collectivities and their articulations of power.[6]

In contrast, the power resource model assumes a social actor who already has accumulated power resources. The essential argument of this chapter is that the process of identity formation itself is crucial for understanding the ability of collectivities to articulate claims and exercise power in welfare states. The purpose of this study is to develop strategies for analyzing women's collective agency and their articulations of power. This involves bridging different theoretical terrains: first, to connect feminist research on citizenship to power resource theory; and, second, to introduce new social movement perspectives on identity formation into power resource theorizing. Though I focus on women's collectivities and claim making, my analytical model (see figure 7.1) illustrates the interdependencies in composing constituencies, deployment of power resources, and extending social citizenship.

This chapter applies this model to a specific case of women's mobilization, Swedish women's mobilization during the 1930s, which is compared to the current wave of women's political activism in the 1990s. This comparison of two periods of feminist activism illustrates path dependencies in how social groups frame citizenship rights and shows that their discursive and organizational resources are embedded in a political culture that reflects the evolution of institutional features of welfare states. The 1930s and the 1990s are inter-

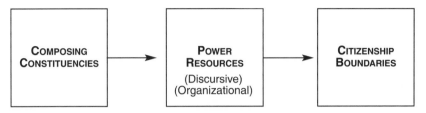

Fig. 7.1. Collective Identity Formation and Power Resources

esting because they are periods of welfare state formation and restructuring, when social and political citizenship is being recast or reconfigured. Sweden is an interesting case from which to analyze women's collective identity formation. It is a society in which inequalities are framed in terms of class, and it is a welfare state in which gender issues have been visible on the policy agenda..

Sweden is also a case in which women's collectivities framed their citizenship rights in terms of participatory rights at a time when much of the first-wave feminist mobilization posited an essentialist women's identity based upon women's experiences as mothers. Also, in Sweden, women's movement and collective identity formation occurred after suffrage. The postsuffrage era everywhere revealed, contrary to the beliefs of suffrage leaders, that women did not vote as a bloc and many did not vote at all; this was true of Swedish women in the 1920s.[7] Because I was looking for a case in Western industrialized societies that could reveal the process of framing citizenship and forging political identities, I chose Sweden, where women's organizations and mobilization were greater in the 1930s than in the presuffrage period.

My analysis fits neither policy regime theories nor feminist interpretations of the gendered dimensions in Swedish welfare state formation. In the former, women's interests are subsumed under class interests or represented in the concept of the family's role in welfare provisioning.[8] The feminist account maintains that women were objects but not subjects of policymaking, that Sweden is a case of feminism without feminists.[9] Another variant of this position among Swedish feminists, the patriarchal explanation, argues that male norms dominate the power structures so that women, even when integrated in the Swedish political sphere, have been ghettoized into female sectors of policymaking.[10]

Before turning to my case study, I want to clarify some of the terms and assumptions in the model. To describe the process of forming collective identities, I have coined the term "composing of constituencies," which is suggestive of a process-oriented approach.[11] "To compose" literally means to come together in a place, and in applying it to movements to extend citizenship rights, I sought to encompass two facets of mobilizing constituencies: (1) the process of creating shared meanings and consciousness among diverse individuals within a social category—in this case, diverse groups of women (collective identity formation); (2) the representation of constituencies' goals and grievances in public arenas (collective agency). Here I am using "constituencies" broadly as the representation of social groups in discursive arenas and politics within and across parties.

Introducing the composing of constituencies into the conceptual framework offers an antidote to a priori categories, such as women or workers. It undercuts the notion that women's power resources are directly correlated with women's right to vote, a notion that is a given in comparative analysis of welfare states for analyzing policy formation around gender issues and/or family issues.[12] My position reflects a current strand in feminist political theory that assumes that no fixed interests of women can be known outside of politics.[13]

Women's power resources are derived from women being recognized as a constituency whose leaders can represent women's interests in the discursive arena of politics as well as threaten to reward friends and punish enemies with women's votes. The deployment of power resources comprises two fields: (1) the representation of women's claims in discursive arenas and (2) the building of cross-class and cross-party alliances that enable women's collectivities to speak for a majority constituency—women's interests. To accumulate power resources, women's collectivities have to be able to represent themselves as a constituency with unity willing to act in concert. To be recognized as such by political elites is crucial for their ability to exercise power.[14]

The standard paths and organizational channels have directly or indirectly excluded women. Even when unions and political parties, the traditional organizational forms of mobilization and power resource investments, did not deny women membership (as was true in much of the British and American craft labor union movement), they marginalized women's role in these organizations.[15] Thus women's collectivities have developed their own discursive and organizational resources. By introducing the concept of discursive resources into the model, I underscore the fact that social groups engage in struggles over the meanings and the boundaries of political and social citizenship. This includes the cultural narratives and metaphors that social actors exploit in their public representations as well as the contesting ideological stances that they take on dominant themes and issues on the political agenda. Because women's collectivities can comprise members from political and social groups that are often seen as having opposing class interests—for example, women in business and professional associations and women members of industrial unions— organizational links and coalition building are essential components of the power resources of women's collectivities.

The model does not assume that composing constituencies inevitably leads to the power to define or extend citizenship rights. Rather, I argue that it is the recognition of a constituency with power resources (discursive and organizational resources) that has the potential to produce new policies and citizenship rights.

Implicit in this analysis is an assumption that institutional contexts are not stable configurations in which gender is encoded, the point of departure in policy regime theorizing. Rather, they are dynamic systems in which historical contingency, social actors, and new discursive fields destabilize and reconfigure institutional arrangements. Within my framework, political opportunities appear as recursive. I suggest that political configurations not only influence the capacity of groups to mobilize and the likelihood of failure or success in shaping social policy but also that mobilized groups can create political opportunities through discursive resources and patterns of mobilization.

Finally, my research contests feminist analyses of welfare states that assume that women are inherently politically weak actors in a closed patriarchal system.[16] Moreover, I implicitly argue against a view of women's agency that is embedded in recent historical studies of the American welfare state, namely, that women's ability to make claims on the state emerged when institutional structures were weak.[17]

Composing Constituencies

Finding a shared set of values and meanings to bind together groups with divergent class backgrounds and political party affiliations has been a challenge for feminist movements in making and remaking women's collective identities that vary in time and space. If one rejects the idea of primordial identities and assumes that individuals have multiple identities and loyalties, then the question of how the individual belief system is conjoined to the larger goals of collectivity is a key component in composing constituencies. (See figure 7.2.)

I argue that the cultural framing of social movements is a prefigurative stage of collective agency. The cultural framing of a movement is the basis for forming group loyalties. Analyzing the frames of feminist movements enables us to avoid dichotomizing them into oppositional cultures of difference and equality.[18] This dichotomy does not allow for contextual variations in the formation of collective identities. Nor does it permit an analysis of the process by which feminist movements forged a common vision and created shared meanings. There are many frames in the history of women's movements. In the nineteenth century, for example, the notion of the equality of souls was a frame embodied in religious women's movements that viewed women's oppression

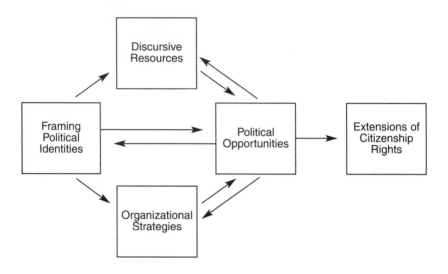

Fig. 7.2. Interdependencies in Composing Constituencies, Political Opportunities, and Citizenship Rights

as a construction of man-made laws and conventions.[19] As was true of many movements in the 1960s and 1970s, second-wave feminism mobilized around the paradigmatic frame, the frame of injustice.[20]

Scholars of women's movements in the first decades of the twentieth century adopted the term "maternalist" to express women's activism that sprang from a recognition of women's interests as mothers. Maternalism is used in many different senses, as an ideology, a women's movement, and as a type of welfare state.[21] These different formulations share at least two common assumptions: (1) that women's identity revolved around care for children and that the vast majority of women believed that this was their contribution to society and that it was valued; (2) that because of their unique capacity for care, women were responsible for all families in their roles as social mothers.[22]

To characterize feminist activism as maternalist in this period distorts the varied politics, identities, and goals of women's movements.[23] Furthermore, maternalism did not capture the varied landscapes in which feminists articulated their versions of women's multiple identities as mothers, citizens, and workers. Citizenship and participatory democracy formed the framework of feminist movements in Sweden and other Scandinavian countries.[24]

At the heart of the participatory citizenship frame is a belief that women have been denied participatory rights in democratic societies. Thus feminist organizations argued that women could not fulfill their roles as citizens because they lacked a political voice or representation in political, legal, and economic institutions. In the words of one Swedish feminist who insisted that women had worked hard for the party in the name of Social Democracy and now demanded democracy: "We believe it is both unjust and poor tactics to treat women as political zeros."[25]

Issues involving motherhood were part of feminist claim making, women's groups put forward demands for maternal health care, paid vacations for mothers, and public-supported child care. But the basis for women's activism was bound, not by a maternalist worldview that women had unique political identities based upon their motherly roles, but rather by a perception that women were a constituency with varied social roles as democratic citizens, workers, and mothers. The Swedish case reveals how participatory citizenship as a citizenship frame laid the foundation for composing a women's constituency in the twentieth century after the realization of suffrage.

Historical Background

Prior to the 1930s, Swedish women had neither the grassroots organizations nor the influence on public policy that Anglo-American feminists had achieved. The coalition of Swedish women's groups united around suffrage did not result in the kind of extensive local and national networks of feminist participation existing in America or Britain. Nor did Swedish political parties appear to perceive women as a collectivity with a political identity or as potential voting bloc, which was more the case in the United States in the era before and after suffrage.[26]

Like so many European feminist movements during the first decades of the twentieth century, Swedish women's groups were divided by class, political loyalties, and ideological disagreements around protection and rights.[27] Suffrage was a magnet that drew disparate groups together around a single-issue campaign, and their differences were reactivated and intensified after the enactment of suffrage. Among Swedish women's organizations, the fractures around ideological positions cut deeper because of long-standing class antagonisms. Bourgeois women feared talk of revolution and class conflict, while working-class women distrusted middle-class organizations. For instance, when the Swedish National Association of Housewives (Husmödersförbundet) was founded in 1919, members of the Social Democratic Women's Union asked, "Does this mean they have become the voice for all women? We have to watch their activities very carefully."[28] Numerous articles in the Social Democratic women's journal, *Morgonbris* (Morning breeze), reflect socialist women's animosity toward bourgeois pretensions. One such article rallied working-class women's support by criticizing the vapidity of other women's organizations: "Dear friends, let us not become so animated, cultural, intellectual, or elevated that our mouths only drip with beautiful but empty phrases instead of simple and natural expressions of a true-hearted commitment to a common purpose and solidarity."[29]

However, by the mid-1930s, numerous opportunities for cooperation had reduced class tensions among women's groups. Middle-class women, in an effort to demonstrate their allegiance to egalitarianism and democracy, recruited working-class women to their organizations.[30] Working-class women became engaged in gender equality issues and no longer viewed the women's movement as a purely bourgeois phenomenon.[31] The decade of the 1930s was a turning point; Swedish women's groups proliferated and moved from political marginality to influence.

Participatory Citizenship and the Active Citizen

Swedish feminists in the 1930s viewed participation as both the means and the end for women's empowerment. Feminists seeking to mobilize women faced a situation in which a significant proportion of women did not even exercise their right to vote. Thus the main task was to make women aware of their citizenship rights and duties. An important strategy in this mobilization was the creation of an informed woman citizen who understood the policy debates and could influence the policy arena. Women's journals provided extensive coverage of political debates, and parliamentary proceedings were published verbatim in several women's journals to keep readers informed.

In 1936, twenty-five women's organizations, ranging from the Organization of Female Postal Workers to the Organization of Swedish Christian Young Women, signed a public letter, "A Call to Swedish Women," asking women to work.[32] Published in both women's trade union journals and bourgeois women's journals, it also urged women to contribute to the advancement of women by joining a party—any political party—and actively campaigning for female politicians. The letter laid the basis for the Swedish Women's Citizen's Union, whose goals were to "Make Sweden's women worthy citizens of society; Push for equality between men and women, socially and economically; Protect the new rights that women have won; Strengthen solidarity among women."[33]

A maternalist tradition existed in Swedish feminism. Its main proponent was an international figure, Ellen Key, who claimed that a woman's power derived from her maternal role and female consciousness. However, this essentialist stance lost ground in Sweden in the 1930s. Key had more influence abroad in the postsuffrage era.[34]

Given that working-class women and Swedish Social Democrats were the key actors in the Swedish women's mobilization in this period, it is not surprising that they did not frame women's political identities around women's role as mother and caregiver. They wanted to affirm the roles of women as workers, mothers, and citizens. The majority of Social Democratic women in the 1930s not only recognized that many women had to work for economic survival, but also they viewed work as a basic citizenship right in a political configuration where citizen and worker were bound together.

The Worker-Citizen

In the 1930s married women's right to work was threatened in many countries.[35] In Sweden, the number of unemployed rose more than fivefold between 1931 and 1932, reaching its maximum in 1933, when over 186,000 Swedes were registered as unemployed.[36] The reaction against married women's employment was so strong that every party from left to right demanded restrictions, and at least nine motions were presented in the Swedish parliament proposing limitations on married women's employment. Some politicians hoped to legislate restrictions that permitted only one spouse to hold public sector employment; they claimed that working married women not only robbed men of jobs but also created unfair competition by accepting low wages.[37] The conservative opposition also incorporated national fertility goals into their argument, blaming women's work outside the home for Sweden's negative population growth.

Some Swedish women had a practical stake in maintaining the right to employment (in the 1930s, 10 percent of employed women were married), yet many more realized the symbolic significance of defending a basic citizenship right. Swedish women's organizations during this period not only prevented the assault on married women's right to work but also in fact achieved the passage of legislation that increased women's rights as workers in a depression decade when women throughout Europe and North America were losing the right to work. A law passed in 1938 prohibited the firing of women who were married, pregnant, or single mothers. The whole spectrum of women's organizations, including the National Housewives Association, defended women's right to work on the basis that it was a citizenship right. Although the association's preference was for mothers to be at home, its spokespersons even came out against a proposal to offer married women early retirement with some severance pay.[38]

The frame of participatory citizenship allowed Swedish feminist groups to mobilize against the threat to women's right to work without pitting housewife and mother against working mother. In Sweden, the right to work was a core citizenship right in Social Democracy. To deny women that right represented a threat to their claims for recognition as citizens.

Clearly, grievance or threat can be a catalyst in mobilizing groups as well as the perception of opportunity; this is the essence of Tilly's classic formulation.[39] But if specific grievances are not linked to the framing of mobilized constituencies' political identities, they may not be able to activate supporters and may even fracture a social movement.

To demonstrate this point, we might turn to the failure of the American feminist campaign against restrictions on married women's work enacted during the depression era. In the 1930s, national and local laws were passed barring married women from working in public sector jobs.[40] Women's groups were unified in their opposition, but earlier ideological disagreements impeded mobilization and the efficacy of the campaign. Throughout the 1920s, American feminists, operating within a maternalist frame, sought to improve women's position through special legislation for mothers: widows' pensions, maternal health, protection for mothers at workplaces, and restrictions on hours and types of work.[41] In the depression era, it was hard to recast women's interests in terms of the right to work.

Not to be underestimated are the cleavages created by competing mobilizing frames that expressed different political identities in American feminist movements. When the American Women's Party introduced the Equal Rights Amendment (ERA) in the 1920s as the main strategy for altering inequality between men and women, the American women's movement became divided into factions of mainly middle-class feminists. On one side were those who believed that the ERA threatened the programs targeted to mothers, specifically for working-class mothers, such as protective labor legislation. On the other side were those who saw these gender-differentiated laws and programs as barriers to women's equal participation in labor market work.[42]

Women's movements that appear divisive and fractured forfeit a crucial resource, their collective agency and discursive power, the ability of leaders and spokespersons to claim that they speak for a women's constituency. Thus, as shown in figure 7.2, women's collective agency, which is a reflection of the failure or success of social groups to compose a broad-based constituency, shapes both the discursive resources available to collectivities and their organizational potential. As the American example suggests, the framing of political identities is path dependent; that is, it can leave its imprint on the future articulation of claims and grievances.

Discursive Resources

Lacking durable institutional bases or reservoirs of power resources, women's activism has been highly dependent on discursive resources for actualizing policy goals.[43] By discursive resources, I mean not merely political discourse but a broad discursive terrain that includes cultural narratives and metaphors that social actors exploit in their public representations as well as the contesting ideological stances that they take on themes and issues on the political agenda.

Swedish feminist groups linked their frame of participatory citizenship to the Swedish *Folkhem* (people's home), a cultural narrative that emerged as the dominant idiom in social democracy.[44] The Swedish Folkhem is a narrative that reverberates in Swedish society and has accrued symbolic value over the years. First used in public Swedish debate by the right-wing politician, Rudolph Kjell, the Folkhem metaphor was co-opted by Social Democrats as part of a strategy to rebuild and extend their political base of support.[45] In 1928, Social Democrats suffered a serious defeat, referred to by the Conservatives as the "cossack election." This defeat convinced the party to abandon strict socialist rhetoric.

The Folkhem was a metaphor that embraced both past and present images and harkened back to the romantic idea of the traditional Byalag, a community collective found in preindustrial Swedish society where village custom held that men and women of the community were duty-bound to help one another, regardless of material background.[46] The Folkhem also personified a caring state that would reproduce a sense of community, a world that was disappearing with the decline of agriculture. It would offer protection against all that was foreign and changing in Swedish society at a time of rapid industrialization.[47] Per Albin Hansson's oft-repeated homily is replete with these images: "The basis of the good home is community and solidarity. In the good home there are no privileged or deprived members, no pets and no step-children. In the good home there is equality, solicitude, cooperation and helpfulness."[48] During the 1930s, Social Democrats advocated an expansive program of social reform under the banner of a Folkhem.

Feminists recognized the symbolic value of the Folkhem for advancing their own political goals, and it provided them with the discursive space to articulate their demands for more influence in shaping the nascent Swedish welfare state. The metaphor of the people's home appears over and over again in articles in the women's publications. A typical example from the Social Democratic women's journal, *Morgonbris*, explicitly links the image of the home with women's participatory roles: "Now there is hardly anyone who will publicly oppose us in what has been the central goal in our agitation, that it is necessary and desirable from democracy's and society's own welfare interest to provide a larger arena for women's contributions in the co-operative project of building a sunny, healthy, safe, and pleasant home for all."[49] One finds examples with more strident tones: "We women do not wish to be invited into the Folkhem once it is finished and ready. We will only be satisfied if we are welcome to help lay the groundwork and build it."[50]

Certainly, the idea of the people's home is a Janus-faced metaphor that could also be used to circumscribe women's influence within the domestic sphere.[51] On the other hand, that the central metaphor for Social Democracy was a home evidently provided discursive resources for women to make claims in the political arena around issues involving care, child rearing, and unpaid domestic work. The domain of home and family and women's concerns, defined in liberal notions of citizenship as outside public or political institutions, emerged in the Swedish welfare state as the foundation and rationale for political legitimacy.

The Citizen-Worker-Mother

Gamson and Modigliani maintain that at any particular moment in a given society, one political theme will emerge and contesting groups will encase it in different ideological packages.[52] The population crisis that dominated Swedish public debates for nearly a decade exemplifies this kind of discursive resource. In 1934, Alva Myrdal and Gunnar Myrdal's *Kris i Befolkningsfrågan* warned that Swedes were not reproducing themselves and asserted that population growth could be achieved through social reforms and the redistribution of resources.[53] The popularity and incredible political influence of their book have to be understood in terms of its fit into other ideological packages. Per Albin Hansson was among the first to embrace the Myrdals' agenda, perhaps because, as Gunnar Myrdal claimed, "The detailed welfare program that we put forward lay so completely in line with Per Albin's dream of the good people's home."[54]

Many Social Democrats, including the Myrdals, exploited the fear of population decline to institute social reforms. Despite their suspicion, the majority of women activists came to realize its potential to push through reforms that they had been advocating for years. Issues that had previously been relegated to women's organizations and congresses, such as parental leave benefits, child care, better housing, and married women's right to work, became a part of mainstream political discourse.

Feminists were able to repackage the population crisis and fit it to their own agenda of participatory rights, the right to employment, and motherhood. Alva Myrdal herself was aware that concerns over high unemployment in the depression era and fears about low birthrates created a dangerous political constellation. Yet the Myrdals asserted that women were the victors in the ideological battles over population:

The remarkable thing is that in this crucial moment the population argument was wrenched out of the hands of the antifeminists and instead used as a new formidable weapon for emancipation ideals. The old debate on married woman's right to work was turned into a fight for the working women's right to marry and have children. The change in public opinion was tremendous.[55]

Feminists in other Western welfare states, such as France and Germany, sought to repackage the population question to fit their own agenda,[56] but they faced formidable opposition and counterdiscourses. Swedish feminists reclaimed the population issue and used it as a discursive resource to extend claim making for social citizenship. They situated themselves in a discursive landscape that enabled them to fuse population issues with citizenship rights (the right of working women to be mothers). Moreover, they interwove with the modern-day politics of the Folkhem images of the lost agrarian society where work, leisure, and family were more integrated; the challenge was to solve the dilemma of how women could combine paid work with having a family.[57] The policy that emanated from the population debates never realized the full implications of this dilemma; however, it laid the foundation for a set of "women-friendly" policy initiatives that emerged in the 1970s that gave working parents the most generous parental leave benefits in the world.[58]

For women's collectivities that lack institutional bases, discursive resources are crucial forms of power resources. They enable leaders to represent the visions and claims of their constituencies. In the case of Swedish feminists, the Folkhem opened up political space for recasting vocabularies of citizenship, and the population crisis became a means of articulating claims for social rights. Discursive resources are crucial power resources for women's collectivities because they gain recognition for a group's power to mobilize its constituency and thus make it a force to be reckoned with politically. Finally, discursive resources provide public arenas for mobilizing and recruiting new members to organizations, as well as for winning public support.

Organizational Alliances

Women's movements have tended to inhabit a region between the free spaces of autonomous networks and permanent mobilizing structures. In practice, feminist movements often have pursued organizational structures that transcend class and party lines, either in autonomous organizations or in coalitions that cut across party politics. Suffrage is the classic example of the former; and examples abound of coalitions of women's groups that extended the boundaries of welfare state policymaking into areas of maternal health and child and family benefits. Although women rarely have invested their power resources in political parties, they have sustained long-standing organizations, some that have been linked to political parties and others that have remained independent.

Attempts to organize women's parties or put forward women's lists have often proved disastrous for women's collectivities. This was true in the 1927 election in Stockholm where women received less than 0.5 percent of the vote.[59] These kinds of efforts actually can undercut women's power resources, something that was understood by the Swedish feminists in the 1990s who used the mere threat of forming a women's party as a means of strengthening their political leverage.[60]

Women's groups have characterized their social activism as apolitical (outside party politics)—what Paula Baker has described as domesticated politics—because of their moral stance and their view of politics as corrupt, as well as their exclusion from an arena dominated by men.[61] But this is truer of Anglo-American than of Swedish feminists. Many of the most active Swedish groups in the 1930s were women's federations connected to the Social Democratic or Liberal Parties.

Throughout the 1930s, feminist groups charted a dual strategy: (1) using their influence as party members and (2) forming cross-party alliances in which they represented women's issues and interests in public debate and policymaking channels. As a form of power resource deployment, this dual strategy had several advantages for Swedish feminists. Cross-party alliances enabled them to represent, and act in behalf of, a "women's constituency." Party membership allowed them to be power brokers in their parties. Ulla Lindström, for instance, claimed that she and other women in the Social Democratic Party were able to push feminist concerns: "Our people were in government and thus it was natural that we frequently promoted these issues in channels we held outside the organization."[62]

The dramatic growth of women's organizations in the 1930s is an important factor in assessing women's power resources. Sweden's Social Democratic Women's Union increased its membership fourfold over the decade, growing to more than twenty-six thousand members. In 1937 the Fredrika Bremer Society, a feminist organization, had thirty-seven local chapters with over six thousand members, and the Swedish Women's Business Organization boasted four thousand members at the end of the 1930s.[63] This is remarkable when one considers that these figures show that almost twice as many women were organized as in the suffrage campaign.[64]

Beyond the actual numbers within organizations, there was networking and dialogue among feminists in different organizations that represented women with varied social backgrounds, political orientations, and reform agendas. These groups did not represent themselves as a formal women's coalition or as a modern-day women's caucus. However, they did have a core set of issues that they mutually supported and lobbied for that reflected a broad constituency: vacations for housewives, sex education, and legalization of contraceptive technologies and information.[65] They were influential in gaining support for improved housing, increased support for single mothers, the right to work for all women, and greater political representation for women. Among the issues espoused by women's groups in this period, women's increased political representation had the broadest appeal.

When Swedish feminists began to devise a set of core issues fitted into an inclusive frame of citizenship, they had to take into account diverse backgrounds and different political orientations of established women's groups. In this instance, we might conduct a thought experiment and imagine what would have happened if a policy on mothers' pensions, such as the one sponsored by feminists in the United States, had been proposed by a group of feminists in Sweden.[66] It is important to keep in mind that the U.S. plan applied in most states only to worthy widows; in some cases divorced and abandoned wives were able to receive benefits, but never-married mothers were excluded.[67] Such a policy would have destroyed the alliance among Swedish feminist groups, since Social Democratic women could never have supported a policy that left out unwed mothers, whom they viewed as a group that had been unjustly treated and stigmatized.[68] The first income-maintenance legislation passed in Sweden in the 1930s gave the same entitlements and social rights to divorced, abandoned, and never-married women with children.

When considering women's collectivities, we have to construct criteria for the deployment of power resources different from those shaped by the dominant paradigm of class mobilization. Women are not viewed as bloc voters. Women's mobilization more often than not cuts across party lines. Only in our own day, with the coining of the term "gender gap," have political analysts made women as a voting constituency visible. However, as my case illustrates, women's power resources are increased through their ability to compose broad-based constituencies, deploy discursive resources, and develop organizational coalitions. From this perspective the politics of numbers applies when women appear as a recognized constituency with the potential to mobilize against parties that do not support their agenda and policy initiatives. This was particularly important during the 1930s in Sweden when political parties did not have huge majorities and the long tenure of the Social Democratic Party was not assured.

Political Opportunities and the Extension
of Citizenship Boundaries

Sidney Tarrow astutely concludes that there is a nonlinear relationship between social movement organization and state responsiveness.[69] Numerous historical studies of feminist movements offer evidence for this; mobilization can be paralyzed by the lack of allies in the legislative arena or defeated by competing discursive resources of oppositional groups. Also well documented are cases of highly mobilized feminist movements that capture the discursive arena but lack the policy channels to ensure implementation of their programs, resulting in laws without teeth or implementation of laws through agencies that alter the meaning and intent of policies that sprang from movements with transformative goals. Here political opportunity comes into play—particular historical conjunctures, changing political agendas, and fluid political fields and allies.

What was the political context in which women's politics emerged? First, it is important to keep in mind that the lengthy political dominance of the Swedish Social Democratic Party often belies the fact that the route toward Social Democratic ascendancy was not always direct and that party leaders continually redrafted the blueprints of the Social Democratic model.[70] Second, the well-known Saltsjöbaden agreement that created a corporatist power structure with business, unions, and government was not signed until 1938. Historical analyses of the impact of this agreement on other social movements conclude that the centralized wage-bargaining system that institutionalized and strengthened solidarity in both business and labor gave little latitude for the recognition of social groups and their interests.[71]

Throughout the 1920s, class issues and heightened class tensions dominated the political arena. Nevertheless, during this period, Swedish Social Democrats ascribed to a mass-membership formula that recognized the numerical importance of women. That the Social Democrats wanted individual women to vote for them and join the party, however, did not mean that women's issues were part of their political platform.[72]

But by the end of the 1930s, there was a noticeable shift in the perception of women as a mobilized constituency. The most powerful in the Social Democratic Party acknowledged that women were a constituency with specific issues and the power to make claims on the basis of women's interests. In 1936, Prime Minister Per Albin Hansson reflected this in his speech on the Social Democratic political platform for the upcoming year: "I suspect women will notice with great satisfaction the way in which women's issues have received attention. Essentially all our issues are your issues."[73]

These were merely hollow political phrases, but they reflected the centrality of women's issues in the main policymaking forum in the 1930s, the Royal Committee on Population, appointed in 1935, in which national debates concerning welfare reform were orchestrated. The Population Committee debated issues such as prenatal care, maternity benefits, child care, health insurance, family taxation, housing, and married women's right to work.[74] These were issues that women's organizations had been discussing in their own circles. Now suddenly they became the focus of national politics. Thus, one feminist could write in 1938, "If one reads the protocol from the first meetings of the Women's Trade Union or Social Democratic Women's Club in 1907, it's almost like reading today's Population Committee Report."[75]

The legitimacy and public visibility that feminists acquire in a parliamentary commission should not be underestimated.[76] Two feminists were selected to lead a two-year commission (1936–1938) on married women's right to work, a subcommittee within the Royal Population Commission. The chair, Kerstin Hesselgren, and the secretary, Alva Myrdal, were central figures in the feminist movement of the 1930s. The committee produced a five-hundred-page report with masses of statistics that drove home the extent of gender inequality in the labor market.[77] But more to the point, the report laid out some of the basic contours of women's social citizenship, the right to participate in work and family life. That two feminists were on this commission was not a coincidence. The very fact that such a commission was inaugurated reflects the power resources of feminist groups.

One could say that Hesselgren and Myrdal were the prototypes of the so-called femocrats, a term coined in our own day and applied to women with feminist orientations who have chosen to enter public life and work within the system to promote women's interests.[78] Whether femocrats are able to promote feminist goals within a policy constellation is dependent upon the power resources accumulated in women's movements—more concretely, the political capital that has accrued from composing a constituency that represents women's interests across a wide spectrum of class and party alliances.

Swedish women's organizations were successful in pushing through policies that became the core of women's social citizenship in the Swedish welfare state: maternity leave and job security, protection of married women's right to work, income-maintenance for single mothers, and universal maternal health care. A mother's benefit based on needs was also enacted, but it included the vast majority of mothers.[79]

During this nascent period of welfare state formation, Swedish women were recognized as a constituency, and feminist spokespersons were making claims on behalf of women. The inclusive frame of citizenship as participatory rights enabled feminists to reach a broad constituency, to use strategically discursive resources, and to open up political opportunities. Through their collective agency, women extended the boundaries of the Swedish welfare state into domains that enhanced women's social citizenship as workers, as family members, as single mothers. What Swedish feminists did not achieve in the 1930s was redistribution of power and decision making within institutions. In the following decades, women's claim making could find little institutional or discursive space in the corporatist system composed of labor, employers, and the state that came out of the historic Saltsjöbaden agreement of 1938.

Path Dependencies in Women's Mobilization

Path dependencies in the mobilization of social groups can be seen in repertoires for social action, forms of claim making, and discursive strategies. They reflect the importance of political learning and collective memory. They also reveal policy legacies and the evolution of institutional features of welfare states, which were shaped by the successes and failures of social groups and, in this case, their interpretations of gendered interests. The Swedish feminist mobilization of the 1990s illustrates this process.

In the 1990s there has been a resurgence of feminist activism in Sweden that has posed more thoroughgoing challenges to the gendered distribution of power in different spheres—state, market, and family—than the second-wave feminism of the 1970s in Sweden. In the 1970s, women mobilized, but the movement did not make the kinds of direct challenges to male privilege and power that characterized much of second-wave feminism in many Western societies. The concept of sexual equality that emerged in this period reflects this. *Jämställdhet,* which translates as "gender equality" or "equal status," was a vision that embraced ideal relations between women and men in society.[80] Gender equality meant the participation of men and women in the family, paid work, and politics. Throughout the 1970s and 1980s, a range of family and parental benefits and sexual antidiscrimination laws was initiated, and an equal opportunity ombudsman was created. One policy, established in 1974, that was considered very important for gender equality was individual taxation, since it laid the foundation for the dual-earner family, the participation of women in paid work, and the demise of the male-breadwinner family.[81] However, none of these reforms directly addressed the redistribution of power and decision making in economic or political institutions.[82]

The catalyst for Swedish feminist mobilization in the 1990s was a dramatic drop in the proportion of women in parliament, which fell from 38 percent to 33 percent in the 1991 election, when a Conservative Party coalition took power. But there were other issues on the agenda in the 1990s: economic decline, a surge in unemployment, and the question of membership in the European Union (EU), all of which brought to the forefront deep divisions over the meaning of citizenship with regard to democratic participation, accountability, social rights, the environment, and gender equality.

There are many parallels between women's mobilization in the 1990s and the 1930s. Participatory citizenship was the frame of women's collective action. However, it has taken on new meanings in a period of welfare state restructuring and in the wake of Sweden's membership in the European Union.

Whereas in the 1930s, women faced the possible denial of the civil right to work through laws that would have affected married women, in the 1990s, women are confronted with a threat to their social right to work. Downsizing of the public sector has meant a decline in women's employment, the spread of temporary employment, and reductions in social services, such as day care and care for the elderly.[83] These social services have enabled women to combine employment and family responsibilities, which is reflected in the fact that women have nearly the same levels of labor force participation as men. The composing of a women's constituency in the 1990s was orchestrated around women's multiple identities as democratic citizen, worker, and mother.

The European Union has been a powerful forum for mobilizing Swedish women's collectivities. Women were key actors in public debate in the referendum held in 1994; opinion polls underscored women's opposition, which cut across parties, regions, and ages. The gender gap was pronounced in the election: 52 percent of women voted against joining the EU; 40 percent of men were opposed.[84] A significant proportion of Swedes view the EU as a threat to democracy, as political and economic decisions are removed from citizen oversight and influence[85] Swedish feminists have highlighted the low proportion of women representatives in policymaking bodies and the total absence of women judges on the European Court, which is not accountable to any elected body.[86] In her first days, Swedish European Commissioner Anita Gradin, one of the few women in the EU hierarchy, "expressed dismay at the overwhelming number of 'gray-suited men' in the upper echelons of the European Commission."[87]

In public debate and the media, feminists contrasted the Swedish woman's identity as a working mother who earns her own income with that of the German wife who is dependent on her husband's earnings or benefits. For Swedish women, the convergence in social policy could threaten the level of benefits and services, since EU directives and European Court decisions offer proposed minimum standards of protection. The European Court cases and directives may appear progressive and forward looking to European women in societies where there are minimal or no parental leave benefits, public services, or protections in the labor market. Convergence could also impose alternative models of family and gender relations, based upon a male-bread-winner wage.[88] Since the 1970s, the construction of gender equality in Sweden has been coupled with participation in paid work.

As in the 1930s, the 1990s has spurred a flowering of grassroots organizations on both local and regional levels that have embraced a range of issues—health, education, bodily integrity, participation, and representation—that appeal to a broad spectrum of women.[89] The composing of a women's constituency took the form of loosely coordinated organizations that were represented in the public arena as a network that called itself the Support Stockings, a multilayered symbol. It expressed the strategy of the group to support women in politics, political parties, and policymaking roles. It brought together images of the bluestockings, the upper-class feminists of the late nineteenth century, and the 1970s leftist "red stockings," the feminist label of that era.[90]

In the 1994 election the leaders of the Support Stockings network were a dominant voice in the public debate. For the first time since the 1927 election when a group of women ran on a separate list in Stockholm, feminist groups in the 1990s raised the specter of a women's party. However, they considered it as a last resort on both strategic and ideological grounds. One leader of the movement has claimed that women in the network rejected the idea of a women's party for ideological reasons since they argued that parties ought to be parties for men and women.[91] For strategic reasons, the network never revealed its actual numbers; this secrecy actually increased its power resources. When one opinion poll found that over 40 percent of the voters said that they would consider voting for a women's list, a small network speaking for scattered grassroots activists and local organizations appeared to be an orchestrated women's campaign, recognized as a constituency with power.

For the first time since the 1930s there was a public affirmation of women's gendered interests across parties; a separate network of women parliamentarians agreed to work together for women's interests.[92] In the 1990s the coalition was broader than in the 1930s, since women from the Conservative Party were part of the network.

There are clear path dependencies in the discursive resources available to feminists in the two eras. Though the Folkhem is no longer an idiom called forth in Swedish political debate, the image of the active democratic citizen and the cultural narrative of people's movements remain in Swedish culture and political discourse. Feminists in the 1990s tapped into this imagery both in their anti-EU rhetoric and in their claims for more representation in politics. The slogans in the 1990s use more assertive terms than in the 1930s, and the links between participation and power are more clearly articulated. Feminist groups in the 1990s used the slogan of "Every Other Seat," a demand that emerged from a rejected proposal by feminists on the Commission on Power

and Democracy in the late 1980s for quotas to ensure women's equal representation. Another slogan, "Half the Power, All the Pay," although it expressed a
more radical politics, was reminiscent of the 1930s "Call to Swedish Women"
to push for equality between men and women, socially and economically.
Instead of the circular letter signed by women's organizations in the 1930s,
Swedish women's groups in the 1990s organized a public tribunal that charged
the state with neglect of women's issues, such as violence against women,
health research, care for the elderly, and child care.

Whereas in the 1930s, Swedish feminists faced a women's movement
divided by class and party loyalties, the barrier to mobilizing Swedish feminism in the 1990s was an oft-repeated refrain in public discussions of gender
equality: Swedish women were already emancipated, Sweden was the paradigm of the women-friendly society. Here discursive power was a crucial
resource for composing a women's constituency and representing women's
claims for participatory citizenship. In their public presentations, feminists
were able to link issues of representation and power to inequalities in the labor
market and the family. The latter, issues of power in the family, were not
broached by the earlier feminist movement. Emerging from this discourse on
power in different spheres of women's lives was a large-scale public government commission "om fördelning av ekonomisk makt och ekonomisk resurser
mellan kvinnor och män" (on the division of economic power and resources
between women and men) that produced twelve books on the unequal gendered distribution of resources in the workplace, the family, sex-segregated
markets, public sector organizations, and welfare state policymaking.[93]

As was true of the 1930s, political opportunities came into play in the 1990s
in electoral politics. But unlike the 1930s, the Social Democratic Party in the
early 1990s was not recruiting women voters; instead, it counted on the votes
of women, who have been a crucial and loyal group of voters for the party.[94]
Thus, after the party's loss in 1991, the mobilization of women as a constituency that threatened to form its own party was not taken lightly by party
regulars. Women's issues were brought onto the agenda, and, most important,
changes were made in candidate lists. In past elections women were put on
party lists as one of many interest groups and were given token seats. But in
the 1994 election the Social Democratic Party made the decision to alternate
women and men on all their lists. This meant equal representation. In the campaign, all parties promoted women candidates, and women not only won back
their lost seats but increased their representation to 41 percent. Half the ministers appointed to the cabinet by the Social Democratic government after this
election were women.

In some respects it was easier to compose a women's constituency in the
1990s because of the similarity in women's everyday lives and choices. Most

notable were the vast numbers of women in the labor market. Whereas in the 1930s only 10 percent of married women were in the labor market,[95] in the 1990s, 81 percent of women between twenty and sixty years old were employed; among married women, the figure is 87 percent. Though there are social differences among women around class, religion, ethnicity, and age, there are basic similarities in women's experiences. Most children go to day care, which is totally or partly publicly funded. Older people receive informal care from their municipalities. Most couples need two incomes to maintain a household, as a result of high taxes and the high cost of living. The high rate of divorce has meant that single mothers are dependent upon the state for support in the form of social transfers as well as services that allow women to combine work and family.[96] Thus, for Swedish women, participatory citizenship embraces the right to one's own income and the right to form an independent household.[97] The policies that support this aspect of women's citizenship have shaped a women's constituency that aligns itself with the social service state.[98] In effect, this process reflects a common assumption in welfare state research: that policy can make politics and can create new social actors and constituencies who are loyal to welfare state institutions.[99]

One significant difference between women in the 1930s and the 1990s is that the women's mobilization in the 1990s is occurring in a period of welfare state retrenchment, while the 1930s was a period of expansion.

Sweden's entry into the European Union also has broader implications for women's collective agency and their ability to articulate claims and exercise power. That policy is made across national borders raises several questions. How do mobilized constituencies use their power resources when the elected body, such as the European Parliament, has little or no power? What kinds of discursive resources can be deployed in supranational contexts? More to the point, mobilizing women across national borders not only poses enormous logistical problems but also raises the question of finding a common frame of citizenship that will resonate among women who have different histories and institutional contexts and dissimilar visions of what women's empowerment would mean.

Obviously, women's collective agency in the 1930s existed in a different historical context from the 1990s, with varied political constellations, family organization, gender relations, educational choices, and labor markets. It is not surprising that there are differences. What is striking are the linkages between the feminist mobilizations; the framing of citizenship rights and the articulation of claims and grievances; and the institutional orientation, parties, and politics. These path dependencies reflect the ways in which women's agency has shaped gendered forms of citizenship in welfare states.

Conclusion

In this study I sought to develop a framework for analyzing women's collective agency and the articulation of power in welfare states. The model presented reveals the interdependencies in women's collective identity formation, power resources, and extensions in citizenship rights. It introduces social movement perspectives into a power resource theory, through an analysis of the production of meanings as sources for mobilizing constituencies (in this case, the framing of citizenship). Discursive resources are shown to be sources for women's agency and articulation of power in welfare states. In both periods of feminist mobilization, the 1930s and the 1990s, I showed how women as social actors were able to use discursive resources and encode their programs into hegemonic cultural forms and ideologies—in effect, to manipulate and extend the meanings of existing vocabularies, such as the metaphor of the people's home and the worker-citizen in social democracy, through engendering frames of citizenship. To view the Swedish welfare state through this lens in early stages of policy formation in the 1930s is to gain some theoretical purchase on its distinctive features, referred to as women friendly policies.

To develop a theory on women's agency and power resources, more research is needed to track the ways in which patterns of political identity formation shape the strategies and opportunities of collectivities over time. In presenting women's mobilization in the 1990s, I have found some evidence of path dependencies in the formation of political identities, repertoires for social action, and forms of power articulation and claim making. These can be seen in the composing of constituencies around issues of policymaking roles, participation in local and national politics, and claims of citizenship with regard to rights to employment. Another distinctive feature of Swedish women's political identities found in both periods emerges in the organizational strategies and the orientation toward formal politics and policymaking bodies. This has been characterized as state feminism,[100] but I would like to suggest that Swedish feminist activism encompasses a broader approach to politics and participation that is rooted in democratic traditions of active citizenship. The main discursive idiom in Swedish women's movements continues to be participatory citizenship.

The framework presented of women's agency and power resources offers some analytical strategies for incorporating new social actors in the casting and recasting of citizenship rights. The keys that I have found—the links between the framing of movements and the power resources of women's collectivities—have implications for comparative research on welfare states, past and present.

More research and comparative cases are needed in order to construct theories of women's agency in periods of state transitions. Given the current period of welfare state retrenchment and restructuring and the rise of new democracies and societies in transition in East and Central Europe, there is a need to develop dynamic models that make visible new social movements and struggles for recognition. There is also a need for analyses of supranational policy-making arenas and their implications for women's mobilization and articulation of power.

Notes

This chapter is a revision and expansion of an earlier published article in collaboration with Marika Lindholm, "Collective Identities, Women's Power Resources, and the Making of Welfare States," *Theory and Society* 26 (1997): 475–508. It has benefited from discussions on both sides of the Atlantic. I am grateful to Shmuel Eisenstadt, Evelyn Huber, Walter Korpi, Diane Sainsbury, John Stephens, Charles Tilly, and Bjorn Wittrock for their comments. I also want to thank Michael Hanagan for his superb editorial work and Sheila Shaver for her comments on the final draft of this article.

1.   T. H. Marshall, *Citizenship and Social Class and Other Essays* (Cambridge: Cambridge University Press, 1950).

2.   Some feminists have turned to Hanna Arendt's vision of politics as dynamic open political spaces; see Joan B. Landes, "Novus Ordo Saeculorum: Gender and Public Space in Arendt's Revolutionary France," in *Feminist Interpretations of Hanna Arendt,* ed. Bonnie Honnig (University Park: Pennsylvania State University Press, 1995). For discussions of civic republicanism and feminism, see Ruth Lister, "Tracing the Contours of Women's Citizenship," *Policy and Politics* 2, no. 1 (1993): 2–16.

3.   Kathleen B. Jones, "Identity, Action, and Locale," *Social Politics: International Studies in Gender, State, and Society* 1, no. 3 (1994): 256–71; Birte Anne Phillips, *Engendering Democracy* (Cambridge: Basil Blackwell, 1991); Birte Siim, "Engendering Democracy: Social Citizenship, and Political Participation for Women in Scandinavia," *Social Politics* 1, no. 3 (1994): 286–305.

4.   J. M. Bystydzeinski, *Women Transforming Politics: Worldwide Strategies of Empowerment* (Bloomington: Indiana University Press, 1992). Nira Yuval Davis makes both these points in her discussion of ethnic identities and empowerment; see Nira Yuval Davis, "Women, Ethnicity, and Empowerment," in *Who's Afraid of Feminism?* ed. Ann Oakley and Juliet Mitchell (London: Hamish Hamilton, 1997), 77–98.

5.   Walter Korpi, "Power Politics and State Autonomy in the Development of Social Citizenship," *American Sociological Review* 54 (1989): 309–28; Walter Korpi, "Contested Citizenship: Social Rights, Class, and Gender" (paper presented at the conference on Comparative Research on Welfare Reforms, Research Committee 19 of the International Sociological Association, Canberra, Australia, August 1996); Gösta Esp-

ing-Anderson, *The Three Worlds of Welfare Capitalism* (Princeton: Princeton University Press, 1990), 105–7.

6. See the collection of essays *Feminist Organizations: Harvest of the New Women's Movement*, ed. Myra Marx Feree and Patricia Y. Martin (Philadelphia: Temple University Press, 1995).

7. Theda Skocpol, *Protecting Soldiers and Mothers* (Cambridge: Harvard University Press, 1992); Barbara Hobson, "Frauenbewegung für Staatsbürgerechete: Das Beispiel Schweden," *Feministische Studien* 14, no. 2 (1996): 18–34.

8. Esping-Andersen, *Three Worlds.*

9. Mary Ruggie, *The State and Working Women* (Princeton: Princeton University Press, 1984); Joyce Gelb, *Feminism and Politics: A Comparative Perspective* (Berkeley and Los Angeles: University of California Press, 1989).

10. Yvonne Hirdman, *Att Lägga livet till rätta: Studier i svenskt folkhems politik* (Stockholm: Norstedts Förlag, 1989). However, recent feminist research in Sweden modifies and challenges this position. See Maud Eduards, "Toward a Third Way: Women's Politics and Welfare Policies in Sweden," *Social Research* 58, no. 3 (Fall 1991): 677–705; Christina Bergqvist, "Mäns makt och kvinnors intressen" (Ph.D. diss., Uppsala University, 1994); and Christina Florín and Bengt Nilsson, "'Something in the Nature of a Bloodless Revolution . . .': How New Gender Relations Became 'Gender Equity Policy' in Sweden in the 1960s and 1970s" (paper presented at Humanistiska Samhällsvetenskapliga Fosrkningsrådets Conference on Research in Europe, Prague, 17–19 October 1997).

11. Hobson, "Frauenbewegung"; Hobson and Lindholm, "Collective Identities."

12. Alan Siaroff, "Work, Welfare, and Gender Inequality: A New Typology," in *Gendering Welfare States,* 82–100; Irene Wennemo, "Sharing the Costs of Children: Studies on the Development of Family Support in the OECD Countries" (Stockholm: Swedish Institute for Social Research Dissertation Series, 1994), 25. This is to suggest, not that feminist groups have not sought to mobilize women's votes as a power resource, but that the mobilizing costs are high.

13. Phillips, *Engendering Democracy.*

14. For a discussion of this point in the Swedish context, see Gunnel Gustafsson, "Ringing the Changes for an Unknown Future," in *Towards a New Democratic Order? Women's Organizing in Sweden in the 1990s,* ed. Gunnel Gustafsson, Maud Eduards, and Malin Rönnblom (Stockholm: Publica, 1997), 169–84.

15. Gunnar Qvist, *Konsten att Blifva en God Flicka* (Stockholm: Liberförlag, 1978); Alice Cook, Val Lorwin, and Arlene Daniels, *The Most Difficult Revolution: Women and Trade Unions* (Ithaca: Cornell University Press, 1992).

16. Some examples of studies that have made this type of argument are: Gillian Pascall, *Social Policy: A Feminist Analysis* (London: Tavistock, 1986); Hirdman, *Att Lägga livet.*

17. Skocpol, *Protecting Soldiers,* in labeling the American welfare state as maternalist and other European welfare states as paternalist, does not leave much theoretical space for a theory of women's power resources in European welfare states; see Kathryn Kish Sklar, "The Historical Foundations of Women's Power in the Creation of the

American Welfare State, 1830–1930," in *Mothers of a New World* (New York: Routledge & Kegan Paul, 1993), 43–93.

18. For a more developed argument against these dichotomies, see Carol Lee Bacchi, *Same Difference: Feminism and Sexual Difference* (Sydney: Allen & Unwin, 1990); Wendy Sarvasy, "Beyond the Difference Equality Debate: Postsuffrage Feminism, Citizenship, and the Quest for a Feminist Welfare State," *Signs* 17 (1992): 329–62.

19. Barbara Hobson, *Uneasy Virtue: The Politics of Prostitution and American Reform Tradition* (Chicago: University of Chicago Press, 1988).

20. William A. Gamson, *Talking Politics* (New York: Cambridge University Press, 1992).

21. Linda Gordon (*Pitied But Not Entitled: Single Mothers and the History of Welfare* [New York: Free Press,1994]) and Sonya Michel (*Children's Interests /Mothers Rights: The Shaping of America's Child Care Policy* [New Haven: Yale University Press, 1998]) describe maternalism as an ideology; Molly Ladd-Taylor (*Mother-Work: Women, Child Welfare, and the State, 1890–1930* [Urbana: University of Illinois Press, 1994]) analyzes "maternalist" women's movements; and Skocpol (*Protecting Soldiers*) uses "maternalist" to depict a type of welfare state.

22. Gordon, *Pitied But Not Entitled*; Ladd-Taylor, *Mother-Work*; and Michel, *Children's Interests*.

23. Sonya Michel, "The Limits of Maternalism: Policies toward American Wage-Earning Mothers during the Progressive Era," in *Mothers of a New World,* 277–320.

24. Norway is the exception, since maternalist issues formed the basis of feminist activism there. See Arnlaug Leira, *Welfare States and Working Mothers* (Cambridge: Cambridge University Press, 1992).

25. Disa Västberg, "Islossning," *Morgonbris*, May 1938, 5.

26. Marika Lindholm, "Gender Identities and Class Coalition Building in the Rise of the Swedish Welfare State, 1870–1976" (Ph.D. diss., University of New York, Stony Brook, 1994).

27. See Marika Lindholm, "Swedish Feminism, 1835–1945: A Conservative Revolution," *Journal of Historical Sociology* 4, no. 2 (1991): 121–42.

28. Brita Åkerman, *Vi Kan, Vi Behövs! Kvinnorna går samman i egna föreningar* (Stockholm: Förlaget Akademilitteratur, 1983), 135.

29. Disa Västberg, "Manlig Konservatism och Kvinnlig Sterilitet," *Morgonbris*, March 1931, 9.

30. Åkerman, *Vi Kan,* 195.

31. *Morgonbris*, December 1939, 5.

32 *Arbetets Kvinnor* 2 (1936): 21–22.

33. "Svenska Kvinnors Medborgarsforbund" (flyer), Hanna Rydh Archive, Women's Historical Collection, Gothenburg University, Box A12, I 20 (1931), 23.

34. Ellen Key can be seen as the ultimate maternalist; she was highly critical of all feminist movements that sought influence in the male domains of politics and the labor market. See Ellen Key, *The Woman Movement* (New York: Putnam, 1912).

35. Barbara Hobson, "Feminist Strategies and Gendered Discourses in Welfare

States: Married Women's Right to Work in the U.S. and Sweden during the 1930s," in *Mothers of a New World*, 396–429.

36. Herbert Tingsten, *The Swedish Social Democrats: Their Ideological Development*, trans. Greta Frankel and Patricia Howard-Rosen (Bedminster, N.J.: Bedminster Press, 1973), 285.

37. Hobson, "Feminist Strategies," 5.

38. Statens offentliga utredningar (SOU) (1938): 2.

39. Charles Tilly, *From Mobilization to Revolution* (Reading, Mass.: Addison-Wesley, 1978), 55.

40. The national law, called the Economy Act, forbade employing two persons from the same household in the civil service. Numerous communities enacted laws that led to wholesale firing of married teachers. For a more detailed discussion, see Hobson, "Feminist Strategies."

41. Skocpol, *Protecting Soldiers*; Molly Ladd-Taylor, "My Work Came Out of Agony and Grief: Mothers and the Making of the Sheppard-Towner Act," in *Mothers of a New World*, 321–42.

42. Cynthia Harris, *On Account of Sex: The Politics of Women's Issues* (Berkeley and Los Angeles: University of California Press, 1988).

43. Nancy Fraser, *Unruly Practices, Power Discourse, and Gender in Contemporary Social Theory* (Minneapolis: University of Minnesota Press, 1989).

44. David A. Snow and Robert D. Benford, "Master Frames and Cycles of Protest," in *Frontiers in Social Movement Theory*, ed. A. D. Morris and C. M. Mueller (New Haven: Yale University Press, 1992), 140–42. The cultural narrative exemplifies what Snow and Benford refer to as "master frames," or narratives that resonate with larger belief systems in a society, which, because they are "syntactically flexible and lexically universalistic," allow numerous aggrieved groups to tap into them.

45. Lindholm, "Swedish Feminism."

46. Wilhelm Moberg, *A History of the Swedish People from Pre-History to Renaissance*, trans. P. Britten Austen (New York: Pantheon Books, 1972), 197.

47. Orvar Löfgren and Jonas Frykman, *Culture Builders: A Historical Anthropology of Middle-Class Life*, trans. Alan Crozier (New Brunswick, N.J.: Rutgers University Press, 1987).

48. Quoted in Tingsten, *Swedish Social Democrats*, 265.

49. *Morgonbris*, May 1938, 1.

50. Quoted in Gunnel Karlsson, *Manssamhället till behag?* (Stockholm: Tidens Förlag, 1990), 36; see also "Kvinnans Rätta Plats är i folkhemmet!" *Hertha*, April 1938, 98.

51. This was the case in the 1940s and 1950s when women's political influence was limited to commissions on surveys of household consumption and scientific management of the home. See Ann-Katrin Hatje, *Befolkningsfrågan och välfärden: Debatten om familjepolitik och nativitetsökning under 1930 och 1940 talen* (Stockholm: Allmänna förl., 1974); Hirdman, *Att Lägga livet*; Ann-Sofie Ohlander, "The Invisible Child: The Struggle over Social Democratic Family Policy," in *Creating Social Democracy: A*

Century of the Social Democratic Party in Sweden, ed. Klaus Misgeld, Karl Molin, and Klas Åmark (University Park: Pennsylvania State University Press, 1992).

52. William A. Gamson and Andre Modigliani, "The Changing Culture of Affirmative Action," in *Research in Political Sociology,* ed. Richard D. Braungart (Greenwich, Conn: JAI Press, 1987), 137–77.

53. Alva Myrdal and Gunnar Myrdal, *Kris i Befolkningsfrågan* (Stockholm, People's edition, 1934).

54. Quoted in Tim Tilton, *The Political Theory of Swedish Social Democracy* (Oxford: Clarendon Press, 1991), 147.

55. Alva Myrdal, *Nation and Family* (London: Routledge, Kegan Paul, Trench, Trubner, 1941).

56. Theresa Kulawik, "Autonomous Mothers: West German Feminism Reconsidered," *German Politics and Society,* nos. 24–25 (Winter 1992); Susan Pedersen, *Family, Dependence and the Origins of the Welfare State: Britain and France, 1914–1945* (New York: Cambridge University Press, 1993).

57. Myrdal, *Nation and Family.*

58. Helga Hernes coined the term "women friendly" in her book *Welfare State and Woman Power: Essays in State Feminism* (Oslo: Norwegian University Press, 1987).

59. Jarl Torbacke, "Kvinnolistan 1927–1928: ett kvinnopolitiskt fiasko," *Historisk Tidskrift* 2 (1969): 151.

60. Agneta Stark, "Combating the Backlash: How the Swedish Won the War," in *Who's Afraid of Feminism?* 224.

61. Paula Baker, "The Domestication of Politics: Women and American Political Society, 1780–1920," in *Women, the State, and Welfare,* ed. Linda Gordon (Madison: University of Wisconsin Press, 1990), 55–91.

62. *Arbetarhistoria* (Stockholm: Arbetarrörelsens Arkiv, 1987), 61.

63. Margaretha Lindholm, *Talet Om Det Kvinnliga* (Gothenburg, Sweden: University of Gothenburg, 1990), 88, 99, 108.

64. Beata Losman, "Kvinnoorganisering och kvinnororelser i Sverige," in *Handbok I Svensk Kvinnohistoria,* ed. Gunhild Kyle (Stockholm: Carlssons, 1987), 199.

65. Abortion for social reasons was included in the original demands by Social Democratic Women but was dropped after the Myrdals' book appeared dramatizing the population crisis. It was political suicide to support abortion legislation. See Ohlander, "Invisible Child."

66. Skocpol, *Protecting Soldiers*; Ladd-Taylor, *Mother Work.*

67. Gordon, *Pitied But Not Entitled.*

68. Barbara Hobson and Mieko Takahashi, "Lone Motherhood and Weak Male Breadwinner Models: The Case of Sweden," in *Lone Mothers and Welfare Policy Regimes,* ed. Jane Lewis (London: Jessica Kingsley, 1997): 121–39.

69. Sidney Tarrow, *Power in Social Movements, Collective Action, and Politics* (Cambridge: Cambridge University Press, 1994).

70. Carlsson, *Swedish Experiment,* 110.

71. Klas Åmark, "Social Democracy and the Trade Union Movement: Solidarity and the Politics of Self-Interest," in *Creating Social Democracy*; Gelb, *Feminism and*

Politics. More relevant to women's collectivities, Joan Acker, in "Två Diskurser om Reformer och Kvinnor i den Framtida Välfärdsstaten," (in *Kvinnors och Mäns Liv och Arbete* [Stockholm: SNS Förlag, 1992], 283), argues that the Saltsjöbaden accord was the beginning of a long tradition of male discursive power.

    72. Torbacke, "Kvinnolistan," 183.

    73. *Arbetets Kvinnor,* 1936, 4.

    74. Analyses of Swedish welfare state formation have concentrated on the passage of unemployment insurance and pensions (Esping-Andersen, *Three Worlds*) and have ignored the gender-specific policymaking spheres attached to the population committee that dominated in the 1930s.

    75. Gunborg Alexandersson, "Vad ville Kvinnorörelser Förkämpar?" *Morgonbris,* June 1938, 20.

    76. Although government commissions are not unique to Sweden, they play a special role in Swedish policymaking. Existing for over 150 years, the parliamentary commission of experts is the site of a vital stage of policymaking that has become a prerequisite for formulating new proposals made to parliament.

    77. SOU (1938): 2.

    78. Betina Cass, "Citizenship, Work, and Welfare: The Dilemma for Australian Women," *Social Politics* 1, no. 1 (1994): 106–24; Hester Eisenstein, "The Australian Femocrat Experiment: A Feminist Case for Bureaucracy," in *Feminist Organizations,* 69–83.

    79. Ohlander, "Invisible Child."

    80. Florín and Nilsson, "'Something of a Bloodless Revolution.'"

    81. Edmund Dahlström, "Analys av könsrolldebatten," in *Kvinnors liv och arbete,* ed. Edmund Dahlström (Stockholm: Studieförbundet Näringsliv och Samhälle, 1962), 189–268; Annika Baude, "Public Policy and Changing Family Patterns in Sweden, 1930–1977," in *Sex Roles and Social Policy: A Complex Social Science Equation,* ed. Jean Lipman-Bluman and Jessie Bernard (London: Sage, 1979), 145–75.

    82. These issues were raised in several Swedish Power Commission reports. See SOU, 1988, nos. 15, 16, 44. See also Eduards, "Toward a Third Way."

    83. Agneta Stark and Åsa Regnér, "Arbete: vem behöver, vem utför, vem betalar? En analysmodell med genusperspektiv," in *En ljusnande framtid eller ett långt farväl?* ed. Agneta Stark (Stockholm: SOU 1997), 115; Lena Gonäs and Anna Spånt, *Trends and Prospects for Women's Employment in the 1990s* (Stockholm: Arbetslivsinstitutet, 1997); Stina Johansson, "Women's Paradise Lost? Social Services and Care in the Quasi-Markets in Sweden," in *Crossing Borders: Gender and Citizenship in Transition,* ed. Barbara Hobson (Basingstoke, England: Macmillan, forthcoming).

    84. Mikael Gilljam and Sören Holmberg, *Ett Knappt Ja Till EU, väljarna och folkomröstningen 1994* (Stockholm: Norstedts Juridik AB, 1996), 372.

    85. The vote for the referendum was fairly close; 52.3 percent voted for and 48.6 voted against. Recent surveys show that if the referendum were held today, the majority of voters would vote no. See Gilljam and Holmberg, *Ja till EU,* 1.

    86. Hobson, *Crossing Borders.*

87. Catherine Hoskyns, *Integrating Gender: Women, Law, and Politics in the European Community* (London: Verso, 1996), 1.

88. Barbara Hobson, "Economic Citizenship: Reflections through the European Union Policy Mirror," in *Crossing Borders;* Lena Gonäs, "Towards Convergence: On Economic Integration and Women's Employment," in *Engendering Citizenship,* 107–18; Ingallil Montanari, "Harmonisation of Social Policies and Social Regulations in the European Community," *European Journal of Political Research* 27, no. 1 (1995): 21–45.

89. Eduards, "Interpreting Women's Organizing."

90. Stark, "Combatting Backlash," 229.

91. Eduards, "Interpreting Women's Organizing," 241–42.

92. During the past two decades, there have been examples of cross-party alliance around specific issues of peace, nuclear power, rape legislation, and general support for greater political representation of women, but they have been the exception rather than the rule. See Diane Sainsbury, "The Politics of Increased Women's Representation: The Swedish Case," in *Gender and Party Politics,* ed. Joni Lovenduski and Pippi Norris (London: Sage, 1993); Eduards, "Interpreting Women's Organizing."

93. *Rapport till Utredningnen om fördelning av ekonomisk makt och ekonomiska resurser mellan kvinnor och män,* SOU (Stockholm: 1998), see nos. 83, 87, 113, 117, 135.

94. In the 1997 election a significant proportion of women abandoned the Social Democratic Party for the more radical Left Party, headed by a woman. Women's proportion of the Social Democratic vote was 31.3 percent, 2 percent less than men's.

95. That married women and adult daughters working on the family farm or store or selling their handicrafts were never reported in the census underestimates women's work in the 1930s. Women working part time and in housecleaning were also underreported. This changed after 1970. See Anita Nyberg, "Tekniken-kvinnors befriare? Hushållsteknik, Köpevaror, gifta kvinnors hushållsarbetstid och förvärvsdeltagande, 1930 talet to 1950 talet" (Ph.D diss., Linköping Universitet, 1989).

96. Hobson and Takahashi, "Lone Motherhood."

97. Barbara Hobson, "Solo Mothers, Policy Regimes, and the Logics of Gender," in *Gendering Welfare States,* 170–87; Ann Shola Orloff, "Gender and the Social Rights of Citizenship: The Comparative Analysis of State Policies and Gender Relations," *American Sociological Review* 58, no. 15 (1993): 303–28.

98. Hernes, *Welfare State and Woman Power*; Leira, *Working Mothers.*

99. Paul Pierson, "The New Politics of the Welfare State," *World Politics* 48, no. 2 (1996): 143–79.

100. Helga Hernes coined this term, but she maintained that in the Swedish context it encompassed both politics from above and politics from below. See also Hernes, *Welfare State and Woman Power,* 135–63.

8

The Prospects for Transnational Social Policy: A Reappraisal

Abram de Swaan

This paper deals with transnational social policies, that is, provisions financed by rich countries for the poor inhabitants of poor countries. The focus is on the prospects for social policies funded by the European Union (EU) or its member states not for the benefit of its own inhabitants but for the sake of those living in poor countries beyond its borders. The next section recapitulates an earlier argument,[1] and the main body of the chapter assesses the degree to which the conditions for transnational social policy are indeed realized in the contemporary world, almost seven years after my article "Perspectives for Transnational Social Policy" appeared.[2]

The Collectivizing Process

Transnational social policies represent a transformation of benefit schemes to a scale that transcends the borders and the jurisdiction of particular states. National welfare states emerged in the past hundred years as the most recent stage in the long-term process of state formation in the West. In the course of four centuries, collective arrangements to cope with individual deficiency and adversity had gradually grown in scale, scope, and compulsory potential. Initially, parish poor relief was restricted to the village, covered a narrow range of needs, and depended heavily on the consent of the providers. Poorhouses, asylums, and the urban dole functioned on a regional scale and required taxes to support the poor to be levied on the citizenry. The nationwide, encompassing, and legally compulsory insurance and assistance arrangements of the modern welfare state are the latest phase in this "collectivizing process."

The dynamics of this process come from a double interdependency. First, the rich are affected by the external effects of poverty in their society. The presence of the poor in their midst causes the wealthier citizens to fear contagion (in modern medical or more magical terms), vagrancy, crime, and rebellion. But the poor also present them with opportunities: they may be useful as workers or recruits, and in later stages of collectivizing as voters and potential consumers (strictly speaking, such "reserve armies" constitute a "joint" rather than a "collective" good). The capacity of the poor to "threaten" the rich, involuntarily or through concerted action and also their potential usefulness determine the pressure upon the rich to apply some remedies.

The second interdependency operates among the rich themselves. Since they believe they cannot on their own ward off the threats that the poor evoke nor exploit individually the opportunities that the same poor represent, the rich must coordinate their efforts in collective action. The familiar conundrum of collective action ensues: how to create collective arrangements to control the external effects of poverty while preventing some of their peers from sharing the benefits without contributing to the effort? The very suspicion that some may opt for a profiteering course is sufficient to dissuade others from joining the collective effort, leaving the external effects of poverty unremedied, to the disadvantage of everyone.

This dilemma of collective action characteristically emerges in a transitional stage, when agents are interdependent and are aware of their interdependence, but there does not as yet exist an agency that can effectively coordinate their actions. By engaging in collective action, actors strive both to bring about the intended collective good and to shape their collectivity with respect to this good. The collectivizing process may be initiated if and only if initial suspicions are somehow overcome. Once collective action gets under way, in the course of the collectivizing process itself, a collectivity emerges that may apply informal sanctions against defectors and reward collaborators at low cost (through punishment or ostracism), at no cost, or even at a premium (through shaming, reproach, and gossip).

The history of welfare before the welfare state is in good part determined by the ways in which the dilemma of collective action was overcome: through the manipulation of mutual expectations by charitable entrepreneurs, such as priests; through optimistic illusions, for example, the misguided expectation that workhouses would turn a profit; through the intervention of big towns in the role of large actors willing to underwrite the collective venture on their own even while being "exploited" by the small actors, the surrounding villages; and, most of all, through external pressure ranging from moral suasion to legal compulsion.

By the end of the nineteenth century, European states increasingly applied their capacities for taxation, regulation, inspection, and adjudication to the implementation of nationwide, compulsory collective arrangements to remedy the deficiencies and adversities of industrial workers. Activist regimes sought the support of large employers or workers' organizations (new actors on the historical scene), or both. They had to overcome the opposition of small, independent entrepreneurs, such as farmers, shopkeepers, manufacturers, and tradesmen.

Within the confines of the national polity, the coercive apparatus of the modern state can effectively impose and enforce the contributions and requirements that the insurance and assistance schemes demand. But transnational social policy by definition transcends the jurisdictional space of single states. In the absence of an effective coordinating agency, the dilemmas of collective action reassert themselves with a vengeance. This time the game is played on a global scale, with wealthy states in the role of the rich, and poor states—or, rather, poor people in poor countries—in the complementary role.

The theory of the collectivizing process allows us to identify a number of necessary conditions for the emergence of care arrangements that transcend state borders.

Conditions for Collective Action of Transnational Scope

The question that suggests itself at this point is whether in a subsequent stage of collectivization analogous arrangements will emerge at the transnational level, covering subcontinents, continents, or even the entire globe. At this transnational level of integration (nation-)states are the actors. Rich states are faced with the dilemmas of collective action in controlling the external effects of poverty in remote lands. There they confront at one level the governments of poor states and at another the poor inhabitants of these poor states, whose leaders may have interests that diverge sharply from those of the indigent citizens.

For transnational social policies to emerge from this constellation, at least these four conditions must be fulfilled:

1. There must be interdependence between rich states and (the poor inhabitants of) poor states: the rich must somehow be affected by the external effects of poverty in poor countries.

2. There should exist widespread awareness of this interdependence among the rich (sociologists specialize in the rhetoric of warning the rich about the indirect effects of poverty and the need for them to fight it). The external effects must be believed to be intrusive and persistent (i.e., they cannot easily be undone), and they must appear to be beyond the control of any single state actor.

3. The rich countries must either somehow overcome their mutual suspicions or be effectively coordinated by some "suprastate" agency (e.g., the European Union).

4. Rich citizens must believe that there exist social policies that are both feasible and effective in controlling the externalities of remote poverty.

Increasing Global Interdependencies

At the end of the twentieth century, the actual externalities from poverty that operate on a global scale may be grouped under four headings.

1. *Migration.* The rich countries are confronted with mass immigration by poor people from poor countries.

2. *Military threats.* The rich countries do not so much fear direct attack by poor states as worry about the consequences of violent confrontation between and within very poor countries as a consequence of persistent economic stagnation and intensified competition for scarce resources. Such large-scale violence may threaten foreign plants, personnel, or supply lines and erode regional and even global stability.

3. *Environmental degradation.* Rich countries are concerned about the consequences of massive devastation of tropical forests, the burning of wood for fuel and the resulting desertification, and the extermination of plant and animal species. Poor countries are affected even more by the external effects of fuel combustion in the richer parts of the world: greenhouse effects, acid rain, rising sea levels, holes in the ozone layer, and so on.

4. *Opportunity.* For the rich in rich countries, the poor in poor countries constitute an opportunity, as they can employ healthy, somewhat skilled, and disciplined workers, applying advanced technologies of transport, communication, and management to link remote production plants to global distribution and control networks.

Increasing Awareness and the Control of External Effects

In the wealthy countries, increasing factual information and an improved understanding of ecological, economic, and sociological links with poor countries have greatly increased the awareness of the threats and opportunities connected with global poverty. However, many of the external effects of remote poverty may be effectively warded off through the exclusion of poor populations and thus fail to trigger any impetus toward transnational collective action.

Migration can be controlled to some degree through collective measures of exclusion such as the Schengen agreement among a number of member states of the EU.[3] The immigration of citizens from former colonies seems to have run its course, but refugees from violence and misery keep migration pressure on Western countries at a high level (although the rich in rich societies do not fear immigration nearly as much as do indigenous unemployed and unskilled workers, who must compete with the newcomers for cheap housing and low-paying jobs).[4]

Further, as long as the rich countries mutually agree not to interfere in local conflicts among poorer countries, they need not much fear that war will cause uncontrollable external effects or extend to their own borders (although foreign property is under threat, and streams of refugees may increase immigration pressure even upon faraway rich countries).[5]

Ecological disturbances are hardest to ward off. The consequences of global warming or the extinction of species may still be quite remote, but pollution, deforestation, and desertification do have immediate and palpable consequences for the rich countries also. These dangers might persuade rich countries to subsidize poor people in poor countries for switching from harmful to sustainable modes of exploiting their natural environment. However, such initiatives are often thwarted by local government or by corporations in these poor countries that continue their detrimental practices or pocket the grants-in-aid as a reward for abandoning them. In the end, poor people all too often find themselves cut off from their resources and excluded from any compensation.

Finally, rich people in rich countries might choose to help improve health services and education in poor countries for positive reasons, rather than to ward off a threat; for example, they may choose to help in order to increase the supply of able workers in those countries from which they may recruit employees. However, while long-term, large-scale reforms of health and education may improve the living conditions of the faraway indigent, paradoxically, they may well enable and encourage the beneficiaries to emigrate in search of still better opportunities. If, on the other hand, they choose to stay, their availability might also benefit entrepreneurs whose governments did not contribute to the reforms: the dilemma of collective action in *optima forma*.

Problems of Coordination: The Case of the European Union

The third overall condition for collective action among the rich countries towards social policies for the benefit of the poor in poor countries requires either an *effective coordinating agency or some mechanism to overcome the mutual suspicions* that prevent collective action from getting under way. Clearly, the European Union is such an effective coordinating agency when it comes to imposing taxes on member states and disbursing grants for internal redistribution, for example, in support of peasants (not always the poorest) or as structural aid to underdeveloped regions. Whether the redistribution policy is efficient or fair is another matter, but it is, in effect, carried out.

The European Union—or at least the countries that signed the Schengen agreement—has succeeded in establishing a collective policy of selectively adopting deserving strangers (i.e., political refugees) and selectively excluding immigrants from outside the Community (rather than sending them across the border to the next country, as has been the custom ever since in premodern times parishes tried to shunt their vagrants off to their neighbors). These policies are effective to some degree. Yet, a steady stream of illegal immigrants continues to enter the Community and to pass from one member state into another. Nevertheless, at present, pressure on the European Union does not unleash a collective effort to put in place social policies that could dissuade potential immigrants by improving their living conditions at home. But such notions are timidly advanced in public debate and play a minor but growing role in Union policies towards the countries of Central and Eastern Europe and the Maghreb.

When it comes to collective military enterprises for preventing or containing armed conflicts elsewhere that might affect the European Union, the record is dismal. No collective campaigns have been waged, no joint foreign policy has been sustained for any length of time, even in the former Yugoslavia, which borders on the territory of the Union. More distant cases, in Central Asia and Central Africa, did not even provoke an attempt to coordinate diplomatic efforts or military containment. In foreign policy and conflict control, the dilemmas of collective action operate with undiminished force among the members of the European Union; only a large actor can overcome the stalemate, and that role is not reserved for a major European power, such as Germany or France, but is played exclusively by the United States.

Under the conditions that have prevailed since the disintegration of the Soviet empire, no coalition without the United States can realize its objectives. A coalition led by the United States can subdue almost all organized military opposition, but it cannot or will not mobilize the collective effort required to carry out domestic pacification and reform in the defeated country. The United States, as a large actor, is the one indispensable ally; all other states must compete for its support—a constellation that Norbert Elias has characterized as one of "monopolistic competition." At the same time, its position exposes the United States to exploitation by small powers that may profit from its military ventures (and the diplomatic interventions predicated upon that military potential) without contributing to them.

The danger that poverty in faraway lands may cause large-scale violence that could eventually threaten the interests of wealthy and powerful countries apparently does not do much to persuade politicians to intervene and improve the conditions of the remote poor (although some development aid may be motivated by such concerns). Measures to control the threat of rebellion by the poor are much more often repressive in nature, consisting of military aid to help the affected government defeat the revolt.

With minor exceptions, the situation is similar when it comes to environmental policy. Internally, the Union is capable of effective coordination, and even if it does not always choose to impose its full weight, it often sets its standards beyond even the strictest national regulations. The EU has enacted numerous import restrictions motivated by environmental concerns (e.g., restrictions on importing rare animal species, ivory, wood from scarce tree species). The most important instances of positive collective environmental policies are the projects providing expert assistance and substantive grants for major clean-up operations and the removal of chemical and nuclear waste in ex-Communesia. But the program of the 1992 United Nations Conference on Environment and Development in Rio de Janeiro that alluded to grants-in-aid to help poor people beyond the confines of the EU find alternative, more sustainable resources to prevent further environmental degradation has hardly resulted in collective enterprises on the part of the rich countries. The strongly collective nature of the potential environmental benefits and the long time span required discourage immediate action by single states or even regional organizations, the EU included.

Have the rich countries embarked upon collective initiatives towards positive intervention in education and health in the poor countries? In fact, UNESCO, the World Health Organization, and other agencies funded by the richer member states have provided expertise and some funds to implement reforms. The EU plays a part in these endeavors, as do individual member countries. Aid by rich countries to the UN High Commissioner for Refugees and other agencies that support refugees in their region of origin is another collective effort to improve the life of poor residents of poor countries in situ. As a matter of fact, it might also be mentioned as an instance of positive social policy aimed at preventing immigration into the European Union.

On balance, the member states of the European Union are quite effectively coordinated by that central authority when it comes to the solution of collective problems *within* the Community. But when it comes to collective problems originating *outside* the Community, coordination is much less effective and mostly limited to measures of a protective, negative nature, such as the exclusion of immigrants; positive policies turn out to be much harder to realize collectively. Current developments in transnational social policy within the EU may provide some idea of what can be expected if such policies were ever devised for countries outside the Union.

Within the EU, social policy decisions are increasing in number and scope, as Leibfried and Pierson have documented.[6] In the case of Germany, the authors show that many new rules ensue from decisions by the European Court applying treaty texts or committee rulings to specific cases, spelling out their implications in the field of social policy even though the original texts were not intended to apply there. Many of the Court's rulings pertain to discriminatory practices (especially in gender issues), the restriction of free movement across internal borders, and the implementation of health protection or labor safety measures. Streeck provides an explanation of the relative facility with which these issues could be regulated by a Community entirely geared to creating an all-European labor market.[7] In Majone's terms, the Community and the present European Union have produced "social regulation" rather than social security measures in the proper sense of the term. Except in the field of agriculture, no legislation has been adopted that involves actual social transfers to citizens of the EU, and such transfers, after all, constitute the core of social policy.[8] Agricultural policy in the EU may well be interpreted as a form of social policy aimed at a specific category, European farmers. As agricultural policy shifts from production subsidies and restrictions toward income maintenance measures, its social character becomes more visible. In all other respects, though, social security has predominantly been dealt with by the separate member states. The welfare state still is essentially national in character.[9] Nevertheless, as the single market is gradually realized, the respective national welfare states and social regulations at the level of the Union increasingly constitute a single interdependent system in which decisions in any one part are taken with an eye on their repercussions upon the other parts. At the same time, the growing integration in other fields—for example, monetary policy with a single European currency managed by a European central bank—may also operate at the all-European level against maintaining or extending social policies either at the national or the Union level. Much depends on the speed and efficacy with which wage earners and claimants can transform their national organizations into movements that operate on the corresponding European level.

Taken together, these points convey some sense of the potential for social policies directed by the EU to countries outside its confines. The Union will be more prone to promote transnational social regulation (e.g., the proposal to impose minimum standards of pay and working conditions in low-wage countries through the GATT mechanism)[10] and much more hesitant to initiate or join programs that would entail social transfers to other countries. If the Union were one day to subscribe to a scheme of this kind, it would prefer not to deal directly with the citizens of the receiving states but to work with their national governments or through nongovernmental organizations (NGOs), in much the way it does at present when providing structural development subsidies or incidental disaster relief grants. The same preference for dealing with national authorities or NGOs also characterizes interventions by the World Bank, the International Monetary Fund, and related agencies. This is, of course, to be expected, as receiving states tend to guard their sovereignty and will not readily allow outsiders to deal directly with their citizens. This makes poor people in poor countries hostage to their leaders.

Confidence in the Efficacy of Transnational Schemes

As a fourth condition for transnational social policy, there should be some faith in the feasibility and efficacy of global-scale social interventions. In the long run, the remarkable fact was the secular increase of confidence in organized action on a massive scale and with ever widening scope. Throughout the nineteenth century and up to World War I, states initiated concerted campaigns, beginning with the effort to abolish slavery and culminating in a sequence of international conventions and organizations. After a brief revival of internationalist activism after World War I, this cosmopolitan optimism emerged once more after the close of World War II, spawning the United Nations and a host of related international organizations whose vicissitudes were determined largely by the vagaries of the cold war.

In hindsight, the transition spelled a brief and intense revival of global activism: the nuclear holocaust had been avoided after all, and Communist dictatorship had disappeared more or less of its own accord. Democracy and capitalism appeared triumphant across the globe. But this mood was soon to be superseded by one of resignation and disillusionment. Since 1989, time and again the Western powers have failed in their efforts at collective intervention: the "Marshall plan" for ex-Communesia, the aftermath of the Gulf War, the campaign in Somalia, and, most tragically, the hesitant interventions in Bosnia and the inaction in Rwanda.

Increasingly, the impression prevails that states per se are losing power. A series of recessions has increased unemployment in a number of European economies, ratcheting up one notch after each cycle. As a consequence, many states find themselves in a fiscal crisis, under strong pressure to limit their spending and with much less opportunity to stimulate employment and reinforce social policies. The movement towards a common European currency certainly has strengthened this tendency towards welfare curtailment.

As governments become less effective in creating jobs and disbursing benefits or subsidies, their citizens tend to lose confidence in the potential of state intervention and turn away from government. And yet the implicit promises of market liberalization, deregulation, and privatization have not materialized for the underprivileged sections of society. Even when economic expansion resumed, it turned out to be jobless growth; even when the domestic national income increased, no "trickle down" resulted as the new wealth disproportionately benefited the higher-income groups; even when employment opportunities improved, the new positions overwhelmingly offered minimal salaries for unskilled work with little job security and even less prospect of promotion.

The demoralization of workers and trade unions came with the remoralization of capitalism.[11] As the Soviet Union broke down and "independent models of socialism" as represented by Yugoslavia and Cuba disintegrated or stagnated, the idea of an alternative to capitalist, free-market economies began to appear entirely utopian. In their totality, these developments seem to suggest that established nation-states are becoming weaker vis-à-vis transnational corporations and regionalist separatist movements and with respect to violent domestic criminal and (anti-)ethnic groups. Whatever the actual shift in this multiple power balance may be, these developments are most germane to the prospects for transnational social policy. In the original argument, states appeared as the actors in a—halting—collectivizing process.

States have become more interdependent, and they are well aware of it, but they still lack an effective coordinating agency—hence their dilemmas. One such transnational coordinating agent is the European Union. And, remarkably, while the impression prevails that European states have been losing power, there also is a widely held conviction that the European Union has not gained in power, either vis-à-vis its member states or with respect to external entities, since its relative power gain after the demise of the Soviet bloc. If one country has become more powerful within the overall European equilibrium, it is no doubt newly united Germany. As a result, it appears that European states are now considered too weak politically and economically and their coordinating agencies insufficiently effective even to consider engaging in global collective action of the magnitude required to enforce a regulatory regime of environmental protection, sustain a major pacification campaign, or carry out transnational social policies.

Much of this current opinion is fashion and fancy. It is not at all clear whether in the totality of power relations the balance is indeed shifting away from established states in favor of other entities. Supranational and international agencies certainly do not appear to come out victorious—suffice it to mention the UN or the EU. The most likely winners in this process are transnational corporations, who, operating as they do on a global scale, can more easily play one government off against another when it comes to tax privileges, labor conditions, environmental controls, social regulation, and so forth. But internationalization also increasingly exposes firms to competition and thus should allow states to make corporations vie for their favors. More than internationalization per se, it may be one of its specific consequences, unemployment, that weakens governments in their dealings with international corporations.

But it is not only power relations that may have shifted. The argument can also be made that a change in mentality has occurred. Claims based on universal commitment and solidarity appear to lose their appeal, while the vindications of sectarian and exclusive loyalties are gaining force. Once again, these are huge generalizations: welfare states were based on national redistribution and on national loyalties; if workers now take a protectionist stance and protest immigration, they may not carry out a universalist, humanist program, but they do defend exactly the implicit national contract on which the welfare state was based from the outset. On the other hand, cosmopolitan commitments to international development aid, always rather tenuous, were meant to be essentially discretionary and never implied that those faraway strangers could come and make their claims heard in the welfare states themselves, even less that they would be sustained by these same states in their country of birth.

Future Prospects for Transnational Social Policy

Serious economic recessions notwithstanding, many countries in Latin America and in East, South, and Southeast Asia appear to be on the road to fully functioning economies and are now in a position to design and finance their social policies themselves. The issues in these societies are predominantly of a domestic and political nature: whether to invest more in "human capital," adopt more egalitarian income and tax policies, and create collective health care and pension funds. Such countries can do without transnational social policy. The question is, rather, why they do not adopt national, collective, and compulsory care arrangements to improve living conditions and control the external effects of poverty.

Those countries that have failed to develop a viable economy often did so not primarily for economic reasons but because of violent extortion and warfare by domestic or foreign military groups. Pacification of these lands is a necessary condition for any kind of development. This too requires collective action, of a more costly and risky nature than poor relief. And even when peace prevails, good governance is a necessary condition for economic growth, one that is not easily furthered by intervention from outside.

Under conditions of war, tyranny, or rampant corruption, transnational social policies can hardly alleviate poverty. But once peace and the rule of law are restored, such policies may not be needed, as the newly released forces of the market may generate opportunities for the poor also. But in a number of countries the economy nevertheless remains stagnant or a considerable part of the poor remain excluded from the expanding economy. In these cases, transnational social policies may stimulate growth by fostering demand and help to integrate the poorer sections of society. Such countries are mostly located in sub-Saharan Africa and Central Asia.[12] Measured against the criteria discussed here, these countries tend not to be very threatening, nor do they hold much promise of opportunity for the rich nations. As a result, they will not easily elicit collective action from a caucus of rich countries, even if that effort might well turn out to be feasible and effective.

On a global scale, a limited but very persistent and especially needy category remains: the poor in poor societies with a stagnant or shrinking economy. They constitute a problem of quite manageable proportions but one that does not impose itself with much urgency upon the community of nations, except as a human tragedy that begs a humanitarian solution.

A major problem in providing relief to poor individuals is the notorious inability of formal institutions in poor countries to deliver money, goods, or expertise to the needy.[13] Schemes for low-interest credit on favorable loan conditions, for example, designed to serve the neediest, almost invariably fail to reach their targeted population.[14]

A research program on transnational social policy should give priority to projects investigating the possibilities of reaching the poorest individuals. It is almost certain that new aid agencies, created from scratch, will fail at that task. Rather, the search should be for existing financial arrangements at the grassroots level.[15] This suggests at least two promising topics: informal savings associations and—a much less investigated phenomenon—money transfers from emigrant workers to their relatives at home.[16] The informal savings associations are similar to nineteenth-century Western mutual societies, except that the latter also had an insurance function.[17]

The school system may also serve as a network for delivering provisions. Even the poorest and most remote villages now have schools. Public health services are best established in their immediate vicinity, where they can most easily reach young children and their parents. Schools may also form the locus where elementary provisions in kind are delivered: school meals and uniforms, for example, which may be supplied by the villagers with local resources and funded by outside agencies.

In the short run, the poor in the poor areas of the globe do not constitute a "clear and present danger" for the inhabitants of the wealthy nations, often not even for the rich citizens of those poor countries themselves. Nor do the poor hold much promise as potential workers, consumers, or voters in countries with a stagnant economy and no elections, where they can expect at best to be employed as recruits for the military. In the long run, large-scale poverty, even in remote areas, is bound to cause problems for the less indigent part of humanity. This may yet persuade the inhabitants of the wealthier countries to support transnational social policies for the residents of poorer lands. Under what conditions, if any, they would be ready to do so is an issue with a long pedigree in the study of the welfare state in the national context. There, the issue is often defined in terms of altruism and solidarity, notions that are notoriously difficult to capture in empirical terms.[18] Yet, these ideas can be combined fruitfully with the notion of a collective interest in controlling the externalities of poverty in a broad context and in the long run. It may well be that the propensity to engage in collective action to improve the living conditions of the poor requires not only an awareness of the actual interdependencies between the poorer and the wealthier sections of society—that is, of the externalities that operate between them—but also a sense of identification with the poor as human beings who are not very different from those who are better off. If the poor are considered less than human, or somehow incurably and necessarily indigent, what use can it be to try to improve their lot at all?

Some recent essays reflect upon transnational identifications with suffering strangers.[19] Such dispositions manifest themselves in an emerging transnational society in the web of connections that link human beings across borders, directly or mediated by firms, states, and international agencies. The "remote sufferer" is one "character" in this transnational society, presented and represented in the media by agencies specializing in charitable relief, fund-raising, and "conscientization." In many respects this drama is a continuation of the European charitable tradition by different means.

It is the task of sociologists to help design transnational policies that, on the one hand, are oriented towards consumption, as is charitable emergency relief but, on the other hand, are of a more structural and binding character, like development aid. Such policies should be implemented by international agencies that coordinate the collective effort of the wealthy nations. This prospect is a matter not of years but of decades. At present it seems to be receding into an ever more distant future. But transnational social policies may come to be accepted as a fair, feasible, and effective way to improve the lot of the poor in poor countries through the collective action of the rich nations.

Notes

1. See Abram de Swaan, *In Care of the State: Health Care, Education, and Welfare in Europe and the USA in the Modern Era* (New York: Oxford University Press; Oxford: Polity Press, 1988).

2. See Abram de Swaan, "Perspectives for Transnational Social Policy," *Government and Opposition* 27, no. 1 (Winter 1992): 33–51, first published, in Dutch, as the Den Uyl lecture (7 December 1989), here summarized in the sections "The Collectivizing Process" and "Conditions for Transnational Collective Action."

3. See Paul Kapteyn, *The Stateless Market: The European Dilemma of Integration and Civilization* (London: Routledge, 1995).

4. See Aristide R. Zolberg, Astri Suhrke, and Sergio Aguayo, *Escape from Violence: Conflict and the Refugee Crisis in the Developing World* (New York: Oxford University Press, 1989).

5. Moral concern about the suffering and misery among the victims of violent conflict is widespread and intense among the populations of the rich countries, and it generates pressure on governments for humanitarian and armed intervention in the affected area, which can be quite effective at times. However, as soon as the expeditionary force suffers casualties, public opinion, out of the same humanitarian sensibility that made it demand intervention, now insists that the boys be brought home at the earliest opportunity.

6. Stephan Leibfried and Paul Pierson, "The Prospects for Social Europe," in *Social Policy beyond Borders: The Social Question in Transnational Perspective*, ed. Abram de Swaan (Amsterdam: Amsterdam University Press, 1994), 15–58. See also various contributions to Stephan Leibfried and Paul Pierson, eds., *European Social Policy: Between Fragmentation and Integration* (Washington, D.C.: Brookings Institution, 1995); and in *Social Policy in a Changing Europe*, ed. Zsuzsa Ferge and Jon Eivind Kolberg (Frankfurt am Main: Campus; Boulder, Colo.:Westview Press, 1992); for a recent discussion of the implications of the Social Charter and the Social Protocol, see Gilles Sintes, *La politique sociale de l'Union européenne* (Brussels: Presses Interuniversitaires Européennes, 1996).

7. See Wolfgang Streeck, "From Market-Making to State-Building? Reflections on the Political Economy of European Social Policy," in *European Social Policy*, 389–431.

8. Giandomenico Majone, "The European Community between Social Policy and Social Regulation," *Journal of Common Market Studies* 31, no. 2 (June 1993): 153–70.

9. Leibfried and Pierson, "Prospects for Social Europe," 35 n 44, ascribe to me the assumption that national barriers are insurmountable for welfare states. My argument is that *so far* welfare states have been national arrangements, and that assessment still stands. At issue is the open question of whether and how social policy will transcend this level of the member states.

10. See G. van Liemt, "Minimum Labor Standards and International Trade: Would a Clause Work?" *International Labor Review* 128, no. 4 (1989): 433–48.

11. Globalization per se, by decreasing the state's power to control domestic condi-

tions for labor, weakens the working class, according to Charles Tilly, "Globalization Threatens Labor's Rights," Working Paper Series 182 (New York: Center for Studies of Social Change, New School for Social Research, March 1994).

12. For a survey of poverty in developing countries, in the context of an impressive discussion of the philosophical and economic issues involved, see Partha Dasgupta, *Well-Being and Destitution* (Oxford: Clarendon Press, 1993).

13. The problems of delivery and "entitlement" have been discussed most lucidly by Amartya K. Sen, *Poverty and Famines: An Essay on Entitlement and Deprivation* (Oxford: Oxford University Press, 1981); see also Jean Drèze and Amartya Sen, *Hunger and Public Action* (Oxford: Clarendon Press, 1989).

14. See F. J. A. Bouman, *Small, Short and Unsecured. Informal Rural Finance in India* (Oxford: Oxford University Press, 1989); see also Shirley Ardener and Sandra Burman, eds., *Money-Go-Rounds: The Importance of Rotating Savings and Credit Associations for Women* (Oxford: Berg, 1995).

15. See D. W. Adams and D. A. Fitchett, eds., *Informal Finance in Low-Income Countries* (Boulder, Colo.: Westview Press, 1992); and D. W. Adams and D. A. Fitchett, eds., *Banking the Unbankable: Bringing Credit to the Poor* (London: Panos, 1989); Monika Huppi and Gershon Feder, "The Role of Groups and Credit Cooperatives on Rural Lending," *World Bank Observer* 5, no. 2 (1990): 187–204; Heru-Negroho Soegiarto, *The Embeddedness of Money, Moneylenders, and Moneylending in a Javanese Town: A Case Study of Bantul-Yogyakarta Special Province* (Ph.D. diss., University of Bielefeld, 1993); Pieter H. Streefland, "Credit and Conscientization: Effects of Different Development Approaches in Bangladesh," *Public Administration and Development,* 13 (1993): 153–69; Michel Lelart, ed., *La tontine: Pratique informelle d'épargne et de crédit dans les pays en voie de développement* (Paris: Libbey, 1990).

16. See the research program of the Amsterdam School for Social Science Research, *Social Policy in a Transnational Context* (Amsterdam: ASSR, 1994; rev. ed., 1996).

17. See Marcel van der Linden, "The Historical Logic of Mutual Workers' Insurance," *International Social Security Review* 46, no. 3 (1993): 5–18; de Swaan, *In Care of the State,* 143–51. On the comparison of nineteenth-century mutual societies in Europe and the United States with contemporary savings clubs in developing countr[ies, see my introduction and other contributions to Marcel van der Linden and Jacqueline van der Sluijs, eds., *Onderlinge hulpfondsen* (Mutual funds) (Amsterdam: International Institute for Social History, 1996).

18. See Cranford Pratt, *Internationalism under Strain: The North-South Policies of Canada, the Netherlands, Norway, and Sweden* (Toronto: University of Toronto Press, 1989); Brian H. Smith, *More than Altruism: The Politics of Private Foreign Aid* (Princeton: Princeton University Press, 1990).

19. See, e.g., Thomas L. Haskell, "Capitalism and the Origins of the Humanitarian Sensibility," parts 1 and 2, *American Historical Review* 90, no. 2 (1985): 339–61; and no. 3 (1985): 547–66; Luc Boltanski, *La souffrance à distance* (Paris: Métailié, 1993); Abram de Swaan, "Widening Circles of Identification: Emotional Concerns in Sociogenetic Perspective," *Theory, Culture, and Society* 12, no. 1 (1995): 25–39; Abram de

Swaan, "Widening Circles of Disidentification: On the Psycho- and Sociogenesis of the Hatred of Distant Strangers: Reflections on Rwanda," *Theory, Culture, and Society* 14, no . 2 (1997): 105–22.

9

From *Special* to *Specialized* Rights: The Politics of Citizenship and Identity in the European Union

Antje Wiener

When citizenship in the European Union (EU) was established with Article 8 of the treaty establishing the European Community (EC Treaty), two decades of citizenship policy making had contributed to defining very little in legal terms. Minimalist legal observers have criticized the citizenship article as not adding much to the rights that Union citizens already enjoyed and creating a "pie in the sky."[1] According to these comments, Union citizenship does not change much. Yet, the years between the intergovernmental conferences (IGCs) of Maastricht (1991) and Amsterdam (1997) suggest a different interpretation. Indeed, the high degree of mobilization among Union citizens, interest groups, and so-called third-country nationals suggests that Union citizenship had a politically stimulating impact. Why did people mobilize around the newly created legal institution of Union citizenship? Was their interest or concern caused by the contents of Article 8 of the EC Treaty, which after all is pretty much limited to granting political rights? How does this political interest fit in with the early intentions of the makers of EU citizenship policy?

This chapter takes on the task of elaborating on these questions. To that end, it will situate the rising visible notion of citizen mobilization within the larger context of EU citizenship policy. The decision to bring citizenship policy onto the EC's agenda was originally made in the early 1970s, when the EC was in desperate need of being acknowledged as an actor on the world stage. Since then, citizenship policy has been shaped by the influence of a whole variety of different actors within the emerging Euro-polity. In the process, what I will call "citizenship practice" (i.e., citizenship policy and politics) helped institutionalize the specifically "European" terms of citizenship, thus contributing to building the Euro-polity. The following account of European citizenship practice begins with the strong impact on policy in the early 1970s and then follows the process of shaping citizenship policy throughout the 1980s and 1990s to demonstrate the critical shift from policy to politics of citizenship.

To understand the content and changed meaning of citizenship, this chapter takes a sociohistorical perspective on citizenship, focusing on the societal context—the input of ideas, normative considerations, and values—and on the institutionalized terms of citizenship as the output of citizenship practice. A constructive approach to the institution of the *acquis communautaire,* the common principles and legal properties of the European Union, helps to evaluate these terms. If Union citizenship exists alongside national citizenship of the EU member states, and if it is true that the meaning of citizenship is greater than the sum of its parts, then EU citizenship requires a perspective that leaves theoretical space for construction. On this premise I argue that the case of Union citizenship contributes to an eventual reconceptualization of citizenship as fragmented and deterritorialized.

The chapter has four sections. The first section provides a brief introduction to the sociohistorical context of citizenship; the second section introduces an analytical approach to the institution of *acquis communautaire*; the third encompasses the case study of citizenship practice over four stages; and the fourth section summarizes the findings of the case study with a view to answering the questions about Union citizenship raised above.

Citizenship: The Sociohistorical Context and Content of a Concept

The academic community and European institutions as well as a number of interest groups voice concern and curiosity about the meaning of Union citizenship, its political potential, and its organizational feasibility. They draw attention to the fact that this type of citizenship seems to lack crucial characteristics of modern liberal concepts of citizenship. Indeed, Union citizenship does not grant full rights to democratic participation or representation,[2] and it is granted on the basis of member state nationality not European nationality. That is, specific European political and sociocultural dimensions seem to be lacking. Beyond the political and organizational aspects, these observations raise questions about the community of belonging and, more specifically, about how to define borders of belonging. Who has a legitimate right to belong legally to this Union has become a much debated issue.[3] Legal approaches characterize Union citizenship as a compilation of previously existing rights, and it seems indeed "difficult to understand which meaning this new element of the EC Treaty may have for the process of European integration, and which stamp it might imprint on the character of the emergent European Union."[4]

The European case represents a dramatic deviation from modern concepts of citizenship. The constructive perspective of this paper is, however, based on another observation that suggests that Union citizenship is not the only challenge to the concept; rather the explosion of interest in citizenship has been building for some time. Processes of decolonization and migration as well as social movement mobilization around questions of ethnicity, race, and gender have pointed to the existence of other than nation-state boundaries and mobilized other than national identities to change exclusive definitions of citizenship. They represent a second challenge to the concept of citizenship, suggesting that the "language of citizenship" is becoming outdated.[5] More radical contributions demand that "democratic citizenship ought to be disentangled from citizenship as state membership" altogether.[6] At any rate, as the borders of citizenship are challenged both internally and externally, central aspects of citizenship such as belonging and identity have moved onto shaky ground. An analysis of Union citizenship within the context of a "postmodern" polity is assumed to shed fresh light on the contested boundaries of belonging and the related citizenship identities.[7]

The most striking difference between Union citizenship and modern citizenship is the lacking dimension of nationality. Union citizenship calls into question the link between the concept of nationality and that of citizenship and hence problematizes the myth of national identity that was crucial for erecting borders around national states.[8] How has the concept of nationality so far been methodologically linked with the concept of citizenship? And how does this affect the evolving concept of Union citizenship? These are crucial questions that challenge national conceptions of citizenship. While national identity was—and often still is—considered important for the representation of states in the international state system, its conceptualization as nationality needs to be clearly distinguished from the concept of citizenship.[9]

Social movements emphasize the importance of collective identities that do not depend on nationality but develop in relation with internal boundaries that mark class, gender, race, age, and other cleavages.[10] Such collective identities produce, and are the product of, boundaries within national states. As such they represent both inequalities and differences. They may lead to citizens' claims and may inversely be mobilized to enforce citizenship identity. However, identities are never generated by the institutions of the state but are created through practice.[11] As an increasing number of individuals (citizens and noncitizens) share economic, social, and cultural spaces, tensions emerge that are not rooted in conflicts over national-state boundaries but over boundaries within states. This specific situatedness challenges the familiar modern geography of citizenship with its external borders and policies to erect and protect these borders.[12] The citizenship model presented in figure 9.1 is thus called into question.

NO ⇒ OUT

Individual ⇒ **Nationality**

YES ⇒ IN

⇓

Citizen ⇐ **Rights**   • **political**

                               • **civil**

                               • **social**

Fig. 9.1. The Modern Geography of Citizenship

They suggest that borders appear not only as visible but also as invisible means of inclusion and exclusion. For example, they may be considered on the one hand as physical borders defined by rules of entry to a country (one crosses the border upon entering a country by land, air, or sea; one has to pass border posts, show one's passport). On the other hand, they also exist as informal boundaries specified by a feeling of belonging to a collectivity that is defined according to structural (i.e., racial, gender, class, ethnic, sexual preference, age, or physical ability) or interest (e.g., environment, consumption) factors. This chapter argues that as these borders become more and more visible, the necessity of incorporating this new geography of citizenship into citizenship theory has become an issue of political power that reaches beyond social movement activities. The post-Maastricht citizenship debates, for example, have acquired the character of constitutional politics. They advance a notion of citizenship as constitutive for a community.[13] Understood in this way, Union citizenship includes a constructive dimension.

This possibility has been explored on two grounds. One approach relies on the concept of additionality. In concurring with the European Commission, it finds that Union citizenship "adds to the first group of nationality rights enjoyed within a Member State a second circle of new rights enjoyed in any Member State."[14] The other approach draws on the concept of historicity. It is based on the assumption that citizenship does not have an objective meaning and must therefore be deconstructed in order to explain how "real historical participants use it in historical contexts."[15] Hence, a reconstruction of citizenship in different contexts allows for an understanding of "the meanings of citizenship over time."[16] Given the observed gap between the language and the history of citizenship, I propose to address the puzzle of Union citizenship by confronting the *language* of citizenship (as in theory) with the new developing *discourse* of citizenship (as in practice) in the EC/EU. Central to this analysis is a sociohistorical approach that assumes that the practice of citizenship is historically variable and is interrelated with

individual

⇑

　　　⇒　**citizenship practice**

⇓

community/state

Fig. 9.2. The Constitutive Elements
of Citizenship

the establishment of state institutional arrangements.[17] This approach draws on the notion of citizenship as a relational concept.[18] I elaborate on this notion of practice and propose a way of incorporating it into traditional conceptions of citizenship. To that end, I first characterize the constitutive elements and subsequently the historical elements of citizenship and argue that both facilitate an analytical context for an appreciation of changing geographies of citizenship.

In the broadest terms, citizenship defines a relation between the individual and the political community. It concerns the entitlement to belong to a political community, which has the right and the duty to represent community interests as a sovereign vis-à-vis other communities and vis-à-vis the citizens. This model of a relationship between two entities, namely, the individual on one side and the representative of a larger community on the other, has provided modern history with a basic pattern of citizenship.[19] It follows from these observations that at least three elements need to be considered in the conceptualization of citizenship: the individual, the community, and the relation between the two.[20] Since all studies of citizenship have so far referred to these three elements in one way or other, they may be termed the three *constitutive elements of citizenship* (see figure 9.2).

Whereas the first two elements, the individual and the community, have been stressed by contractarian approaches to citizenship in particular, so far the third—relational—element has not received much attention.[21] Yet, there is an increasing awareness of the fact that citizenship cannot be dealt with on the basis of formal criteria alone. Instead, citizenship always represents more, and at the same time less, than the sum of its parts.[22] That is, citizens contribute to the creation of a community, yet not all persons who reside within the same geographical spaces enjoy the same citizenship privileges. This is where the tension lies; the current mobilization of (non)citizens in the European Union is a case in point. To assess these underlying dynamics, the focus shifts to the dynamic aspect of citizenship that develops from the interplay of the constitutive elements across time and space and contributes layers of historically derived meaning to the concept. Both citizens' action, expressed as political struggles, and state policies have contributed to changes in political organization within and among communities.

Three *historical elements* of citizenship allow for a conceptualization of citizenship that takes account of historical variability and thus avoids presupposing a specific situatedness of the constitutive elements. These historical elements are rights, access to participation, and belonging. *Rights* refers to the legal entitlements of an individual from the community. This element comprises various types of rights, civil, political, and social. The perspective of citizenship as the incremental addition of rights has been most prominently associated with T. H. Marshall. Civil rights include the rights to liberty of the person; freedom of speech, thought; and faith, ownership of property; and the freedom to make valid contracts. Political rights include the right to participate in the exercise of political power. Social rights amount to the right to receive a modicum of social welfare and security, to share in social heritage, and to live the life of a civilized being.[23]

Access, the second element of citizenship, is about the conditions for practicing the relationship between citizen and community and may be understood as access to political participation. Conditions of access are set by regulative policies including social policy, market policy, and visa policy, for example. They are crucial determinants as to whether or not individuals are fit to participate politically. Access therefore hinges on sociocultural, economic, and political mechanisms of inclusion and exclusion. That is, while rights may have been stipulated, access may be denied because the means to use citizenship rights, such as proper education, communication, or transportation, may not have been sufficiently established.

The third historical element encompasses two modes of *belonging* to a community. One is identity based, the other hinges upon legal linkages to an entity that are currently based on either the law of soil or of blood (*jus solis* and *jus sanguinis,* respectively), or, as in the European Union, on nationality of one of the member states. Every person residing within a particular area potentially has the opportunity to participate in the creation of collective identities. These identities may be created through participation at the workplace, in cultural matters, or in other spaces of the community. Accordingly, residence is the crucial aspect for participation. Apart from the residence criterion, a person's legal status defines whether or not he or she is considered a full citizen. This status has always been exclusive, mostly according to the criteria of gender, age, and nationality. This dimension of belonging is therefore also about borders, as citizens derive certain rights and opportunities of access based on their belonging to a bounded sphere. More specifically, this feeling of belonging depends on a previous process of "drawing boundaries" around terrains designated for those citizens who belong.[24]

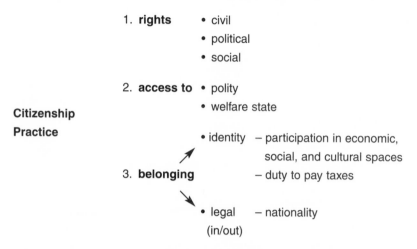

Fig. 9.3. Citizenship Practice: Rights, Access, Belonging

While it is possible to single out the three historical elements, it is important to keep in mind that they are always interrelated. The three aspects bear a process-oriented or dynamic notion of citizenship. They add contextualized meaning to the concept of ideal citizenship, defining citizenship as stipulating rights, providing access, and creating a feeling of belonging and identity. Beyond the creation of a concrete citizenship that is particular to each community, they contribute to the crafting of distinct institutional networks. They are thus important factors for successful governance within and among communities. Figure 9.3 provides a schema for such a constructive approach to citizenship practice.

In sum, I propose a concept that understands citizenship as the practice that leads to the establishment of rights, access, and belonging as three interrelated historical elements of citizenship. In principle this concept does not follow either a state-centric (top-down) or a society-centric (bottom-up) perspective. It encompasses both policymaking and politics with respect to the establishment or change of citizenship.[25] The prevalence of one mode of action over the other varies according to context. Both modes of citizenship practice are always possible.

If the establishment of access to rights contributes to the mobilization of identities that enhance the creation of a feeling of belonging, then an analysis of the process through which access to rights has been established in the EC/EU will provide insights into the creation of belonging. Based on the concept of citizenship practice, this analysis of Union citizenship does not begin from an approach that defines citizenship legally according to citizenship rights, nor does it seek to assess the potential of European citizenship to develop a European *national* identity. Instead it aims at an understanding of characteristic features of European citizenship and assumes citizenship to be constructed in practice particular to time, place, actors, and institutions. It seeks to identify Union citizenship in its own context. Citizenship is thus understood as more than a status based on rights. It is conceptualized as a dynamic rather than a static concept.

A Reflective Approach to the Acquis Communautaire

In the fractured Euro-polity policymaking rests on the Treaty on European Union as a quasi constitution and tangible institutional framework that also helps to define the acquis communautaire.[26] The "accession" acquis was the oldest concept of acquis that defined "the whole body of rules, political principles and judicial decisions which new Member States must adhere to, in their entirety and from the beginning, when they become members of the Communities."[27] According to the European Commission the acquis communautaire is understood as "the contents, principles and political objectives of the Treaties, including the Maastricht Treaty; the legislation adopted in implementation of the Treaties, and the jurisprudence of the Court; the declarations and resolutions adopted in the Community framework; the international agreements, and the agreements between member states "connected with the Community's activities."[28] It therefore is an important institution of the Euro-polity that any analysis of EC/EU politics cannot avoid considering. While member states might "deplore certain aspects of Community policy, there is no question that all find themselves locked into a system which narrows down the areas for possible change and obliges them to think of incremental revision of existing arrangements."[29]

However, the substance of the acquis is often difficult to pin down. It is like "something that everybody has heard about it, but nobody knows what it looks like."[30] There is something else beyond the formal rules, regulations, and procedures of the Euro-polity. Even though the acquis is often known by the participating actors in the Euro-polity, this knowledge about shared principles and norms does not necessarily mean visibility. It can therefore be assumed that the processes of constructing meaning that contribute to the construction of knowledge add another dimension to the acquis. To make such processes visible, I propose to include informal resources and the routinization of citizenship policy in the assessment of the citizenship acquis.

According to figure 9.1, the acquis potentially comprises informal resources such as constructed meaning and practices, on the one hand, and formal resources such as rules, regulations, and procedures, on the other. The informal resources often are the part of a proposal that has been debated for some time, such as the right to vote, which has not been codified, pending final adoption by the European Council. In contrast, the formal resources include the regulations, directives, and decisions that have been adopted by the Council. While the acquis entails both informal and formal resources, it is important to note that not all informal resources immediately form part of the acquis. This model suggests that they are only considered part of the acquis once they have acquired a degree of routinization that structures the policy process.

While the formal resources of the acquis are largely subject to a consensus, the informal resources are much more likely to be contested. They will therefore most often be debated in the appropriate forums of the Euro-polity depending on the policy's link with the EU's pillar structure and the respective approach (Community or intergovernmental) that applies.[31] The acquis changes over time. These changes are expressed in the debates in between "history-making" Council decisions or "snapshots."[32] The dynamic of these debates is most likely based on the often contradictory interests between two largely differing approaches to the process of European integration, most clearly distinguished as integrationists, who will more often push for the adoption of a proposal, and the intergovernmentalists, who will attempt to keep the status quo.

The resources contribute crucial information for policymakers because the formal resources may be mobilized, on the one hand, and the informal resources may be transformed into legally established principles or share norms, on the other, once the opportunity is right. Providing opportunities and constraints, they thus invisibly structure policymaking. It follows that a change of the acquis potentially involves two processes. One includes the expansion of formal resources (changes in the treaty provisions, directives, regulations); the other involves the routinization of practices or the constitutionalization of informal resources (ideas, shared principles, practices as suggested by European Parliament resolutions and Commission proposals or other documents). In general, the change of the acquis depends on changes in the political opportunity structure that facilitate the mobilization of resources for the establishment of a policy or its components. The analysis of the multidimensional jigsaw puzzle of EU citizenship policy therefore hinges on the systematic assessment of changes of the acquis communautaire. Historical institutionalism thus offers an important methodological access point for a sociohistorical account of citizenship policy by providing a way to assess the immediate institutional context on the basis of the formal and informal resources that compose the acquis communautaire.

Four Stages of "European" Citizenship Practice

Since the early 1970s, policymaking with respect to Union citizenship has unfolded on the basis of two policy packages whose objectives were "special rights" for Community citizens and "passport union." [33] Both policy packages touch crucial aspects of modern citizenship, such as borders and how to cross them (passport union) and citizens' right to vote and stand for elections (special rights). They have been central to the debates over citizenship, European identity, and political union that took place over two decades in the Euro-polity. [34] The step-by-step development and application of the two policy packages not only provides insight into how citizenship eventually turned into Article 8 of the EC Treaty twenty years later but also suggests that Union citizenship acquires a specific meaning once it is put into context. [35]

While citizenship practice in the EC/EU remained largely invisible until it was spelled out as citizenship of the Union and legally grounded in the 1993 Treaty of the European Union, the roots of citizenship policy and actual citizenship practice can be traced over a period of about two decades. From the analytical framework laid out in this chapter, it follows that we need to focus on the development of citizenship policy in order to reconstruct the making of Union citizenship as a practice. The following section summarizes the story of unfolding citizenship practice based on the expanding citizenship acquis communautaire since the early 1970s. It focuses on the gradual fragmentation of rights, access, and belonging as special rights and passport policy emerged as ideas or practices and were eventually turned into rules and procedures that added to the substantial basis of Union citizenship.

Paris

In the early 1970s, European politicians and practitioners expressed the need to develop a stronger European presence on the global stage. To that end, they proposed to work towards a stronger European identity. The Community documents of that period demonstrate that the debate over how to achieve a European identity received central attention. Out of these debates were generated the policy objectives of special rights for European citizens and a passport union, both aimed at creating a feeling of belonging and identity. The adoption of the 1976 Council decision to implement direct universal suffrage [36] and the first European elections in 1979 and the adoption of a Council resolution on the creation of a single European passport in 1981 [37] were crucial first steps that expanded the institutionalized acquis. Besides these institutional changes, the acquis was expanded on a discursive level as the idea of "Europeanness" that had been introduced with the document on European identity in 1973.

Thus, both political union and the creation of a European identity were put on the agenda as new overarching goals in Community policymaking.[38] During the turbulence that followed the breakdown of the Bretton Woods system, EC policymakers stressed the necessity to establish a European voice in the global realm. Commission President Xavier Ortoli stated after the 1972 Paris summit that "the economic crisis and the changes in international relations, far from strengthening Community solidarity and leading to an assertion of *Europe's identity vis-à-vis the rest of the world,* have marked a further check, and perhaps a retreat, in the process of European construction."[39] According to Commissioner Davignon, the crisis was largely rooted in the EC's lack of organic political growth, which was also reflected in meager support from European citizens.[40] His discourse regarding the problem stressed the theme of *belongingness* when he stated that "we don't feel that we belong to a new entity. *Europe should be personalized.* . . . Another dimension should be added to Europe, the new Europe must be *more human.*"[41] In a similar vein Belgian Foreign Minister Van Elslande pointed to the missing link between citizens and the Community as one reason for the crisis. In order to establish that link, he recommended that the Belgian presidency aim at creating the "first concrete stage towards establishing *European citizenship,*" which would include mobility for students, exchanges of teachers, and harmonization of diplomas, with a view to giving "young people . . . the chance of feeling truly part of a vast network covering the whole of the Community."[42] Italy's Altiero Spinelli demanded "a constitutional procedure for European identity," which could be based on the nine leaders' expression of "their Governments' political obligation to bring forward the deadline for preparing the European political Union and to specify the form of such preparation."[43]

These contributions set out ideas for a twofold approach to the creation of belonging. One was based on the experience of national states and understood belongingness as evolving from the making of a nation-state-like entity. Accordingly, policymaking was geared towards the goal of a supposedly federal political union. The other understood belongingness as emerging from participation in Community affairs. That approach was not necessarily based on the vision of a federal union. Both lines were reflected in the subsequent changes in the resources of the citizenship acquis. For example, as a first step towards the creation of a sense of belonging, a paper on European identity was issued at the 1973 Copenhagen summit.[44] It broadly defined European identity as based on a "common heritage" and "acting together in relation to the rest of the world," while the "dynamic nature of European unification" was to be respected.[45] This general modern idea of Community development was to be carried out through a citizenship practice that included the adoption of the two policy objectives of special rights for European citizens and a passport union.

Special working groups were assigned the task of producing draft reports for the development of the passport union, special rights, universal suffrage, and a concept of European union.[46] Importantly, in the Council's final document, citizens were for the first time considered participants in the process of European integration, not as consumers, but as citizens.[47] The notion of citizen thus turned into a new informal resource of the acquis communautaire.

The Commission's report on special rights pointed out that "special rights of a political nature are essentially the rights to vote, to stand for election and to hold public office."[48] They were defined as the "political rights traditionally withheld from foreigners."[49] The report suggested that European citizenship should not be achieved on the basis of the process of "naturalization," since this process would involve the loss of the previous nationality by substituting a new European nationality. Instead, citizens' rights should be defined according to the principle of equality, thus providing the citizens with the possibility of adding "rights relating to the original nationality . . . to the rights in the host State." It is important to note that at this stage of citizenship practice, it remained to be decided whether foreigners should be granted special rights "on the foreigner's status as a worker . . . [or] as a citizen of another Member State."[50] The Commission did, however, point out that equal treatment for foreigners would not be easily accepted by the public, and thus the Commission favored a step-by-step approach.[51] In turn, the Tindemans Report brought to the fore the interrelation between member state nationality and a new European dimension. It proposed to overcome the idea of the national as predominant and to break "intellectual barriers" by constantly including a "European dimension" in daily politics.[52] The European Parliament's perception of special rights was clearly grounded in a federal vision. As defined by the Bayerl Report, "[s]pecial rights are 'subjective' public rights, in other words rights which the citizen possesses as a legal subject vis-à-vis the State and which may be asserted at any time."[53]

These conceptually crucial discussions remained as ideas among the informal resources of the acquis until they were dusted off more than a decade later. In the meantime, citizenship practice included the creation of further resources for the establishment of voting rights. On 8 October 1976, the Council adopted an "Act concerning the election of the representatives of the Assembly by direct universal suffrage."[54] The Parliament adopted a resolution on a "draft uniform electoral procedure for the election of Members of the European Parliament" on 10 March 1982.[55] And in 1983 the European Parliament's Legal Affairs Committee prepared the "Report on the right of citizens of a Member State residing in a Member State other than their own to stand for and vote in local elections."[56]

In addition to policymaking within the special rights package, the passport package was developed. A uniform passport was assumed to contribute in a twofold way to the construction of ties between the Community and its citizens. It was not only aimed at increasing awareness of Europe as a new political actor on the international stage, but it was also expected to create a feeling among European citizens of belonging to the Community. The final communiqué of the 1974 Paris summit clearly stated, first, that "the fact remains that the introduction of such a passport would have a psychological effect, one which would emphasize the feeling of nationals of the nine Member States of belonging to the Community";[57] and second, "that such a passport might be equally justified by the desire of the nine Member States to affirm vis-à-vis non-member countries the existence of the Community as an entity, and eventually to obtain from each of them identical treatment for citizens of the Community."[58]

However, the practice of carrying common passports within this new community involved, among other things, the reduction of border controls and the introduction of spot checks at internal Community borders. When the European passport was created in 1981, it turned out that the creation of the passport and its actual use were two different matters. The peculiarity of the policy situation was rooted in the Janus-faced characteristics of this enterprise. On the one hand, successful foreign and economic policy performance depended on the acknowledgment of Europe as an actor in the global arena. On the other hand, the creation of this feeling of belonging—as one aspect of creating a European identity—depended among other things on the practice of border crossing. That is, it was part of a third pillar, justice and domestic policy, which was an essentially diplomatic matter. Yet, by carrying burgundy-colored passports at intra-Community borders, citizens of EC member states were crucial to the creation of this type of belonging. As the story of citizenship practice in the 1980s will show, this approach to the creation of belonging remained a seemingly insurmountable hurdle for member states' security concerns.

Fontainebleau

Citizenship practice during the next stage of Community development in the 1980s included a changed policy paradigm. A decade of economic uncertainty, widespread concerns over "ungovernability" in the member states, and an increasing fear of "Euro-sclerosis" as EC policymaking remained largely blocked by unsolved budgetary problems had contributed to an overall feeling of "Euro-pessimism"[59] and put market-making on top of the Community agenda in the 1980s.[60] The new policy paradigm involved a focus on negative integration (i.e., eliminating obstacles to the project of creating a market without frontiers) stressing movement of worker-citizens as one basic condition for economic flexibility. Positive integration, which would involve, for example, access to the polity (i.e., the political right to vote) lagged behind access to participation in socioeconomic terms or, for that matter, access to an emergent European social space, which became a major aspect of citizenship practice during this period of market-making. The slogan that contributed to the dynamic of this process was Jacques Delors's "Europe without Frontiers by 1992."[61] Apart from abolishing internal Community frontiers, the Europe '92 program included new strategies to make the best use of Europe's human resources in the creation of European identity.[62]

This access was extended group by group as a new mobility policy targeted groups other than workers, such as young people, academics, and students.[63] Three new directives established the right of residence for workers and their families and students.[64] Two types of special rights were now negotiated by Community policymakers and the member states' politicians. First, a series of social rights such as health care, the right to establishment, old-age pensions, and the recognition of diplomas were defined with the Social Charter. These rights were the economic and social requirements to prevent social dumping (i.e., circumventing social costs of production by transferring the productive process to another member state). However, crossing borders to work in another member state meant that so-called foreigners (i.e., Community citizens who worked in a member state of which they were not nationals) and nationals shared the work spaces but remained divided in the polity. This situation evoked an increasing public awareness of a "democratic deficit" in the European Community. The Commission identified the impact of economic integration as being a loss of status. That is, once citizens moved, they lost access to political participation. To overcome this dilemma, the Commission negotiated the second type of special right and proposed the establishment of voting rights for "foreigners" in municipal elections.[65] This proposal for a Council directive on the right to vote and stand for election in municipal elections suggested closing the gap between foreigners and nationals by reviving an informal resource of the acquis, namely, the shared principle of equal political rights for European citizens.

The interrelation between the free movement of worker-citizens and the political right to vote and stand for election represented a decisive discursive shift in EC citizenship practice. By linking normative ideas to the politics of market-making, citizenship practice highlighted two different expressions of belonging. One was the modern type of belonging based on legal ties between citizens and a community defined by political citizenship rights and nationality. The other type of belonging is more subtle. It rests on a feeling of belonging that emerges from participation. European citizenship practice suggests that the two types of belonging stand in tension with each other, as participation in another member state created identity-based ties with a Community to which worker-citizens were not legally entitled to belong. The functionalist policy of negative (economic) integration thus created a link to the arguments for positive integration based on citizenship as they had been introduced to the citizenship acquis in the early 1970s.

The passport policy package was also significantly changed in the context of the new policy paradigm when the Commission decided to put the responsibility for difficult and unpopular decisions on the shoulders of the member states. In light of the member states' security concerns about borders, the bulk of border politics as one aspect of the passport package was passed on to intergovernmental bargaining among the member states that participated in the Schengen agreements.[66] Despite this move, Community citizenship practice still involved passport policy as it worked on implementing freedom of movement for workers, thus making clear the Commission's duty to come forward with policy proposals on the matter.[67] Indeed, the profoundly modern security concerns of the member states contributed to an unintended emphasis on the creation of belonging through worker-citizens' participation in the creation of a common market. In this context the Community Charter of Fundamental Rights for Workers was adopted.[68] The Commission's white paper had established a timetable for economic policy making by setting the 1992 time limit for creating an internal market without frontiers.[69] Beyond that, by means of an intergovernmental conference it had elaborated a plausible reason for a treaty reform.

Maastricht

The demands for greater access to participation in both political and socioeconomic terms were renewed in the changed political opportunity structure of the 1990s. With the finalized Maastricht Treaty and the end of cold war politics, Union building reemerged on the agenda of the Euro-polity. The 1990s resulted in the adoption of political citizenship rights as well as the stipulation of the rights of free movement and residence not only for the employed and their families but also for other persons, such as pensioners, job seekers, or students, so long as they are nationals of a member state.

Together the three periods of citizenship practice reveal that the meaning of Union citizenship cannot be identified as the sum of the member states' national citizenship rights and practices, nor can it be deduced from modern citizenship alone. Instead, it is necessary to understand Union citizenship as constructed anew and with its own characteristic features. While the 1990s clearly contributed to the final steps towards the institutionalization of political citizenship rights, this third period of the developing practice of European citizenship also meant another step away from modern citizenship.

The contested aspect of nationality in Union citizenship was brought to the fore by the Community's suddenly changed geopolitical position.[70] "From the outset, the Community had considered itself as synonymous with 'Europe'. With the Cold War over, [the question became] could the Community foster a sense of pan-European solidarity and genuinely pan-European integration?"[71] This was a serious question that also problematized the discourse on a "European" identity that had been so crucial for the emergence of citizenship practice in the early 1970s. At that time European identity meant Western Europeans (including the citizens of potential Western European new member states). Now the fall of the Berlin Wall clearly challenged the use of that term, and, more important, it suggested that some Europeans had been left out all along, as non-Community nationals had been excluded from the special rights policy for years.[72] Now it was "no longer possible to talk of Western Europe as a clearly defined region in world politics."[73] With the meaning of "European" thus challenged, the Community's future was as uncertain as ever.[74] Also significant for further citizenship practice was the shaking of the Paris-Bonn axis—which had proved quite successful for EC politics thus far—as Germany's Chancellor Kohl pushed for fast German unification, while President Mitterrand of France was "torn between an instinctive antipathy toward German unification, . . . and an equally instinctive affinity for European integration."[75] One way of facing this tension was to forge a link between German unification and European integration. This solution seemed feasible to the majority of the member states and led to a renewed interest in political integration.[76] The policy paradigm was then determined by concerns about legitimacy and political integration.

Citizenship practice during this period was strongly influenced by a series of Spanish letters and proposals. These documents suggested a "concept of Community citizenship [that] was different from the notion of the Europe of citizens that had been introduced at the Fontainebleau summit" in that it would include political, economic and social citizenship rights.[77] They contributed to a debate over Community citizenship that could draw on the resources that had become part of the acquis communautaire since the early 1970s. Two types of resources were mobilized during these citizenship negotiations preceding Maastricht. First, citizenship was to grant rights that were special to the different levels of the Community as a polity and as a social space (rights to free movement, residence, and establishment, and the right to vote and stand for municipal and European elections at one's place of residence). Second, the visible sign of citizenship while traveling outside the Community was the uniform passport (which offered reduced border checking and diplomatic protection while abroad). Some of these resources were formalized with the establishment of Article 8 of the EC Treaty.

The debate unfolded over four stages. It was triggered by a letter from Prime Minister Felipe Gonzalez of Spain written on 4 May 1990 for an interinstitutional conference to prepare the IGC on political union.[78] Then a "Foreign Ministers' Note for Reflection" included the idea of citizenship in its recommendations for the Dublin II Council on 25–26 June 1990. This note stated that the upcoming IGC had to deal with the "transformation of the Community from an entity mainly based on economic integration and political cooperation into a union of a political nature, including a common foreign and security policy." Three main aspects were considered important for this goal: (1) the transfer of competencies, (2) Community citizenship, and (3) the free circulation of persons.[79] The second stage included the time between the Dublin II Council and the first meeting of the IGC on 14–15 December 1990. In this period, the concept of European citizenship became part of the Community discourse as policymakers reacted to the Spanish proposal (see table 9.1). The third stage lasted until the Maastricht European Council in December 1991 and was mostly dedicated to developing a legal definition of citizenship to be included in the treaties. The fourth stage began after Maastricht and ended with the first citizenship report of the Commission in 1993. During this stage, the practical aspects of citizenship policy, such as voting rights, were refined. The four stages represent the negotiation of a number of documents leading to the final wording of the Maastricht Treaty.

In time for the IGC on political union on 28 February, the Spanish delegation came forward with a second proposal on citizenship. It proposed to embed citizenship in the treaty by way of a new title to provide a framework for a dynamic concept of citizenship. The rights mentioned in the title included, first, the social right of a citizen to "enjoy equal opportunities and to develop his abilities to the full in his customary environment"; second, the civil rights to movement and residence "without limitation of duration in the territory of the Union"; third, the political rights to "take part in the political life of the place where he lives, and in particular the right to belong to political associations or groupings and the rights to vote in and stand for local elections and elections to the European Parliament"; and, finally, the right to "enjoy the protection of the Union and that of each member State" while in third countries.[80]

The discourse on citizenship practice in the early 1990s showed that although the historical element of belonging was continuously addressed, the focus shifted from creating a *feeling* of belonging to establishing the *legal ties* of belonging. Not only were these legal ties important for defining anew the relation between citizens and the Community, but they also raised questions about the political content of nationality. Along the lines of the Spanish

Table 9.1. Central Documents of Citizenship Policy in the 1990s

Date	Document
20 Feb. 1991	Second Spanish proposal for citizenship[1]
30 March 1991	Commission contribution on citizenship to the IGC on political union[2]
12 April 1991	Non-paper "with a view to achieving political action" drafted by the Luxembourg Presidency[3]
23 May 1991	Interim report on "Union citizenship" by the EP Committee on Institutional Affairs[4]
20 June 1991	Draft treaty on "the Union," used as a reference document until Maastricht[5]
15 July 1991	EP resolution on "Union citizenship"[6]
3 Oct. 1991	Dutch draft treaty "towards European Union"[7]
6 Nov. 1991	Final report on "Union citizenship" by the EP (Bindi Report)[8]
11 Dec. 1991	Maastricht Council conclusions[9]
13 Dec. 1991	Final Dutch draft of the Treaty on Political Union as modified by the Maastricht summit[10]

[1]CONF-UP 1731/91, 20 Feb. 1991.
[2]SEC(91) 500, 30 March 1991; and Bull. EC, supp. 2, 1991, 85–88
[3]Written 12 April 1991. For full text, see *Europe Documents*, no. 1709/1710, 3 May 1991.
[4]PE 150.034/fin, 23 May 1991. Rapporteur: Mrs. Rosamaria Bindi
[5]*Europe Documents*, no. 1722/1723, 15 July 1991
[6]*OJ EC*, C 183, 15 July 1991, 473–76
[7]*Europe Documents*, no. 1733/1734, 3 Oct. 1991
[8]PE 153.099/fin, 6 Nov. 1991
[9]*European Report*, doc. no. 1728, 11 Dec. 1991
[10]*Europe Documents*, no. 1750/1751, 13 Dec. 1991

proposal, Parliament demanded that Union citizenship be included in the treaty as a separate title comprising the following central aspects: "social rights including a substantial widening of the proposals contained in the Social Charter; equal rights between men and women; the political right to vote and stand for election in local and EP elections at one's place of residence, as well as the political right to full political participation at one's place of residence; and the civil right to free movement and residence in all Member States."[81] Importantly, the report repeatedly emphasized the necessity to rethink citizenship, as it could no longer be reduced to the "traditional dichotomy between citizen and foreigner or to the exclusive relationship between the state and the citizens as individuals."[82] Once individuals enjoyed different types of rights in this new world that reflected flexibility and mobility, it became increasingly difficult to define citizenship practice on the basis of nationality.[83]

Amsterdam

The institutionalization of "thin" citizenship meant an institutionalized fragmentation of citizenship. The fourth period shows a growing mobilization around, and a rising confusion over, the consequences of this fragmentation. The European Parliament had, for example, organized hearings in Brussels during which nongovernmental organizations (NGOs) could express their demands to the IGC. While NGOs were not formally entitled to participate in the IGC process, nor were there formally established democratic channels for participation, these hearings nevertheless provided space for discussion.[84] After Maastricht a new debate unfolded over the gap between politically included and excluded residents—that is, between citizens who had legal ties with the Union and so-called third-country citizens, or individuals who did not have legal ties with the Union but who might have developed a feeling of belonging. The debate was pushed by interest groups and the European Parliament in particular.

With respect to the new dynamic in the debate over third-country nationals, it is important to recall that with the fall of the Berlin Wall, the Community had to face a new challenge in the area of border politics; namely, the question of visa and asylum policy, which now involved the question of East-West migration, and how it was to be dealt with by the upcoming Schengen renegotiations.[85] One way of approaching this potential political problem was to establish place-oriented citizenship. It was brought to the fore by social movements' demand to change the citizenship legislation of the treaty. For example, instead of granting citizenship of the Union to "[e]very person holding the nationality of a Member State" (Article 8[1]), the ARNE (Antiracist Network for Equality in Europe) group requested citizenship for "[e]very person holding the nationality of a Member State *and every person residing within the territory of the European Union.*"[86]

The Amsterdam draft treaty of 19 June 1997 did not, however, reflect these demands. On the contrary, the nationality component of citizenship was reinforced with the changed Article F(4) of the Treaty on European Union, which states that the national identities of the member states will be respected. The potential flexibility of the citizenship article (Article 8 of the EC Treaty) has not been used by the practitioners. While the formal institutional aspects of the citizenship acquis thus remained largely the same, the Amsterdam stage of citizenship practice produced more changes with regard to the routinization of informal resources, as Brussels institutions began to work with national representatives, national parliaments, and NGOs on the citizens' demands in order to fight the rising discontent that had begun to replace the "permissive consensus" of earlier decades. Such reactions include campaigns, such as Citizens First, which have been initiated by the European Parliament and transferred by the Commission to the member states to bring Europe closer to the citizens.

The citizens' mistrust is, however, not only a reaction to the distance between Brussels and the citizens but also a reflection of a new way of practicing citizenship. The EU has brought a new model of fragmented citizenship to the fore. As the Second Report from the Commission on Citizenship of the Union states: "this diverse set of rights (entailed in Union Citizenship) is subject to different conditions. Generally speaking the rights stemming from citizenship of the Union cannot, for instance, be invoked in domestic situations which are purely internal to a Member State. Some of the entitlements such as the electoral rights can only be exercised in a Member State other than that of origin, whilst others such as access to the Ombudsman or to petition the European Parliament are extended to all natural and legal persons residing or having their registered office in a Member State."[87]

While early European citizenship policy did not aim at this institutional setting, the 1990s brought an institutional fragmentation to the fore that is yet to be matched by day-to-day experiences on the ground. The EU's new decentralized institutional framework thus contributes to increasing an already "challenged confidence in the progressive and unifying force of democratic politics and value."[88] Indeed, Union citizenship contributes to the dissolution of centered (citizenship) politics. At the same time, and "despite certain limitations, in practice the introduction of a citizenship of the Union has raised citizens' expectations as to the rights that they expect to see conferred and protected especially when they move to another Member State."[89] The expectations of citizenship have now been raised, the genie is out of the bottle, and the EU institutions feel the pressure to act. As the Commission's second report on citizenship stresses, "(P)enalty for failure [to apply citizens' rights in practice] is that citizenship of the Union may appear to be a distant concept for citizens engendering confusion as to its means and objectives *even fueling anti-EU feelings.* "[90]

From *Special* to *Specialized* Rights

Clearly, the EU is not the only polity that has to confront a new style of policy and politics with a fading center. Even if it is a sui generis case so far, it is the most dramatic example of this deviating form, as the story of citizenship practice has shown. It raises the question of how to conceptualize decentered, fragmented, and transnational citizenship practice in the long run without losing sight of its moral and ethical underpinnings. First and foremost, this story of making citizenship implies that Union citizenship means much more than a simple compilation of rights; it also turns out to be a story about identities. While both types of belonging (legal and identity-based) have been the target of EC/EU policy, it was the question of belonging in the meaning of identity that was first mobilized by policymakers. This identity was, however, not applied to replace national identity with a European one. Citizenship practice also suggests that the phenomenon of belongingness to the EC/EU was based on what individuals did or might aspire to do with reference to economic and political participation. Crossing national borders as economically active citizens, waving closed passports at internal Community borders as travelers, exchanging knowledge as scholars and students, voting in common for the European Parliament, and sharing municipal governance as Union citizens were aspects of this process of creating belongingness as it was generated step by step and area by area. The comparison of EC/EU citizenship to the characteristic pattern of citizenship in modern European nation-states reveals both similarities and differences.

To recall briefly: Modern citizenship practice was embedded in a centralized institutional organization of the nation-state. Both citizenship policy and citizenship politics led to the establishment of civil, political, and social *rights*, to a shared understanding of legal and identity-based *belonging* to a community, and to the ongoing struggle for *access* to participation. Characteristic of this type of national citizenship practice was that demands were directed towards the state[91] and policy was directed to citizens who were nationals of the state.[92] As a whole, this process of interaction between state and societal forces forged the institutions of modern national states. In the European Union, no central union with "state" institutions was established. The Union is not a centrally organized state, nor does it follow state-centric types of policymaking.[93] It may be identified as a union-state (as opposed to city-state or nation-state) with its own characteristic features. The citizenship practice related to this union generated a fragmented type of citizenship: Union citizens direct demands to the member states and to the Union as well; they also may belong to a local community of one member state (in terms of their social, cultural, economic, and political activities) and at the same time to a national community of another member state (legal/national ties and political activity). Figure 9.4 shows the fragmented citizenship practice in the EU.

One of the particularities of this story of the developing practice of European citizenship is that citizenship rights were understood as special rights in the sense that they were meant for Europeans only. Over time and through practice,

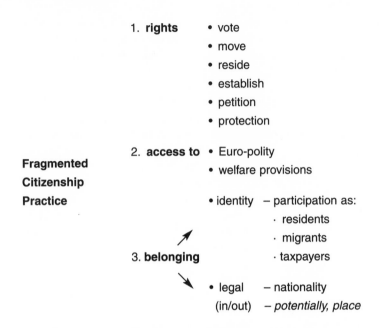

Fig. 9.4. Fragnented Citizenship Practice in the European Union

however, special rights acquired the meaning of being accessible only to special groups of Community citizens. That is, they became literally *specialized.* Citizenship rights were now defined according to what individuals did or what they were (workers, old, young, unemployed) rather than according to the fact that they were human beings.[94] The fragmented character of Union citizenship is underscored by another phenomenon. Both types of citizenship—national and EC/EU—are linked with, and embedded in, large processes of transformation.[95] However, while the citizenship practice of nation-states developed historical characteristics closely related to the societal changes during the industrial revolution and an emerging world system of interacting nation-states, citizenship practice of the EC/EU acquired characteristic meaning during a time of increasing globalization of the economy. This process indicated that both "the concepts of 'union' and 'citizenship' are undergoing wholesale and simultaneous changes in Community Europe. . . . the actual attribution of the status of Community citizen to citizens of the member States becomes a central element of the reforms and a reference point in determining the level of integration achieved by the Union which is being established."[96] In other words, both the type of citizenship practice and the institutions that are created in relation to it bear the historical imprint of their times.

This case study has not only located the historical elements of rights, access, and belonging in their Euro-specific appearances, but it has also facilitated a view of tensions that evolved during the process of citizenship practice. In a nutshell, the establishment of special rights of movement for European citizens and the desired establishment of an area without internal frontiers did two things. First, it guaranteed the civil right of free movement; and, second, it created political and social inequalities between those who moved to another member state and those who were citizens of that state. This tension led initially to the establishment of social rights and, in the long run, to the establishment of the political right to vote. Subsequently, those who could not move freely because they did not belong to the group of wage earners or were not related to them also requested freedom of movement. Prior to Maastricht, the difference between so-called Community foreigners (i.e., nationals living in a member state with which they had no legal ties of loyalty but to which they might have developed a feeling of belonging) and nationals, (i.e., those who possessed legal ties to that particular member state) was at stake. It was addressed by guaranteeing to these foreigners the right to vote and stand for election in European and municipal elections. Foreigners thus acquired equal, albeit limited, access to political rights based on their status as nationals of a member state. This change of status shifts the emphasis of political tension towards the struggle of third-country nationals—often longtime residents of a member state—for access to political participation.

Notes

An earlier version of this chapter was previously published in *Theory and Society* 26, no. 4 (1997): 529–60, under the title "Making Sense of the New Geography of Citizenship: Fragmented Citizenship in the European Union."

1. This view on creating a legally unsustained hope is presented, e.g., in Siofrà O'Leary, "The Relationship between Community Citizenship and the Protection Of Fundamental Rights in Community Law," *Common Market Law Review* 32 (1995): 519–54. For the latter citation, see Hans Ulrich Jessurun d'Oliveira, "Union Citizenship: Pie in the Sky?" in *A Citizens' Europe: In Search of a New Order*, ed. Allan Rosas and Esko Antola (London: Sage, 1995), 58–84.

2. See Philippe C. Schmitter, "Is It Really Possible to Democratize the Euro-Polity?" (paper presented at the European Forum workshop "Social and Political Citizenship in a World of Migration," European University Institute, Florence, 22–24 February 1996); and Svein S. Anderson and Kjell A. Eliassen, "Introduction: Dilemmas, Contradictions, and the Future of European Democracy," in *The European Union: How Democratic Is It?* ed. Svein S. Andersen and Kjell A. Eliassen (London: Sage, 1996), 1–12.

3. The debate over exclusion and inclusion and Union citizenship has developed most visibly over the issue of the exclusion of "third-country nationals" (i.e., individuals who live within the territory of the Union but are not nationals of a member state). Debate has, however, also occurred over exclusion along the lines of gender, sexual preference, and economic participation. See, e.g., the European Parliament's Bindi Reports of 1991 and 1993 (PE 207.047/fin.), as well as the Imbeni Report of 1993 (PE 206.762), and the Banotti Report of 1993 (PE 206.769/fin.).

4. See Michelle C. Everson and Ulrich K. Preuss, *Concepts, Foundations, and Limits of European Citizenship,* ZERP-Diskussionspapier 2, Bremen, 1995, 8. Legal attempts to grapple with Union citizenship do, however, often point to the important dimension of a possible evolution of Union citizenship based on Article 8e of the EC Treaty. See David O'Keeffe, "Union Citizenship," in *Legal Issues of the Maastricht Treaty,* ed. David O'Keeffe and Patrick M. Twomey (London: Wiley Chancery Law, 1994), 106.

5. David Held points to this important gap between the language (as in theory) and the practice of citizenship when he writes: "[T]o what political entity does the democratic citizen belong? Everywhere the sovereignty of the nation state itself—the entity to which the *language of citizenship* refers, and within which the claims of citizenship, community and *participation* are made—is being eroded and challenged." David Held, "Between State and Civil Society: Citizenship," in *Citizenship,* ed. Geoff Andrews (London: Lawrence & Wishart, 1991), 24.

6. See Veit Bader, "Citizenship and Exclusion: Radical Democracy, Community, and Justice. Or, What's Wrong with Communitarianism?" *Political Theory* 23, no. 2 (1995): 224.

7. I apply the term "postmodern" similarly to Ruggie (1993) and Caporaso (1996) as a means of expressing newly emergent models of political organization that build on modern ones but cannot be fully understood in modern terms only. See John G. Ruggie. "Territoriality and Beyond: Problematizing Modernity in International Relations," *International Organization* 47, no. 1 (1993): 139–74; and James Caporaso. "The European Union and Forms of State: Westphalian, Regulatory, or Post-Modern?" *Journal of Common Market Studies* 34, no. 1 (1996): 29–52.

8. Indeed, the inverse situation has been recently stated with regard to the "debordernization" of states and global politics as a process that renders the notion of citizenship equally problematic. See Lothar Brock and Mathias Albert, "Entgrenzung der Staatenwelt: Zur Analyse weltgesellschaftlicher Entwicklungstendenzen," *Zeitschrift für Internationale Beziehungen* 2 (1995): 269.

9. Recent work on European citizenship has emphasized the conceptual importance of this distinction. See, e.g., Ulrich K. Preuss, "Citizenship and Identity: Aspects of a Political Theory of Citizenship," in *Democracy and Constitutional Culture in the Union of Europe,* ed. Richard Bellamy, Vittorio Bufacchi, and Dario Castiglione (London: Lothian FP, 1995), 109. On the importance of the identity of states, see Alexander Wendt, "Identity and Structural Change in International Politics," in *The Return of Culture and Identity in IR Theory,* ed. Yosef Lapid and Friedrich Kratochwil (Boulder, Colo.: Lynne Rienner, 1996), 47–64.

10.   Feminist and antiracist contributions to the citizenship debate have also emphasized the problematic equalization of nationality and citizenship, pointing to the fact
that this conceptualization hides boundaries of inclusion and exclusion within nations
—a blind spot with serious consequences for theory, politics, and policy of citizenship.
Elizabeth Meehan, *Citizenship and the European Community* (London: Sage, 1993),
22; and Nira Yuval-Davis, "Gender and Nation," *Ethnic and Racial Studies* 16, no. 4
(1993): 621–32.

11.   According to Jane Jenson and Susan D. Phillips, "[S]tate institutions never
have the power to establish identities"; they may "choose to recognize some claims,
and thereby to shore up some identities." In other words, "identity remains the property
of the claimant, a creation of collective action." Jane Jenson and Susan D. Phillips,
"Redesigning the Citizenship Regime: The Roots of the Current Reconfiguration in
Canada" (paper presented as "Répresentation sociale et citoyenneté au Canada" at the
Colloque International, Intégration Continentale, Recomposition Territoriale, et Protection Sociale, Université de Montréal, 25–27 October 1995), 15.

12.   Examples of such policies are migration policy and security policy. Thus, some
consider citizenship an "instrument of social closure" between and within states. See
William Rogers Brubaker, ed., *Immigration and the Politics of Citizenship in Europe
and North America* (Lanham, Md.: University Press of America, 1989). On citizenship
as the "border of order," see Friedrich Kratochwil, "Citizenship: The Border of Order,"
Alternatives 19 (1994): 485–506.

13.   Constitution making in the EU has become the subject of a number of analyses.
See, e.g., Renaud Dehousse, "Constitutional Reform in the European Community: Are
There Alternatives to the Majoritarian Avenue?" *West European Politics* 18, no. 2
(1995): 118–36; Dieter Grimm, "Does Europe Need a Constitution?" *European Law
Journal* 1, no. 3 (1995): 282-302; and J. H. H. Weiler, "Journey to an Unknown Destination: A Retrospective and Prospective of the European Court of Justice in the Arena
of Political Integration." in *Economic and Political Integration in Europe,* ed. S. Bulmer and A. Scott (Oxford: Blackwell, 1995), 131–60. The question at hand is whether
it is possible to think about citizenship as constitutive for a community. See Preuss,
"Citizenship and Identity," 108.

14.   Carlos Closa, "Citizenship of the Union and Nationality of Member States."
Common Market Law Review 32 (1995): 493.

15.   See Jean Leca, "Immigration, Nationality, and Citizenship in Western Europe
(paper presented at the Conference on Social Justice, Democratic Citizenship, and Public Policy in the New Europe, ECPR/Erasmus University, Rotterdam, 1991); and Meehan, *Citizenship and the European Community,* xiii.

16.   Meehan, *Citizenship and the European Community,* xiii.

17.   Reinhard Bendix. *Nation Building and Citizenship* (New York: John Wiley,
1964); Jenson and Phillips, "Redesigning the Citizenship Regime"; T. H. Marshall. *Citizenship and Social Class* (Cambridge: Cambridge University Press, 1950); Margaret
Somers, "Rights, Relationality, and Membership: Rethinking the Marking and Meaning of Citizenship," *Law and Social Inquiry* 19 (1994): 63–112; Charles Tilly, ed., *The*

Formation of National States in Europe (Princeton: Princeton University Press, 1975); and Meehan, *Citizenship and the European Community.* .

18.   For an approach to citizenship practice that aims at encompassing the complex set of relations that underlies citizenship, see, e.g., Somers, "Rights, Relationality, and Membership."

19.   As Evans and Oliveira point out, citizenship is "a concept denoting the legal consequences which attach to the existence of a special connection between a defined category of individuals and a state" and thus essentially "a provision which is made for participation by a defined category of individuals in the life of a state." See A. C. Evans and H. U. Jessurun d'Oliveira. *Nationality and Citizenship. Rapport realisé dans le cadre d'une recherche effectuée à la demande de la Communautée européenne,* Strasbourg, 20–21 November 1989, 2.

20.   Similar elements have been identified by Tilly as basic criteria for state making. He writes, "[i]n its simplest version the problem [of state making] has only three elements. First, there is the *population* which carries on some collective political life—if only by virtue of being nominally subject to the same central authority. Second, there is a *governmental organization* which exercises control over the principal concentrated means of coercion within the population. Third, there are *routinized relations* between the governmental organization and the population." Tilly, *Formation of National States,* 32.

21.   More recent contributions to the citizenship debate point to this informal link between citizens and the state as a problem for the study of citizenship. Accordingly, much of the new debate on citizenship aims at an assessment of this theoretical problem that focuses on the question of how informal aspects of citizenship rather than formal criteria may be included in citizenship analysis. See Will Kymlicka and Wayne Norman, "Return of the Citizen: A Survey of Recent Work on Citizenship Theory," *Ethics* 56, no. 1 (January 1994): 352–81; Jürgen Habermas, "Staatsbürgerschaft und nationale Identität," in *Faktizität und Geltung,* ed. Jürgen Habermas (Frankfurt am Main: Suhrkamp, 1991), 632–60; Meehan, *Citizenship and the European Community*; Somers, "Rights, Relationality, and Membership"; and Iris M. Young. "Polity and Group Difference: A Critique of the Ideal of Universal Citizenship," in *Feminism and Political Theory,* ed. Cass Sunstein (Chicago: Chicago University Press, 1990), 117–42. While this is not the place to engage in a debate about different schools of thought, it is important to note an overall concern about problematic citizen-state relations.

22.   As Kratochwil argues, e.g., in order to solve questions about obligations to our fellow citizens and our country, the Kantian categorical imperative is not helpful. See Kratochwil, "Citizenship: The Border of Order," 495.

23.   See Marshall, *Citizenship and Social Class,* 10–11.

24.   Kratochwil notes that "[i]t is perhaps best to conceive of citizenship as a space within a discourse on politics that institutionalized identities and differences by drawing boundaries, both in terms of membership and in terms of the actual political practices that are connected with this membership. An explication of the concept, therefore, is not governed by the atemporal criteria of adequacy or correspondence. It necessarily

becomes historical, requiring an examination of the genealogy of the concept and its temporary reconciliations." Kratochwil, "Citizenship: The Border of Order," 486.

25. Turner suggests an approach that includes active (society-centered) and passive (state-centered) citizenship. According to his model, the French Revolution is considered the prime example of active citizenship politics, whereas the Bismarckian citizenship policy would be considered passive. See Bryan S. Turner. "Outline of a Theory of Citizenship." *Sociology* 24, 2 (1990): 189–217.

26. This section is taken from Antje Wiener, "Accessing the Constructive Potential of Union Citizenship," *European Integration online Papers (EIoP),* http://eiop.or.at/eiop/texte/1997-017a.htm.

27. Michalski and Wallace note that "the *acquis communautaire* is composed of the treaties of the EC and the regulations, directives, decisions, recommendations derived from them, as well as the case law from the European Court of Justice (ECJ). It comprises policies, the legal framework and the institutional structure which a country must accept when it aims at membership in the Community." See Anna Michalski and Helen Wallace, *The European Community: The Challenge of Enlargement* (London: Royal Institute of International Affairs, 1992), 36. Yet, while being incremental is part of the acquis communautaire, the Maastricht Treaty provides reason for caution, because a "number of protocols of the Union Treaty . . . damage the *acquis communautaire*"; see Deirdre Curtin, "The Constitutional Structure of the Union: A Europe of Bits and Pieces," *Common Market Law Review* 27 (1993): 18. On the concept of acquis communautaire, see Carlo Curti Gialdino, "Some Reflections on the *Acquis Communautaire,*" *Common Market Law Review* 32 (1995): 1090. Knud Erik Jørgensen, "The Social Construction of the *Acquis Communautaire:* A Cornerstone of the European Edifice" (paper presented at the International Studies Association Meeting, Minneapolis, Minn., 17–21 March 1998); and Antje Wiener, "The Embedded *Acquis Communautaire:* Transmission Belt and Prism of New Governance," *European Law Journal* 4, no. 3 (1998): 294–315.

28. European Commission, cf. Michalski and Wallace, *European Community,* 38.

29. See Michael Shackleton, "The Community Budget after Maastricht," in *The State of the European Community,* vol. 2, *The Maastrict Debates and Beyond,* ed. Alan W. Cafruny and Glenda G. Rosenthal (Boulder, Colo.: Lynne Rienner, 1993), 2:20. See also Paul Pierson, "The Path to European Integration: A Historical Institutionalist Perspective," *Comparative Politics* 29, no. 2 (1996): 144, on the emergence of a "restrictive" acquis that grows with the enactment of new policies.

30. See Michalski and Wallace, *European Community,* 35.

31. The pillar structure of the EU was introduced by the Maastricht Treaty on European Union (TEU). It involves (1) the three communities, i.e., the European Coal and Steel Community, the European Community (formerly the European Economic Community), and the European Atomic Energy Community; (2) Common Foreign and Security Policy; and (3) Cooperation on Justice and Home Affairs. See Jo Shaw, *Law of the European Union* (London: Macmillan, 1996), 7.

32. See John Peterson, "Decision-Making in the European Union: Towards a

Framework for Analysis," *Journal of European Public Policy* 2, no. 1 (1995): 69–93; and Pierson, "Path to Integration," 123–63, respectively.

33. These policy objectives were adopted within the final communiqué of the 1974 Paris summit meeting. See *Bulletin of the European Communities* [hereafter *Bull. EC*] 12 (1974): 8–9.

34. For the term "Euro-polity," see Gary Marks et al., eds., *Governance in the European Union* (London: Sage, 1996).

35. For elaborations on contextualized citizenship practices and their effect on the meaning of citizenship in different contexts, see Marshall, *Citizenship and Social Class,* for the British context; and, for the EU context, Meehan, *Citizenship and the European Community.*

36. On 8 October 1976, the Council adopted an "Act concerning the election of the representatives of the Assembly by direct universal suffrage." See *Official Journal of the European Communities* [hereafter: *OJ EC*] no. L 278, 8.10.76, 1–11.

37. *OJ EC,* no. C 241, 19.9.81, Council resolution.

38. As the final communiqué of the 1972 Paris summit stated, "The member states of the Community, the driving force of European construction, affirm their intention before the end of the present decade to transform the whole complex of their relations into a European Union." Commission, 1972, General Report, point 5(16) cf. Desmond Dinan. *Ever Closer Union? An Introduction to the European Community.* (Boulder, Colo.: Lynne Rienner, 1994), 81.

39. *Bull. EC,* Supp. 5, 1975, 5, Report on European Union (emphasis added).

40. As Davignon observed: "One of the difficulties of European construction is that historical stages have to be missed out. It is necessary to behave as if Europe already existed, as a political entity. In history, all countries passed through a phase of exclusively national development. Yet in this instance Europe has to act and intervene at the international level before having completed the phase of its internal development." See *Agence Europe (AE),* no. 713, 5 January 1973, 7.

41. *AE,* no. 713, 3–4 (emphasis added).

42. *Europe Documents,* no. 752, 17 July 1973, 1–2.

43. *Europe Documents,* no. 775, 3–5.

44. *Europe Documents,* no. 779, for the document on European identity. Clapham also stresses the link between the document on European identity and setting the policy objectives for the creation of Community citizenship. See Andrew Clapham. *Human Rights and the European Community: A Critical Overview.* (Baden-Baden: Nomos, 1991), 66.

45. *Europe Documents,* no. 779, 1.

46. The Commission's report "Towards European Citizenship" specified policy-related problems regarding the granting of special rights and the introduction of passport union. See *Bull. EC,* supp. 7, 1975. Another report, prepared by Prime Minister Leo Tindemans of Belgium, proposed guidelines for policymaking on European Union. See *Bull. EC,* supp. 1, 1976.

47. The Commission's report stressed the importance of the political nature of the special rights objective, stating that "granting special rights to the citizens of Member

States [was] an allusion to the citizen—basically a political concept which was substituted for the term national, which is always used in Community texts—[and provided] a first clue to the civil and political nature of the special rights." See *Bull. EC,* supp. 7, 1975, 26; see also Guido Van den Berghe. *Political Rights for European Citizens* (Aldershot, England: Gower, 1982), 31.

48.   With respect to policies regarding special rights, it is important to note that, from the Commission's perspective, special rights included only those rights of member states' nationals that had not yet been acquired by foreigners. See *Bull. EC,* supp. 7, 1975, 28. It is important to note that at that time, the term "foreigner" was used in Community documents to desginate nationals of EC countries who lived in a member state where they were not passport holders. For example a Belgian passport holder living in France would be a foreigner in France; the French Member State was considered the "host country."

49.   *Bull. EC,* supp. 7, 1975, 27

50.   *Bull. EC,* supp. 7, 1975, 32

51.   In its report "Towards European Citizenship" the Commission reasoned "that European citizenship, which does not exist at the present, will take the first step towards becoming a reality only with the election of the European Parliament on the basis of universal suffrage and the implementation of point 11 on special rights." This cautious step-by-step approach was based on the observation that "[e]qual treatment for foreigners in the economic and social fields is accepted by public opinion, since this has long been a subject for frequent negotiation between States [but t]he same does not apply to equal treatment for foreigners in the political field. *This is a new idea* and the public will have been given an opportunity to get used to it." See *Bull. EC,* supps. 7, 16, and 30, respectively. (Emphasis added.)

52.   *Bull. EC,* supp. 1, 1976, 26–27

53.   See Bayerl Report; cf. European Parliament, *Proceedings of the Round Table on Special Rights and a Charter of the Rights of the Citizens of the European Community and Related Documents. Florence, 26–28, October 1978* (Luxembourg: European Parliament, 1979). According to this report, special rights policy meant that "all the constitutional rights on which the legitimacy of a democratic State depends are conferred upon the citizens of the European Community vis-à-vis the European Community and, secondly, to include those rights which citizens of a particular Member State possess but which have not hitherto been granted to other citizens of the Community." European Parliament, *Special Rights,* 86–87. The Legal Affairs Committee of the European Parliament later specified that migrant workers "should as far as possible be placed on an equal footing with the citizens of the host country; in particular, they should have the means of influencing, through their vote, the running of public affairs in the place in which they have opted (or have been obliged) to establish their residence." See European Parliament, PE 81.688/fin, 9. This idea was to become an important informal resource for the making of Union citizenship and was to be taken up again by a Commission proposal on voting rights. See *Bull. EC,* supp. 7, 1986.

54.   *OJ EC,* no. L 278, 8.10.76, 1–11.

55.   *OJ EC,* no. C 87, 5.4.82, 64; for the text of the draft act, see 61–62.

56. European Parliament, 29 April 1983, PE 81.699 final [Rapporteur: Mrs. M.-A. Macciocchi].

57. *Bull. EC,* no. 12, 1974, 8–9.

58. *Bull. EC,* Supp. 7, 1975, 7.

59. See George Ross, "The European Community and Social Policy: Regional Blocs and a Humane Social Order," *Studies in Political Economy,* 40 (1993): 44–45; Loukas Tsoukalis, *The New European Economy.* (Oxford: Oxford University Press, 1993); and William Wallace, "Rescue or Retreat? The Nation State in Western Europe, 1945–93," *Political Studies* 42, special issue (1994): 64–65.

60. For the term "market-making," see Wolfgang Streeck, "European Social Policy: Between Market-Making and State-Building," in *European Social Policy: Between Fragmentation and Integration,* ed. Stephan Leibfried and Paul Pierson (Washington, D.C.: Brookings Institution, 1995), 389–431.

61. *Bull. EC,* supp. 7, 1985, 9.

62. As a Commission program explained: "Recognition as a 'Community centre of excellence' for establishments giving additional training or conducting very advanced research in specialized areas would help towards *the increased mobility of students and research scientists* within the Community. The European Council should express its support for these types of activity, which *will promote the European identity* in the eyes of the economic and social decision-makers of the future of the Community." See *Bull. EC,* 3, 1985, 101. (Emphasis added.)

63. Among these programs were, e.g., the European Community Action Scheme for the Mobility of University Students (ERASMUS), (Coimbra Report, PE, May 1986, Doc. A 2–22/86) and the Young Workers' Exchange Scheme (YES) (Fontaine Report, PE, November 1986, Doc. A 2–109/86). The European Parliament stressed the importance of such programmes towards building an ever closer union when it observed "[c]ooperation among the Member States of the Community in the field of education and culture is inherent to the process of the construction of Europe, and reflects the spirit of the Treaties, since there is no doubt that it promotes closer relations between peoples." See European Parliament, Directorate General for Research, *Action Taken Series* 3, 11, 1988, 103; see also Brigid Laffan. "The Politics of Identity and Political Order in Europe," *Journal of Common Market Studies* 34, no. 1 (1996): 97.

64. *OJ EC,* no. L 180, 13.7.90. These directives were to survive the Maastricht Treaty. They were, however, later partially challenged by the European Parliament and came increasingly under attack once the TEU entered into force. See Official Common Document (COM)(93) 702 final, 21 December 1993, 4; and the Opinion of the Committee on Women's Rights, PE 206.769/fin., 2 December 1993.

65. Another aspect of the "democratic deficit" was a question of democratic procedure. Both aspects are rooted in different contexts. Bulmer and Scott identify a *procedural deficit,* consisting of the "Community's decision-making procedures" and the lack of "democratic legitimacy" as regards the legislative process. See S. Bulmer and A. Scott, eds., *Economic and Political Integration in Europe* (Oxford: Blackwell, 1994), 7. From the passport policy process, it is evident that the lack of transparency after the split into a Schengen and a Community approach to border politics also con-

tributed to the notion of a democratic deficit. See, e.g., the European Parliament's Out-rive Report I, PE 156.390. In turn, the Commission's demand for the political right to vote was based on historical experience of citizenship practice in nation-states, thus suggesting a n*ormative deficit.* For the Commission proposal, see *Bull. EC,* supp. 7, 1986, "Voting Rights in Local Elections for Community Nationals."

66. For observations of this process, see esp. Hans Claudius Taschner, "Die Abschaffung der Personenkontrollen an den Binnengrenzen der Europäischen Gemein-schaft und ihre Folgen," in *Das Europa der Bürger in einer Gemeinschaft ohne Binnen-grenzen,* ed. Siegfried Magiera (Baden-Baden: Nomos, 1990), 229–235; and Hans Claudius Taschner. "Schengen oder die Abschaffung der Personenkontrollen an den Binnengrenzen der EG," Vortrag vor dem Europainstitut der Universität des Saarlandes, Saarbrücken 11 Dezember 1990; J. J. Bolten, "From Schengen to Dublin: The New Frontiers of Refugee Law," in *Schengen: Internationalization of Central Chapters of the Law on Aliens, Refugees, Privacy, Security, and the Police,* ed.. J. D. M. Steenber-gen (Leiden: Stichting NJCM, 1992); and H. Meijers, "Schengen: Introduction," In *Schengen,* 1–7; and Antje Wiener, *Building Institutions: The Developing Practice of "European" Citizenship* (Boulder, Colo.: Westview Press, 1998). The Schengen agree-ment on the gradual abolition of border controls was first signed by the governments of the Benelux economic union, the Federal Republic of Germany, and the Republic of France, on 14 June 1985 in the town of Schengen, Luxembourg.

67. According to Article 49 of the EEC Treaty, the Council was to issue directives or make regulations setting out the measures required to bring about, by progressive stages, freedom of movement for workers, on the basis of a proposal from the Commis-sion and acting by a qualified majority.

68. COM(89) 568 final, which was adopted at the European Council meeting at Strasbourg, 8–9 December 1989.

69. The clear definition of the 279 directives prescribed by the Commission's 1992 white paper provided the point of departure for this type of policymaking, which led to a new era in Community politics that soon became known under the slogan of "Europe '92." While the white paper went beyond market policy making, it was nonetheless conceptualized to operate within a market paradigm. Behind a quite technical appear-ance, the white paper had in store for the member states a whole series of legal com-mitments that were part of the implementation of the directives. It therefore required basic agreement on the legal basis for resolving intra-Community disputes.

70. See Bolten. "From Schengen to Dublin," 11; and Soledad Garcia, ed., *European Identity and the Search for Legitimacy* (London: Royal Institute of International Affairs, Pinters, 1993), 2.

71. Dinan, *Ever Closer Union?* 158.

72. T. Hoogenboom, "Free Movement of Non-EC Nationals, Schengen and Beyond," in *Schengen,* 74–95.

73. Brigid Laffan, "The Treaty of Maastricht: Political Authority and Legitimacy," in *The State of the European Community,* vol. 2, *The Maastricht Debates and Beyond,* ed. Alan W. Cafruny and Glenda G. Rosenthal (Boulder, Colo.: Lynne Riener, 1993), 35–52, 36.

74. Dinan, *Ever Closer Union?* 158.

75. Dinan, *Ever Closer Union?* 163.

76. The "[l]inkage between German unification and deeper political integration and between EMU [European Monetary Union] and European Political Union (EPU) emerged explicitly at the Strasbourg Summit in early December 1989." See Dinan, *Ever Closer Union?* 161n34. In 1990 a now famous letter signed by Chancellor Kohl and President Mitterrand addressed to the Irish Council Presidency of the Community suggested calling an IGC on political union. This letter reflected the policy paradigm of legitimacy and union building, saying that the goals for such an IGC would be "to strengthen the democratic legitimation of the union, to render its institutions more efficient, to ensure unity and coherence of the union's economic, monetary and political action and to define and implement a common foreign and security policy." See AE, no. 5238, 20 April 1990, 6.

77. SG(90) D/06001, 1–4.

78. For the letter see SEC(90) 1084 and *AE*, no. 5252, 11 May 1990, 3. This "interinstitutional" conference included the main Community institutions. It was thus different from the IGC format, which restricted the negotiation process to the member states.

79. *Europe Documents*, no. 1628, 2

80. See Permanent Representation of Spain to the European Communities, "Economic and Social Cohesion in Political, Economic, and Monetary Union: The Spanish Viewpoint, 5 March 1991," in *The Intergovernmental Conference on Political Union: Institutional Reforms, New Policies, and International Identity of the European Economy,* ed. Finn Laursen and Sophie Vanhoonacker (Maastricht: European Institute of Public Administration, 1992), 326–27.

81. PE 150.034/fin., 6–10.

82. PE 150.034/fin., 9.

83. Meehan captured this fragmenting aspect of European citizenship noting that it is "neither national nor cosmopolitan" but that it is "multiple in the sense that the identities, rights and obligations associated . . . with citizenship are expressed through an increasingly complex configuration of common Community institutions, states, national and transnational voluntary associations, regions and alliances of regions." See Meehan, *Citizenship and the European Community,* 1.

84. The hearings were organized by the institutional committee of the European Parliament on 18–19 October 1995 "with a view to preparing the Dury and Maij-Weggen Reports on revision of the Maastricht Treaty" (*AE*, 18.10.95, 4). According to *AE*, the hearings were attended by "dozens of NGOs" while "over 300 NGOs had asked to take part" (*AE* 18.10.95, 4; and *AE*, 19.10.95, 4, respectively).

85. Bolten, "From Schengen to Dublin"; and Hoogenboom, "Free Movement."

86. See ARNE (Antiracist Network for Equality in Europe), "Modifications to the Maastricht Treaty in Sight of the 1996 Inter-Governmental Conference," Rome, 14–15 July 1995, 4. (Emphasis in original.)

87. COM(97) 230 final, Brussels 27.05.1997, 6.

88.   See Michael Salter, "Habermas's New Contribution to Legal Scholarship," *Journal of Law and Society* 24, no. 2 (1997): 285.

89.   COM(97) 230 final, 6.

90.   COM(97) 230, 6. (Emphasis added.)

91.   As Turner summarizes: "Citizenship is, as it were, pushed along by the development of social conflicts and social struggles within . . . a political and cultural arena, as social groups compete with each other over access to resources. Such a theory of citizenship also requires a notion of the state as that institution which is caught in the contradictions between property rights and political freedoms." See Turner, "Theory of Citizenship," 195.

92.   Indeed, the distinctive features of a modern state included that it was "an organization which controls the population occupying a defined territory . . . in so far as (1) it is differentiated from other organizations operating in the same territory; (2) it is autonomous; (3) it is centralized; and (4) its divisions are formally coordinated with one another." See Tilly, *Formation of National States,* 70.

93.   See Liesbet Hooghe and Gary Marks, "Theoretical Foundations of Multi-level Governance" (paper presented at the Annual Meeting of the American Political Science Association, Chicago, 31 August–4 September 1995.

94.   As Meehan put it, they were "citizens-as-workers, not citizens-as-human-beings." See Meehan, *Citizenship and the European Community* 1993, 147.

95.   Tilly characterizes political rights of citizens as "political rights in a large sense—political in that they constitute binding claims on the agents of government, rather than some other groups"; he continues that "that specification clarifies a large historical transformation. The European national revolutions of the last few centuries did not so much expand political rights as concentrate them in the state and reduce their investment in other sorts of governments. A large part of the process consisted in the state's abridging, destroying or absorbing rights previously lodged in other political units: manors, communities, provinces, estates." See Tilly, *Formation of National States,* 37.

96.   PE 150.034/fin., 10.

10

From Center to Periphery and Back Again: Reflections on the Geography of Democratic Innovation

John Markoff

Struggling for Change: Two Social Movements Challenge the Old Order

In the late 1830s, a movement for radically democratizing Britain's parliamentary politics rapidly flowered and for a decade challenged the established order.[1] This was a time of strikes and lockouts in the industrializing towns, of debate over conditions in the factories, of conflict over the rights of Irish Catholics in England (and in Ireland), and of threats to traditional family relationships constituted by child labor. The Reform Bill of 1832 dramatized the exclusion of Britain's working people from the political institutions within which these awesome changes might be addressed. The Reform Bill had extended the right to vote in parliamentary elections, but not so far as to include any women or most of the people working in the factories, workshops, fields, mines, or at home. The ensuing bitter popular mobilizations acquired a focus with the publication by the two-year-old London Working Men's Association in 1838 of the People's Charter, whose Six Points proclaimed a simple and powerful program that provided adherents with an identity as Chartists. The next decade saw the deployment of meetings and demonstrations, newspapers, pamphlets, hymns, prayers and poems, appeals to Parliament—the National Petition had more than a million signatures—and bills introduced in Parliament, the founding of organizations, and open debates about tactics ("moral force" versus "physical force"). Clashes with police and judicial authorities unfolded in a climate of fears of revolution; many were imprisoned and some were transported to Australia. The movement probably provided Marx and Engels with much food for thought as they were developing their notions of working-class consciousness.[2]

The first two provisions of "The Six Points of the People's Charter" demanded universal suffrage for adult men (other than the mentally ill or criminals) and the institution of the secret ballot.[3] The general thrust of the Six Points taken collectively was the elimination of differential claims to the political rights of citizenship deriving from distinctions of wealth and property. Such measures have become part of what is now meant by democracy everywhere and eventually became institutionalized in Britain. It is striking, however, that while, despite the enormous efforts of the Chartists, these measures went unrealized in Britain in the 1840s, they were actually realized at a substantially earlier point in some of Britain's overseas colonial offshoots.

Although the British elite successfully resisted Chartist demands at home, transported Chartists carried their radicalism to Australia, where they found familiar enough conflicts in their new country's towns and gold fields. They found as well an Australian elite whose leaders might decry the "spirit of democracy" that threatened "British principles."[4] Nonetheless, along with suffrage expansion, the secret ballot was introduced in most Australian colonies between 1856 and 1859, although Western Australia held out until 1877. Already by the mid-1850s one former member of the legislature in New South Wales held the Australian colonies the "most advanced democracies in the world."[5] The Australian ballot, as it was soon known in the debates that developed in other countries, crossed to New Zealand in 1870 before its adoption in Britain in 1872.[6]

The elimination of property and wealth qualifications proceeded in several steps in Britain, and the reform of 1912 eliminated most remaining restrictions. By then, such restrictions were long since nonexistent in Australia and New Zealand, not to mention the early escapee from British dominion, the United States, most of whose states had eliminated such distinctions early in the nineteenth century. Even 1912 was not the British terminal point on this matter, for some plural voting—an extra vote for university graduates and for those with business assets above a certain threshold—remained in force in Britain until 1948.[7]

As Chartists were mounting their last major actions in England in 1848, on the other side of the Atlantic, champions of women's rights were initiating a new phase in their own continuing campaign.[8] Women were long-standing participants in transatlantic antislavery activism and had been employing the language and social analyses of that movement in debates about organization, strategy, and tactics. For some, egalitarian commitments made particularly galling the subordinate status of women within the world of antislavery activism itself, a circumstance that galvanized independent organizing by, and on behalf of, women. At the Seneca Falls Convention of 1848, a number of broad principles and more specific objectives were endorsed, of which the most contentious was voting rights for women, the only proposal, in fact, that was not unanimously approved by the participants.[9]

Over the next decades, U.S. activists mounted campaigns and deployed a variety of tactics in the pursuit of their objectives in many states. Brochures, meetings, petitions, dramatic violations of law, forging of alliances with champions of other causes, lobbying, actions in the juridical arena, and the founding of a diverse range of organizations were parts of campaigns for property rights; educational and professional opportunities; autonomy from husbands, brothers, and fathers; recognition of women's capacity to participate in public life; and voting equality. Competition, sometimes acrimonious, among organizations that differed deeply in preferred tactics and in their definitions of problems and solutions (such as the National Woman Suffrage Association, the American Woman Suffrage Association, and the Women's Christian Temperance Union [WCTU]) generated a broad array of actions. Despite the eastern origin of the major organizations—the three just named were launched in New York, Boston, and Cleveland[10]—the early triumphs were far to the west. By 1869, Wyoming enacted women's suffrage, and Utah followed in the next year.

Despite all this activism, however, on a national scale women's suffrage took decades. The WCTU, for example, was founded in 1874 and organized tens of thousands of participants in most states for a variety of actions linking moral reform and women's political rights.[11] Nevertheless, for nearly half a century all this effort by the WCTU and other campaigners was producing victories only in the West. By the eve of Word War I, roughly the western quarter of the country had equal voting rights for women (eleven states plus the territory of Alaska). The ratification of a constitutional amendment enfranchising women throughout the country did not take place until 1920.

But other political systems were considerably less resistant. A decade after its founding in the United States, a WCTU organizer traveled abroad and helped establish chapters in New Zealand and Australia. These chapters participated in promulgating ideas and mounting actions of a kind quite familiar in the American context, but with notably greater and more immediate success. From its founding in 1885, the New Zealand Women's Christian Temperance Union injected itself into the major debates about women's issues in that country, from dress norms to property rights.[12] It held meetings, petitioned parliament, sponsored clubs as alternatives to pubs, promoted poor relief, organized classes, supported unionism for women workers. And it became the major women's organization promoting suffrage. Only eight years after the WCTU's implantation, New Zealand enfranchised women in national elections, the first large country to do so. An array of other legal disabilities was soon removed by new legislation that ranged from legalizing divorce to granting women the right to enter the medical and legal professions.[13] Meanwhile, women were gaining the franchise in Australia, beginning with South Australia in 1894. Australian women got voting rights in national elections in 1902 (although women could not vote in all elections in all states until 1908).[14] At the moment when Australian women joined those in New Zealand in voting for the first time in national elections, U.S. women could vote in state elections in Wyoming, Utah, Colorado, and Idaho.

A Big Generalization: The Polycentric but Not Random Geography of Democratic Innovation

Although some comparativists seem to think that major democratic innovations come from the great powers and are imitated by, or imposed upon, the lesser, participants in political struggles have often thought otherwise.[15] In debating the secret ballot in the United States in the late nineteenth century, it was a commonplace to name the institution under debate "the Australian ballot"; in similar debates in England, a parliamentary commission called on Australians to testify.[16] There was also much discussion of New Zealand's example by suffragists and antisuffragists alike in Britain and the United States. British champions of women's suffrage, for example, could use New Zealand's combination of precocity in women's rights with the Maori franchise to play the race card in their own cause; the British activist Millicent Fawcett asked in 1909, "Why should the Maori women be in a superior position to that held by the women of England?"[17]

Despite the vigor of activism on behalf of the secret ballot in nineteenth-century England and on behalf of women's voting rights in the nineteenth-century United States, the late-nineteenth-century breakthroughs to actual implementation on a national scale were first achieved at considerable distance from those two economic powerhouses, to some extent, in fact, propelled by the very same actors—transported Chartists in Australia and the WCTU in New Zealand (and Australia, too). Rather than try to identify the distinctive features of the two Pacific states as a route to understanding their innovative openness to secret ballots and women's voting rights, I will focus here on a more general empirical claim: Democratic innovations since the late eighteenth century have been pioneered in many places but have been especially prone to take place away from the world centers of wealth and power. The innovating places in the world history of modern democracy have tended to be in lesser players on the world stage.

In addition to ballot secrecy and women's suffrage, consider the following:[18]

- *Constitutionalism.* Founding government on a document setting out the decisions of living human beings on the powers and responsibilities of governing authorities and on the rights of citizens was pioneered on the western fringe of the European world, in the newly independent United States, which ratified its document in 1789; the first European state to follow suit was Poland in 1791, well to the east of imperial Europe's Atlantic center of economic gravity. (The most significant immediate precursor state was Sweden, far to the north, in 1772.)

- *Accountability of governments to publics.* The late-eighteenth-century United States was an important pioneer here in subjecting all holders of governing power to scrutiny by electorates, directly or indirectly (through appointment by a person or body subject to electoral processes).[19] But we should recall as well the distinctive republican traditions of Holland, Switzerland, and Poland, hardly at the center of world power in the eighteenth century.

- *Equality of rights, especially rights of active participation in political life.* In suffrage rights the United States was a world leader in removing property and wealth qualifications; Switzerland was the European leader.[20] New Zealand was developing voting rights for Maoris while the U.S. South was developing Jim Crow restrictions. In the realm of personal freedom, Denmark abolished its slave trade before England, while Haiti and Chile were early to abolish legal slavery and Spanish America more generally was well in advance of the United States in abolition.

- *Democratic identification.* The word "democrat," whose use indicates that some people are claiming themselves, or others, champions of the advance of democratic institutions, seems to come from the Low Countries in the 1780s, before being taken up by some of the radicals in the French Revolution.

Because of definitional ambiguity, selectivity in choice of indicators, gaps in the scholarly literature, or my oversight, some readers might challenge some of these particular claims or invoke some element of democratization not considered here. But the overall pattern seems too persistent to be overturned by such specific errors. The places where democracy was invented since the late eighteenth century include the new, thinly populated, and militarily inconsequential (at that moment) United States, the Low Countries, Switzerland, Poland, Australia, and New Zealand.

It turns out, then, that the geographic aspect of the realization of women's suffrage or of ballot secrecy is not just part of some distinctive history of women's rights or of election procedures but is typical of the entire modern history of democratic innovation.[21] We also notice that places that are innovative in some ways are not necessarily so in others. The United States pioneered in constitutionalism, accountability of powerholders to publics, multiparty competitive elections, and abandonment of property and wealth qualifications for the franchise, yet it did not effectively assure voting rights for the descendants of slaves until the 1960s; Switzerland, early in Europe to abandon property and wealth qualifications, was extremely late to abandon gender qualifications; Australia, pioneer in secret ballots and very early in women's suffrage, was quite late in extending voting rights for its original inhabitants (or even in counting them in its census).[22] The world history of democracy, then, is the history, not of a single but complex innovation, but of many innovations that were developed at different moments in different places, including places that were quite laggard in some ways. Nonetheless, there is the general pattern: democratic innovations for the past two centuries have tended to take place in countries that are not, at the time, world centers of wealth and power.

This large point is part of a still larger one. The history of modern democracy is not simply the sum of the separate histories of democratizations in separate national states, which may be considered as "cases" in comparative analyses. There is a world history of democracy in which initiatives have flowed from place to place, in which social movement challengers and powerholding elites have both played important roles, and in which national dialogues of challengers and powerholders have taken place, not within isolated national contexts, but within webs of transnational connection. For many purposes, the traditional tools of comparative analysis remain invaluable sources of insight.[23] These include the search for similarities that reveal the common working of strong forces in differing contexts and the search for differences that reveal either nationally distinctive paths or the range of national variation. But for other purposes, what is essential is to understand the interconnectedness of social processes across national frontiers and the ways in which national political processes are part of interacting, and larger, transnational wholes.[24] The observations offered here about the interplay of movements rooted in Britain or the United States with political change half a world away are not directed especially at illuminating the particular histories of Britain, the United States, or Oceania but at pointing to a little-noted aspect of democracy's global history, the geographic patterning of innovation.

Transnational Aspects of Democratizations: The Role of Major Powers

Although social scientists have often tended to explain episodes of democratization as processes endogenous to the states under study, there is much to be said for considering a broader canvas. In transnational perspective, the role of the greater powers in propelling political change has been as considerable as it is unmysterious. The multiple forms of influence exerted by the centers of economic and political power reshape the political arrangements of smaller and weaker states. This may sometimes happen even without deliberate effort on the part of the powerful states' elites because the constraints and opportunities open to weaker states may recommend imitating the stronger. To review briefly a few of the mechanisms:

- *Military dominance* may be used as an instrument of political cloning, as in the creation of satellite republics by revolutionary France in the 1790s and the democratizations carried out under U.S. military auspices at the end of the World War II.

- *Models of success* in the economic or political realm may make powerful states seem worthy of emulation to those grappling with difficult problems elsewhere. In the wake of the World War I, in which only the Western democracies emerged with their political regimes intact, the prestige accruing to sanguinary triumph helps explain why so many of the European states that emerged from the ruins of the Hohenzollern, Habsburg, Romanov, and Ottoman empires adopted democratic institutions; why Europe's colonies acquiring independence at that moment did likewise (Ireland and Iceland); and why other states undergoing political upheaval were apt to incorporate democratic features into their new structures (Mexico and Turkey).

- *Hope of support* by the wealthy and powerful is a strong inducement to conspicuous displays of pleasing symbols, including institutions. Thus in the 1990s some political figures in very poor places hoped claims of democracy would attract U.S. largesse, now that there was no longer a Soviet alternative; Eastern European statesmen saw democracy as the only route into the European Union; and Islamicist movements in some countries may have found some Western governments less hostile to the possibility of their accession to power if they claimed the mantle of democracy.

- *Socialization* of elites from elsewhere in the values of the powerful countries may also play a role, particularly in the form of education in those countries' universities, where formal classroom study of those states' political institutions and culture may be reinforced by a climate of disdain for the benighted institutions of other places. Thus graduate students from antidemocratic regimes who studied in the United States in the

1970s and 1980s often found themselves semiapologetically having to explain their own country's political folkways to fellow students, to professors, and perhaps to themselves, a state of affairs that contributed in a small way to the delegitimation of their own country's political institutions (even in places whose governments had been installed with U.S. support).

Why Has So Much Innovation Taken Place in Lesser Powers?

Such processes inject a very important transnational element into the entire history of democratization. But they hardly exhaust the transnational dimension, for the crucial empirical point that is addressed in this chapter is the innovative role of lesser powers. Why have the innovative centers of modern democracy been so often such places? Perhaps we can get some clues by reviewing the place names that have come up in this essay: the Low Countries and Poland in the late eighteenth century, the United States in the late eighteenth and early nineteenth centuries, Denmark and Sweden in the late eighteenth century, Switzerland in the mid-nineteenth, New Zealand and Australia in the late nineteenth—not by any means world centers of wealth and power, but hardly the poorest or weakest places on the planet. And, perhaps as significantly, these were places that were intensely interacting with the centers of power. Several were present or recent settler colonies, with many recent or continuing connections to Britain in particular. Others were intensely involved in the European state system, sometimes as battlefields for others' armies, sometimes courted as potential military allies, often important as rivals or partners in commerce.

These were not, in short, places that are autonomous and insulated from the politics of the world centers of economic and political power. Repertoires of contention, in Charles Tilly's expressive phrase, are not bounded by national frontiers. General ideas about social justice, models of organization for engaging in conflict, reflection on strategies and tactics—these can all cross national frontiers through the movement of information and of people. Transported Chartists were one link between British and Australian conflicts. The proselytizing of the Women's Christian Temperance Union linked U.S. patterns of conflict with Oceania, and the experiences of English-speaking Pacific states in turn struck a chord in the core English-speaking countries. The web of transnational interconnection may run in more than one direction, and the innovative experiences of some places may enter into the political life of connected but more central places. Secret ballots and women's suffrage in Oceania, for example, were more readily incorporated into British political debate than, let us say, the even earlier, if temporary, women's suffrage in Velez, Colombia.[25]

But connectedness is not the whole story. It only helps us understand the flow of ideas and personnel. If British or U.S. patterns of conflict were readily echoed in Australia and New Zealand (and vice versa), we still need to understand why similar pressures yielded institutional change more readily in the late nineteenth century in those Pacific states. Here I advance a highly speculative hypothesis: It is among intermediate players on the world stage that elites are particularly prone to take up major innovations as their own. First of all, in such countries a mix of threat and opportunity may run particularly strong. The possibility of losing out in transnational competition, economically or militarily, is joined with the possibility of advance. Second, the elites are not only likely to be intensely connected to the elites of some of the more centrally located countries but also to see some realistic possibilities at home of maintaining or mimicking the culture and recreating the institutions of those important models. Third, achieving a more central position on the world stage, or cultivating alliances with states already so favorably placed, may be experienced as demanding a break with existing practice.

By contrast, consider elite response to threat in the most and in the least powerful states. In the core countries, elites under threat have valued cultural models from the national past and command the resources to support those models. Conservative attempts to return to past traditions and the power to pass burdens on to lower classes may therefore be more characteristic of elite responses to challenges in core countries than innovation. Of course change happens, but given the greater resistance of centers of power, the initial places of political innovation are likely to be somewhere else than there. They will be the second, or the third, or the tenth to take such innovative steps.

But in the very poorest and weakest of states, significant institutional change is likely to threaten present elites with ruin, while dissidents are unlikely to successfully contest elite intransigence without support from some powerful external ally that may well serve as a model or even be able to impose one. In short, elites in power and oppositions are less likely to be innovators on the world stage than to be, if not necessarily conservative, imitative of external powers. In the course of their political upheavals these states may borrow the institutional forms of the powerful, especially if previously oppositional elites arrive at power and seek externally recognizable legitimating formulae. This borrowing may be superficial or more profound.[26] And innovations in such very poor states are not likely to be imitated in the core, at least not without passing through that middle tier.

Let us look a bit more closely at the geography of women's suffrage within the British Empire.

Searching for as remote a place to hide out as they could find, the notorious mutineers from H.M.S. *Bounty* and the Tahitians who, voluntarily or otherwise, went with them colonized the uninhabited Pitcairn Island in 1790. A British captain, stopping by in 1838, took it upon himself to give the islanders "a few hasty regulations," which included, among many provisions about the island's cats and dogs, a magistrate "to be elected by the free votes of every native born on the island, male or female, who shall have attained the age of eighteen years." Captain Elliott's journal makes clear that his concern was how to "least involve my own government, of whose intention in respect to the Pitcairn islanders I am ignorant" in the affairs of this imperial Pacific flyspeck.[27] When this captain codified the practices fashioned by the descendants of British sailors, transplanted Tahitians, and occasional new arrivals, he produced the first modern constitutional prescription of women's voting rights, in a remote part of an indifferent empire.[28]

Eighteen years later, the imperial government relocated the Pitcairners to Norfolk Island, considerably nearer Australia and New Zealand. When the British governor in whose turf the new Norfolkers found themselves got around to giving them a set of regulations, he left intact women's suffrage, betting that this institution could be contained on such a distant outpost of empire. "I left untouched the rule which gave the women, as well as the men, a vote in the annual election of the Chief Magistrate. I hope, however, that this experiment on a small scale, will not be assumed as a precedent in favor of the claims now made on the part of our 'better halves' to have a say in the government of the country. . . . I should most certainly not have proposed even this small amount of petticoat government had I not found it already in existence."[29]

A generation after Sir William expressed the hope that women's suffrage could be successfully contained far offshore, the expansion of women's rights to New Zealand and Australia drew the notice of some much closer to the imperial core.[30] Paralleling Sir William's earlier outlook, some observers, following events from Britain, now reassured themselves that the situation of such distant Pacific colonies was so different from that of the British Isles themselves that there need be no necessary diffusion from the former to the latter. While feminists tried to use New Zealand's precedent to bolster their case elsewhere, some conservatives in Britain suggested that it was a mere "experiment," an experiment, moreover, carried out in a remote state too insignificant to serve as such a precedent. One conservative member of Parliament observed in the British House of Commons in 1897: "Generally speaking, the children follow the example of the parent, not the parent the example of the children."[31]

As the debates about women's political rights continued in late nineteenth-century Britain, women's rights activists in England could take heart from a breakthrough into suffrage equality a great deal closer to home than Oceania. The Isle of Man, whose residents had their own parliament (the House of Keys), in some improbable toponymic irony, enfranchised their women in 1881—or at least those who met the property qualifications then in force—considerably before London women could vote for the House of Commons.[32]

In summary, although specific democratic innovations have been pioneered in a wide variety of specific locations, these locations tended to have in common an intermediary position in the world in wealth and power as well as considerable interconnections with the centers of world wealth and power.[33] I have offered the hypothesis that the cause of such a geographic patterning to innovation is the mix of tensions and possibilities (both hopeful and threatening) that tend to go with such a location, and a consequent openness to innovation on the part of elites.

The Geography of Innovation: Challenge and Response

The basic lines of this explanation are not novel. At its core is a model of "challenge and response," which has a way of turning up in a wide variety of efforts at large-scale macrosocial explanation. In William McNeill's book *The Rise of the West*, for example, the flow of social innovation often involved some challenge to adjacent "civilized" cultures posed by the persistent raiders of the Eurasian steppe, who spur considerable innovation at the point of contact, which then may diffuse far from its origin.[34] Thus, in McNeill's argument, the mounted warrior in heavy armor was invented on the Iranian plateau as a defensive adaptation against steppe raiding; the military technology, along with social practices that could support costly animals and a class of men who could own both such costly animals and costly armor, diffused westward, ultimately becoming a constituent element in Western feudalism.

The great theoretical and empirical problem of such challenge-and-response models is distinguishing among (1) the challenge that is insufficient to provoke innovation at all, (2) the challenge that is so great as to be overwhelming rather than stimulating, and (3) the challenge that, like Little Bear's bed for Goldilocks, is just right. We see this issue clearly posed in Alexander Gerschenkron's influential theory of "economic backwardness in historical perspective."[35] Under pressure of English industrial advance, Gerschenkron argues, various organizations or even states in continental Europe attempted to do likewise. As we move east in Europe, conditions are increasingly different from those nurturing English industrialization, so more easterly and later industrializers follow patterns of capital mobilization and productive organization that differ increasingly from England's. Innovation, not simple imitation, is the response to the challenge. The greater the challenge, the more innovative the response. But the argument poses the question of what happens if conditions get too remote, if, in other words, the challenge is too great.

A very interesting systematization of such arguments has been carried out by Christopher Chase-Dunn and Thomas Hall, who make use of, and extend, the conceptual framework formulated by Immanuel Wallerstein.[36] A rich network of transnational interconnections—economic, political, military, cultural—links the regions of the world into a hierarchically organized whole. Within this whole, the *core* regions are those able to extract the greatest benefits from participation, while the *periphery* is the least favored portion. In between, and of particular importance to us, is a *semiperiphery*. This semiperiphery may be constituted in many ways; it includes places that combine core and peripheral characteristics, it includes places dominated by core regions but capable of dominating peripheral ones, it includes formerly core regions in significant economic and political decline, and it includes formerly peripheral regions in significant economic and political ascent. By these criteria, it includes most of the places—maybe all of them—that have turned up in our account here, at least at the moments of their democratic innovations.

In the Chase-Dunn and Hall account, the contradictory pulls and pushes on semiperipheral places, from without and from within, have made such places prime zones of social innovation, the places new models of governance and new forms of economic organization are launched. Indeed, as they sift through histories of ancient empires and multicentric interacting interstate systems, Chase-Dunn and Hall find that it has generally been such semiperipheral zones that are the sources of transformation of the larger systems in which they are embedded. We do not need here to consider these questions on nearly so grand a scale, but their work suggests that the geographical distribution of political creativity that we have found to characterize the history of modern democracy is an instance of a very much more general process.

Let me be clear about the important things this thesis does not explain. It does not explain why equal voting rights for women, specifically, were institutionalized so early in Oceania in particular. It does not explain why the secret ballot, specifically, was mandated at such an early date in Australia in particular. Still less does it explain why Poland was the first European state to follow the U.S. lead in constitutionalism, why the United States pioneered in legitimizing political party election-contesting, why Switzerland was abolishing property restrictions on voting rights in the 1830s and 1840s, why Denmark was the first European state to abolish the slave trade and Chile the first state in South America to abolish slavery. The specifics of innovation, the time, place, and nature of new democratic institutions have not been explained here at all; and these specifics are important, for as we have noted, countries that have innovated have generally been innovative only in some ways and at some moments. But in demonstrating that many of the major innovations in democratization have been made in particular kinds of countries—those of intermediate levels of wealth and power—and in suggesting a broad explanation for this broad pattern, I hope to have demonstrated the interest of moving on towards these more specific questions of the conjunction of time, place, and form of democratic innovation. And more important still, I hope I have shown that it is important to begin to think of democracy as something invented, and reinvented, and, if it is not to become trivialized, in need of being reinvented yet again.

Conclusion

At the end of the twentieth century, the attention of many social scientists is focused on a great wave of democratizations. Some are confident that democracy is now the wave of the future, others see that "they" are well on the way to acquiring the same institutions that "we" have and that, therefore, we may glimpse an end to history.[37]

It is a bit sobering to return, as Arthur Schlesinger Jr. has urged, to an eminent student of politics from the late nineteenth and early twentieth centuries. Finishing up his two-volume survey, *Modern Democracies,* in 1920, James Bryce pondered "the universal acceptance of democracy as the normal and natural form of government." Alternative forms of rule over large territorial states had collapsed as "four great empires in Europe—as well as a fifth in Asia—all ruled by ancient dynasties, crash to the ground, and we see efforts made to build up out of the ruins new States, each of which is enacting for itself a democratic constitution." And Bryce goes on: "China, India, and Russia contain, taken together, one half or more the population of the globe, so the problem of providing free government for them is the largest problem statesmanship has ever had to solve."[38] Bryce had the sense to see that history had not come to an end, although he did not anticipate that in the years ahead the initiatives on the world stage were very quickly to pass to Mussolini, Hitler, Stalin, and assorted antidemocratic monarchs, militaries, and movements. Although democracy had, by 1920, spread over an unprecedented geographic range, and, as Bryce noted, the great empires had collapsed, for two and a half decades after Bryce wrote, democracy was embattled and its continued existence very much in doubt.

In considering, then, the present moment, when once again there are unprecedentedly widespread claims of democracy and the sudden collapse of rival systems of rule, and with the future of Russia, India, and China once again much on everyone's minds, it is well worth asking whether it is enough to be examining the degree to which increasing numbers of states are acquiring the sorts of institutions by which the older democracies announce their democratic character. The historical record suggests that the places where creative breakthroughs have occurred have tended to be lesser powers on the world stage. Alongside our efforts to see to what extent previously less democratic places are, at the end of the twentieth century, becoming more democratic by developing institutions that resemble those of prestigious, wealthy, and powerful democratic states, we need to be looking for the ways in which democracy might be altered, renewed, and re-created. And in *that* investigation, the historical record suggests that we are more likely to find what we are looking for in those lesser powers. Is Chile's late-twentieth-century reorganization of its social security system a precursor of new models of the relation of citizen and state?[39] Is the postapartheid constitution of South Africa beginning the institutionalization of new kinds of citizens' claims in its declaration of gay rights?[40] If there is a meaningful future for democracy, it will require, as it always has, renewal and reinvention; if, as scholars, we want even a blurry glimpse of what that future might be, we shall have to go beyond considering how, to what extent, and why, places like Chile and South Africa have been acquiring the institutions that have come down to us out of democracy's past and look for clues to the institutions that we hope, or fear, may be part of that future.

Notes

This paper has benefited considerably from critical comments on a different paper by readers who, for the most part, have not seen this one. I do not know what the norms for acknowledgments are in such a case, but I am grateful for valuable suggestions on that other essay to Michael Hanagan, Juan Linz, John Marx, Verónica Montecinos, Richard Rose, Arthur Stinchcombe, Charles Tilly, and Sasha Weitman.

1. For the background, see Asa Briggs, ed., *Chartist Studies* (London: Macmillan, 1969); David Jones, *Chartism and the Chartists* (New York: St. Martin's Press, 1975); Dorothy Thompson, *The Chartists: Popular Politics in the Industrial Revolution* (New York: Pantheon Books, 1984); John Charlton, *The Chartists: The First National Workers' Movement* (London: Pluto Press, 1997).
2. See the observations of Dorothy Thompson in *The Chartists,* 311.
3. F. C. Mather, *Chartism and Society: An Anthology of Documents* (New York: Holmes & Meier, 1980), 47–48.
4. The quotes are from William Charles Wentworth, who was advocating an upper house of peers for New South Wales. When that plan for an Australian aristocracy went

down to defeat, Wentworth relocated to England. See I. D. McNaughtan, "Colonial Liberalism, 1851–1892," in *Australia: A Social and Political History,* ed. Gordon Greenwood (London: Angus & Robertson, 1955), 103–4; *Collins Australian Encyclopedia,* (Sydney: Collins, 1984), 686–87.

5. Quoted in McNaughtan, "Colonial Liberalism," 102. On early Australian receptivity to a range of democratic procedures, some of Chartist inspiration, see W. G. McMinn, *A Constitutional History of Australia* (Melbourne: Oxford University Press, 1979), 62–65.

6. J. F. H. Wright, *Mirror of the Nation's Mind: Australia's Electoral Experiments* (Sydney: Hale & Ironmonger, 1980), 24 ff.; Lionel E. Fredman, *The Australian Ballot: The Story of an American Reform* (East Lansing: Michigan State University Press, 1968); I. D. McNaughtan, "Colonial Liberalism," 98–144; Spencer D. Albright, *The American Ballot* (Washington, D.C.: American Council on Public Affairs, 1942); *The Modern Encyclopedia of Australia and New Zealand* (Sydney: Horwitz-Graham, 1964), 24.

7. Thomas T. Mackie and Richard Rose, *The International Almanac of Electoral History* (Washington, D.C.: Congressional Quarterly, 1991), 439.

8. On the transnational history of women's suffrage, see Caroline Daley and Melanie Nolan, eds., *Suffrage and Beyond: International Feminist Perspectives* (New York: New York University Press, 1994); and Richard J. Evans, *The Feminists: Women's Emancipation Movements in Europe, America, and Australasia, 1840–1920* (New York: Barnes & Noble, 1977).

9. Eleanor Flexner and Ellen Fitzpatrick, *Century of Struggle: The Woman's Rights Movement in the United States* (Cambridge: Harvard University Press, Belknap Press, 1996), 71.

10. Cleveland, Ohio, was the site of the WCTU's first convention, planned a few months earlier in Chatauqua, New York. See Janet Zollinger Giele, *Two Paths to Equality: Temperance, Suffrage, and the Origins of Modern Feminism* (New York: Twaye Publishers, 1995), 64, 114.

11. Giele, *Two Paths to Equality*; Joseph Gusfield, *Symbolic Crusade: Status Politics and the American Temperance Movement* (Urbana: University of Illinois Press, 1963).

12. Patricia Grimshaw, *Women's Suffrage in New Zealand* (Auckland: Auckland University Press, 1972).

13. Erik Olssen, "Towards a New Society," in *The Oxford History of New Zealand,* ed. Geoffrey W. Rice (Auckland: Oxford University Press, 1992), 264.

14. Kristen Lees, *Votes for Women: The Australian Story* (St. Leonard's, Australia: Allen & Unwin, 1995).

15. E.g., Barrington Moore Jr., *Social Origins of Dictatorship and Democracy: Lord and Peasant in the Making of the Modern World* (Boston: Beacon Press, 1966), xi–xiii.

16. Fredman, *Australian Ballot,* 4–5, 13.

17. Raewyn Dalziel, "Presenting the Enfranchisement of New Zealand Women Abroad," in *Suffrage and Beyond,* 42–64; quote on 57.

18. Much more detail and references to relevant literature are provided in John Markoff, "Where and When Was Democracy Invented?" *Comparative Studies in Society and History* (forthcoming).

19. Alternative practices have included hereditary monarchs with extensive powers; membership by right, including inheritance or occupancy of some other position not subject to public accountability, in a legislative body; presidency-for-life; plebiscitary affirmation of authority when the plebiscites are held only at times and under conditions chosen by the powerholder.

20. We ignore here some important, but very temporary, innovations in revolutionary France in the 1790s.

21. Some skeptical readers might object that we ought to consider local or regional innovation, not just the national scene, and therefore ought to stress the precocity of women's suffrage in parts of the U.S. territory. If we pursue such a direction, however, we must note that before Wyoming and Utah enfranchised women in 1869 and 1870, Colombia's province of Velez did so in 1853; and before Velez, the residents of tiny Pitcairn Island in the Pacific had done so by 1838.

22. Susan Magarey, "Why Didn't They Want to Be Members of Parliament? Suffragists in South Australia," in *Suffrage and Beyond,* 70.

23. Theda Skocpol and Margaret Somers, "The Uses of Comparative History in Macrosocial Inquiry," *Comparative Studies in Society and History* 22 (1980): 174–97.

24. Charles Tilly's exploration of "encompassing comparisons" helps sort out some of the important issues. See Charles Tilly, *Big Structures, Large Processes, Huge Comparisons* (New York: Russell Sage, 1984), 125–43.

25. Tiza Rivera-Cira, *Las mujeres en los parlamentos latinoamericanos* (Valparaiso: Universidad Católica de Valparaiso, 1993), 24–25.

26. Thus Juan Linz has argued that many regimes in weaker countries are mimetic; despite superficial resemblances, their political institutions could often be characterized as pseudofascism, pseudosocialism, or pseudodemocracy, depending in significant degree on the currently prestigious models on a world scale. See Juan Linz, "Totalitarian and Authoritarian Regimes," in *Macropolitical Theory,* vol. 3 of *Handbook of Political Science,* ed. Fred I. Greenstein and Nelson W. Polsby (Reading, Mass.: Addison-Wesley, 1975), 175–411.

27. Captain Elliott's account is reproduced in Walter Brodie, *Pitcairn's Island and the Islanders in 1850* (London: Whittaker, 1851); quotes on 83–84.

28. It is not evident to me whether Captain Elliott's document marks the instant that woman's suffrage was created or whether he was simply writing down the already existing practice of the Pitcairners. It is hard not to wonder whether back behind Pitcairn practice, as precursor and model, there were the democratic elements in the governance of pirate crews, almost certainly known to the *Bounty* sailors, including occasional defiance of landside gender norms. See Marcus Rediker, *Between the Devil and the Deep Blue Sea: Merchant Seamen, Pirates, and the Anglo-American Maritime World, 1700–1750* (Cambridge: Cambridge University Press, 1987), esp. 261–66; and Marcus Rediker, "Liberty beneath the Jolly Roger: The Lives of Anne Bonny and Mary Read, Pirates," in *Iron Men, Wooden Women: Gender and Seafaring in the Atlantic*

World, 1700–1920, ed. Margaret S. Creighton and Lisa Norling (Baltimore: Johns Hopkins University Press, 1996), 1–33.

29. Sir William Denison, *Varieties of Vice-Regal Life* (London: Longman's, 1870), 1: 411–12.

30. Women in New Zealand's protectorate, the Cook Islands, got to vote a bit before the women of New Zealand proper. See Dick Scott, *Years of the Great Pooh-Bah: A Cook Islands History* (Rarotonga: Cook Islands Trading Corp., 1991), 59.

31. Quoted in Dalziel, "Presenting the Enfranchisement," 60.

32. Melissa A. Butler and Jacqueline Templeton, "The Isle of Man and the First Vote for Women," *Women and Politics* 4, no. 2 (Summer 1984): 33–47. When local political arrangements permitted regional differences in the breakthrough to women's suffrage, countries' pioneering localities have often been far from the national power centers. Not only did women on the Isle of Man get to vote for the local parliament before London women could vote for the House of Commons, and Wyoming women get the vote before women in New York, but women in New Zealand's distant protectorate of the Cook Islands voted before women in Auckland; women in Velez had, briefly, the right to vote long before women in Bogotá; women in Yucatán before Mexico City; women in Rio Grande do Norte before Rio de Janeiro or São Paulo; a woman in Loja before any woman in Quito or Guayaquil. (See Markoff, "Where and When?")

33. For some Australian-British interconnections within the women's suffrage movement, see Lees, *Votes for Women*, 169–79. Some might argue that the technology of the "globalized" late twentieth century makes specific interconnections less significant. The new technologies—TV, e-mail, fax—have so increased the density of communication in all directions that structured transnational networks have been replaced by a protean, amorphous interconnectedness of everyone and everything. Michael Hanagan's work, however, makes a strong case that social movement activism depends on personal, not virtual, contacts, and therefore the study of specific networks of interaction remains as pertinent as ever. See Michael Hanagan, "Irish Transnational Social Movements, Deterritorialized Migrants, and the State System: The Last One Hundred and Forty Years," *Mobilization* 3, no. 1 (1998): 107–26.

34. William H. McNeill, *The Rise of the West: A History of the Human Community* (Chicago: University of Chicago Press, 1963).

35. Alexander Gerschenkron, *Economic Backwardness in Historical Perspective* (Cambridge: Cambridge University Press, 1962), 5–51.

36. Christopher Chase-Dunn and Thomas D. Hall, *Rise and Demise: Comparing World-Systems* (Boulder, Colo.: Westview Press, 1997). Immanuel Wallerstein, "The Rise and Future Demise of the World Capitalist System: Concepts for Comparative Analysis," *Comparative Studies in Society and History* 16 (1974): 387–415; Immanuel Wallerstein, *The Modern World-System*, vol. 1, *Capitalist Agriculture and the Origins of the European World-Economy in the Sixteenth Century* (New York: Academic Press, 1974).

37. Francis Fukuyama, "The End of History?" *National Interest* 16 (Summer 1989): 3–18.

38. James Bryce, *Modern Democracies* (New York: Macmillan, 1921), 1: 4–5. For

Schlesinger's comments on Bryce, see his "Has Democracy a Future?" *Foreign Affairs* 76, no. 5 (1997): 2 ff.

39.   In the 1980s, Chile began to move towards the privatization of its national pension system. By the 1990s, a number of other Latin American countries were introducing similar policies, the British government was announcing that it would follow suit, and U.S. economists were debating the relevance of the Chilean model to their country. See Peter Passell, "How Chile Farms Out Nest Eggs," *New York Times,* 21 March 1997, D1.

40.   Under the South African constitution of 8 May 1996, the third item under the heading "Equality" states: "The state may not unfairly discriminate directly or indirectly against anyone on one or more grounds, including race, gender, sex, pregnancy, marital status, ethnic or social origin, colour, sexual orientation, age, disability, religion, conscience, belief, culture, language, and birth" (Constitution of the Republic of South Africa 1996, chap. 2, sec. 9). Among the wealthier countries, the most extensive personal rights for gays in the late 1990s were probably found in Holland, where "registered partnerships" had acquired most (but not all) the rights of marriage ("When My Old Dutch Is a Man," *Economist*, 24–30 January 1998, 52).

11

Conclusion: Why Worry about Citizenship?

Charles Tilly

Since the later eighteenth century, new political regimes have developed the habit of advertising their newness by enacting written constitutions. These days new constitutions address at least three audiences: a population that is supposed to live by its provisions, an international community that must deal with its leaders, and an array of people who will actually run the country. Each of these audiences, furthermore, typically has more than a single ear. Constitutional definitions of citizenship unavoidably speak simultaneously to all three audiences and their diverse internal claques.

The post-Soviet Republic of Kazakhstan offers a striking case in point. The republic's 1995 constitution stresses rights and obligations of Kazakh citizenship. In a day when a claim to be a coherent indigenous nation forms a crucial part of any bid for internationally recognized sovereignty, how constitution writers answer the question "Who are you?" matters to all three audiences. Savor the preamble's assertive tone:

> We, the people of Kazakstan, united by a common historic fate, creating a state on the indigenous Kazak land, considering ourselves a peaceloving and civil society, dedicated to the ideals of freedom, equality and concord, wishing to take a worthy place in the world community, realizing our high responsibility before present and future generations, proceeding from our sovereign right, accept this Constitution.[1]

The constitution's Article 7 specifies that "1. The state language of the Republic of Kazakstan shall be the Kazak language. 2. In state institutions and local self-administrative bodies the Russian language shall be officially used on equal grounds along with the Kazak language. 3. The state shall promote conditions for the study and development of the languages of the people of Kazakstan." One begins to detect that who is Kazakh and who is not, matters intensely in the politics of Kazakhstan. As it turns out, who is Kazakh also matters to Kazakhstan's neighbors.

Small wonder. The constitution's drafters worked against a backdrop of vigorous, often violent contention over national autonomy. The territory that people now call Kazakhstan centers on the steppe crisscrossed for centuries by caravans between China and Europe. Today's Kazakhstan touches the Caspian Sea, Turkmenistan, Uzbekistan, Kyrgyzstan, and China. Across a vast border with the Russian federation it also abuts Siberia, the Urals, and the Volga region. Over most of the last millennium, nomadic Turkic pastoralists have predominated within its territory. But they have endured conquest after conquest.

Conquered by an expanding Mongol empire in the thirteenth century, the region sustained its own khan from the later fifteenth century. Forcible integration of the region into the Russian empire during the eighteenth and nineteenth centuries, followed by extensive immigration of Russian-speaking farmers from the north, greatly increased Russian cultural and political presence in Kazakhstan: "About 1.5 million new colonists from European Russia came to Kazakhstan at the end of the nineteenth century and in the beginning of the twentieth century."[2] Those changes marginalized the region's nomadic herders and drove many of them into settled agriculture. Self-identified Kazakhs took advantage of the Bolshevik Revolution to create an autonomous republic that lasted from 1918 to 1920. Those Kazakh nationalists, however, soon succumbed to Soviet military might.

Come to power, Stalin eventually established his characteristic pattern of governing the region through Moscow-oriented Kazakhs and created a full Soviet republic of Kazakhstan in 1936. But Stalin and his successors also built an economic system that made Kazakhstan's major industrial and commercial nodes tributaries of centers in Russia and Uzbekistan rather than connecting them with each other. The early 1930s brought forced collectivization of agriculture and fixed settlement of the remaining Kazakh nomads. Successive Soviet regimes shipped in technicians, peasants, and political prisoners from Russia, Belorussia, Poland, Ukraine, and the Caucasus as displaced Turkic nomads died out or fled to China. Unsurprisingly, Russian-speakers concentrated in and around the Russian-oriented nodes, which meant that ethnic balances varied enormously by region within Kazakhstan. Kazakhs themselves divided into three large and sometimes hostile clans, or *zhus*: a Great Horde concentrated chiefly in southern Kazakhstan, a Middle Horde in the north-central region, and a Lesser Horde, in the west.

Ethnic Kazakh Dinmukhamed Kunaev became regional party boss in 1964 and eventually acquired full membership in the Soviet Union's Politburo. Kunaev brought a number of Kazakhs (especially from his own Great Horde) into his administration. In 1986, however, reformer Mikhail Gorbachev replaced Kunaev with Gennadi Kolbin, an ethnic Russian unconnected with Kazakhstan. Students and others thereupon demonstrated against the regime in the capital, Almaty; perhaps two hundred people died in street confrontations and subsequent repression.[3] By 1989, Gorbachev had replaced Kolbin with another ethnic Kazak, Nursultan Nazarbaev.

Having ridden the rapids of the Soviet Union's downstream rush, Nazarbaev still rules Kazakhstan with a heavy hand. While tolerating (and possibly benefiting from) a great deal of rent-seeking by former and present state officials, Nazarbaev has attempted to advance a definition of Kazakh national identity without alienating either a large domestic Russian minority or the great Russian power to his north. No doubt with an eye to the intermittent civil war in nearby Tajikistan and the volatility of ethnic, linguistic, regional, and religious factions in neighboring Uzbekistan and Kyrgyzstan, Nazarbaev has handled ethnic-linguistic divisions with kid gloves.[4] The only nationalist group his regime has actively suppressed is the militant Alash party, which advocates a great state uniting all the Turkic peoples. Meanwhile, the regime resists pressure from outside (especially Russia) for recognition of dual citizenship and presses its self-identified Russians to declare themselves either foreigners or dedicated citizens of a Kazakh state.

For whoever can claim to control the country, the stakes are high. Including its share of the Caspian, Kazakhstan contains enormous potential wealth in minerals, including estimated oil reserves of 40 billion to 178 billion barrels, equivalent to a quarter-century of total U.S. oil consumption.[5] Cocaine, other drugs, and a wide range of valuable contraband flow across the country, with mobsters and officials dividing large profits. Before the economic crises of the 1990s, furthermore, Kazakhstan supplied a substantial portion of the Soviet Union's commercial grains. If the state ever establishes an effective system of taxation and investment, it will have abundant revenues to spend, not to mention fortunes to be made in capitalist enterprises.[6]

Claimants to that state divide sharply by ethnic category. As of the mid-1990s, demographers enumerated 44 percent of the republic's population as Kazakh, 36 percent as Russian, and about 10 percent as "Europeans" of other varieties; the remaining tenth fell into a hundred other nationalities, chiefly Asian in origin.[7] Although the proportion identified as Kazakh was rising through a combination of differential fertility, exits of Russians, in-migration from other parts of Central Asia, and (I speculate) shifts of declared identity on the parts of people with mixed ancestry, the constitution's drafters had to contend with the fact that the country's ostensible nationality accounted for a minority of its population and that the country's lingua franca was not Kazakh, but Russian. Hence great sensitivity to definitions of citizenship.

Referring to subjects of the Kazakh state, the constitution speaks of the following human entities (and nonentities): The People, citizens, everyone, no one, foreigners, stateless persons, persons, and individuals. It also makes distinctions between minors and full adults, with only full adults (those twenty and over in the case of elections to local assemblies) having the right to vote and hold office. Some rights and obligations apply to everyone, but many of those specified apply to citizens alone. Citizens, according to the constitution, enjoy the right:

- to change citizenship (a concession to domestic Russians and representatives of Russia who pressed for recognition of dual citizenship)

- not to be extradited except as provided by international treaty

- not to be exiled, and to return freely from abroad

- to the state's protection and patronage outside its boundaries

- to access to documents, decisions, and other sources of information concerning the citizen's rights and interests

- to form associations. Exceptions: (a) the military, employees of national security and law-enforcement bodies, and judges must not join parties, trade unions, or actions in support of any political party; (b) no associations are permitted that are "directed toward a violent change of the constitutional system, violation of the integrity of the Republic, undermining the security of the state, inciting social, racial, national, religious, class and tribal enmity, as well as formation of unauthorized paramilitary units"; (c) no political parties, trade unions, or religious parties based in or financed by foreign countries, foreign individuals, or international organizations are permitted.

- to housing at an affordable price

- to ownership of legally acquired property

- to a minimum wage, pension, and social security in old age as well as in case of disease, disability, or loss of breadwinner

- to protection of health, including free extensive medical assistance

- to free secondary education and access to higher education on a competitive basis

- to pay for and receive education in private establishments

- to assemble; hold meetings, rallies, demonstrations, and street processions; and picket peacefully and without arms

- to participate in state affairs directly and through representatives, including collective appeals to public and local self-administrative bodies

- to elect and be elected to public offices. Exceptions: (a) "citizens judged incapable by a court as well as those held in places of confinement on a court's sentence" may not vote or hold office; (b) the "age of a government employee must not exceed sixty years and sixty-five years in exceptional cases"; and (c) restrictions on minimum age, residence, and professional qualifications apply to specific offices.

As compared with these many rights of citizens, the Constitution stipulates only a handful of obligations:

- not to violate rights and freedoms of other persons or infringe on the constitutional system and public morals

- to attend secondary school

- to defend the Republic of Kazakhstan, and to perform military service "according to the procedure and in the forms established by law"

- to care for the protection of historical and cultural heritage and preserve monuments of history and culture

- to preserve nature and protect natural resources

The constitution applies such weighty obligations as paying taxes not to citizens alone but to "everyone." It leaves unmentioned such common obligations of citizenship elsewhere as submitting to censuses, serving on juries, and registering vital events. Nevertheless, it clearly articulates three principles of citizenship that distinguish our own time's prevailing ideas, if not always its practices, from those of almost any previous historical epoch:

1. Citizenship designates not attributes of individuals but a broad categorical relation between the state's agents and a large share of the population falling under the state's jurisdiction.

2. Ethnic categories other than the official national category have no standing with respect to citizenship.

3. Degrees of citizenship exist, at least when it comes to minors, persons aged sixty and over, incarcerated criminals, and court-declared incompetents.

Such principles appear tediously obvious in today's Western world. Yet, as this book's authors have demonstrated abundantly, the existence of citizenship in something like the sense defined by the Kazakh constitution sets off our era from all other historical eras. It identifies political institutions that first grew up in Europe and by no means flourish everywhere in the world today. In Kazakhstan itself, the current regime repeatedly violates its announced principles of citizenship, notably with respect to political freedom for voices of opposition. Nevertheless, a constitution's announcement of strong citizenship facilitates the formation of alliances between aggrieved citizens and outside powers.

Within its zone of application, effective citizenship establishes the frame for fierce contention over rights and obligations of different categories within populations subject to the same governmental institution. Given substantial citizenship at a national scale, inequalities based on gender, race, national origin, recency of arrival in the territory, employment, income, and welfare become issues of citizenship. In practice, all states compromise citizenship significantly in two ways: (1) by distinguishing among categories and degrees of citizenship that imply different rights, obligations, and relations to authorities; and (2) by advertising as general rights and obligations arrangements that actually differ significantly in their applicability to various segments of the state's subject population. Most contributions to our volume—notably the analyses of Suzanne Shanahan, Michael Hanagan, Barbara Hobson, Abram de Swaan, and Antje Wiener—deal with just such issues. The remainder of this concluding chapter merely draws together the elementary operating principles of citizenship as sketched in earlier chapters then reflects on why and how citizenship matters to human welfare.

A little definitional work clarifies essential connections. Let us take *government* to designate any organization that controls the chief concentrated coercive means within some substantial territory, reserving the name *state* for those governments that (a) do not fall under the jurisdiction of any other government and (b) receive recognition from other governments in the same situation. Sweden and China qualify as states, while municipalities within their perimeters qualify as governments but not as states. In principle, citizenship then refers to a relation between (1) governmental agents acting uniquely as such and (2) whole categories of persons identified uniquely by their connection with the government in question. The relation includes transactions among the parties, of course, but those transactions cluster around mutual rights and obligations. In the case of Kazakhstan, we have already seen that those rights and obligations can cover a wide range of social relations.

What are rights and obligations? Imagine X and Y as social actors, including organizations and whole categories of persons. X's rights with respect to Y include all enforceable claims that X can make on Y, with the crucial feature of enforcement being that authoritative third parties will intervene to promote Y's acceptance of the claims in question. Obligations are nothing but the same enforceable claims seen from Y's perspective. Veterans have rights to pensions to the degree that governmental paymasters have an obligation to pay those pensions, residents of a state have an obligation to pay taxes to the degree that fiscal officials have a right to collect those taxes.

Citizenship designates a set of mutually enforceable claims relating categories of persons to agents of governments. Like relations between spouses, between coauthors, between workers and employers, citizenship has the character of a contract: variable in range, never completely specified, always depending on unstated assumptions about context, modified by practice, constrained by collective memory, yet ineluctably involving rights and obligations sufficiently defined that either party is likely to express indignation and take corrective action when the other fails to meet expectations built into the relationship. As observers, we actually witness transactions between governmental agents and members of broadly defined categories, but we abstract from those transactions a cultural bundle: a set of mutual rights and obligations. Precisely insofar as a bundle of rights and obligations actually distinguishes a whole category of the state's subject population defined by its relation to that state rather than by the category's place in the population's general system of inequality, those categorically defined rights and obligations belong to citizenship.

Citizenship resembles the run of contracts in drawing visible lines between insiders and outsiders yet engaging third parties to respect and even enforce its provisions. It differs from most other contracts in (a) binding whole categories of persons rather than single individuals to each other, (b) involving differentiation among levels and degrees of members, and (c) directly engaging a government's coercive power. To the extent that governments control substantial resources, including coercive means, these three differentials single out citizenship as a potent form of contract liable to fierce contestation. Military service, eligibility for public office, voting rights, payment of taxes, public education, access to public services, and protection of rent-producing advantages—all frequent items in contracts of citizenship, and all explicitly enumerated in Kazakhstan's 1995 constitution—have engaged serious struggle for centuries.

As contributors to this book demonstrate amply, contracts of citizenship have a history at least as tortuous as that of other major contracts, commercial or intellectual. For centuries, as Maarten Prak forcefully points out, citizenship bound most Western European people not to organizations like the large, centralized consolidated states of recent experience but to smaller units such as municipalities. Despite emulation and mutual influence from one local polity to another, the small scale produced great variability in conditions of citizenship from place to place.[8]

As Prak also establishes, between 1750 and 1850, Europe's consolidating states did not so much absorb these earlier forms of citizenship as subordinate or even smash them in favor of relatively uniform categorization and obligation at a national scale. State consolidation thus thinned citizenship significantly for those who already participated in its rights and obligations at the smaller scale. For them, national citizenship offered a narrower range of rights and obligations than had the burghers' militia service, participation in public ceremonies, supervision of poor relief, moral oversight, and involvement in public finance. For those who had previously lacked substantial local or regional citizenship, however, the establishment of national citizenship brought significant gains in rights at the cost of expanded obligations to national authorities. Much of the widespread Western transition from indirect to direct rule between the eighteenth and twentieth centuries consisted, precisely, of national citizenship's establishing priority over local and regional systems of obligation. Those changes squeezed out autonomous middlemen such as warlords and fief-holders or integrated them directly into national administrative hierarchies.

Ariel Salzmann shows us the distinctive Ottoman path toward direct rule, which led perilously away from a rather effective system of indirect rule in which separate religious, military, and property-holding segments maintained distinctive compacts with the imperial center. Ironically, the very Western European powers that were aggressively establishing direct rule within their own domestic territories successfully pressed Ottoman authorities to create special statuses for ostensible nationalities, thus hindering the establishment of direct rule and generalized citizenship in the empire. (Those same powers, of course, employed indirect rule widely in their overseas colonies.)[9] Although Salzmann displays no nostalgia for the old millet system (in which members of different religious categories enjoyed or suffered different collective legal relations to the Ottoman state), she astutely analyzes how its organizational structure shaped efforts to create citizenship in Ottoman territories. Those efforts generally failed until the empire itself collapsed in military defeat.

Not that any state ever established a single contract of citizenship or an impermeable boundary between citizens and noncitizens. Like Kazakhstan, all states differentiate within their citizenries, at a minimum distinguishing between minors and adults, prisoners and free persons, naturalized and native-born. Many make finer gradations—for example, by restricting suffrage or military service to adult males, imposing property qualifications for certain rights, or installing a range from temporary residents to probationary applicants for citizenship to full-fledged participants in citizenship's rights and obligations.

Almost all constitutions define a special subset of citizens who are eligible for high public offices. Kazakhstan's constitution stipulates that:

A citizen of the Republic shall be eligible for the office of the President of the Republic of Kazakstan if he [*sic*] is by birth not younger than thirty-five and not older than sixty-five, has a perfect command of the state language [i.e., Kazakh] and has lived in Kazakstan for not less than fifteen years.

Other stipulations of age and residence restrict citizens' access to other offices, thus creating additional grades within the general category of citizenship.

The European Union (as Antje Wiener documents) is further complicating categories of citizenship by establishing rights that transfer from state to state and by creating some sets of rights connecting whole categories of Europeans not to agents of the states within which they reside but to agents of the Union itself. Just as large capitalist firms establish not one uniform contract with all their workers but numerous contracts connecting managers with different categories of workers, states and citizens maintain multiple categories of relationship.

More visibly than in the case of capitalist firms (where a new firm typically borrows a great deal of its organizational structure, including contracts, from existing firms in the same industry), rights and obligations linking citizens to states have formed through struggle. Schematically, we can distinguish between top-down and bottom-up claims. From the top down, state demands for resources and compliance generate bargaining, resistance, and settlements encapsulating both rights and obligations, as when popularly elected parliaments gain power through their role in raising taxes for warfare. From the bottom, segments of the subject population also acquire rights and obligations by mobilizing to demand state agents' intervention, reorganization, or reallocation of state-controlled resources.

In our own time, we commonly use names like taxation, conscription, and regulation—all of them regularly generating bargaining, resistance, and settlements—for activities falling clearly into the top-down category, reserving names like parties, pressure groups, and social movements for unambiguous members of the bottom-up category. We typically place governmental expenditure, bureaucratic operation, and public services in an intermediate location. Top-down and bottom-up claims often pivot, precisely, on struggles for control over those intermediate locations. Top-down claims regularly generate bottom-up claims, as when military veterans who served reluctantly at the start demand peacetime benefits in recognition of their service, or when dissidents withhold tax payments to back demands for a voice in public expenditure.

Such claims become citizenship rights—enforceable claims—through struggle between governmental agents and categories of the population subject to their governments. Most claim making fails; in this book, Michael Hanagan shows us repeated workers' claims for the right to work, none of which ever achieved full realization in any capitalist country's code of citizenship. Women's claims to political participation, in contrast, have enjoyed dramatic success. Because consolidating states essentially conceded popular electoral participation in return for military service and subjection of male-dominated enterprises to war-driven taxation, voting long remained a male prerogative. Eventually female mobilization and claim making succeeded in opening national polities to women. Barbara Hobson takes that transformation as given, tracing its consequences for further claims on social rights as she criticizes both the idea of more or less automatic expansion of rights she associates with T. H. Marshall and the political-power modification of the scheme she associates with Gösta Esping-Anderson and Walter Korpi.

Bin Wong's analysis of public obligation in China shows us how distinctive is the Western background of the struggles analyzed by Hanagan and Hobson: in imperial China, nothing like the bargaining out of specific rights between local groups and national authorities occurred. No ordinary subject of the Chinese state could call on third parties to enforce his or her categorically defined rights. That legacy of officials bound by virtue but not by enforceable contract carried over into the revolutionary age. Hence recent attempts to define Chinese citizenship proceed against a very different set of assumptions concerning the mutual obligations involved.

We begin to sense why citizenship matters. It encases vital rights and obligations, ones that impinge significantly on life outside the world of constitutional affairs. Effective citizenship imposes strong obligations uniformly on broad categories of political participants and state agents. It thereby mitigates—but by no means eliminates—political effects of inequalities in routine social life. At a national scale effective citizenship is a necessary condition of democracy. The statement holds whether we adopt a substantive definition of democracy (stressing such outcomes as equity and well-being), an institutional definition (stressing such arrangements as contested elections and independent judiciaries), or a political-process definition (stressing relations between a state's agents and people falling under their jurisdiction). In the political-process definition that strikes me as most useful for explanatory purposes, democracy combines four elements: (1) relatively broad public political participation; (2) relatively equal participation; (3) binding consultation of political participants with respect to state policies, resources, and personnel; and (4) protection of political participants (especially members of minorities) from arbitrary action by state agents. Without effective citizenship, no regime provides sufficient breadth, equality, binding consultation, or protection of participants in public politics to qualify as democratic.

Citizenship is by no means, however, a sufficient condition of democracy.

In the West, bargaining over the means of state expansion started generating institutions of citizenship—extensive rights and obligations binding whole categories of their national populations together with state agents—long before broadening, equalization, consultation, or protection reached levels that we might reasonably call democratic. Unlike their tyrannical predecessors, twentieth-century authoritarian regimes have commonly created their own versions of citizenship, stronger on obligations than on rights from the citizen's perspective. The building of patron-client relations into citizenship through exchanges of goods for political support actually inhibits democratization.[10] In Europe as a whole, citizenship began to take democratic forms when conquest, colonization, confrontation, or revolution tore existing webs of privilege. Then those who benefited from undemocratic political arrangements lost the power (sometimes even the incentive) to maintain narrow, unequal political participation, restricted consultation, and arbitrary action by state agents.

By these criteria, independent Kazakhstan has established a precarious sort of citizenship but has remained far from democracy.[11] The 1995 constitution's announced rights for citizens may look good to the constitution's first audience—various international actors—but they do not much constrain the country's current rulers and provide little protection for their domestic opponents. Elected president without opposition, Nursultan Nazarbaev rules by decree in the absence of a parliament that he disbanded—or, more precisely, in the presence of a consultative assembly he created after dismissing the elected parliament. His daughter Dariga Nazarbaeva runs the principal state TV channel, which does not broadcast news of political opposition. His government routinely and massively imprisons political opponents on the basis of forced confessions. Despite constitutional provisions we reviewed earlier, by presidential fiat dissenting political assemblies are largely illegal:

A March 17, 1995 presidential decree issued while parliament was disbanded remains in force and limits the ability of citizens to participate in unsanctioned demonstrations. Gaining permission for such gatherings is difficult, and authorities have jailed violators. Madel Ismailov, leader of the opposition Working Class Movement, for example, was imprisoned for leading an unsanctioned rally on May 30 [1997] that drew thousands of participants, and many others have been fined.[12]

Single-handedly, President Nazarbaev decided to move the national capital from Almaty to Akmola, a raw, mosquito-ridden settlement of three hundred thousand people in north-central Kazakhstan. (Since Akmola means "white tomb," Nazarbaev has since changed the name to Astana, meaning "capital"; Soviet authorities called the place Tselinograd, "city of the virgin lands.") In these and other ways, the regime qualifies as sustaining moderately broad but centrally controlled political participation, unequal and contested citizenship, very limited consultation, and weak protection. The regime operates far from democracy.

In these regards, alas, most of the world's regimes resemble Kazakhstan more than they resemble France or Japan. Even more so than in today's well-established parliamentary democracies, citizenship remains contested. Sri Lanka, Nigeria, Ecuador, Indonesia, and Israel all stand witness to the explosive content of controversies about citizenship. Without broad, relatively equal, binding, well-protected citizenship, however, democracy will flourish nowhere. John Markoff rightly points out how much the history of democracy has depended on waves of innovation outside the core of dominant democracies. Crucial innovations and failures will continue to occur in the efforts of today's poorer undemocratic countries to craft new varieties of citizenship. The future of democratization hangs in the balance.

Notes

I am grateful to Edward Tiryakian and Katherine Verdery for criticism of an earlier version of this paper.

1. Citations from the Kazakh constitution come from the World Wide Web, at www.geocities.com/CapitolHill/Lobby/2171/kzconst.html.
2. Anatoly M. Khazanov, *After the USSR: Ethnicity, Nationalism, and Politics in the Commonwealth of Independent States* (Madison: University of Wisconsin Press, 1995), 157.
3. Martha Brill Olcott, "Democratization and the Growth of Political Participation in Kazakstan," in *Conflict, Cleavage, and Change in Central Asia and the Caucasus,* vol. 4 of *Democratization and Authoritarianism in Postcommunist Societies,* ed. Karen Dawisha and Bruce Parrott (Cambridge: Cambridge University Press, 1997), 206.
4. Muriel Atkin, "Thwarted Democratization in Tajikistan," in *Conflict, Cleavage, and Change*; Dana Fane, "Ethnicity and Regionalism in Uzbekistan: Maintaining Stability through Authoritarian Control," in *Ethnic Conflict in the Post-Soviet World: Case Studies and Analysis,* ed. Leokadia Drobizheva et al. (Armonk, N.Y.: M. E. Sharpe, 1996); William Fierman, "Political Development in Uzbekistan: Democratization?" in *Conflict, Cleavage, and Change*; Eugene Huskey, "Kyrgyzstan: The Fate of Political Liberalization," in *Conflict, Cleavage, and Change*; Gavhar Juraeva and Nancy Lubin, "Ethnic Conflict in Tajikistan," in *Ethnic Conflict in the Post-Soviet World.*
5. Marshall Ingwerson, "Into the Steppe of Genghis Khan Ride the Conquerors of a Sea's Oil Bounty," *Christian Science Monitor,* 18 August 1997, 1, electronic ed.
6. Edgar Feige, "Underground Activity and Institutional Change: Productive, Protective, and Predatory Behavior in Transition Economies," in *Transforming Post-Com-*

munist Political Economies, ed. Joan M. Nelson, Charles Tilly, and Lee Walker (Washington, D.C.: National Academy Press, 1998).

7. United Nations, *Kazakstan: The Challenge of Transition. Human Development Report 1995* (New York: United Nations, 1995), 1:6; www.undp.org/rbec/nhdr/kazakstan.

8. For a convenient orientation, see Wayne te Brake, *Shaping History: Ordinary People in European Politics, 1500–1700* (Berkeley and Los Angeles: University of California Press, 1998).

9. Mahmood Mamdani, *Citizen and Subject: Contemporary Africa and the Legacy of Late Colonialism* (Princeton: Princeton University Press, 1996).

10. Jonathan Fox, "The Difficult Transition from Clientelism to Citizenship: Lessons from Mexico," *World Politics* 46 (1994): 151–84.

11. CSCE (Commission on Security and Cooperation in Europe), *Political Reform and Human Rights in Uzbekistan, Kyrgyzstan, and Kazakstan* (Washington, D.C.: CSCE, 1998), 27–38.

12. CSCE, *Political Reform and Human Rights.*

12

A Bibliography of Citizenship

Teal Rothschild

Ackers, Louise. "Citizenship, Gender, and Dependence in the European Union: Women and Internal Migration." *Social Politics* 3, nos. 2–3 (Summer 1996): 316–30.

Ahrne, Goran. "Civil Society and Civil Organizations." *Organization* 3 (1996): 109–20.

Akarlı, Engin. *The Long Peace: Ottoman Lebanon.* Berkeley and Los Angeles: University of California Press, 1993.

Aminzade, Ronald. *Ballots and Barricades: Class Formation and Republican Politics in France, 1830–1871.* Princeton: Princeton University Press, 1993.

Andrews, Geoff, ed. *Citizenship.* London: Lawrence & Wishart, 1991.

Aron, Raymond. "Is Multinational Citizenship Possible?" *Social Research* 41, no. 4 (1974): 638–56.

Barbalet, J. M. *Citizenship.* Minneapolis: University of Minnesota Press, 1988.

Beiner, Roland, ed. *Theorizing Citizenship.* Albany: State University of New York Press, 1995.

Bendix, Reinhard. *Kings or People: Power and the Mandate to Rule.* Berkeley and Los Angeles: University of California Press, 1978.

———. *Nation Building and Citizenship.* New York: John Wiley & Son, 1964.

Binnie, J. "Invisible Europeans: Sexual Citizenship in the New Europe." *Environment and Planning* 29, no. 2 (February 1997): 237–49.

Birkenbach, Hanne-Margret. *Preventive Diplomacy through Fact-Finding: How International Organisations Review the Conflict over Citizenship in Estonia and Latvia.* New Brunswick, N.J.: Transaction, 1997.

Birnbaum, Pierre, and Ira Katznelson, eds. *Paths of Emancipation: Jews, States, and Citizenship.* Princeton: Princeton University Press, 1995.

Boehm, Tatiana. "The Women's Question as a Democratic Question: In Search of Civil Society." In *Gender Politics and Post-Communism: Reflections from Eastern Europe and the Soviet Union,* edited by Nanette Funk. New York: Routledge, 1993.

261

Bossenga, Gail. "Rights and Citizens in the Old Regime." *French Historical Studies* 20, (1997): 217–244.

———. *The Politics of Privilege: Old Regime and Revolution in Lille.* Cambridge: Cambridge University Press, 1991.

Bouamama, Said. "Egalité-equité: Fondement du lien social." In *Le citoyenetté dans tous ses états: De l'immigration à la nouvelle citoyenneté,* edited by Said Bouamama, Albana Cordiero, and Michel Roux. Paris: Ciemi L'Harmatan, 1992.

Brubaker, Rogers. *Citizenship and Nationhood in France and Germany.* Cambridge: Harvard University Press, 1992.

———. "Citizenship Struggles in Soviet Successor States." *International Migration Review* 26, no. 2 (Summer 1992): 269–91.

Buckley, Mary, and Malcolm Anderson, eds. *Women, Equality, and Europe.* Basingstoke, England: Macmillan, 1988.

Bulmer, Martin, and Anthony M. Rees, eds. *Citizenship Today: The Contemporary Revolution of T. H. Marshall.* London: UCL Press, 1996.

Bulmer, Simon, Stephen George, and Andrew Scott, eds. *The United Kingdom and EC Membership Evaluated.* London: Pinter, 1992.

Butler, Fiona. "Social Policy and the European Community: Proposals for Worker Participation Legislation." *Public Policy and Administration* 6, no. 1 (1991): 72–79.

Cannan, Crescy. "A Europe of the Citizen: a Europe of Solidarity? A Social Policy in the European Union." In *Citizenship and Democratic Control in Contemporary Europe,* edited by Barbara Einhorn and Mary Kaldor. Brookfield, Vt.: Edward Elgar, 1996.

Carter, Robert, Marci Green, and Rick Halpern. "Immigration Policy and the Racialization of Migrant Labour: The Construction of National Identities in the USA and Britain." *Ethnic and Racial Studies* 19, no. 1 (1996): 135–57.

Cass, Betina. "Citizenship, Work, and Welfare: The Dilemma for Australian Women." *Social Politics* 1, no. 1 (1994): 106–24.

Cerruti, Simona, Roberta Descimon, and Maarten Prak, eds. "Cittadinanze." *Quaderni Storici* 30, no. 89 (1995): 281–514.

Cesarani, David, and Mary Fullbrook, eds. *Citizenship, Nationality, and Migration in Europe.* London: Routledge, 1996.

Chalmers, Douglas A., et al. *The New Politics of Inequality in Latin America: Rethinking Participation and Representation.* Oxford: Oxford University Press, 1997.

Chun, Lin. "Citizenship in China: The Gender Politics of Social Transformation." *Social Politics* 3, nos. 2–3. (Summer 1996): 278–90.

Clarke, Paul Barry, ed. *Citizenship.* London: Pluto Press, 1994.

Cleveland, William. *Islam against the West: Shakib Arslan and the Campaign for Islamic Nationalism.* Austin: University of Texas Press, 1985.

Close, Paul. *Citizenship, Europe, and Change.* London: Macmillan, 1995.

————. "Towards a Framework for Analyzing Modern European Citizenship." In *Citizenship, Europe, and Change*. London: Macmillan, 1995.

Coenen, Henry, and Peter Leisink, eds. *Work and Citizenship in the New Europe*. Brookfield, Vt.: Edward Elgar, 1993.

Coleman, David. "The United Kingdom and International Migration: A Changing Balance." In *European Migration in the Late Twentieth Century*, edited by Heinz Fassman and Rainer Munz, 37–66. Laxenburg, Austria: Edward Elgar, 1994.

Dalziel, Raewyn. "Presenting the Enfranchisement of New Zealand Women Abroad." In *Suffrage and Beyond: International Feminist Perspectives*, edited by Caroline Daley and Melanie Nolan. New York: New York University Press, 1994.

Davison, Roderic H. "The Advent of the Principle of Representation in the Government of the Ottoman Empire." In *Essays in Ottoman and Turkish History, 1774–1923*. Austin: University of Texas Press, 1990.

————. *Reform in the Ottoman Empire, 1856–1876*. Princeton: Princeton University Press, 1963.

Deacon, Bob, ed. *The New Eastern Europe: Social Policy*. London: Sage, 1992.

Deem, Rosemary, Kevin J. Brehony, and Sue Heath. *Active Citizenship and the Governing of Schools*. Buckingham, England: Open University, 1995.

Demaine, Jack, and Harold Entwistle. *Beyond Communitarianism: Citizenship, Politics, and Education*. New York: St. Martin's Press, 1996.

Deringil, Selim. *The Well-Protected Domains: Ideology and the Legitimation of Power in the Ottoman Empire, 1876–1909*. London: I. B. Tauris, 1998.

Dewey, John. *Liberalism and Social Action*. New York: G. P. Putnam's Sons, 1935.

Dietz, Mary. "Context Is All: Feminism and Theories of Citizenship." *Dimensions of Radical Democracy, Pluralism, Citizenship, Community*, edited by Chantal Mouffe. London: Verso Press, 1992.

Einhorn, Barbara. *Cinderella Goes to the Market: Gender and the Women's Movement in East Central Europe*. London: Verso Press, 1993.

————. "Gender and Citizenship in East Central Europe after the End of State Socialist Policies for Women's 'Emancipation.'" In *Citizenship and Democratic Control in Contemporary Europe*, edited by Barbara Einhorn and Mary Kaldor. Brookfield, Vt.: Edward Elgar, 1996.

Eldersveld, Samuel, and Bashiruddin Ahmed. *Citizens and Politics: Mass Political Behavior in India*. Chicago: University of Chicago Press, 1978.

Esseveld, Johanma. "From Welfare State to Cultural Turn: Swedish Sociology." *Contemporary Sociology* 26, no. 3 (May 1997): 285–88.

Falkenheim, Victor, ed. *Citizens and Groups in Contemporary China*. Ann Arbor: University of Michigan Press, 1987.

Fuchs, Dieter, Jürgen Gerhards, and Edeltraud Roller. "Nationalism versus Eurocentrism? The Construction of Collective Identities in Western Europe." In *Migration,*

Citizenship, and Ethno-National Identities in the European Union, edited by Marco Martiniello. Aldershot, England: Avebury Press, 1995.

Garrigou, Alain. *Le vote et la vertu: Comment les Français sont devenus électeurs.* Paris: Presses de la Fondation Nationale des Sciences Politiques, 1992.

George, Stephen. *Politics and Policy in the European Community.* Oxford: Clarendon Press, 1991.

Geyer, Georgie Anne. *Americans No More.* New York: Atlantic Monthly Press, 1996.

Giddens, Anthony. *A Contemporary Critique of Historical Materialism.* Vol. 2. Berkeley and Los Angeles: University of California Press, 1981.

Gilbert, Alan. *Marx's Politics: Communists and Citizens.* New Brunswick, N.J.: Rutgers University Press, 1981.

Gold, Steven J. "Transnationalism and the Vocabularies of Motive in International Migration: The Case of Israelis in the United States." *Sociological Perspectives* 40, no. 3 (1997): 409–26.

Gordon, Daniel. *Citizens without Sovereignty: Equality and Sociability in French Thought, 1670–1789.* Princeton: Princeton University Press, 1994.

Gorham, Eric. "Social Citizenship and Its Fetters." *Polity* 28, no. 1 (Fall 1995): 25–47.

Grahl, John. "Economic Citizenship in the New Europe." *Political Quarterly* 65, no. 4 (October-December 1994): 379–97.

Grasmuck, Sherri, and Ramon Grosfoguel. "Geopolitics, Economic Niches, and Gendered Social Capital among Recent Caribbean Immigrants in New York City." *Sociological Perspectives* 40, no. 3 (1997): 339–64.

Habermas, Jürgen. *The Structural Transformation of the Public Sphere: An Inquiry into a Category of Bourgeois Society.* Cambridge: MIT Press, 1992.

Hadjimichalis, Costis, and David Sadler. *Europe and the Margins: New Mosaics of Inequality.* Chichester, England: John Wiley & Sons, 1995.

Hammar, Tomas. *Democracy and the Nation State: Aliens, Denizens and Citizens in a World of International Migration.* Aldershot, England: Avebury Press, 1990.

Hanagan, Michael, and Charles Tilly. "Special Issue on Recasting Citizenship." *Theory and Society* 26, no. 4 (1997): 397–604.

Harrop, Jeffrey. *The Political Economy of Integration in the European Community.* New York: Edward Elgar, 1991.

Headrick, Daniel R. *The Tentacles of Progress: Technology Transfer in the Age of Imperialism, 1880–1940.* New York: Oxford University Press, 1988.

Heater, Derek. "Citizenship: A Remarkable Case of Sudden Interest." *Parliamentary Affairs* 44 no. 2 (April 1991): 140–56.

———. *Citizenship: The Civic Ideal in World History, Politics, and Education.* London: Longman, 1990.

Held, David. *Democracy and the Global Order: From the Modern State to Cosmopolitan Governance.* Stanford, Calif.: Stanford University Press, 1995.

Hernes, Helga. "Scandinavian Citizenship." *Acta Sociologica* 31 (1988): 199–215.

Hill, Greg. "Citizenship and Ontology in the Liberal State." *Review of Politics* 55, no. 1 (Winter 1993): 67–85.

Hobson, Barbara. "Remaking the Boundaries of Women's Citizenship and the Dilemma of Dependency." In *Unresolved Dilemmas: Women, Work, and Family in the United States, Europe, and the Former Soviet Union,* edited by Tuulo Gordon and Kaisa Kauppinen-Toropainen, 33–56. Aldershot, England: Ashgate, 1997.

Hoff, Joan. "Citizenship and Nationalism." *Journal of Women's History* 8, no.1 (Spring 1996): 6–13.

Ignatieff, Michael. "The Myth of Citizenship." *Queen's Quarterly* 99, no. 4 (Winter 1987): 966–85.

Ireland, Patrick. "Socialism, Unification Policy, and the Rise of Racism in Eastern Germany." *International Migration Review* 31, no. 3 (Fall 1997): 541–68.

Janoski, Thomas. *Citizenship and Civil Society: A Framework of Rights and Social Democratic Regimes.* Cambridge: Cambridge University Press, 1998.

Janoski, Thomas, and Elizabeth Glennie. "The Integration of Immigrants in Advanced Industrialzed Countries." In *Migration, Citizenship, and Ethno-National Identities in the European Union,* edited by Marco Martiniello. Aldershot, England: Avebury Press, 1995.

Jelin, Elizabeth, and Eric Hershberg, eds. *Constructing Democracy: Human Rights, Citizenship, and Society in Latin America.* Boulder, Colo.: Westview Press, 1996.

Jenson, Jane. "De-constructing Dualities: Making Rights Claims in Political Institutions," *New Approaches to Welfare Theory,* edited by Glenn Drover and Patrick Kerans. Aldershot, England: Edward Elgar, 1993.

Jordan, Bill. *The Common Good: Citizenship, Morality, and Self-Interest.* Oxford: Basil Blackwell, 1989.

Kahn, Jonathan. *Budgeting Democracy: State Building and Citizenship in America.* Ithaca: Cornell University Press, 1997.

Kaldor, Mary. "Nation-States, European Institutions, and Citizenship." *Citizenship and Democratic Control in Contemporary Europe,* edited by Barbara Einhorn and Mary Kaldor. Brookfield, Vt.: Edward Elgar, 1996.

Kammon, Michael. *Sovereignty and Liberty: Constitutional Discourse in Culture.* Madison: University of Wisconsin Press, 1988.

Keane, John. *Democracy and Civil Society.* London: Verso Press, 1989.

Keatinge, Patrick., ed. *Ireland and EC Membership Evaluated.* London: Pinter Publishers, 1991.

Kelly, George Armstrong. "Who Needs a Theory of Citizenship?" *Daedalus,* State Issue 108, no. 4 (Fall 1979): 21–36.

Kerber, Linda. "A Constitutional Right to Be Treated like American Ladies: Women and the Obligations of Citizenship." In *U.S. History as Women's History: New Fem-*

inist Essays, edited by Linda Kerber, Alice Kessler-Harris, and Kathryn Sklar, 17–35. Chapel Hill: University of North Carolina Press, 1995.

————. "The Meanings of Citizenship." *Dissent* 44, no. 4 (Fall 1997): 33–37.

————. "The Paradox of Women's Citizenship in the Early Republic: The Case of *Martin vs. Massachusetts,* 1805." *American Historical Review* 97, no. 2 (April 1992): 349–78.

————. *Toward an Intellectual History of Women: Essays.* Chapel Hill: University of North Carolina Press, 1997.

King, Desmond. *The New Right: Politics, Markets, and Citizenship.* Chicago: Dorsey Press, 1987.

Klusmeyer, Douglas. *Between Consent and Descent: Conceptions of Democratic Citizenship.* Washington, D.C.: Carnegie Endowment for International Peace, 1996.

Klusmeyer, Douglas, and Sophie H. Pirie. "Membership, Migration, and Identity: Dilemmas for Liberal Societies." *Stanford Humanities Review* 5, no. 2 (1997): 2–315.

Korpi, Walter. "Power Politics and State Autonomy in the Development of Social Citizenship." *American Sociological Review* 54 (1989): 309–28.

Kratochwil, Friedrich. "Citizenship: On the Border of Order." *Alternatives* 19 (1994): 485–506.

Kymlicka, Will. *Multicultural Citizenship.* Oxford: Oxford University Press, 1995.

————. "Return of the Citizen: A Survey of Recent Work on Citizenship Theory." *Ethics* 104 (January 1994): 352–81.

————. "Three Forms of Group-Differentiated Citizenship in Canada." In *Democracy and Difference: Contesting the Boundaries of the Political,* edited by Seyla Benhabib. Princeton: Princeton University Press, 1990.

Laffan, Brigid. "The Politics of Identity and Political Order in Europe." *Journal of Common Market Studies* 34, no. 1 (1996): 97.

Lake, Marilyn. "Personality, Individuality, Nationality: Feminist Conceptions of Citizenship, 1902–1940." *Australian Feminist Studies* 19 (1994): 25–38.

Landes, Joan B. "The Performance of Citizenship: Democracy, Gender, and Difference in the French Revolution." In *Democracy and Difference: Contesting the Boundaries of the Political,* edited by Seyla Benhabib. Princeton: Princeton University Press, 1990.

Lansing, Carol. "Gender and Civic Authority: Sexual Control in a Medieval Italian Town." *Journal of Social History* 31, no. 1 (Fall 1997): 33–60.

Layton-Henry, Zig., ed. *The Political Rights of Migrant Workers in Western Europe.* London: Sage, 1990.

Lehning, Percy B., and Albert Weale. *Citizenship, Democracy, and Justice in the New Europe.* London: Routledge, 1997.

Lemons, J. Stanley. *The Woman Citizen: Social Feminism in the 1920s.* Urbana: University of Illinois Press, 1973.

Lewis, Jane, ed. *Women and Social Policies in Europe: Work, Family, and the State.* Cheltenham, England: Edward Elgar, 1993.

Lewis, Michael. *Rioters and Citizens: Mass Protest in Imperial Japan.* Berkeley and Los Angeles: University of California Press, 1990.

Liebich, André, and Daniel Warner. *Citizenship, East and West.* London: Kegan Paul International, 1995.

Lucien, Jaume. *Le discours jacobin et democatie.* Paris: Fayard Publishers, 1989.

Ludden, David, ed. *Contesting the Nation: Religion, Community, and the Politics of Democracy in India.* Philadelphia: University of Pennsylvania Press, 1996.

Magiera, Siegfried. "A Citizens' Europe: Personal, Political, and Cultural Rights." in *The State of the European Community: Policies, Institutions, and Debates in Transition Years,* edited by Leon Hurwitz and Christian Lequesne. Harlow, England: Longman, 1991.

Maltese, Paolo. *La terra promessa: La guerra Italo-Turca e la conquista della Libia, 1911–1912.* Milan: Arnoldo Mondaduici, 1968.

Mamdani, Mahmood. *Citizen and Subject: Contemporary Africa and the Legacy of Late Colonialism.* Princeton: Princeton University Press, 1996.

Marden, Peter. "Geographies of Dissent: Globalization, Identity, and the Nation." *Political Geography* 16 (1997): 37–64.

Marks, Shula, and Stanley Trapido, eds. *The Politics of Race, Class, and Nationalism in Twentieth-Century South Africa.* London: Longman, 1987.

Marshall, T. H. *Class, Citizenship, and Social Development.* Westport, Conn.: Greenwood Press, 1973.

Martiniello, Marco. *Migration, Citizenship, and Ethno-National Identities in the European Union.* Aldershot, England: Avebury Press, 1995.

McClain, Charles, ed. *Asian Indians, Filipinos, and Other Asian Communities and the Law.* New York: Garland, 1994.

Miller, David. "Citizenship and Pluralism." *Political Studies* 43, no. 3 (September 1995): 432–50.

Miller, Mark J. *Foreign Workers in Western Europe: An Emerging Political Force.* New York: Praeger, 1981.

Montgomery, David. *Citizen Worker: The Experience of Workers in the United States with Democracy and the Free Market during the Nineteenth Century.* Cambridge: Cambridge University Press, 1993.

Mottier, Veronique. "Citizenship and Gender Division in the Swiss Direct Democracy: From Structures to Political Action." *Western European Politics* 18, no. 1 (January 1995): 161–72.

Mouffe, Chantal, ed. *Dimensions of Radical Democracy: Pluralism, Citizenship, and Community.* London: Verso Press, 1992.

Nalbandian, Louise. *The Revolutionary Movement: The Development of Armenian*

Political Parties through the Nineteenth Century. Berkeley: University of California Press, 1965.

Ndegwa, Stephen N. "Citizenship and Ethnicity: An Examination of Two Transition Moments in Kenyan Politics." *American Political Science Review* 91, no. 3 (September 1997): 599–616.

Neunreither, Karlheinz. "Citizens and the Exercise of Power in the European Union: Towards a New Social Contract?" In *A Citizen's Europe: In Search of a New Order,* edited by Allan Rosas and Esko Antolz. London: Sage, 1995.

Nicolet, Claude. *La république en France: Etat des lieux.* Paris: Seuill, 1992.

Noiriel, Gerard. *The French Melting Pot: Immigration, Citizenship, and National Identity.* Minneapolis: University of Minnesota Press, 1996.

Nugent, Neil. *The Government and Politics of the European Community.* Basingstoke, England: Macmillan, 1991.

Oliveira, Miguel Darcy de, and Rajesh Tandon. *Citizens: Strengthening Global Civil Society.* Washington, D. C.: Civicus, 1994.

Ong, Aihwa. "Cultural Citizenship as Subject-Making: Immigrants Negotiate Racial and Cultural Boundaries in the United States." *Current Anthropology* 37, no. 5 (December 1996): 737–63.

Oommen, T. K. *Citizenship and National Identity: From Colonialism to Globalism.* London: Sage, 1987.

Orloff, Ann Shola. "Gender and the Social Rights of Citizenship: The Comparative Analysis of Gender Relations and Welfare States." *American Sociological Review* 58 (1993): 303–28.

———. "Reply to Louise Tilly: Citizenship, Policy, and the Political Construction of Gender Interests." *International Labor and Working-Class History* 52 (Fall 1997): 35–50.

Palma, Giuseppe de. *To Craft Democracies: An Essay in Democratic Transitions.* Berkeley and Los Angeles: University of California Press, 1990.

Pamplona, Marco A. *Riots, Republicanism, and Citizenship: New York City and Rio de Janeiro City during the Consolidation of the Republican Order.* New York: Garland, 1996.

Peled, Yoav. "Ethnic Democracy and the Legal Construction of Citizenship: Arab Citizens of the Jewish State." *American Political Science Review* 86 (1996): 432–43.

Pharr, Susan J. *Losing Face: Status Politics in Japan.* Berkeley and Los Angeles: University of California Press, 1990.

Pocock, J. G. A. "The Ideal of Citizenship since Classical Times." *Queen's Quarterly* 99, no. 1 (Spring 1992): 35–55.

Prak, Maarten. "Citizen Radicalism and Democracy in the Dutch Republic: The Patriot Movement of the 1780s." *Theory and Society* 20 (1991): 73–102.

Putnam, Robert D. *Making Democracy Work: Civic Traditions in Modern Italy.* Princeton: Princeton University Press, 1993.

Ramirez, Francisco O., Yasemin Soysal, and Suzanne Shanahan. "The Changing Logic of Political Citizenship: Cross-National Acquisition of Women's Suffrage Rights, 1890–1990." *American Sociological Review* 62 (1997): 734–45.

Rees, Anthony M. "T. H. Marshall and the Progress of Citizenship." In *Citizenship Today: The Contemporary Relevance of T. H. Marshall,* edited by Martin Bulmer and Anthony M. Rees, 14–17. London: UCL Press, 1996.

Riesenberg, Peter. *Citizenship in the Western Tradition: Plato to Rousseau.* Chapel Hill: University of North Carolina Press, 1992.

Roche, Maurice. *Rethinking Citizenship: Welfare, Ideology, and Change in Modern Society.* Cambridge, England: Polity Press, 1992.

Rokkan, Stein. *Citizens, Elections, Parties.* Oslo: Universitetsforlaget, 1970.

Safran, William. "Citizenship and Nationality in Democratic Systems: Approaches to Defining and Acquiring Membership in Political Community." *International Political Science Review* 18, no. 3 (July 1997): 313–35.

Salvatore, Nick. "Some Thoughts on Class and Citizenship in America in the Late Nineteenth Century." In *In the Shadow of the Statue of Liberty: Immigrants, Workers and Citizens, 1880–1920,* edited by Marianne Debouzy. Urbana: University of Illinois Press, 1992.

Saraceno, Chiara. "Reply to Louise Tilly: Citizenship Is Context-Specific." *International Labor and Working-Class History* 52 (Fall 1997): 27–34.

Savarsy, Wendy. "Beyond the Difference versus Equality Policy Debate: Post-Suffrage Feminism, Citizenship, and the Quest for a Feminist Welfare State." *Signs* 17, no. 2 (Winter 1992): 329–62.

Schnaper, Dominique. *La communauté des citoyens: Sur l'idée moderne de nation.* Paris: Gallimard, 1994.

Schuck, Peter, and Rogers Smith. *Citizenship without Consent: Illegal Aliens in the American Polity.* New Haven: Yale University Press, 1990.

Scott, Joan W. *Only Paradoxes to Offer: French Feminists and the Rights of Man.* Cambridge: Harvard University Press, 1996.

Seidman, Gay W. "No Freedom without the Women: Mobilization and Gender in South Africa, 1970–1992." *Signs* 18, no. 2 (1993): 291–300.

Silver, Allan. "Democratic Citizenship and High Military Strategy: The Inheritance, Decay, and Reshaping of Political Culture." *Research on Democracy and Society* 2 (1994): 317–49.

Silverman, Maxim. "Citizenship and the Nation-State in France." *Ethnic and Racial Studies* 14, no. 3 (July 1991): 333–49.

Smith, Rebecca. "Creating Neighborhood Identity through Citizen Activism." *Urban Geography* 5 (1984): 49–70.

Smith, Rogers M. *Civic Ideals: Conflicting Visions of Citizenship in U.S. History.* New Haven: Yale University Press, 1997.

Smith, Trevor. "Citizenship and the Constitution." *Parliamentary Affairs* 44, no. 4 (1991): 429–41.

Solinger, Dorothy. *Contesting Citizenship in Urban China: Peasant Migrants, the State, and the Logic of the Market.* Berkeley and Los Angeles: University of California Press, forthcoming.

Somers, Margaret. "Citizenship and the Place of the Public Sphere: Law, Community, and Political Culture in the Transition to Democracy." *American Sociological Review* 58 (October 1993): 587–620.

Soysal, Yasemin. *Limits of Citizenship: Migrants and Postnational Membership in Europe.* Chicago: Chicago University Press, 1994.

Springer, Beverly. *The European Union and Its Citizens: The Social Agenda.* Westport, Conn.: Greenwood Press, 1994.

Stevenson, Nick. "Globalization, National Cultures, and Cultural Citizenship." *Sociological Quarterly* 38, no. 1 (Winter 1997): 41–66.

Taylor, Paul. *The Limits of European Integration.* New York: Columbia University Press, 1983.

Thomas, Robert J. *Citizenship, Gender, and Work: Social Organization of Industrial Agriculture.* Berkeley and Los Angeles: University of California Press, 1985.

Tilikainen, Teija. "The Problem of Democracy in the European Union." In *A Citizens' Europe: In Search of a New Order,* edited by Allan Rosas and Esko Antolz. London: Sage, 1995.

Tilly, Charles. *Citizenship, Identity, and Social History.* Cambridge: Cambridge University Press, 1995.

Tilly, Louise A. "Women, Work, and Citizenship." *International Labor and Working-Class History* 52 (Fall 1997): 1–26.

Turner, Bryan. *Citizenship and Capitalism: The Debate over Reformism.* London: Allen & Unwin, 1986.

———. "Outline of a Theory of Citizenship." *Sociology* 24, no. 2 (1987): 189–217.

Twine, Fred. *Citizenship and Social Rights: The Interdependence of Self and Society.* London: Sage, 1992.

Van den Berghe, Guido. *Political Rights for European Citizens.* Aldershot, England: Gower, 1982.

Van Steenberger, Bart, ed. *The Condition of Citizenship.* London: Sage, 1994.

Vogel, Ursula, and Michael Moran, eds. *The Frontiers of Citizenship.* Basingstoke, England: Macmillan, 1991.

Waldinger, Renée, Philip Dawson, and Isser Woloch, eds. *The French Revolution and the Meaning of Citizenship.* Westport, Conn.: Greenwood Press, 1993.

Waylen, Georgina. "Women and Democratization: Conceptualizing Gender Relations in Transition Politics." *World Politics* 46, no. 3 (1994): 327–54.

Webster, Eddie. "Democratic Transition: South African Sociology." *Contemporary Sociology* 26, no. 3 (May 1997): 279–82.

Weil, Patrick. *La France et ses étrangers: L'aventure d'une politique de l'immigration, 1938–1991.* Paris: Calmann-Levy, 1991.

————. *European Citizenship Practices: Building Institutions of a Non-State.* Boulder, Colo.: Westview Press, 1997.

————. "Making Sense of the New Geography Citizenship: Fragmented Citizenship in the European Union." *Theory and Society* 26, no. 4 (1997): 529–60.

Wiener, Antje. "Assessing the Constructive Potential of Urban Citizenship: A Socio-Historical Perspective." *European Integration Online* (EIOP) 1, no. 017, 1997). http://eiop.or.at/eiop/texte/1997-0179.htm.

Wiener, Antje, and Vince Della Sala. "Constitution-Making and Citizenship Practice-Bridging: The Democracy Gap in the European Union?" *Journal of Common Market Studies* 35, no. 4 (December 1997): 595–614.

Wihtol, Catherine de Wenden. *Citoyenneté, nationalité, et immigration.* Paris: Arcantere, 1987.

Will, Pierre-Etienne, and R. Bin Wong. *Nourish the People: The State Civilian Granary System in China, 1650–1850.* Ann Arbor: University of Michigan Center for Chinese Studies, 1991.

Wong, R. Bin. *China Transformed: Historical Change and the Limits of European Experience.* Ithaca: Cornell University Press, 1997.

Young, Iris Marion. "Polity and Group Difference: A Critique of the Ideal of Universal Citizenship." *Ethics* 99, no. 2 (January 1989): 250–74.

Yuval-Davis, Nira. "The Citizenship Debate: Women, Ethnic Processes, and the State." *Feminist Review* 39 (Autumn 1991): 58–68.

Zolberg, Ari. "Ethical Dilemmas of Immigration Policy in the New Europe." In *The Conference on Social Justice, Democratic Citizenship, and Public Policy in the New Europe.* Rotterdam: ECPR/Erasmus University, 1991.

Index

Abdulhamid II, sultan of Ottoman Empire, 49–51, 52
access, citizenship and, 200, 201; European Union citizenship and, 215
accession, Bois-le-Duc citizenship and, 20
accountability of governments to publics, as democratic innovation, 233
acquis communautaire, European Union citizenship and, 11, 196, 202–3, 204, 206, 208, 209, 210, 213, 221n27
Al-Afghani, Jamal al-Din, 51
Alien Registration Act of 1914 (Great Britain), 74
aliens: Bois-le-Duc citizenship and, 21–23; British citizenship and, 74; Netherlands citizenship and, 26. *See also* immigration, citizenship and
Aliens Act of 1905 (Great Britain), 71
American Woman Suffrage Association (United States), 231
American Women's Party, 158
Andorra, national anthem of, 1
anthems. *See* national anthems
Anti-Socialist Union (Great Britain), 128
Anti-Sweating Exhibition (Great Britain), 128–29
Asquith, Herbert, 131, 136
Asylum Act of 1993 (Great Britain), 81, 82–83
Austin, John, 8
Australia: democratic innovation in, 233, 236; men's suffrage in, 230; secret ballot in, 230, 234, 236–37; women's suffrage in, 231–32, 234, 236–37, 238
Australian ballot. *See* secret ballot
Austria, national anthem of, 2

authoritarian regimes, citizenship in, 257–58
Aves, Ernest, 129

Baker, Paula, 162
balance of power, end of, 4
Balfour, Arthur, 131
Barnett, Canon, 129, 137
Bayerl Report (European Union), 206
Belgium: European Coal and Steel Community and, 3; federal union of, as transnational state, 13
belonging, citizenship and, 200–201; European Union citizenship and, 205–6, 207, 208–9, 211, 215
Beveridge, William, 129, 137–39, 140
Board of Trade, Labour Department of (Great Britain), 129, 136–37, 139
Bois-le-Duc, (the Netherlands), citizenship rights in, 6, 17–18, 19–24, 27–28, 29
Booth, Charles, 129, 137
Box, Congressman, 85
Bremer, Fredrika, Society (Sweden), 162
Bron, Kenneth, 133
Bryce, James, 241
Bulgaria, national anthem of, 1
bureaucracy: Chinese citizenship and, 105, 110–11; social policy and, 136–37
burgher trade, Bois-le-Duc citizenship and, 19–20
Buxton, Sidney, 136

Campbell-Bannerman, Henry, 130–31
capital: consolidated state formation and, 4–5; in contemporary Europe, 5

central government, Chinese citizenship
and, 105, 107–8
challenge-and-response model, of democratic innovation, 239–41
Chamberlain, Joseph, 125, 126–27, 130
Charity Organization Society (COS)
(Great Britain), 132–33, 134, 136,
137
Chartists: in Australia, 232, 236; in Great
Britain, 229–30
Chase-Dunn, Christopher, 240
child labor, Great Britain and, 128, 134
Chile: abolition of slavery in, 233; democratic innovation in, 246n39; social
security system in, 242
China, citizenship in, 8–9, 97–122, 256;
anti-opium campaign and, 103;
bureaucracy and, 105, 110–11; central
government and, 105, 107–8; civil
rights and, 104, 108, 109–10, 112;
claims on state and, 98–100, 101;
commitments and, 8–9, 98–99,
100–101, 102–4; Communist China
and, 109–18; cultural activities and,
116; economic entitlements and,
111–12, 113–14; European citizenship versus, 8–9, 97, 99, 100, 101–2,
104, 108–9, 111–12, 113, 114, 115,
116, 117, 118; imperial China and,
98–104; local government and,
105–7, 109, 116–17, 118; mass movements and, 111, 115; military and,
107; officials and elites and, 100–101,
102–8, 116; paternalism and, 100,
112; peasants and, 111–12, 113; political rights and, 104, 107–8, 110,
114–17; protests and, 8–9, 98–100,
115; provincial government and, 105,
107, 116, 118; representative assemblies and, 102, 104, 107; Republican
China and, 104–9; social rights and,
104, 112–14; taxation and, 98–100,
101, 107
Churchill, Randolph, 126

Churchill, Winston, 136, 137, 139
Citizens First (European Union), 214
citizens' oath, Bois-le-Duc citizenship
and, 19–20
citizenship: access and, 200, 201; authoritarian regimes and, 258–59; belonging and, 200–201; constitutive elements of, 199, 220nn19–22; contracts
of, 253; controversies about, 258; definition of, 17–18, 97–98, 199,
220n19, 252; democracy and,
256–57, 258; European, *see* European
Union (EU), citizenship in; historical
elements of, 200–201; importance of,
256–58; language of, 197, 198,
218n5; rights of, 200–201, *see also*
citizenship rights and obligations;
civil rights; political rights; social
rights; sociohistorical context of,
196–202
Citizenship and Nationality Act of 1935
(Ireland), 89–90
Citizenship Law of 1869 (Ottoman
Empire), 45
citizenship rights and obligations, 3,
200–201, 252–53; constitutions of
new political regimes defining,
247–52, 253, 254–55, 257–58; current threats to, *see* right to work; Sweden, feminist power in; future and,
see democratic innovation; European
Union (EU), citizenship in; transnational social policies; historical parallels and, 5; struggle and formation of,
255; variations of from regime to
regime, *see* China, citizenship in;
immigration, citizenship and. *See also*
civil rights; Netherlands, the, citizenship during revolutionary era in;
Ottoman Empire, citizenship in; political rights; social rights
civil rights, 200, 201; Chinese citizenship
and, 104, 108, 109–10, 112; European
Union citizenship and, 211, 212, 215

civil service, Ottoman citizenship and, 43
claims, 253, 255–56; Chinese citizenship and, 98–100, 101; feminist power within Sweden and, 10, 149–78; right to work and struggle against unemployment in Great Britain and, 9–10, 123–47
collective agency, feminist power within Sweden and, 10, 149–78
collectivizing process, transnational social policies and, 180–81
Commission on Power and Democracy (Sweden), 168–69
commitments: Chinese citizenship and, 8–9, 98–99, 100–101, 102–4; right to work and struggle against unemployment in Great Britain and, 9–10, 123–47
Committee of Union and Progress (CUP), Ottoman citizenship and, 52–54
Common Market, 3–4
Commonwealth Immigrants Acts of 1962 (Great Britain), 76–77
Communists, U.S. immigration policy and, 86
Conservative Party (Great Britain), right to work and, 9, 125, 126, 127, 128, 129, 130, 131, 133–34, 141
Conservative Party (Sweden), women and, 166, 168
consolidated state, 3–5, 253–54; capital and, 4–5; conditions producing, 3–4; definition of, 2–3; feminist power within Sweden and, 10, 149–78; historical context of, 5; military competition and, 4; national citizenship in the Netherlands and, 6, 17, 18–19, 24–29
constitutions: citizenship of new countries defined in, 247–52, 253, 254–55, 257–58 as democratic innovation, 232–33
crosscutting jurisdictions, in Europe, 5

cultural activities, Chinese citizenship and, 116
Cultural Revolution (China), 109, 111, 115
culture, immigration and citizenship debates and, 69–70
Czechoslovakia, national anthem of, 2

Dahrendorf, Ralf, 123
Davison, Roderic, 49
Delors, Jacques, 208
democracy: citizenship as necessary for, 256–57, 258; European Union citizenship and, 208, 224n65; Netherlands citizenship and, 29
democratic innovation, 13–14, 229–46; accountability of government to publics and, 233; in Australia, 230, 231–32, 233, 234, 236–37, 238; challenge and response model of, 239–41; in Chile, 233, 242, 246n39; constitutionalism and, 232–33; democratic identification and, 233; in Denmark, 233, 236; elites in lesser powers and, 237–39; equality of rights and, 233; in Great Britain, 229–30, 232, 236; in Haiti, 233; in Holland, 233; interconnectedness and, 239, 245n33; in Isle of Man, 239, 245n32; lesser powers and, 232–34, 236–41; in Low Countries, 233, 236; major powers and, 234–36; men's suffrage and, 230; in New Zealand, 230, 231, 232, 233, 236–37, 238, 245n32; in Norfolk Island, 238; in Pitcairn Islands, 238, 244n28; in Poland, 233, 236; secret ballot and, 230, 232, 236–37; in South Africa, 242, 246n40; in Sweden, 233, 236; in Switzerland, 233, 234, 236; in United States, 230–31, 232, 233, 234, 236, 245n32; women's suffrage and, 230–32, 236–39, 245n32

Denmark: abolition of slavery and, 233; democratic innovation in, 236; national anthem of, 1; right to work in, 142

deportation, U.S. immigration policy and, 86

Dewey, John, 14

discursive resources, feminist power within Sweden and, 10, 149–78

Dittmer, Lowell, 8

divided sovereignty. *See* immigration, citizenship and

economic entitlements: Chinese citizenship and, 111–12, 113–14; Ottoman citizenship and, 45–48

education: Ottoman citizenship and, 43, 57; transnational social policies and, 182, 183, 185

Eire. *See* Ireland

Elias, Norbert, 184

elites: Chinese citizenship and, 100–101, 102–8, 116; democratic innovations in lesser powers and, 237–39

employment. *See* right to work

England. *See* Great Britain

Enlightenment, national citizenship in the Netherlands and, 23–24, 28

environmental degradation, transnational social policies and, 182, 183, 185

Equal Rights Amendment (ERA) (United States), 158

Esping-Anderson, Gösta, 150, 256

Estonia, national anthem of, 2

ethnicity. *See* racism/ethnicity

Europe: Chinese citizenship versus citizenship in, 8–9, 97, 99, 100, 101–2, 104, 108–9, 111–12, 113, 114, 115, 116, 117, 118; foreign aid and, *see* transnational social policies; fragmented sovereignty and crosscutting jurisdictions and, 5; Holy Roman Empire and state order in, 4–5; national anthems of, 1–2; rights tradi-

tion in, *see* citizenship rights and obligations. *See also* European Union (EU), citizenship in

European Coal and Steel Community (ECSC), 3

European Community, 3

European Court of Justice, 5, 12

European identity, European Union citizenship and, 207–8, 210, 224nn62, 63

European Union (EU): anthem of, 1, 2; capital and, 4; consolidated state versus current, 3–4; as economic and monetary union, 5; feminist power and Sweden's membership in, 10, 167–68, 170; fragmented sovereignty and crosscutting jurisdictions and, 5; Ireland in, 91; right to work and, 141, 142, 143; transnational social policies coordinated by, 11, 182, 183–87; unemployment in, 123

European Union (EU), citizenship in, 11–13, 195–228, 255; access and, 215; *acquis communautaire* and, 11, 196, 202–3, 204, 206, 208, 209, 210, 213, 221n27; additionality and, 198; Amsterdam and, 195, 213–14; belonging and, 205–6, 207, 208–9, 211, 215; civil rights and, 211, 212, 215; democracy and, 208, 224n65; European identity and, 207–8, 210, 224nn62, 63; fragmented citizenship and, 214–16; German unification and, 210, 225n76; historicity and, 198; Maastricht Treaty and, 5, 195, 202, 209–13; mobility and, 208–9, 211, 213, 224nn62, 63, 226n83; nationality and, 197–98, 210, 213, 219nn10–12, 226n83; 1970s and, 195, 204–7, 222n38; 1980s and, 195, 207–9; 1990s and, 195, 204, 209–13; Paris summit (1972) and, 204–7, 222n38; passport union and, 204, 205, 206–7, 209, 210–11, 222n46, 224n65; political rights and, 195, 196, 208, 209,

211, 212, 215, 227n95; social rights and, 211, 212, 215; sociohistorical perspective on citizenship and, 196–202; Spanish letters and proposals and, 210–12; special rights and, 204, 205, 206, 208, 210, 222nn46, 47, 223n48; specialized rights and, 214–16; stages of, 204–14; students and, 208, 224nn62, 63; third-country nationals and, 195, 206, 208, 213, 218n3, 223n53; Treaty of the European Union (1993) and, 195, 202, 204, 211, 213, 218n4; voting rights and, 206, 208, 210, 211, 212, 224n65; workers and, 208–9, 225n67
European Union, Treaty of the (1993), 195, 202, 204, 211, 213, 218n4
Fabian Society (Great Britain), 127–28
Fang Lizhi, 116
Fawcett, Millicent, 232
feminists: in France, 161; in Germany, 161; in Great Britain, 127; power of, 5; in United States, 158. *See also* Sweden, feminist power in; women's suffrage
femocrats, in Sweden, 165
Folkhem (people's home), Swedish feminist groups using, 159–60, 161
foreign aid. *See* transnational social policies
fragmented citizenship, European Union citizenship and, 214–16
fragmented sovereignty, in Europe, 5
France: citizenship in Old Regime, 18; European Coal and Steel Community and, 3; feminists and population issue in, 161; fragmented sovereignty and crosscutting jurisdictions in, 5; migrant workers and, 143; national anthem of, 1; Ottoman Empire citizenship and, 38, 39, 43, 47, 50; right to work in, 142. *See also* French Revolution
franchise. *See* voting rights

French Revolution: French citizenship and, 18; Netherlands citizenship and, 6, 17, 24–29
frictional unemployment, Great Britain and, 138–39, 140

General Agreement on Tariffs and Trade (GATT), 4
General Federation of Trade Unions (Great Britain), 135
George, David Lloyd, 136, 137
Germany: British citizenship and, 74; European Coal and Steel Community and, 3; feminists and population issue in, 161; right to work in, 142; rights tradition in, 5; unification of and European Union and, 210, 225n76
Gerschenkron, Alexander, 239
Gladstone, Herbert, 126, 127, 130, 134
globalization, citizenship and, 67–68
Gonzalez, Felipe, 211
Gorbachev, Mikhail, 248–49
Gradin, Anita, 167
Great Britain: immigration and citizenship in, 70–71, 72, 73–83, 87, 92; Irish immigration to, 77; men's suffrage in, 125, 229–30; Ottoman Empire citizenship and, 38, 39, 43, 47, 50; right to work and struggle against unemployment in, 9–10, 123–47; rights tradition in, 5; secret ballot in, 230; voting rights in, 125, 126; women's suffrage in, 232
Great Leap Forward, 111, 115
guild membership, Bois-le-Duc citizenship for, 21
Gülhane Rescript of 1839 (Ottoman Empire), 39, 41, 46, 47, 48,

Haiti: abolition of slavery and, 233; voting rights in, 13
Hall, Thomas, 240
Hamidian regime, Ottoman citizenship and, 50–53, 55, 57, 58

Hansson, Per Albin, 159, 160, 164
Hardie, Keir, 139
Harris, José, 138
He, Baogang, 114–15
health, transnational social policies and,
   182, 183, 185
Hesselgren, Kerstin, 165
high politics, 11
Hobbes, Thomas, 3
Hoffman, Stanley, 11
Holy Roman Empire, state order in
   Europe and, 4–5
human rights: British citizenship and, 83;
   citizenship and, 68; U.S. immigration
   policy and, 87

identity formation, women in Sweden
   and, 10, 149–78
immigration: in Bois-le-Duc, 21, 22;
   transnational social policies and, 182,
   183, 184. *See also* immigration, citizenship and
Immigration Act of 1917 (United States),
   83–84
Immigration Act of 1924 (United States),
   84, 85
Immigration Act of 1965 (United States),
   87–88
Immigration Act of 1990 (United States),
   88–89
Immigration Bill of 1971 (Great Britain),
   77
immigration, citizenship and, 7–8,
   67–69; culture and, 69–70; in Great
   Britain, 70–71, 72, 73–83, 87, 92; in
   Ireland, 72, 73, 74, 76, 77, 80, 89–91,
   92; language and, 69; League of
   Nations and, 72–73; in United States,
   67, 68, 71–72, 73, 80, 83–89, 92
Immigration Commission Report of 1911
   (United States), 83
Immigration Reform Act of 1986 (United
   States), 88

imperial citizenship, vernacular politics
   in Ottoman Empire and, 39–45
Independent Labour Party (ILP) (Great
   Britain), 128, 135
interconnectedness, democratic innovation and, 239, 245n33
International Monetary Fund (IMF), 4
international trade, transnational unions
   and, 4
Iraq, invasion and annexation of Kuwait
   and, 4
Ireland: immigration and citizenship in,
   72, 73, 74, 76, 77, 80, 89–91, 92;
   immigration from to Great Britain,
   77; national anthem of, 1
Isle of Man, women's suffrage in, 239,
   245n32
Italy: capital-intensive path of development by urban oligarchies in, 4; right
   to work in, 142

Jews: British citizenship and, 74; immigration of to Ireland, 89; Netherlands
   citizenship and, 22–23, 27
Jordan, Barbara, 67
Jospin, Lionel, 142
judicial rights: Bois-le-Duc citizenship
   and, 20, 21; Ottoman citizenship and,
   42–43
jus sanguinis, 200; Irish citizenship and,
   72; Ottoman citizenship and, 45
jus soli, 200; British citizenship and, 71,
   77, 81; Ottoman citizenship and, 45;
   U.S. citizenship and, 71

Kang Youwei, 102
Kazakhstan, citizenship in, 247–52, 253,
   254–55, 257–58
Kemal, Mustafa, 55, 56
Kennedy, Edward, 88
Key, Ellen, 156
Kisrawan uprising, Ottoman citizenship
   and, 47
Kjell, Rudolph, 159

Kohl, Helmut, 210, 225n76
Kokubun Ryosei, 114–15
Kolbin, Gennadi, 249
Korpi, Walter, 150, 256
Kunaev, Dinmukhamed, 248–49
Kuwait, Iraq's invasion and annexation of, 4

labor movement, power of, 5. *See also* right to work
Labour Department of the Board of Trade (Great Britain), 129, 136–37, 139
Labour Party (Great Britain), right to work and, 9, 128, 130, 131, 133–35, 136, 137, 139, 140–41
Land Code of 1858, Ottoman citizenship and, 45, 46–47
language, immigration and citizenship debates and, 69
Lansbury, George, 139
Le Pen, Jean-Marie, 143
League of Nations, nation-states and, 72–73
Liang Qichao, 102
Liberal Party (Great Britain), right to work and, 9, 125, 126, 127, 128, 129, 130–31, 133, 134, 135, 136, 137–39, 141, 143
Liechtenstein, national anthem of, 1
Lindström, Ulla, 162
Link, Perry, 110
literacy, U.S. immigration policy and, 84
Lithuania, national anthem of, 2
Liu Binyan, 116
Local Government Act of 1884 (Great Britain), 125
local governments, Chinese citizenship and, 105–7, 109, 116–17, 118
London Trades Council, 131
Long, Walter, 130, 131
Low Countries, democratic innovation in, 233, 236
low politics, 11

Maastricht Treaty, citizenship and, 5, 195, 202, 209–13, 221n31
McClellan, Senator, 88
MacDonald, James Ramsay, 128, 130, 134, 135, 140, 141
MacDonald, Margaret Ethel, 128–29
McNeill, William, 239
Mahmud II, sultan of Ottoman Empire, 41, 44
Mao Zedong, 111, 115, 117
Marshall, T. H., 99, 102, 112, 114, 200, 256
mass movements, Chinese citizenship and, 111, 115
maternalist tradition: American feminists and, 158; Swedish feminists and, 155, 156
men's suffrage: in Australia, 230; in Great Britain, 229–30; in New Zealand, 230
migrant workers: power of, 5; right to work and, 143
military: Chinese citizenship and, 107; consolidated state formation and, 4; Ottoman citizenship and, 6, 7, 41, 43, 44, 50–53; transnational social policies and, 182, 183, 184–85
millet system, Ottoman citizenship and, 44–45, 49
Mitterrand, François, 142, 210, 225n76
mobility, European Union citizenship and, 208–9, 211, 213, 224nn62, 63, 226n83
Monaco, national anthem of, 1
moral law, 8
Morgonbris, 155, 159
multinational corporations, 4
municipal citizenship, 253; in the Netherlands, 6, 17–18, 19–24, 27–28, 29
Murad V, sultan of Ottoman Empire, 49
Myrdal, Alva, 160, 165
Myrdal, Gunnar, 160

National Acts of 1988 (Great Britain), 81, 82
national anthems, European, 1–2
national citizenship, 254; in the Netherlands, 6, 17, 18–19, 24–29
National Housewives Association (Sweden), 157
National Liberal Federation (NLF) (Great Britain), 127
national origin quotas, U.S. immigration policy and, 84–85, 87–88
National Right to Work Council (Great Britain), 128
National Union of Women Suffrage Societies (Great Britain), 129
National Union of Women Workers (Great Britain), 128
National Woman Suffrage Association (United States), 231
nationalism, immigration and citizenship and, 69–70
nationality, European Union citizenship and, 197–98, 210, 213, 219nn10–12, 226n83
Nationality Act of 1940 (United States), 86
Nationality Act of 1948 (Great Britain), 71, 75, 76
Nationality Act of 1981 (Great Britain), 81–82
nation-states, 2–3; League of Nations and citizenship and, 72–73; Versailles treaty and, 73. *See also* consolidated state
Naturalization Act of 1790 (United States), 71
Nazarbaev, Nursultan, 249, 257
Nazarbaeva, Dariga, 257
Netherlands, the: accountability of government to publics in, 233; capital-intensive path of development in, 4; national anthem of, 1
Netherlands, the, citizenship during revolutionary era in, 6, 17–35; in Bois-le-

Duc, 6, 17–18, 19–24, 27–28, 29; Enlightenment and, 23–24, 28; French Revolution and, 6, 17, 24–29; Jews and, 22–23, 27; national citizenship and, 6, 17, 18–19, 24–29; Patriot revolution and, 24, 28; urban citizenship and, 6, 17–18, 19–24, 27–28, 29
New Zealand: democratic innovation in, 233, 236; men's suffrage in, 230; secret ballot in, 230, 236–37; voting rights to Maoris in, 232, 233; women's suffrage in, 231, 232, 236–37, 238, 245n32
Norfolk Island, women's suffrage in, 238
Norway, right to work in, 142
Nunn, T. Hancock, 129

obligations. *See* citizenship rights and obligations
Offe, Klaus, 123
officials, Chinese citizenship and, 100–101, 102–8
opium, campaigns against in China, 103
Opium War, 103
opportunity, transnational social policies and, 182, 183
Organization of Female Postal Workers (Sweden), 156
Organization of Swedish Christian Young Women, 156
Ortoli, Xavier, 205
Ottoman Empire, citizenship in, 6, 7, 37–66, 254; Citizenship Law of 1869 and, 45; Committee of Union and Progress and, 52–54; and constitutionalism, derailment of (1878–1907) and, 49–52; foreign intervention and, 37, 38–39, 43, 45, 47–49, 50–51; Gülhane Rescript of 1839 and, 39, 41, 46, 47, 48; Hamidian regime and, 50–53, 55, 57, 58; Land Code of 1858 and, 45, 46–47; military power and, 6, 7, 50–53; millet system and, 44–45, 49; Pan-Islam and, 51–52, 56; precar-

ious state (1908–1914) and, 51–55;
Reform Rescript of 1856 and, 41,
44–45; social and economic rights
(1839–1877) and, 45–48; Tanzimat
and, 39, 41, 42, 43–49, 54, 55, 56, 58;
vernacular politics to imperial citizenship (1800–1869) in, 39–45

Paine, Thomas, 134
Pan-Islam, Ottoman citizenship and,
51–52, 56
Parliamentary Committee of the Trades
Union Congress (Great Britain), 129
participatory citizenship, feminist power
within Sweden and, 10, 149–78
passport union, European Union citizenship and, 204, 205, 206–7, 209,
210–11, 222n46, 224n65
paternalism, Chinese citizenship and,
100, 112
path dependencies, in women's mobilization in Sweden, 166–70
Patriot revolutionaries, national citizenship in the Netherlands and, 24, 28
peasants, Chinese citizenship and,
111–12, 113
Pirandello, Luigi, 37
Pitcairn Island, women's suffrage in,
238, 244n28
Poland: accountability of government to
publics in, 233; constitutionalism and,
233; democratic innovation in, 233,
236; national anthem of, 1
political citizenship, derailment of in
Ottoman Empire, 49–52
political office, Bois-le-Duc citizenship
and, 20
political rights, 200, 201; Chinese citizenship and, 104, 107–8, 110,
114–17; European Union citizenship
and, 195, 196, 208, 209, 211, 212,
215, 227n95, *see also* specialized
rights; special rights; right to work in

Great Britain and, 9–10, 123–47. *See
also* voting rights
Poor Law of 1834 (Great Britain), 133
Poor Law Unions (Great Britain), 132
poor states, rich states helping. *See*
transnational social policies
population, feminists and, 160–61
Portugal, voting rights in, 13
power resources, feminist power within
Sweden and, 10, 149–78
proletarians, right to work in Great
Britain and, 124–31
protectionism, right to work in Great
Britain and, 130–31
protests, Chinese citizenship and, 8–9,
98–100, 115
provincial governments, Chinese citizenship and, 105, 107, 116, 118

Quota Law of 1921 (United States),
84–85

racism/ethnicity: British citizenship and,
76–80, 82; immigration and citizenship and, 92; U.S. immigration policy
and, 84–86, 87–89
real law, 8
Reed, Senator, 84
Reform Bill of 1832 (Great Britain), 229,
230
Reform Rescript of 1856, Ottoman citizenship and, 42, 44–45
religion, Ottoman citizenship and, 44, 49
representative assemblies, Chinese citizenship and, 102, 104, 107
restriction, U.S. immigration policy and,
85–87
revolutionary era, national citizenship in
the Netherlands and, 6, 17, 23–29
rich states, poor states helped by. *See*
transnational social policies
Rifkin, Jeremy, 123

right to work, 256; Great Britain and, 9–10, 123–47, 256; Swedish women and, 157–58
Right to Work Council (Great Britain), 135
rights, citizenship and, 200, 201. *See also* citizenship rights and obligations; civil rights; political rights; social rights
Royal Committee on Population (Sweden), 165
Rueschemeyer, Dietrick, 136

Saltsjöbaden agreement (Sweden), 164
Schlesinger, Arthur, Jr., 241
Schoppa, Keith, 106
secret ballot, 233; in Australia, 230, 236–37; in Great Britain, 230; in New Zealand, 230, 236–37; in United States, 232
Selim III, sultan of Ottoman Empire, 41
Seneca Falls Convention of 1848 (United States), 230
settler society, United States as, 71
Sino-Japanese War, 103
Skocpol, Theda, 136
Smith, Hubert Llewellyn, 129, 137, 139
Social Democratic Federation (SDF) (Great Britain), 128
Social Democratic Party (Sweden), 149–66, 169
Social Democratic Women's Union (Sweden), 155, 162
social reform, right to work in Great Britain and, 9–10, 123–47
social regulation: Bois-le-Duc citizenship and, 21–23; Ottoman citizenship and, 42–43
social rights, 200, 201; Bois-le-Duc citizenship and, 21; Chinese citizenship and, 104, 112–14; European Union citizenship and, 211, 212, 215; Ottoman citizenship and, 46–49; right

to work in Great Britain and, 9–10, 123–47
South Africa, postapartheid constitution in, 242, 246n40
sovereignty: divided, *see* immigration, citizenship and; fragmented, 5; transnational unions and, 4; undiluted, 5
Soviet Union, collapse of, 4
Spanish Empire, fragmented sovereignty and crosscutting jurisdictions and, 5
special rights, European Union citizenship and, 204, 205, 206, 208, 210, 223n48, 224nn46, 47
specialized rights, European Union citizenship and, 214–16
Spinelli, Altiero, 205
Steadman, W. C., 129
students, European Union citizenship and, 208, 224nn62, 63
Suavi, Ali, 49
subversion, U.S. immigration policy and, 86
suffrage. *See* voting rights
Sun Yatsen, 108
Support Stockings (Sweden), 168
Sweden: constitutionalism and, 233; democratic innovation in, 236
Sweden, feminist power in, 10, 149–78, 256; European Union membership and, 10, 167–68, 170; 1930's and, 155–66, 167, 168–70, 171; 1990's and, 166–70, 171; right to work for women and, 157–58
Swedish National Association of Housewives, 155
Swedish Women's Business Organization, 162
Swedish Women's Citizen's Union, 156
Switzerland: accountability of government to publics in, 233; democratic innovation in, 233, 236; migrant workers in, 143; voting rights in, 233, 234

Tanzimat, citizenship in Ottoman Empire and, 39, 41, 42, 43–49, 54, 55, 56, 58
Tarrow, Sidney, 12, 125
Tawney, R. H., 129
taxation: Chinese citizenship and, 98–100, 101, 107; Ottoman citizenship and, 41–43
territorialism, as European anthem theme, 1, 2
Thane, Pat, 140
Thatcher, Margaret, 141
thick rights, national citizenship in the Netherlands and, 6, 17, 18–19, 24–29
thin rights: municipal citizenship in the Netherlands and, 6, 17–18, 19–24, 27–28, 29; Sweden and, 10
third-country nationals, European Union citizenship and, 195, 206, 208, 213, 218n3, 223n53
Tilly, Charles, 4, 17, 97–98, 99, 118, 158, 236
Tindemans Report (European Union), 206
Toynbee Hall, 129, 137
trade unionism, right to work in Great Britain and, 126, 128, 133, 134, 135, 141–42
Trades Union Congress (Great Britain), right to work and, 135
Trades Union Council (Great Britain), 127
transnational social policies, 10–11, 179–94; awareness of rich countries about poverty for, 181, 182–83; collectivizing process and, 179–80; conditions for, 181–89; confidence in efficacy of, 182, 187–89; coordination of and European Union, 11, 182, 183–87; education and health and, 182, 183, 185; environmental degradation and, 182, 183, 185; future prospects for, 189–91; global interdependencies for, 181, 182; immigration and, 182, 183, 184; military threats

and, 182, 183, 184–85; opportunity and, 182, 183, 185
transnational unions: Belgium and, 13; sovereignty limited by, 4
Tsin, Michael, 103
Turner, Bryan, 101

Unemployed Workmen Act of 1905 (Great Britain), 130, 140
unemployment. *See* right to work
Unemployment: A Problem of Industry (Beveridge), 137–39
Unemployment Act of 1911 (Great Britain), 136–41
unemployment insurance, Great Britain and, 136–41
Unemployment Insurance Act (Great Britain), 129
Unionists (Great Britain), 128, 131
United Nations: Committee for the Elimination of Racial Discrimination, 79; Conference on Environment and Development in Rio de Janeiro (1992), 185; High Commissioner for Refugees, 185; UNESCO, 185; Universal Declaration of Human Rights of 1948, 75, 123
United States: abolition of slavery and, 233; accountability of government to publics in, 233; constitutionalism and, 232–33; democratic innovation in, 233, 236; equality of rights in, 233; feminist movement in, 158; immigration and citizenship in, 67, 68, 71–72, 73, 80, 83–89, 92; men's suffrage in, 233; military power of, 4; secret ballot in, 232; voting rights in, 230–31, 233, 234; women's suffrage in, 230–31, 232, 245n32
U.S. Commission on Immigration Reform (1997), 67
urban citizenship, in the Netherlands, 6, 17–18, 19–24, 27–28, 29
Urwick, E. J., 129

Van Elslade, Foreign Minister, 205
vernacular politics, in Ottoman Empire,
    39–45
Versailles Treaty, nation-states and, 73
voting rights: European Union citizen-
    ship and, 206, 208, 210, 211, 212,
    224n65; in Haiti, 13; in Portugal, 13;
    in Switzerland, 233, 234. *See also*
    Australia; Great Britain; men's suf-
    frage; New Zealand; United States;
    women's suffrage

Wales, national anthem of, 2
Wallerstein, Immanuel, 240
Walter-McCarran Nationality Act of
    1952 (United States), 86–87
warmaking, as European anthem theme, 1
Webb, Sidney and Beatrice, 129, 137,
    139, 140
welfare state, feminist power within
    Sweden and, 10, 149–78
Whig party (Great Britain), right to work
    and, 126–27, 133
Women Industrial Council (Great
    Britain), 128
Women Labour League (Great Britain),
    128
women, power of, 256. *See also* femi-

nists; Sweden, feminist power in;
    women's suffrage
Women's Christian Temperance Union
    (WCTU): in New Zealand, 232, 236;
    in United States, 231
women's rights, Ottoman citizenship
    avoiding, 43
women's suffrage, 233, 245n32; in Aus-
    tralia, 230, 231–32, 236–37; in Great
    Britain, 232; in Isle of Man, 239,
    245n32; in New Zealand, 230, 231,
    232, 236–37, 245n32; in Sweden,
    155; in United States, 230–31, 232,
    245n32
work. *See* right to work
workers, European Union citizenship
    and, 208–9, 225n67
Workers Representation Committee
    (Great Britain), 129
working class, right to work in Great
    Britain and, 123
World Bank, 4
world citizenship, 67–68
World Health Organization, 185

Yujiro, Murata, 106

Zürcher, Erik, 54

About the Contributors

MICHAEL HANAGAN is adjunct professor at the New School for Social Research. His research interests focus on labor history, social movements, violence and collective action, and world history. With Leslie Page Moch and Wayne te Brake, he has edited a collection, "Challenging Authority: The Historical Study of Contentious Action." With Miriam Cohen, he is currently working on a comparative study of the welfare state in England, France, and the United States, 1870–1950.

BARBARA HOBSON is an associate professor in the Sociology Department at Stockholm University and director of the Advanced Research School in Comparative Gender Studies. She is a founder and a current editor of *Social Politics: International Studies of Gender, State, and Society*. She has published articles on the themes of gender and citizenship, women's power resources and welfare state formation, and women's economic dependency and social citizenship. Her edited collection *Crossing Borders: Gender and Citizenship in Transition* is forthcoming from Macmillan.

JOHN MARKOFF is professor of sociology, history, and political science at the University of Pittsburgh. He is the author of *Waves of Democracy, The Abolition of Feudalism,* and (with Gilbert Shapiro) *Revolutionary Demands. The Abolition of Feudalism* received prizes from the Society for French Historical Studies, the Social Science History Association, and the American Sociological Association.

MAARTEN PRAK is professor of social and economic history at the University of Utrecht. His research interests focus on social dimensions of urban life in early modern Europe. His contribution to this book is part of a larger project, soon to be published, about social transformations during the Revolutionary era.

TEAL ROTHSCHILD is a Ph.D. candidate in sociology and historical studies at the New School for Social Research. She is adjunct lecturer in the sociology department at John Jay College of Criminal Justice, City University of New York. Her research interests focus on labor movements, comparing immigration, gender, and identity through cross-ethnic and cross-skill alliances in New York City during the nineteenth and twentieth centuries.

ARIEL SALZMANN teaches early modern Middle Eastern and world history in the Department of Middle Eastern Studies of New York University. In addition to writing on comparative and cultural history, she is now completing a monograph on politics, finance, and society in the eighteenth-century Ottoman Empire.

SUZANNE SHANAHAN received her Ph.D. in sociology from Stanford University and is an assistant professor of sociology and North American studies at Duke University. Her research centers on the relationships among and between collective identity formation, social inequality, and political mobilization. Current projects include "Sovereignty and the Changing Boundaries of Social Membership"; "Irish Adoption Policy: Issues of National and Individual Identity"; "The Degendering of Political Citizenship" (with Francisco Ramirez); and "Immigration, Diversification, and Ethnic Conflict in U.S. Cities from 1850–1990" (with Susan Olzak).

ABRAM DE SWAAN is cofounder of the Amsterdam School for Social Research. He served as its dean from 1987 to 1997 and is presently its chairman. He has been professor of sociology at the University of Amsterdam since 1973. In 1997–1998, he held the European Chair at the Collège de France in Paris.

CHARLES TILLY teaches social sciences at Columbia University. His most recent books are *Roads from Past to Future* (1997), *Work under Capitalism* (with Chris Tilly, 1998), and *Transforming Post-Communist Political Economies* (coedited with Joan Nelson and Lee Walker, 1998).

ANTJE WIENER received her Ph.D. from Carleton University in 1995. She is an assistant professor at the Institute for Political Science, University of Hanover, where she teaches European integration and international relations theory. She recently published *"European" Citizenship Practice: Building Institutions of a Non-State* (Westview Press, 1998). Her current work includes a coedited volume (with Karlheinz Neunreither), *Amsterdam and Beyond: Institutional Dynamics and Prospects for Democracy in the European Union* (Oxford University Press) and a monograph on border conflicts under the new EU Schengen politics.

R. BIN WONG, professor of history and social sciences at the University of

California, Irvine, has recently published *China Transformed: Historical Change and the Limits of European Experience* (Cornell University Press, 1997) and a coedited volume, *Culture and State in Chinese History* (Stanford University Press, 1997). His current projects include studies of Chinese economic history, political economy, and social change.